MW00532281

CIVIL WAR INFANTRY TACTICS

The 36th Pennsylvania ployed in a simple column, one company battle line behind the other, at its winter camp. (LC-DIG-ppmsca-03308)

CIVIL WAR
INFANTRY
TACTICS

TRAINING, COMBAT, AND SMALL-UNIT EFFECTIVENESS

EARL J. HESS

LOUISIANA STATE UNIVERSITY PRESS

BATON ROUGE

Published with the assistance of the V. Ray Cardozier Fund

Published by Louisiana State University Press
Copyright © 2015 by Earl J. Hess
Manufactured in the United States of America
First printing

DESIGNER: *Mandy McDonald Scallan*
TYPEFACE: *Whitman*
PRINTER AND BINDER: *Maple Press, Inc.*

All line diagrams not otherwise credited are by the author.

Library of Congress Cataloging-in-Publication Data
Hess, Earl J.
  Civil War infantry tactics : training, combat, and small-unit effectiveness /
Earl J. Hess.
    pages cm
  Includes bibliographical references and index.
  ISBN 978-0-8071-5937-8 (cloth : alk. paper) — ISBN 978-0-8071-5938-5
(pdf) — ISBN 978-0-8071-5939-2 (epub) — ISBN 978-0-8071-5940-8 (mobi)
1. United States—History—Civil War, 1861–1865—Campaigns. 2. United
States. Army. Infantry—Drill and tactics—History—19th century. 3. Confed-
erate States of America. Army. Infantry—Drill and tactics. 4. Infantry drill and
tactics—History—19th century. I. Title.
  E470.H59 2015
  973.7'3—dc23

                                                                    2014033785

The paper in this book meets the guidelines for permanence and durability of
the Committee on Production Guidelines for Book Longevity of the Council
on Library Resources.♾

As always, dedicated to Pratibha

CONTENTS

PREFACE ... xi

1.
The European Tactical Heritage ... 1

2.
The North American Tactical Heritage ... 19

3.
Tactical Manuals and the Management of Men ... 34

4.
Training ... 61

5.
Moving Forward and the Art of Skirmishing ... 81

6.
Multiple Lines, Echelons, and Squares ... 103

7.
Changing Front ... 123

8.
Columns ... 140

9.
Multiple Maneuvers ... 162

10.
Large Formations ... 176

11.
Tactical Developments after the Civil War ... 202

12.
Comparison and Context ... 226

CONCLUSION: A Tactical Summary of the Civil War ... 239

APPENDIX: A Tactical Glossary of the Civil War ... 243

NOTES ... 249

BIBLIOGRAPHY ... 275

INDEX ... 291

ILLUSTRATIONS

36th Pennsylvania *frontispiece*

1.1. From Column into Line by Processional Method . . . 5
1.2. From Column into Line by Perpendicular Method . . . 6

2.1. Winfield Scott . . . 29
2.2. William J. Hardee . . . 31

3.1. Silas Casey . . . 36
3.2. Formation of a Regiment . . . 39
3.3. Passing Obstacles . . . 46
3.4. Simple Column at Full, Half, and Closed Distance . . . 50
3.5. Double Column at Full, Half, and Closed Distance . . . 50
3.6. Forming a Square . . . 52
3.7. Forming Skirmishers . . . 54
3.8. Breaking by Company to the Right . . . 58

5.1. Company E, 5th New York . . . 82
5.2. 110th Pennsylvania . . . 83

6.1. Comparing Multiple-Lines Formation and Simple Column
        at Full Distance . . . 107
6.2. Actual and Theoretical Confederate Deployment's at Shiloh . . . 108
6.3. Buell's Standard Division Formation . . . 109
6.4. Samuel Beatty's Brigade at Stones River on December 31, 1862 . . . 111
6.5. Echelon Formations . . . 119
6.6. 139th Pennsylvania . . . 121

7.1. Changing Front Forward on a Subunit . . . 125
7.2. Comparing Movement by the Flank and Simple Column
        at Full Distance . . . 128

7.3. Moving by the Flank by Companies . . . 129

7.4. Full Wheel, Half Wheel, and Quarter Wheel . . . 134

8.1. 26th New York in Simple Column . . . 141

8.2. 2nd Rhode Island in Double Column . . . 142

8.3. Mix of Line and Column at Stones River and Pine Mountain . . . 147

8.4. Mix of Line and Column at Chancellorsville . . . 153

8.5. Mix of Line and Column at Fort Wagner, Orchard Knob, and
     Cold Harbor . . . 156

9.1. Multiple Maneuvers at Antietam . . . 168

9.2. Multiple Maneuvers at Burgess's Mill . . . 174

10.1. Large Formations at Chancellorsville, Spotsylvania, and
      Fort Stedman . . . 183

10.2. Fifth Corps Formation at Five Forks . . . 190

10.3. Sixth Corps Formation on April 2 . . . 197

PREFACE

Civil War officers relied on a system of linear tactics to form and maneuver their units on the battlefield. Developed in Europe during the late 1600s and early 1700s, this system reached its height in limited wars fought by professional armies of the eighteenth century. The system involved shoulder-to-shoulder lines, columns, and a range of complicated maneuvers to take a unit from one formation to another. The idea was to wed tactics to the capabilities of the single-shot, smoothbore weapon that all major European armies used by the early 1700s. It had a range of about one hundred yards and involved a fairly complicated process of reloading. Officers needed to mass their men so as to control not only their fire but also their movement on the field. Linear tactics provided them the opportunity to accomplish those goals. In its purest form, the linear system involved an entire field army small enough to be personally controlled by the commanding general. This unitary army reached the peak of its development by the mid-1700s.

The system worked well throughout the eighteenth century, but it had to be adapted to new demands by the late 1700s. French writers discussed the use of divisions as a way to add more flexibility and speed in moving armies toward battle and during combat. The unitary-army concept gave way to a flexible linear system by the time of the French Revolutionary and Napoleonic Wars. The enlarged volunteer and conscript armies of that era also made the shift toward the flexible system feasible. There developed a greater emphasis on skirmishing and on organizing corps to operate as semi-independent units of a larger field army. Generals also loosened up the extended line of battle into segments controlled by subordinates who had authority to conduct operations in their sector within the larger framework of operations set by the army commander.

Civil War armies inherited the modified linear system of the French Revolutionary and Napoleonic era. The biggest difference between the Civil War and previous conflicts was the introduction of the rifle musket. The only technical change, however, was the rifle's effective range, five hundred yards compared to the one-hundred-yard range of the smoothbore. This increased range led contemporaries to predict revolutionary changes in warfare—higher casualties, greater power added to the side fighting on the defensive, and cavalry and field artillery becoming ineffective when confronting infantry armed with rifles.

Historians later accepted this view and established it as a standard interpretation in Civil War historiography. The ultimate expression of this view appeared with Grady McWhiney and Perry D. Jamieson's *Attack and Die: Civil War Military Tactics and the Southern Heritage* in 1982. McWhiney and Jamieson see nearly all characteristics of Civil War military operations as influenced by the use of the rifle musket. Everything from high casualties to the lack of decisive battles and the ineffectiveness of artillery and cavalry on the battlefield are ascribed to the potency of that weapon. This view held sway until a handful of historians began to question a key component, the range at which combat actually took place. Paddy Griffith, Mark Grimsley, and Brent Nosworthy have raised significant questions about that issue, based on research in the official reports clearly indicating that infantry combat normally took place at ranges far less than five hundred yards and similar to or only slightly more than the range of the smoothbore musket.[1]

My study of the issue in *The Rifle Musket in Civil War Combat—Reality and Myth* (2008) thoroughly criticizes the old interpretation and offers a new one—that the rifle musket did not revolutionize Civil War military operations. Its only advantage over the smoothbore was longer range, but the great majority of soldiers did not use it at that distance. The rifle's parabolic trajectory made hitting targets at long range a technical problem that even rifle enthusiasts of the day admitted was difficult to solve. Moreover, one had to see a human target at five hundred yards across a landscape cluttered with trees and obscured by undulating terrain in order to fire at it, much less hit it. The army did not train soldiers how to deal with these issues.[2]

More importantly, there was a very strong predisposition to fight at close range during the Civil War. Officers and men alike believed that it was more decisive to engage the enemy at ranges of 100 yards or less, a belief proven correct by the experience of combat. Brent Nosworthy has argued that the decisive point at which an attack was repelled lay about 80–120 yards in front of the defending line. John Bell Hood lectured his men before the start of the Atlanta Campaign: "Firing on the enemy at long range should never be permitted, since its lack of effectiveness often gives encouragement instead of causing demoralization, as a well-directed fire at short range is certain to do." Benjamin F. Cheatham recalled that on the battlefield of Franklin, where the Army of Tennessee attacked across a broad, open area, bodies of his men lay as far away from the Federals as 400 yards, but the great majority of dead and wounded lay within 50 yards of the defenders.[3]

The evidence is overwhelming that fighting usually took place at very close ranges during the Civil War, far less than is required to argue that the long-range capability of the rifle musket was felt in combat. The casualty rates of these battles also fail to prove the point that the rifle was a more deadly weapon than the smoothbore. In fact, Civil War loss ratios were on the same level as those seen in major smoothbore battles of the eighteenth century. In some cases the latter produced even higher loss ratios than Civil War engagements. At Bunker Hill 47 percent of the British troops were shot down by smoothbore musketry delivered by American militiamen without the assistance of artillery. In contrast, the bloody engagement at Gettysburg produced a casualty rate of about 30 percent among Robert E. Lee's men.[4]

Moreover, infantry combat after the Civil War continued to take place mostly at short range. This knowledge was built into the training regimen of those men preparing to go into battle during World War II, Korea, and Vietnam. Ironically, American soldiers fired their twentieth-century weapons at similarly short ranges as their predecessors had used their smoothbore muskets in the eighteenth century. These were the same distances at which Federals and Confederates fired their rifle muskets in the 1860s. The consistency is remarkable and significant.[5]

Civil War soldiers wanted the newest weapon, but they did not want to fire it at long range. Its trajectory was relatively flat, similar to that of the smoothbore, for the first one hundred yards. After that the ball arced considerably in the air. Thus, at short ranges the rifle musket was as effective as the smoothbore, while at long ranges it proved much more difficult to aim so as to hit the target.

The new interpretation of the rifle musket's significance—that it did not produce a revolutionary change in Civil War operations—opens many new doors in the historiography. No longer are we tied to the notion that this weapon changed everything on the Civil War battlefield. Among other things, dropping the old interpretation and accepting the new allows us to reevaluate the significance of infantry tactics in a more accurate and positive way. If the rifle musket was used mostly like a smoothbore had been used, then there is no reason to believe the linear system was obsolete.

GOALS OF THIS STUDY

This book is a study of infantry tactics in the Civil War, crafted within the context of the new interpretation of the rifle musket and its effect on military operations. I started with an intensive reading of the tactical manuals available to Civil War commanders, those written by Winfield Scott (1835), William J. Hardee (1855), and Silas Casey (1862). It was necessary to understand the complex descriptions of formations and maneuvers well enough to make sense of them for an understanding of Civil War tactics. Then I intensively read the battle reports in the *War of the*

Rebellion: A Compilation of the Official Records of the Union and Confederate Armies to see how well commanders knew the tactics and how effectively they utilized them on the battlefield. Those reports are the foundation of this book; they are the wellspring of any understanding of Civil War military operations.

My interpretation includes an assertion that the linear system was not obsolete; in fact, not only was it relevant to the reality of Civil War operations, it was also the correct system to be used with the rifle musket. No matter what rifle enthusiasts of the day thought about the effect of long-range fire on enemy formations, the reality was that its use did not develop into a widespread phenomenon during the war. The rifle musket's only advantage over the smoothbore was its longer range. It could not be loaded faster, and there is no evidence that it was more accurate at short ranges. It did play a role in the sharp increase of effective skirmishing and sniping during the Civil War, when in the hands of men naturally adept at using firearms. But there was no need to alter the tactical system if the majority of soldiers were unable to use the rifle to fire effectively at long range. Volume of rifle fire might well have compelled a change in linear tactics, but the breech-loading and magazine rifles that were introduced during the Civil War were never issued in large enough numbers to make a difference.

Moreover, I argue that most Civil War commanders took their job seriously, even though they were only volunteer soldiers serving for the duration of the conflict. They recognized that learning the intricacies of drill would pay dividends when under fire. As a result, the official reports demonstrate that most unit commanders could handle their men under duress, choose the correct formations for them, and call up the commands necessary to change the unit's position to meet the difficulties that cropped up when enemy troops suddenly appeared. These reports also demonstrate that some commanders failed the test of tactics, and some units failed to execute maneuvers or assemble the proper formations. I give full attention to the limits of proficiency among Union and Confederate commanders, but that does not invalidate the assertion that most officers attained at least an acceptable level of proficiency in tactical matters, many of them achieving an impressively high level of unit articulation.

It is important to set the story of Civil War infantry tactics within the larger context of Western military history. Thus, chapters 1 and 2 deal with the tactical heritage from Europe and from pre–Civil War North America. Chapter 11 covers post–Civil War tactical developments in the United States and the major nations of Europe. One of the problems with the traditional interpretation of the rifle musket is that historians have assumed that the American Civil War was an exceptional experience in world military history, with revolutionary implications that Europeans were foolish to ignore. This is not my view. In fact, the Civil War was very much a part of international military developments, but it was far less important in those developments than American historians have tended to think.

Chapter 3 discusses the basic formations and maneuvers as described in the three drill manuals available to Civil War commanders, emphasizing their role as ways in which officers could control and manage their men on the battlefield. Chapter 4 details the training process employed by Union and Confederate officers. Chapters 5–10 look at actual practice in the field, especially in combat. These six chapters form the heart of this study and include more than four hundred examples of tactical formations and maneuvers among Union and Confederate units drawn mostly from battle reports. All the major formations and maneuvers are covered, with discussions of their utility, their relative frequency of use, and the preferences of commanders for one way to accomplish a particular task on the battlefield over other options. Chapter 12 compares the experience of Civil War armies to the larger American experience with volunteer military forces. The conclusion summarizes tactical practice in the Civil War, and the glossary defines many tactical terms that were current among Civil War soldiers.

CONTEMPORARIES, HISTORIANS, AND CIVIL WAR TACTICS

It is also important to set this study within the context of Civil War military history. In addition to its new interpretation of linear tactics, it is the first study of what often is called the lower or minor level of tactics, the actual formations and maneuvers used by officers and men. Previous works on the topic have mostly dealt with grand (or battle) tactics, which is a higher level of the story. Grand tactics mostly concern issues such as whether a commander elected to attack or defend a position, and whether he used frontal assaults or flanking maneuvers to seize the tactical offensive. In fact, the main point of McWhiney and Jamieson's book is that the Confederates did not understand the power of the rifle musket and therefore frontally attacked the Federals too often, thereby defeating themselves on the battlefield. That book does not delve into the lower level of tactics in a significant way.[6]

From the beginning, when the rifle musket was initially introduced to the U.S. Army, observers were impressed by its potential. America's first major promoter of the rifle musket was Lt. Cadmus M. Wilcox of the 7th U.S. Infantry. He wrote a book about the new weapon and its possible effects on warfare, *Rifles and Rifle Practice: An Elementary Treatise upon the Theory of Rifle Firing*, published in 1859.

It was an enthusiastic endorsement of the rifle's use but came with a heavy dose of reality. Wilcox argued that all soldiers armed with the new weapon should be scientifically trained to work its adjustments so as to compensate for the parabolic trajectory of the ball. Otherwise, its long-range capabilities would be nullified. Wilcox predicted that the rifle would rule the battlefield if used correctly. After the war there is no evidence that he tried to determine if the weapon had been used correctly or had the predicted effect on combat.[7]

During and immediately after the Civil War, a handful of observers remained convinced that the rifle had revolutionized military affairs. An anonymous reviewer of William Hopkins Morris's book *Field Tactics for Infantry* assumed that the new firearm had rendered traditional modes of attack obsolete. In his view, frontal assaults in column, bayonet charges, and cavalry assaults were reduced to relics of the past under the rain of long-range infantry fire.[8]

The threat posed by breech-loading and magazine rifles became more prominent during the 1880s, prompting Arthur L. Wagner to predict that long-range small-arms fire would rule the battlefield. Wagner, an army theorist who had not participated in the Civil War, argued in *Organization and Tactics* (1895) that infantry formations would be pummeled at incredible ranges (such as 3,000 yards, nearly two miles) before closing on an enemy armed with modern weapons. He studied Civil War military operations to gather data condemning column formations and praising any evidence of dispersed linear order as the wave of the future.[9]

Historians have accepted the evaluations of antebellum, Civil War, and postbellum observers at face value. Marion Joyce expressed this acceptance in the popular magazine *Civil War Times Illustrated* in 1964. Joyce believed that the rifle gave extraordinary power to the army that acted on the defensive, rendering the old linear system obsolete. Commanders on all levels were foolishly oblivious to this basic fact and tens of thousands of men lost their lives needlessly. According to Joyce, shoulder-to-shoulder formations merely placed soldiers "into the configuration of a choice target."[10]

In an unpublished dissertation about Civil War tactics, Thomas Vernon Moseley largely repeats Wagner's conclusions to argue that the linear system was outdated. John K. Mahon continued to repeat those conclusions in an article published in *Military Affairs*. Mahon believed that the rifle musket gave more power to the defense and made combat longer, bloodier, and more indecisive. Carl L. Davis, writing about the procurement of weapons by the Federal government during the Civil War, assumed that the rifle was accurate at very long ranges, thus "close order was becoming a thing of the past." This view was also expressed by Steven Ross, who wrote about the development of the small arms used by Western armies during the past couple of centuries.[11]

As already noted, the most widely read expression of the idea that the rifle musket revolutionized military operations is found in *Attack and Die.* "Casualty lists reveal that the Confederates destroyed themselves by making bold and repeated attacks," McWhiney and Jamieson argue. They stress their point that "tactics lagged behind military technology in the 1860s." The book reinforced a general perception among Civil War students and coincided with the prevailing American assumption that new technology will produce change wherever it is employed.[12]

Henry Jerry Osterhoudt continued the theme in his unpublished dissertation about the development of infantry assault tactics in the American army, which was completed in 1986. The Civil War occurred when "the technology of infantry weapons had far surpassed the tactical concepts with which they were employed. The collision that ensued when improved weapons met outmoded tactics had reverberations which completely changed the face of infantry battle." Osterhoudt assumes a great deal about infantry combat in the Civil War without digging into the reports to prove his assertions, a fault of the McWhiney and Jamieson study as well. For example, Osterhoudt argues that Civil War infantrymen typically fired their muskets at five hundred yards and managed to shoot eight to ten volleys in five minutes, none of which is true. The reports clearly show that fighting normally took place at around one hundred yards and that firing a round every one to two minutes was typical, even during periods of heavy combat. Yet Osterhoudt concludes that "the old fashioned linear attack was little short of murder."[13]

A handful of historians have continued to stretch out this standard interpretation of the rifle musket's effect on operations. Edward Hagerman, in a study stressing that the origins of modern warfare can be found in the American conflict of the 1860s, boldly proclaims that the "classical line and column of Empire and Restoration doctrine faded" on Civil War battlefields. Joseph Allan Frank and George A. Reaves, writing about the experience of combat at Shiloh, assumed the rifle musket had made linear tactics obsolete, but at least they warn that "this effect should not be exaggerated." Andrew Haughton, in a study of training, tactics, and leadership in the Army of Tennessee, continued to assume that the rifle musket was a weapon that produced fundamental changes in military operations.[14]

Historians who have written more generally about the Civil War have always accepted the standard interpretation as fact. The most popular historian of the war, James M. McPherson, has stated: "The tactical predominance of the defense helps explain why the Civil War was so long and bloody. The rifle and trench ruled

Civil War battlefields as thoroughly as the machine-gun and trench ruled those of World War I." Respected military historian Russell Weigley has called Civil War battlefields "a killing ground par excellence" that demonstrated "the devastating effect of the rifled musket in the hands of steady and well-positioned defenders against a frontal attack."[15]

Most historians have given Civil War armies little credit for their use of linear tactics, criticizing officers at all levels for adhering to doctrines scholars believe were outdated by the new weaponry. In that view, Civil War soldiers were the victims of their commanders' inability to understand what should have been obvious to anyone, that linear tactical formations presented massed targets to defenders armed with long-range small arms.

Even Paddy Griffith, who began the process of questioning the revolutionary influence of the rifle musket, thought Civil War officers should have been more innovative and flexible when it came to tactical decisions. He noted that the new chasseur tactics available to regimental commanders, which involved dispersed order and rushes toward the enemy, were never fully learned or used in the conflict. Those tactics demanded much more rigorous training supported by extensive target practice. Given the citizen army with which both sides fought the war, this was not possible. Griffith joined mainstream historians to argue that "the armies either improvised ineffectively" on the battlefield "or reverted to outdated tactics disastrously. They were not usually able to use the most modern tactics available to them—which ironically were incorporated [in a *very limited* degree] in their own drill manuals."[16]

A modified note in this discussion was inserted by a graduate student who published an article in an obscure periodical in 1985, based mostly on the memoir of one man in one regiment, Steve Fratt concluded that mainstream, traditional tactics as explained in Hardee's manual were useful in maneuvering a unit on the battlefield before it came under fire but seemed to be less successfully employed under the stress of combat. He noted that the level of drill and the quality of officers played a role in this, concluding that standard linear tactics, although only imperfectly learned, provided "a framework for maneuvering and training" Civil War regiments both on and off the battlefield.[17]

Brent Nosworthy has recently broken from the standard interpretation of Civil War tactics by agreeing with Griffith that the rifle musket did not have a revolutionary effect on warfare. He rejects the argument of McWhiney and Jamieson that frontal attacks were doomed to fail. Though he admits that rifles "were at least slightly more effective than the weapons they replaced," Nosworthy also notes that many factors other than weaponry affected the outcome of attacks. He also points out that quite a few frontal attacks succeeded in spectacular fashion.[18]

My own take on Civil War tactics has slowly evolved over many years. Early in my career, I accepted the traditional interpretation of the rifle musket and its effect on military operations. But Griffith's book sparked a period of questioning the basic assumptions behind that interpretation. When I finally came around to devoting a great deal of attention to the issue, the evidence popping up about a number of other assumptions making up that interpretation called for a thorough rejection of the old idea.

Moreover, during many years of teaching Civil War history to undergraduate students and to Elderhostel classes as well as lecturing to Civil War round tables and symposia, I have countless times heard the comment that Civil War soldiers used obsolete tactics against modern weapons and paid the price in brutally high casualties. This idea exists alongside the notion that the Americans won their independence by fighting "Indian style" from behind rocks and trees while the British foolishly walked in the open, or that the American way of war is different because we have forests to fight in and European armies have always fought on open ground. Any reading of the campaigns of the American Revolution, and a thoughtful tour of the European countryside, can disabuse anyone of those ideas. Yet they persist in the minds of most casual students of military history.

As Nosworthy has put it, there is a popular notion that disdains linear tactics within the context of modernism. A prejudiced view of the old system sprang up as soon as the idea that new weapons would revolutionize combat took hold. "When compact formations ceased to be practical," Nosworthy has written, "soon almost everyone forgot they had ever been functional at all." Then the idea that linear tactics was "a baroque system whose ultimate origins lay in the intellectual limitations" of the past began to develop. "To express it simply, 'They wouldn't have fought that way, if they knew what we know.'"[19]

As indicated early in this preface, and as explained throughout the rest of this book, I strongly believe that the linear tactical system was not obsolete in the Civil War. That system had been developed in Europe to accommodate the use of a single-shot, muzzle-loading weapon with short range. Its principles were still relevant for the single-shot, muzzle-loading rifle because most soldiers either could not or did not want to utilize that weapon's longer range. Volume of fire, not range of fire, was the cue for developing new tactical formations, and that cue was not fully sounded until the 1880s. In fact, not only were linear tactics relevant to the Civil War, they worked very well. Even poorly trained regiments could execute basic maneuvers laid down in the drill manuals, and the better units utilized a wide variety of basic as well as complex maneuvers under great pressure on the battlefield. A careful reading of battle reports indicates that even volunteer commanders who had no antebellum military experience of any kind could employ their unit's manpower under fire in quite sophisticated ways to achieve their tactical goals. The Civil War was, indeed, the last great American conflict employing close-order linear tactics effectively, and it was the apotheosis of the American volunteer system.

The drill manuals were not ossified relics of the past. They offered Civil War commanders the foundation of their tactical art. The units that did well in combat were those commanded by men who knew their Scott, Hardee, and Casey cover to cover and had the intelligence to quickly choose which maneuver they needed to meet each developing problem. They were also the ones in which the rank and file understood the maneuvers as well as their officers. While there are many other factors that go into an understanding of why some units succeeded and others failed on the battlefield, one of the most important is the level of familiarity with standard tactics.

DEFINING TACTICS

Many developments rendered military operations far more complex and confusing by the early part of the twentieth century than they were during the Civil War. Rising populations coupled with increased centralized authority by national governments made it possible for a general to command huge armies. Those troops now possessed a multiplicity of complicated weapons. Advances in artillery made it the dominant weapon on the battlefield by World War I. The addition of effective aircraft added a new dimension to warfare, and the development of an effective tank as well as the mechanization of infantry units gave unprecedented mobility to armies operating in the field.

As result, managing military resources grew into such a monstrous task that theorists worked hard to develop new doctrines. Soviet writers began the process in the 1920s by coining the term "operational art" to designate the management of men, material, and everything else that made military movement so complex in the modern age. That concept took its place between the level of strategy and tactics and referred to the planning and execution of campaigns to achieve strategic objectives. While some historians still use the term "grand tactics" to describe the larger aspect of maneuvering for battle within reach of the enemy, others simply lump all battlefield aspects of the military art into the term "tactics."[20]

Writers in the Civil War era defined tactics as "the art which teaches how to bring your force to bear upon the enemy to the best advantage in actual combat." In 1863, when the U.S. Army published a condensed version of Casey's manual, it defined tactics as "the movements of armies upon the battle-field, within sight and reach of the enemy." For Henry L. Scott, who authored a military dictionary, tactics was simply "the art of handling troops." The nomenclature began to change significantly only twenty years after the war. Arthur L. Wagner preferred to use the terms "maneuver tactics" for grand tactics and "fighting tactics" for minor tactics.[21]

Most Civil War military studies have tended to focus on the old concept of grand tactics and many aspects of the newer concept of operations as well. Books about campaigns and battles are plentiful, and they necessarily discuss the movement of armies toward contact and the decisions made at high levels about how to deal with the enemy on the battlefield. Historians who write battle studies invariably detail the movements of higher-level commands—corps, divisions, and brigades—but not necessarily the actions of smaller units. Minor tactics have been shortchanged in Civil War military history, admittedly for understandable reasons. The actions of a single regiment or company often do not fit into a study that attempts to compass a large, complicated battle, and much of it would seem repetitious anyway.

There is therefore ample room for new work in the area of minor-tactics history, and not just for the Civil War but for all other conflicts. We can start with an attempt to give it a new name. Rather than being "minor" or at a "lower" level, they were in fact the most important aspect of tactics. Formations and maneuvers were the foundation of infantry success and deserve to be called "primary" tactics. This book can serve as a primer for understanding the basic formations and maneuvers of Civil War infantry regiments. I also hope it will help in the creation of new understandings of combat operations involving those formations and maneuvers under fire. Finally, it is the first substantial study of small-unit effectiveness in the Civil War.

≡
≡
≡

It is time to embrace the welcome opportunity to thank people who have aided me in the research, writing, and production of this book.

While I drafted the diagrams and maps, a friend, who prefers to remain anonymous, computerized one-third of them, and my wife, Pratibha, and I computerized the rest.

I owe many thanks to Prof. Samuel Watson of the Department of History, U.S. Military Academy, for carefully and thoughtfully reading this manuscript for Louisiana State University Press. Professor Watson offered many helpful suggestions for improving it, including the idea for figure 6.2, "Actual and Theoretical Confederate Deployment at Shiloh."

The West Point Museum Collection, U.S. Military Academy, graciously allowed the press to use their painting by James Walker, *Civil War Drill Scene, Militia Regiment, 1861,* as cover art for this book.

I also wish to thank Fred Ray for sending me a copy of Norman Hitchman's report, used in the last chapter of this book. It proved to be very helpful and very interesting.

Rand Dotson ably shepherded this project through the acquisitions process.

Mostly, I owe eternal thanks to my wife, Pratibha.

CIVIL WAR INFANTRY TACTICS

$$\equiv \mathbf{1} \equiv$$

The European Tactical Heritage

The linear system was developed over a long period of time to control and direct the fire of soldiers armed with single-shot, muzzle-loading weapons. It also allowed for tight control of the men themselves and demanded a great deal of intensive drilling. In its purest form in the eighteenth century, this system served the needs of military forces that were comparatively small. The entire battle line of a field army was treated as a rigid structure firmly controlled by the army commander, with relatively little opportunity for subordinates to exercise initiative. This concept of a unitary army "demanded that large groups of formations act together in unison as lengthy linear bodies," according to historian Brent Nosworthy.[1]

THE DEVELOPMENT OF LINEAR TACTICS

Before commanders and theorists began to develop linear tactics, the armies of Europe had to dispense with older weapons such as the pike and to improve the early muskets. The matchlock was in the hands of about two-thirds of all infantrymen in European armies by 1600, a time when the usual tactical formation was the Spanish tercio. This huge formation was many ranks deep and quite broad as well, more akin to the old Greek phalanx than to modern battle lines. The matchlock was heavy, requiring a forked stick to hold up the muzzle, and had a misfire rate approaching 50 percent. Its potential range was impressive, about 250 yards, but soldiers could hardly expect to hit their target beyond about 60 yards.[2]

As the weapons available to European armies improved, so did the tactical formations. Spanish tercios were massive, unwieldy affairs, usually containing 1,500 troops in a solid rectangle of fifty men wide and thirty ranks deep. Generals usually adopted a staggered deployment with wide intervals between the tercios. Maurice of Nassau experimented with smaller formations that were wider than they were deep to allow more of his musket men to fire during the campaigns of the Dutch Revolt (1566–1609). This was the precursor to the development of linear formations. These battle lines, when employed with men armed with pikes and matchlocks during the seventeenth century, tended to be looser and more flexible than those later employed by soldiers armed with flintlocks in the eighteenth century. When yet far from the enemy, Nassau typically placed files three feet apart from each other and ranks thirteen feet apart. When closing with the enemy, his troops closed ranks to five feet apart. A major reason for the more open formation was that, before the cartridge was developed, infantrymen had to load their muskets using loose powder in horns or pouches while their comrades held lighted matches continuously burning; they lessened the danger of accidental discharge by distancing themselves from their neighbors. Also, European armies had not yet developed the concept of cadenced marching. Each individual soldier stepped off and walked on his own, generally keeping pace with his neighbor. They could not march in tight formations until they all learned to step off in unison.[3]

Throughout the seventeenth century, various armies experimented with reducing the number of ranks in the formation. By the 1680s, most military forces used five or six ranks, but there were some units which used only three as early as the Thirty Years' War (1618–48). This became the norm a century later, as any more than three inhibited the free use of the musket. The formation had to be no deeper than the length of a musket barrel, otherwise there was danger of a soldier singeing his comrades or bursting their eardrums with the muzzle blast. With the full employment of the flintlock by the early eighteenth century, the need to improve tactical formations became imperative. As a modern historian has put it, "in the days of short-ranged weapons with a low rate of fire, the exact placing of the weapons and the timing of their use was of supreme importance."[4]

It was just as important to improve the larger formations as well, to find better ways of arranging the position of each unit in relation to the other. Before about 1725, commanders typically arranged their field armies into three lines. The units within each of the lines sometimes maintained substantial distances between one another, called intervals, roughly equal to their frontage. The units of the rear line were positioned facing the intervals between those before them so all lines could have maximum freedom of movement forward and backward. Commanders often organized a small reserve rather than a third line and positioned it at a convenient spot in the rear. They typically placed the second line three hundred paces behind the first. This was considered the optimal distance because it put the second line out of range of hostile fire and allowed ample room for maneuvering its units as needed. Commanders placed their field artillery in the intervals in the first line and sometimes in front of it as well.[5]

Under Louis XIV, the French used the battalion system of organizing their army and replaced the matchlock with the flintlock. They instituted a rigorous training schedule that included not only drilling but also fire practice, although apparently not target practice. In fact the first official drill regulation approved by a French monarch was issued in 1683. The French reduced the depth of their formations from ten ranks in 1622 to three ranks by about 1750. While three-fifths of the men in a typical battalion of 1622 were armed with pikes, all of them carried flintlocks by 1705.[6]

Like all other armies, the French under Louis XIV deployed in multiple lines on the battlefield. They preferred three lines and made the third one a reserve for the others. Normally three hundred paces separated the second line from the first, but six hundred paces was the usual distance between the third line and the second. Their formations maintained large intervals between the flanks of units within each line in the late 1600s but reduced those gaps as flintlocks became more widely distributed, seeking to obtain a greater degree of control over the fire of the troops by massing them together. The French preferred to assault rather than to stop and engage in firefights.[7]

As military men worked out the details of linear formations, they continued to value place of honor in the array. This was an old idea that dated at least to medieval warfare, and the French grasped it more firmly than anyone. They put great store on arranging the twelve companies of their infantry battalions "in order of the rank and the seniority of the officer commanding them." The most senior was placed farthest to the right, all others progressively to the left of the battalion line until the most junior officer's company held the left. The exception was the grenadier company, which always positioned itself on the extreme right. This unit originated as a company armed with hand grenades for siege work and evolved into an elite component of each battalion. The British and Germans worried about grouping their most experienced officers in one wing and started to alternate the pattern, with the second-most-senior commander's company placed on the far left, and the third on the right next to the most senior, and so on. The French came to accept this practice by the 1720s. The concept was still used by the U.S. Army when the Civil War broke out. Even though the volunteer regiments were largely officered by men with no prior military experience, they also made use of this organizational scheme. In Europe the most experienced captain commanded Company A, the second-most experienced led Company B, and so on. In the Civil War, volunteer regiments placed their lettered companies in the same order even if they had no experienced captains to command them. Among the Europeans, the tradition also extended to the placement of individual battalions within the larger battle line. The most experienced ones were put on the right, the next on the left, and alternately until the "most junior regiment by default occupied the middle of the line."[8]

By about the 1740s, the basic components of the linear system had been worked out by the major European armies, but there was room for much refinement to come. After the 1740s, commanders tightened up their formations, putting units closer to each other to better control their movements and their fire. They gradually developed more-sophisticated ways of deploying a battle line from a marching column as the army reached the battlefield. Also, articulation became a concern. This refers to the ability of commanders to handle their units even under difficult circumstances in order to deal with the many problems encountered on the battlefield.

More-sophisticated methods of deployment demanded the adoption of cadenced marching, where "every infantryman advanced his left then his right foot in unison, following the beat of the drums." The Prussians adopted the practice by the 1730s, stipulating sixty-five paces per minute as the marching rate, with a pace measured at two feet. For maneuvering or attacking, they specified a pace of seventy-five to eighty steps per minute, and forty-five steps in a retreat. This and other reforms transformed the Prussian army into the first truly professional military force of the modern era.[9]

Frederick the Great inherited this force from his predecessor and employed several new methods of handling it on the battlefield. The older parallel or "processional" method of deploying from marching column to battle line called for the entire column to turn right or left and move with its flank exposed to the enemy. The column stopped and each unit turned to face the foe. This was simple, though slow and cumbersome. The "perpendicular" method, perfected by the Prussians under Frederick, allowed individual battalions in the column to deploy either right or left from the column itself. It was faster (when employing well-trained units), did not expose any flanks, and provided the army with maneuvers that could be used to avoid obstacles on the battlefield after they deployed into line. The perpendicular method was far more complex than the parallel method and just as vulnerable if conducted within range of enemy artillery. Actually, Frederick rarely

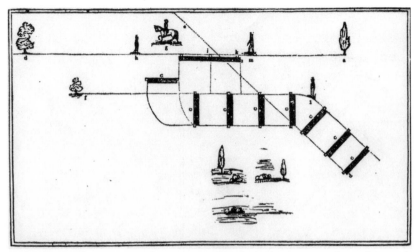

Fig. 1.1. From Column into Line by Processional Method. This diagram indicates how a column deployed for battle by marching parallel to the enemy position, with its units wheeling into line facing the foe. Each bar represents one line, not one rank. (From *Abstract of Infantry Tactics* [1830], 119, plate 14)

used the perpendicular method because it gave too much freedom of action to battalion commanders to suit him. But its development marked a milestone in the refinement of the linear system and a step toward the accelerated deployment of forces onto the battlefield during the French Revolutionary and Napoleonic Wars (1792–1815).[10]

Frederick also developed new methods of moving troops toward the enemy after they deployed on the battlefield. The "march by lines" involved moving a battle line to threaten the enemy's flank. The battalions wheeled to form a temporary column that was as long as the line had been then marched "at a slight angle" that led it to a new position near the opponent's flank and at an angle of about forty-five degrees compared to its former position. Then the battalions wheeled to reform their battle line and attack the enemy flank. Another maneuver, the "attack en echelon," involved extending one wing of the army beyond the enemy's flank in preparation for an assault while the other wing remained in front to keep the opponent occupied. The problem lay in bringing the attacking wing forward and in a different direction in order to strike the enemy flank without exposing its own. Wheeling a long line could prove difficult, so Frederick deployed the striking units

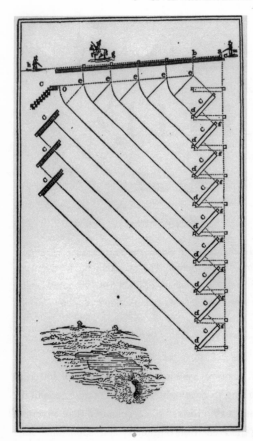

Fig. 1.2. From Column into Line by Perpendicular Method. This diagram indicates how a column deployed for battle by marching perpendicularly to the enemy position, with its units marching obliquely to the left before coming into line facing the foe. Each bar represents one line, not one rank. (From *Abstract of Infantry Tactics* [1830], 123, plate 15)

en echelon, each one about fifty paces forward of its neighbor, to allow them to wheel with more freedom. Of course, this demanded discipline and experience, for all units had to end up aligned and touching flanks to ensure the success of the advance after they finished wheeling. Yet another maneuver, "the oblique attack," involved placing most or all of the field army, not just one wing of it, in a position to hit the enemy flank. This involved using the march by lines or the attack en echelon on a grander scale, further increasing the level of professionalism required to execute the manuever.[11]

These new methods of maneuvering large units on the field helped Frederick win several major battles, but he and many other European generals continued to use the older, processional method of deploying from marching formation into battle line more often than the newer perpendicular method. For commanders who fretted about maximizing their control over all the units of a field army, the parallel method seemed more comfortable. Frederick's innovations helped change the tactical terminology. The older processional method was typically called an evolution, for the battle line seemed to evolve from the column in a slow fashion. The new methods, faster and more spectacular to watch, came to be called maneuvers because one could see small units turning, twisting, and marking geometric patterns as they moved.[12]

With the widespread adoption of cadenced marching, it became possible to close the ranks and files and lessen the intervals that separated battalions. This allowed commanders greater control of the mass. The French mandated "six ordinary paces" between ranks. This was for marching anywhere as a rule, but in an attack, the ranks were to move closer so that only twelve inches separated "the point of the soldier's leading foot and the heel of the soldier to his front." The files had to close as much as possible, the arms of each man touching those of his neighbor "without however making it too confined."[13]

Given the tightly controlled formations, troop density on the battlefield rose with the further development of the linear system. At the Battle of Mollwitz (April 10, 1741), the Prussians covered a two-mile front with 22,000 men deployed in two lines. They packed 65,000 men into a two-and-a-half-mile front at the Battle of Prague (May 6, 1757), and 45,000 men arrayed across only a mile of front at the Battle of Torgau (November 3, 1760). The French deployed 60,000 troops across a front of two and a quarter miles at Fontenoy (May 11, 1745).[14]

Closing those masses of troops on enemy positions was the key element of deciding victory or defeat in battle, and European theorists were divided on whether it was best to stop within range of the defender and weaken him with musketry or simply to move forward without firing until he retired. Frederick the Great preferred the "go through" method for at least the early part of his military career but came to appreciate the value of firefights and to understand the tendency of soldiers to stop and punish the enemy. Prussian regulations advocated a fire by platoons at longer ranges and closing in to deliver concentrated volleys by battalion instead of platoons. At twenty paces from the defender, the tactical manual encouraged commanders to fire a full volley by all available troops and then charge with the bayonet.[15]

While the Prussians and the British retained faith in well-disciplined firepower, the French trusted élan, the spirit of the attack. They emphasized that a well-directed initial volley was the first step to victory, but the battle had to be won at the point of the bayonet. Concentrated, sustained firepower was useful, French officers thought, only on the defensive. Their enemies often suffered little damage in a firefight, even at short ranges, because of the French army's relative lack of firing practice. But on the advance, French troops were trained to move forward quietly, closing ranks and quickening the pace as they neared the enemy. Other armies, such as those of Sweden and Bavaria, also favored spirited assaults but were willing to pause now and then to exchange fire during an advance. All armies, however, tried to conduct attacks with the full battle line on the assumption that the momentum, with its physical and ultimately psychological effect, would more likely produce positive results. This especially was the case if the attacking force extended broadly enough to outflank the enemy.[16]

European armies began to use light infantry to supplement the operations of their main force. Light infantry, in which the Austrians specialized, were independent bodies of men operating in loose order away from the battle line. These units normally ranged across wide areas of countryside, raiding enemy supply lines, conducting surprise attacks on garrisons, and gathering intelligence for their commanders. The important point is that light infantry were usually not tied to the operations of the battle line in an engagement. They performed many of the functions that cavalry executed during the Civil War.[17]

The most intense tactical debate of the eighteenth century centered on the use of columns. Advocates of the *ordre profond,* who believed in the shock value of attacking in deep, heavy columns, argued with advocates of the *ordre mince,* who believed that firepower delivered by lines was more effective. Chevalier de Folard started the debate with the publication of several books beginning in 1727. He also started debate on the *ordre mixte,* the idea of mixing columns and lines in a single formation. Folard held an exaggerated opinion of columns, believing they would be effective in breaking opposing lines by sheer physical force. Baron de Mesnil-Durand published a work supporting this contention in 1755 and providing many more details on how a column could be formed and used than did his predecessor. While Folard assumed the column would attack without firing, Mesnil-Durand argued (without much success) that it was possible for troops in column to deliver fire on the enemy. Despite this interesting debate, the French army retained faith in lines. Not until after the War of the Austrian Succession (1741–48) did the French experiment with columnar tactics. The Ordinance of 1754 allowed for the possible use of columns but mandated a line of three ranks. The idea to use columns of attack was not generally well received in France until the onset of the French Revolutionary Wars nearly forty years later.[18]

Commanders relied on multiple lines throughout the eighteenth century. They normally formed two lines with a reserve to the rear, spacing the first and second lines three hundred paces apart. By the 1740s and 1750s, nearly every European army reduced such formations from four to three ranks. The battalion organization was nearly universal, with typically two field battalions of about eight hundred men each in a regiment. Most armies used fairly broad marching columns ten to thirty men wide. Folard's idea of attacking in column was debated but never really took hold because of the obvious problems associated with it. The front was so narrow that only a small number of men in a column could fire their weapons.[19]

THE SEVEN YEARS' WAR AND ITS AFTERMATH

The Seven Years' War (1756–63) marked the beginning of a transition period between the golden age of the unitary army and the more flexible linear system developed during the French Revolutionary and Napoleonic Wars and used in the American Civil War. Participants in the Seven Years' War experimented with a combination of line and column, extensive use of light infantry, and at least minimal efforts to attempt attacks in column formation. Linear tactics proved to be an adaptable system to a number of new developments, at least as long as the primary infantry weapon remained the single-shot muzzleloader. None of the limited experiments of the Seven Years' War bore much fruit until the outbreak of the French Revolution twenty-nine years later.

The French were responsible for many of the innovative experiments tried during the Seven Years' War. They adopted the division organization to spread out the army into more marching columns, which made it easier to deploy the troops for battle. The division became an organic unit within the army with its own artillery complement. Typically the French division deployed in two battle lines, half of its sixteen battalions in each line, with a small reserve to the rear. Tactical manuals allowed for the use of attack columns only to assault fortified positions. The French developed the "column of waiting" as an intermediate stage between the marching column and the line of battle. It could deploy or continue on to a more threatened part of the army's position as the need arose.[20]

The French continued to form combinations of line and column during this war to create a flexible formation. Columns invariably were placed to the rear of units that were formed in line. This was not the true ordre mixte of Napoleon's era because the mix of line and column was not formed side by side. The French conducted an attack in column at the Battle of Rossbach on November 5, 1756. More accurately, it was a counterattack and may well have been an impromptu response to enemy action. Regardless, the assault in column badly failed that day. French officers employed skirmishers in front of their main battle formation in many major engagements, an idea urged by Marshal Maurice de Saxe several years earlier. The Seven Years' War also saw more individual firing, or firing at will, than was typical of the early eighteenth century due to the widespread adoption of the iron ramrod, which allowed for easier reloading.[21]

The Prussian experience during the Seven Years' War has become almost legendary to students of the conflict. Outnumbered and hedged in by enemies nearly on all sides, Frederick the Great earned his title through a series of campaigns that more often than not resulted in Prussian battlefield victories. Dennis Showalter has written of Prussian "operational virtuosity" at the Battle of Leuthen (December 5, 1757), with effective support of the infantry by artillery and the flanks protected by cavalry. Two Prussian attacks launched at the right place and time proved to be effective that day. In general, Frederick emphasized shock action and sought ways to move nearly his entire battle line to strike at enemy flanks. He also used multiple lines and developed echelon formations to extend his own flanks offensively.[22]

Frederick the Great "brought the old-style unitary army to the peak of its possibilities," Robert S. Quimby argues. That concept, treating the entire field force as one unit, was the culmination of the linear system as developed by the 1750s. The Prussians achieved that goal with intense training and discipline that the French could not match. Thus, the French experimented with a more flexible system, dividing their field forces into divisions to create several columns for faster marching and deployment. This in turn pointed toward future developments shaping how the French Revolutionary conflict, the Napoleonic Wars, and the American Civil War were conducted.[23]

Following the Seven Years' War, the French engaged in fruitful reevaluation of their military system. The Regulations of 1764 continued to mandate lines of battle but more strongly recommended attack columns when feasible. It identified what American Civil War soldiers would recognize as a "double column" for that purpose, smaller than those proposed by Folard and Mesnil-Durand. The regulations also gave "official sanction to the long-standing use of skirmishers," according to Quimby. The revised Ordinance of 1766 continued to support these ideas and provided for passage of deployed lines in ways that also would be familiar to American soldiers a century later.[24]

The intensity of tactical discussion deepened when the Comte de Guibert published *Essai général de tactique* in 1772. Guibert dealt with both primary and secondary tactics, advocating a more fluid, flexible, and mobile form of operations that would inform Napoleon's practice within a few years. He saw firepower as the fundamental tool of infantry and shock as secondary, criticizing Folard and Mesnil-Durand for their exaggerated faith in the physical effect of column attacks. Yet Guibert fully realized the utility of using columns on the battlefield to hold units in readiness for deployment into line when needed. If attack columns were called for, he argued that they should be small double columns. He advocated streamlining the process of moving from marching columns to battle formations and argued that commanders did not have to worry about inverting ranks. If faced to the rear, the rear rank had to face the enemy, inverting the normal formation of the unit; Guibert believed it was not worth the complex and time-consuming maneuvers needed to avoid this situation. He also introduced the concept of marching by the flank, which involved each man turning right or left in place and stepping forward to shift the line laterally until ordered to stop and face to the front again. This was the fastest and easiest way to move a line and became quite popular among Civil War commanders. In another book, *Defense du systeme de guerre moderne*, published in 1779, Guibert endorsed the ordre mixte.[25]

Guibert called for light infantry that could not only operate independently but also in support of main battle formations. The French had used such troops during the Seven Years' War, and the Austrians continued to excel in this area. According to Christopher Duffy, using those troops to conduct raids and ambushes in small-scale operations had become "an established feature of warfare" by the late eighteenth century. But by the 1760s, theorists were calling for training line infantrymen in loose-order formations so they could more closely cooperate with the main line. Light infantry sometimes did this too, but the trend now was toward developing what Civil War soldiers would readily recognize as skirmishing. Rather than ranging across the countryside, light infantry ought to stay within close range of the main line, protect it, and pave the way for its advance. In part, this trend was spurred by a realization that light infantry tended to be expensive and difficult to control. Training line troops to fulfill some of these roles would be more efficient.[26]

THE FRENCH REVOLUTIONARY WARS

Dramatic changes in the tactical system took place during the late eighteenth century. Skirmishing, as it came to be practiced by Civil War troops, flowered during the wars of the French Revolution (1792–1800). Some mixture of line and column formations became standard. The increased size of field armies led to higher levels of organization—divisions and corps became fully functioning subunits of the larger field army, capable of marching and fighting independently on a huge, segmented battlefield. Shoulder-to-shoulder lines still constituted the basic formation, but a great deal more flexibility was introduced to maneuvers, giving commanders on all levels additional opportunity to articulate their units to meet almost any battlefield need. This was the impressive tactical system inherited by Civil War commanders.

The more flexible linear system that replaced the unitary army concept came to full fruition in this period, some historians calling it the impulse system. This allowed a good deal of latitude to battalion, brigade, division, and corps commanders to determine how to achieve their part of a larger plan for each battle. As Paddy Griffith has put it, "the secret of success lay in the operational or grand tactical level of action, not in minor tactics." In short, army commanders had to develop clear instructions for subordinates and then trust in their ability to do their part. Offensives took place along an "axis" of advance and often involved a series of attacks rather than "a single broad-front effort." It became necessary to keep many units in columns of waiting to see how each impulse progressed, allowing the division, corps, or army commander to dispatch reserves where needed. "This allowed a numerically large force to selectively assault a portion of the enemy's line."[27]

Revolutionary armies widely used combinations of line and column by about 1794. The tactical regulations of 1791 suggested the use of columns to move troops but still recommended the three-rank line as the standard formation for engaging the enemy. The regulations also recommended squares for defense against cavalry and advocated columns as the proper organization for attacks on fortified villages and redoubts. Increasingly, subordinate commanders on all levels acquired more freedom to decide for themselves whether to fight in column or line, depending on the objective and the lay of the land where they were operating.[28]

While debates about the usefulness of attack columns had been going on for nearly seventy years, it was not until the 1790s that they were used in significant measure. As John Lynn has put it, the French army employed "the attack column as its characteristic offensive tactic." The Armée du Nord, the largest of the several forces fielded by the Revolutionary government, used these formations frequently by 1794. While not always successful, Lynn believes that "shock assault in column emerged as the decisive element in offensive tactics employed by the Armée du Nord." Commanders still recognized that attack columns limited the amount of firepower troops could deliver, but the formation had a political connotation within the context of the Revolution, representing the power of the people smashing the Revolution's enemies. It also connected the Revolution with the heritage of élan that ran deep in French military culture.[29]

Subunits of the larger field army became bigger and more powerful, fully capable of independent action, which justified the freedom of choice on minor tactical matters allowed their commanders. By 1794 a French division could be as large as 13,000 men, typically divided into three demibrigades and with its own artillery and cavalry force. The demibrigades, also known as half brigades, were the product of a decision to merge the mass of citizen-soldiers with the professional army. Two volunteer or (after 1798) conscript battalions were brigaded with one professional battalion. It was a successful effort to blend the best qualities of these two types of soldiers (in contrast to the Northern government in the Civil War, which kept the regulars separate from the volunteers). Revolutionary France created a national army similar both in size and in general-mobilization policies to the Northern and Southern forces of the Civil War.[30]

The tactical manuals available to Civil War armies had their origins in the French Revolution. The Ordinance of 1791 "was the culmination of all the intellectual fermentation of the French Army during the century," according to Quimby, and many of Guibert's ideas were institutionalized in its pages. This ordinance established the tactical system used by the French for the next three decades. Moreover, the 1791 manual and its revisions would be copied by the Americans for their own use until the 1880s. The Ordinance of 1791 mandated a line of three ranks but allowed for widespread use of columns for many purposes, including attack. It provided improved ways to deploy into battle formations that included wheeling and oblique marching by columns and facilitated the shift from the unitary army concept toward the more flexible linear system that had been slowly developing for decades.[31]

French Revolutionary forces learned the formations and maneuvers described in their tactical regulations of 1791 and used them rather effectively on the battlefield. Commanders alternated column with line, changing from one to the other as demanded by the enemy force and the terrain. They deployed large numbers of skirmishers, concentrated their artillery, attacked with persistence after any initial repulse, and learned to adapt to changing circumstances on the spur of the moment. Unit effectiveness was uneven on the corps and division levels but much more consistent on the battalion and brigade levels.[32]

Modern skirmishing came into its own during this time. With the onset of war in 1792, light troops now began to operate as a screen for the main formation in addition to ranging freely across the countryside to conduct raids. The Armée du Nord mostly employed specially recruited light infantry to skirmish in front of its main line, but at times its commanders also sent line troops out to skirmish. Eventually, line units were trained to specialize in skirmish tactics and received unique designations to indicate that specialty. While light infantrymen tended to operate in swarms and masses when detached and far away from support, they tended to organize a line when fronting the main battle formation. The development of the skirmish line "in support of heavy infantry increased in extent and frequency beyond eighteenth-century experience or expectations," Lynn concludes. Civil War armies inherited this concept sixty years later.[33]

THE NAPOLEONIC WARS

Napoleon thus inherited a war machine that already had instituted many innovations. He honed its new methods to a fine point of execution in the field during the Napoleonic Wars (1800–1815) and was so brilliantly successful that writers afterward often gave him more credit as a military innovator than he deserved. They also tended to refer to "Napoleonic" warfare without explaining exactly what that term meant. Napoleon was a great practitioner rather than a theorist; his success lay in his ability to recognize how to use new methods to accomplish his tactical and strategic goals. Mixing the use of those elements with an uncommon boldness of vision and a surprising degree of risk taking, he both dazzled and frightened the world. Moreover, Napoleon often opposed generals who had none of his abilities and were more easily overcome by these methods. He fought battles that closely resembled those of the Civil War and was a self-conscious model for many Northern and Southern officers.

Napoleon tinkered little with the military machine he inherited from the Revolutionary government, retaining the battalion at nine companies and renaming the demibrigade a regiment. He institutionalized the corps as a permanent feature of his armies and made it the smallest unit to be graced with its own artillery and cavalry. Napoleon preferred to give general instructions, leaving the tactical considerations largely to his subordinates. Corps, division, regimental, and battalion commanders had remarkable leeway to decide when and how to use columns versus lines, how many skirmishers to send out, and whether to stop and fire during an advance or to push straight on without halting. Those worthy of their salt could articulate their units with surprising ease during combat, going from column to battle line and back again as circumstances demanded. This was a brand of warfare very different from that of half a century earlier and remarkably similar to the Civil War half a century later.[34]

Napoleon assiduously drilled his troops during the interim between wars. At Boulogne in 1804–1805, he mandated two days per week for battalion drill and target practice, three days for division drill, and one day for corps drill, with multi-corps maneuvers every two weeks. Intensive training combined with repeated experience on campaign and in battle were key elements of French military effectiveness.[35]

The makeup of Napoleon's forces altered as time passed. Battlefield losses and the growing extent of the empire required him to use more non-French troops. He also standardized the division at two brigades. Each brigade consisted of two regiments of four field battalions, with a fifth battalion stationed at a depot for more efficient funneling of replacements to the parent command. Each battalion consisted of four line companies, one skirmish company, and one grenadier company. Napoleon concentrated artillery at higher command levels to make it easier to mass firepower and promoted the shift toward heavier ordnance. He could achieve a concentration of as many as seventy guns in one position during some engagements.[36]

The size of Napoleon's field armies grew after 1808, with 170,000 men at Wagram (July 5–6, 1809), 120,000 at Dresden (August 26–27, 1813), and 195,000 at Leipzig (October 16–19, 1813). Tactical effectiveness tended to decrease as the size of his field armies grew and drillmasters experienced difficulties while training later conscripts. The French commander came "to rely more on mass and less on maneuver." At Borodino (September 7, 1812) Napoleon simply pushed frontal attacks against the Russians that eventually convinced his opponent to give up the field, but the success cost him horrendous casualties. The degree of articulation suffered as well in these later wars. Units and their commanders "lacked the precision and flexibility of earlier campaigns," according to Brent Nosworthy. "Once under fire, units rarely changed formation to respond to circumstances." Napoleon tried to compensate for these trends by mandating a two-rank line and insisting on more-intense target practice and drill, but his subordinates often could not implement those directives.[37]

One of the many reasons for Napoleon's downfall lay in the fact that his principal enemies learned his methods and successfully used them at a time when his own ability to utilize them deteriorated. They improved their tactical formations along the lines already achieved by the French. The British had adopted a line of two ranks before other European forces and emphasized light infantry. Wellington especially became adept at using terrain features to hide his formations and to deliver concentrated musketry at close ranges to disrupt the advance of enemy columns before they could deploy into lines. The Prussians used columns of two-company frontage to both maneuver and attack, and they greatly expanded their light-infantry force. Their new drill manual called for more target practice to improve volley and individual fire and more skirmish drill for a larger percentage of the line infantry. The Russians also liked the column with two-company frontage, smaller than they typically used, to achieve a greater degree of flexibility in manuevering.[38]

General trends evident in the major Napoleonic-era armies included the tendency to open fire at moderate or longer ranges than was typical of the eighteenth century. Greater amounts of ammunition were available, making prolonged firefights more common as in the American Civil War. This did not mean that aggressive tactics had fallen out of favor. Arguments over whether it was better to fire and damage the enemy before advancing or to assault with little or no softening up continued. A compromise solution was to follow up a few well-placed volleys with a bayonet attack. The French used squares more widely than would be common in the Civil War. Flexible mixing of lines and columns and effective coordination of artillery and cavalry to support infantry formations also highlighted Napoleonic warfare.[39]

A handful of officers argued that the French regulations of 1791 needed revision to eliminate formations and maneuvers that were less useful in the field. Nosworthy has concluded that a number of "ad hoc variants born out of necessity" resulted when officers dealt with these formations and maneuvers. But his research base seems limited. Quimby's more detailed investigation of this issue supports the view that the system as laid out worked very well with little improvisation. He argues that "even the most complex evolutions of the Ordinance of 1791 fitted actual conditions well enough . . . to find occasion for application." The same could be said of the linear system used by Northern and Southern officers during the Civil War.[40]

How often armies of the era used columns and how much they relied on lines has been a source of debate. Napoleon endorsed the ordre mixte, and it seems to have been a fairly common way to organize units on the battlefield, but that does not mean it was common to launch attacks in column. Previously, historians had assumed that the French attacked in columns and the British, in particular, defended in lines, but more recent studies have indicated that even the French more often attacked in lines than in columns.[41]

Detailed methods for moving lines across a cluttered landscape had been worked out long before the arrival of Napoleon. Commanders fixed a prominent point in the terrain ahead as a target to help their troops advance in a straight line. The men touched elbows and guided to the center of their battalion. When more than one unit participated in the movement, one of them was designated as the battalion of direction, and the others had to adjust their movements to it. The British typically designated the rightmost battalion, but it could be any of those in the formation.[42]

If the battle line had to change its front to right or left to meet an enemy threat, it could do so by a number of different ways. Each battalion could pivot in place, using its center or either flank as the pivot point. If the unit had to face to the rear, each man could turn around in his place, inverting the placement of the senior company in the battalion line as well as the order of the ranks. Wheeling a battle line onto a new piece of ground was a bit more complicated. Men were sent out to stand on the spot where the new line was to take shape. The battalion of direction then wheeled to this new spot, to be followed by the others. The difficulty lay in the fact that each battalion had to break contact with its neighbor, move independently and accurately into the new line, and reestablish contact with units to right and left. Of course, the longer the wheel and greater the distance covered, the more time consuming and complex the maneuver.[43]

Commanders had several different ways to advance a line toward the enemy. To attack en echelon, the battalion of direction started first, breaking contact with its neighbors. The next battalion waited until the first was about one hundred paces away before beginning a similar movement, to be taken up by the other units in turn. The commanders had to be comfortable maneuvering independently but in concert with the others. An advance en echelon was useful for covering the exposed flank of a large formation as it moved forward or for attempting to outflank an opposing line if the echelon extended forward rather than backward. Drill manuals allowed units to retreat en echelon as well.[44]

The cluttered nature of a battlefield, often dotted with small villages, farmsteads, and other obstacles, offered many difficulties to a moving line. Subunits such as the platoon, battalion, or brigade could drop back and slide to the rear of the next subunit, usually toward the center of the line, to create an interval in the formation and thereby pass an obstruction. For smaller subunits, the easier method was to form a column as it dropped back to avoid the object, then to wheel back into line when the way was clear. Commanders used a similar method to pass a line through a narrow defile, or opening, in a line of obstructions. The subunits formed a column and lined up to pass through the defile and then redeployed into line on the other side.[45]

Actually, none of these tactical maneuvers were new to the Napoleonic era. All of them had been thoroughly worked out by the Prussians and the French in previous decades. The armies of the American Civil War still used these basic maneuvers. A recent historian of tactics during the Napoleonic Wars has noted that there is little evidence to indicate how closely these maneuvers were followed in practice. That problem does not exist for the Civil War. Official battle reports clearly show that they were known by brigade and regimental commanders who used them quite a lot on the battlefield, and this was most likely true of Napoleonic-era commanders as well.[46]

Tactical formations and maneuvers had developed a great deal from the time of the Spanish tercios to the fall of Napoleon. In the seventeenth century, battlefields were busy, complex arenas filled with several different kinds of soldiers armed with different weapons and organized in massive formations loosely coordinating their movements with each other. In the eighteenth century the human shape of the battlefield was much more streamlined. Uniformity replaced multiplicity, a single weapon dominated the field, and high-ranking officers asserted control over thousands of men. This was the era of the unitary army. By the early nineteenth century, a significant degree of flexibility and control by lower-level officers was achieved, adjusting the tactical system to a more comfortable and viable stage befitting the enlarged armies of the new era. This was the inauguration of the flexible system some historians called the impulse system.[47]

When the Napoleonic Wars came to an end in 1815, only forty-six years before the firing on Fort Sumter, French theory and experience deeply influenced tactical thinking in Europe. American armies shared this military heritage.

The North American Tactical Heritage

The European military experience was the fundamental background of the tactics used by Civil War armies, but the North American military experience was more immediate in the collective memory of the Civil War generation. While officers and men did not necessarily know the details of the American Revolution or the War of 1812, for example, they certainly were aware of those conflicts in a general way. A survey of the North American tactical heritage reveals that the linear system as developed in Europe was used largely intact in the New World, though with some alterations to suit specific circumstances.

The English colonies relied on a militia force to fill their martial needs rather than the professional armies that the linear system was meant to serve. The colonists either imported or reprinted numerous European manuals in the years preceding the outbreak of the American Revolution, but they tended to find them too complex and arcane because the books had been written for professional armies rather than citizen-soldiers. Some Americans wrote their own manuals to appeal to militiamen, but none of these caught on widely with the colonials either.[1]

Lewis Nicola, a French-born veteran of the British army who had moved to Philadelphia before the war, set the tone for many of the manuals produced in North America. In a book designed for use by the Philadelphia militia, he omitted elaborate maneuvers designed for parades and boiled down the rest of the tactical doctrine to suit his amateur audience. Nicola's previous experience in the British army lent credibility to his warnings that the Americans were in for a tough fight. The British, he warned, used a three-rank line, while the Philadelphia militiamen always drilled in two ranks. Nicola urged the colonials to adopt the British practice, instructing that the ranks be separated by "four good paces" and that the tallest men should be in the first rank, the next tallest in the third, and the shortest in the second. Within each rank, the tallest soldier should be on the right. Nicola did not like deep columns with narrow fronts, advocating instead columns of "grand divisions," four per regiment, each of which forming behind the other, thus making a twelve-rank regimental column. If a regiment was deployed in only two ranks, however, he suggested that it form an attack column of half–grand divisions that would be sixteen ranks deep.[2]

But Nicola prescribed some intricate maneuvers for articulating a regiment on the battlefield that were probably too complex for his militia audience. He described how to wheel on the center of a regiment, with each wing of the unit wheeling to right or left. Each man was to feel the elbow of the man next to him toward the side that pivoted while looking down the line toward the flank that moved to keep the line as straight as possible. Nicola also outlined a method whereby a regiment could change front to the rear so that its left flank would still be its left flank in the new facing—maintaining the standard deployment of the unit and avoiding inversion. This involved a tedious process of moving each file separately to the new position, although Nicola admitted it could be done faster if whole platoons and subdivisions did it at a time. He also spelled out how to form squares and to pass defiles.[3]

THE AMERICAN REVOLUTION

The tenor of Nicola's work, and that of other American-produced manuals, was to simplify complex maneuvers for an audience with no previous military experience. No one did this better than another European who enlisted in the American cause, Frederick William Augustus von Steuben. A Prussian who had served in the army of his native land since age sixteen, he resigned his commission at the end of the Seven Years' War to enter the landed gentry. Steuben came to North America in 1777 and offered his services to Washington at Valley Forge, drilling a model company and drafting a manual in French (he spoke little English). It was translated to become the standard American drill manual in 1779 and continued to be used well into the War of 1812. Steuben received command of a division at Yorktown and lived in New York State until his death in 1794.[4]

Steuben's manual, which became known as the "Blue Book" after the Revolution, drew material from several sources. He based much of it on the British regulations of 1764 but also used French and Prussian manuals. Steuben preferred the Prussian seventy-five steps per minute rather than the English sixty steps per minute as the standard marching rate. He prescribed both column and line to increase tactical flexibility, encouraging the use of closed columns for easier handling of troops on the march.[5]

A page-by-page examination of the Blue Book shows it to be the most watered-down version of European linear tactics ever published, yet Steuben managed to convey to his untutored charges the essence of that system. It was a triumph of concise and clear exposition geared to the level of his audience. Steuben also followed the basic format of the tactical manual without copying the words verbatim. He literally rewrote existing European manuals without losing the important instructions contained in them.

Steuben's manual duplicated the outline of all drill manuals of the day. It began with basic information on the organization and composition of the company and regiment. Then, in a section later to be called the "School of the Soldier," he discussed how a recruit should stand and how he should handle, load, and fire his musket. Once the recruit learned these basic tasks, he joined eleven other men so they could form one rank and learn how to deport themselves as a small unit. Steuben also described the basic elements of marching and wheeling in this section.[6]

Moving into what was later termed the "School of the Company," Steuben discussed how to open and close ranks (moving individuals within the ranks closer or farther apart from each other), drilling on rough ground, marching by files, and wheeling by platoons or by companies. He preferred a two-rank line and also prescribed that the tallest men should occupy the rear rank. In the front rank the tallest should occupy the right and left, leaving the center for the shorter men. Steuben divided each battalion into four divisions of two platoons each. In a style to be copied by later manual authors, he used the word *battalion* to refer to the basic unit of the army, which in North America was the regiment. The Americans did not adopt the European practice to make the true battalion (a subunit of the regiment) the basic operating unit of their forces, though, which led to a certain amount of confusion in the terminology of subsequent drill manuals. The Prussian assumed the standard American regiment would consist of eight companies, with one additional company of light infantry that drilled on its own.[7]

Steuben's "Exercise of a Battalion" explained the basic maneuvers for a unit larger than a company. He described how to change a marching column of eight companies into a battle line and back again by forming either on the left, right, or center (fifth) company. Steuben recommended wheeling as the best way to change the front of a regimental line, but if a brigade or division had to do so, it was best to form a close column and march to the spot, then redeploy into line. The simplest way for a marching column to change direction was for the first unit to wheel, followed by each succeeding unit wheeling at the same spot. He explained how files could break off from the marching column and fall back in order to move the column through a narrow defile. Lines negotiated defiles and obstacles in its path by a similar method of breaking off subunits to fall back and go through the gap or around the impediment, then resuming their place in line on the other side. The battle line maintained its alignment during an advance by taking cues from the pace of the flag, from the battalion of direction, or by fixing a point in the landscape ahead as a marker.[8]

Battlefield practice sometimes deviated from the recommendations of the drill manual. Despite the ongoing debate about the number of ranks, both sides typically used two ranks during the Revolutionary War. The British army on campaign in North America used the regulations issued in 1764, which not only mandated three ranks but also recommended a formation of three lines, with the second three hundred paces behind the first, and the third five hundred to six hundred paces behind the second. But commanders often were unable to do this because of severely limited manpower. They often had formed only one line and thinned it out to two ranks, with intervals of eighteen inches between men in the ranks to extend the front and cover more ground. Loss of officers also made a mess of the proper order of companies within regiments.[9]

Historian Matthew Spring has argued that the heavily forested topography of North America compelled the British to adopt many of the tactical alterations described above. Terrain prompted officers "to display an unconventional degree of tactical initiative" compared to European practice. The heavy use of light infantry also characterized warfare in North America, with the patriots outperforming the British in what Spring calls "bush fighting." He also believes British companies acted "as semiautonomous tactical entities" on these battlefields due to the limited size of armies and the often rugged nature of the terrain.[10]

British commanders in North America preferred to avoid prolonged firefights. They commonly ordered one or two volleys at about sixty yards, then pushed their troops into a rapid advance. The American habit of taking up defensive positions on good ground, aided at times by fieldworks, prompted this trend. British officers did not think they could damage the enemy much by prolonged firing and, given their limited manpower, did not want to waste troops in half-hearted measures. Shock assaults therefore became a feature of British operations during the American

Revolution. The officers normally marched their men at the fastest rate feasible, beginning at 120 paces per minute and moving faster when closing on the target. The Americans normally broke and retired before the British came close enough to use the bayonet.[11]

In general, American troops could not match their counterparts in terms of tactical effectiveness during the length of the Revolutionary conflict. State-militia troops served short terms before returning to civilian life. Continental units were raised by the state governments for longer terms, but until the advent of Steuben's training regimen, they received little effective drill instruction. British troops thus often faced opponents who were below their level in terms of tactical acumen. By the latter stages of the conflict, many Continental units approached that level, but even when opposing poor-quality American units, the British normally did not follow up a battlefield victory with an effective pursuit. Exhaustion of the men, the lack of cavalry, and the forested nature of the terrain all played a role in this decision, which helped prolong the conflict into seven years of terrible suffering.[12]

The American military experience in the Revolution was characterized by painful learning over time. In the disastrous New York Campaign, troops were cautioned to fire at very short ranges. A soldier at the Battle of Brooklyn (August 27, 1776) remembered that his officers told the rank and file to wait until their British opponents were fifty yards away before opening fire. Jeremiah Greenman recalled that the 2nd Rhode Island Infantry deployed from marching column to battle line during a skirmish in New Jersey in 1780, employing the old-fashioned processional method.[13]

In some of the later battles, especially in the South, field commanders commonly employed more than one line. At Cowpens (January 17, 1781) Col. Daniel Morgan deployed his less-reliable South Carolina militia in the first line while putting Continental troops in another line behind them. He placed skirmishers 150 yards in front of the militia, which forced the approaching British to attack with inadequate knowledge of Morgan's formation. The militia fired five times by battalions at a range of 30–50 yards before obeying Morgan's instructions to break off contact and fall back to the rear of the second line. The Continentals misunderstood their orders and began to retire when the advancing enemy closed in, only to stop 80 yards away, turn, and deliver a volley at a range of fifteen yards that devastated the 71st Regiment of Foot.[14]

At Guilford Courthouse (March 15, 1781) Nathaniel Greene duplicated Morgan's dispositions, except that he deployed three lines instead of two and the terrain forced him to place his lines farther apart from each other. North Carolina militiamen formed the first line behind a fence with an open field in front. A mixture of mounted troops, light infantry, and militiamen covered both flanks. The second line, consisting of Virginia militiamen, formed in heavy woods 300 yards to the rear of the first. A thin line of riflemen was posted twenty paces behind the Virginians to act as a provost guard, keeping the militiamen in their assigned place. The third line, 500 yards to the rear of the second, took position on a slight hill. Greene put 1,400 Continental troops, the best the Americans had in the South, here. Cleared land fronted them, and two six-pounder field guns bolstered the center of their position.[15]

Lord Cornwallis's British force, a mixture of English and Hessian units, consisted of about 2,200 men compared to Greene's 4,400 troops. The North Carolina militia opened fire at long range, 140 yards, but the British were not affected until they reached within 50 yards of the fence, where they stopped and fired a volley. Then the militia obeyed Greene's instructions to break off the engagement and retire. The woods that fronted the American second line disrupted British formations, so the confrontation with the Virginians devolved into a series of firefights. The eventual result was an American retreat.[16]

The opposing sides, however, grappled in a bloody and stubborn contest at the third line. It started with an ill-prepared attack by the 33rd Regiment of Infantry and some German units against the American right. The Continentals fired at close range, as short as twenty yards, and repelled the attack. Then a battalion of Guards swept across the open space and drove away the 2nd Maryland, which supported the two six-pounders. The guns fell into British hands, bringing the battle to a crisis. A spirited counterattack by the 1st Maryland from the American right to the center retook the guns and resulted in frenzied hand-to-hand fighting. Cornwallis ordered his artillery to fire into the melee, willing to injure his own men to break the tactical stalemate. The Guards retired, but Greene also admitted defeat and pulled away from Guilford Courthouse, leaving the field to the British. Cornwallis lost 24.1 percent of his command in this Pyrrhic victory, while Greene suffered 29.7 percent losses.[17]

Obstinate fighting of this type foreshadowed Civil War combat. The 1st Maryland performed an oblique advance across the battlefield and stubbornly engaged in hand-to-hand combat in an effort to decide the outcome of the battle. This level of articulation and willingness to grapple with a dangerous enemy spoke volumes about how far many regiments of the Continental army had developed into professional units equal in effectiveness to their European counterparts.

THE WAR OF 1812

The U.S. Army was ill prepared to engage the British when the War of 1812 began. Dismal battlefield performances thus characterized much of the conflict. But the level of effectiveness rose sharply because of a rigorous training course that Maj. Gen. Jacob Brown instituted at Buffalo, New York, in the spring of 1814. Regular troops had trained rather ineffectually in 1812 and to greater results the next year, but the troops at Buffalo were put through a much more intense level of drill than previously in the war. Winfield Scott was in charge of the course, using the French regulations of 1791 as translated by a French émigré named Amelot DeLacroix and published in 1810. Scott put his regulars through their paces for ten weeks, and his intense drilling produced results. When Brown took the field with this small army, it was "the most combat-ready force the United States would field during the War of 1812" in the estimation of historian Donald Graves.[18]

The improvement in American tactical effectiveness can be gauged by comparing two late-war battles, one fought before and the other after the Buffalo training camp. At Crysler's Farm (November 11, 1813), which took place on the north bank of the Saint Lawrence River in Canada, the Americans pushed two regular brigades through the woods in columns of regiments. Emerging onto open ground where the defending British were posted, they opened fire at long range. The British returned fire at a range of 100–150 yards, firing by division; that is, the right wing of the depleted 89th Regiment of Infantry, three companies, fired first, followed seconds later by the two companies of the left wing. This fire caught the Americans as they were deploying from column into line. Then the 89th switched to platoon fire to increase the tempo, and the Americans broke and fled. The 49th Regiment of Infantry joined the 89th in a counterattack, both of them continuing to fire by platoons as they moved forward, driving more than double their number of opponents off the field. Crysler's Farm was a dismal American failure that ended James Wilkinson's attempt to capture Montreal. All historians criticize the American performance.[19]

But the Battle of Lundy's Lane (July 25, 1814), fought just inside the Canadian border, involved American units subjected to Scott's training regimen. The result proved the value of units able to articulate their strength under stress. The British took position about two miles from Niagara Falls atop a gentle ridge with a gradual, open ascent. They posted 2,200 men and five guns, while the Americans deployed three regular regiments into a two-rank battle line and advanced to long musket range, where both sides exchanged volleys for forty-five minutes. The Americans suffered more from British artillery fire than from their musketry. Then Scott ordered his First Brigade to advance. The men closed the range until British fire compelled them to halt, suffering heavy casualties (more than 60 percent during the entire battle) and running out of ammunition. Scott was compelled to retire, but Brown quickly brought up Eleazar W. Ripley's Second Brigade. The British commander, Lt. Gen. Gordon Drummond, had failed to post a skirmish line even though most of his regiments included a light-infantry company. This helped Ripley's 21st U.S. Infantry to get close and devastate the British gun crews with a volley at 100 yards or less. The 89th Regiment advanced toward the 21st, and the two units engaged in a firefight at such close ranges that survivors remembered the muzzle flashes crossed between the lines. The 89th was forced to fall back, and the American regiment continued forward to take possession of the British guns.[20]

Drummond carefully formed a counterattack and launched it at about 10:00 P.M. Neither side deployed a skirmish line. The British quietly moved to close range, between thirty and ninety feet, before firing by volley. Drummond's men retired after almost a half hour of this mutual punishment. He attacked again a few minutes later, duplicating the close-range fight. Scott advanced the remnants of his re-formed brigade to help, but in the darkness his men were fired on by fellow Americans. Yet Drummond ordered his troops to retire from their second counterattack only to launch a third effort at about 11:30 P.M. Yet another close-range firefight in the dark, another failed attempt by Scott to push the British away, and hand-to-hand fighting at the captured guns took place, but the British retired again.[21]

The articulation of units, the intensity of sustained fighting, and the repeated attacks at Lundy's Lane were far beyond what had happened at Guilford Courthouse and indicative of what was to come in the Civil War. Also indicative of what was to come, the Americans withdrew despite their bloody victory and retired that night to their forward base of operations at Chippawa. The opponents at Lundy's Lane were on the same level of professional development and commitment to their cause as would be the case nearly fifty years later in the Civil War.[22]

AFTER 1815

The American military groped its way toward adopting a more thorough tactical manual during the period of the War of 1812 and its aftermath. The army relied on Steuben's simple manual for a long while, but several writers worked to replace it. Journalist William Duane published a two-volume study in 1809 that compiled information on all aspects of military knowledge, the first to appear in the United States, including a substantial section on tactics that was translated from the French regulations of 1791. He revised some parts of Steuben's work and reinforced other parts. The points of agreement and disagreement included the pace of the common and quick step and the use of three ranks versus two. Duane also supported a faster way to move units along a diagonal line of advance, preferring the French technique of having each man turn either a half or quarter to the right or the left and then marching the line in that direction.[23]

Duane still believed in the concept of specialized light infantry. He delineated ten duties, ranging from conducting advance patrols to foraging, setting up ambushes, and acting as line infantry if needed. He continued to differentiate between light infantry and skirmishers and specified that rifle companies should send out no more than half their strength to skirmish during a battle, keeping the rest as a skirmish reserve. While Duane thought skirmishers should be 120 paces in front of the main line, the reserve should be placed halfway between the forward line and the main position.[24]

Duane's compilation was on the verge of being adopted by the U.S. Army when its chief sponsor, Secretary of War Henry Dearborn, was replaced in office by William Eustis in 1810. Nevertheless, there were several competitors to Duane's book by that time. As mentioned earlier, Delacroix had translated the 1791 French regulations and published his book in Boston in 1810. In addition, Col. Alexander Smyth of the army's rifle regiment translated and abridged the same French regulations. This effort won favor with Eustis, and James Madison officially adopted Smyth's book by presidential order in March 1812, three months before the war began.[25]

Published as *Regulations for the Field Exercises, Manoeuvres, and Conduct of the Infantry,* Smyth's book was much longer and more complex than Steuben's. Smyth emphasized wheeling more than his predecessor. He retained Steuben's preference for three ranks but allowed that units could drill in two ranks for convenience. He adjusted the rate of the quickstep, slowing it from 120 paces per minute to 100 paces, and urged substantial firing practice so that soldiers could consistently shoot three rounds per minute. Smyth allowed for inversion, the practice of changing a regimental front without maintaining the prescribed order of companies in the linear formation. Inversion put companies out of their normal spot in the lineup but allowed the regiment to change front to the rear to meet a new threat more quickly.[26]

Duane bounced back with another effort to produce an acceptable drill manual. He argued that only Congress, not the president, could officially adopt a tactical system for the army and found favor with John Armstrong, the new secretary of war. Armstrong convinced lawmakers to adopt a new book compiled by Duane, *Hand Book for Infantry*. It also was based largely on the 1791 French regulations, but Duane condensed that manual from three hundred to one hundred pages. Officially adopted in the spring of 1813, the *Hand Book* found little favor among the army's officers, who widely considered it fit only for militia troops.[27]

The army entered a new and more professional phase after the War of 1812 as Winfield Scott began to dominate tactical thinking. James Monroe replaced Armstrong as secretary of war and called for a board to handle the question of adopting a better tactical system for the army. Scott headed the board, which obeyed Monroe's instruction to adopt the 1791 French regulations, selecting John McDonald's translation of the drill manual that had been published in London in 1803. Congress officially approved what came to be known as the 1815 Regulations. But the French drill had not included tactics for light infantry or for riflemen, so another board was convened in 1824 to revise the regulations. Scott headed this board too, which adopted a new French manual that included drill for light infantry and rifle troops in 1825. When another improvement in the French regulations appeared in 1831, Scott translated the work and saw its adoption by the U.S. Army four years later.[28]

The 1835 manual was the crowning achievement of Scott's influence on American tactics. Published in three volumes as *Infantry Tactics, or Rules for the Exercise and Manoeuvres of the United States Infantry*, it was the longest, most thorough drill book yet published in America. Unlike previous manuals, it dealt comprehensively with brigade and division movements. Even though the concept of a corps had been well established by the time of the Napoleonic Wars, Scott failed to include it in his discussion because the U.S. Army had never operated in numbers large enough to justify the creation of a corps. Like Duane and Smyth before him, Scott also spent a good deal of time on the exact pace of quick and double-quick movements and whether three ranks were better than two.[29]

Scott's manual represented a greater degree of professional achievement in American drill literature, but the next generation of army officers came to see it as stultified by the 1850s. They criticized it for being "overloaded by a redundancy of words," as one put it. The critic, who remained anonymous, understood the purpose was to instill a sense of "dignity and grandeur" to the process of giving commands for movements that were "formal and dignified; no unseemly haste, but

Fig. 2.1. Winfield Scott, who dominated American tactical thinking during much of the early nineteenth century. Scott compiled one of the three tactical manuals used by Union and Confederate troops during the Civil War. It was adopted by the U.S. Army in 1835. (LC-DIG-cwpb-04768)

in slow and measured time." Yet the newer generation felt this sort of emphasis had outlived its usefulness.[30]

The growing influence of West Point on instilling a stronger, more sustained sense of tactics in the interwar American army can be seen in the teaching of Dennis Hart Mahan, who fully endorsed French tactics. He supported the use of a two-rank battle line, columns to maneuver and to attack, and the use of light infantry to skirmish.[31]

By 1846 the U.S. Army was able to operate with surprising effectiveness on the battlefields of the Mexican War (1846–48). The Americans continued to use two ranks and often deployed lighter skirmish lines than did the Europeans, even lighter than prescribed in the manuals, perhaps because they had limited troop strength and commanders did not want to disperse manpower. Brig. Gen. David E. Twiggs, for example, screened his division with only two companies of skirmishers at the Battle of Monterey (September 21, 1846). The Americans normally used lines, employing columns only when terrain difficulties called for it, but they usually deployed the columns into lines to bring home an attack. On the few occasions when they used attack columns, the formation consisted of relatively few men. One attack column of 500 men at Molino del Rey (September 8, 1847) and another of 250 men at Chapultepec (September 13, 1847) represent the typical size.[32]

THE RIFLE MUSKET

By the 1850s, Europeans and Americans alike were trying to deal with the introduction of the rifle musket as a general-issue weapon. Capt. Claude Etienne Minié's innovation placed a hollow indentation on the bottom surface of a cylindrical-conical bullet to allow the powder gases to expand the soft lead sides of the ball and fit the spiral grooves inside the barrel. This was the most effective way to add rifling to a standard infantry weapon. The Minié rifle became available by 1846 and was widely introduced into the national armies of several nations over the next decade. Britain adopted the Enfield Model 1853 rifle musket, while Austria employed the Lorenz rifle. The Russians followed their defeat and the French followed their victory in the Crimea with the adoption of Minié rifles. Secretary of War Jefferson Davis approved the Springfield .58-caliber rifle musket, Model 1855, for general distribution to the U.S. Army.[33]

This improved weapon, with a potential range of five hundred yards as compared with the smoothbore's range of one hundred yards, seemed to portend revolutionary changes in combat. European writers predicted many results, including increased power on the skirmish line and a reduction in the ability of artillery and cavalry to battle infantry. More radical observers even predicted the demise of linear tactics and their replacement with open order, skirmish formations. For a time, the French were more enthusiastic about the inherent potential in mass distribution of rifles. They sought to find methods of employing skirmish tactics by the battle line to speed up movement within the apparently deeper killing zone of the rifle musket. British writers tended to be more conservative, noting that long-range firing had built-in limitations. The cluttered nature of most battlefields, where visibility was limited by woods, hills, or buildings, and the difficulties of seeing very far through clouds of powder smoke could limit the ability of soldiers to observe and zero in on distant targets.[34]

The Americans were also enthusiastic about the possibilities of the rifle musket and changed their tactical manual a bit in an effort to accommodate its greater range. Lt. Col. William J. Hardee authored a new book, *Rifle and Light Infantry Tactics*, which was adopted in 1855 to replace Scott's manual, now two decades old.

Fig. 2.2. William J. Hardee, author of the tactical manual that replaced Scott's book in 1855. After he joined the Confederate army, the Federal government replaced his book with a new manual compiled by Silas Casey. (LC-USZC4-7972)

It was hardly a revolutionary book, for Hardee essentially changed only one small aspect of American tactics by increasing the rate of the double quick to 165 steps per minute, which perspiring infantrymen derisively called the "Shanghai Drill." Hardee also increased the rate of the quick step to 110 paces per minute.[35]

The Americans were not as enamored of the new weapon as were the French, nor as aloof as the British. In fact, one of the most enthusiastic American writers, Lt. Cadmus M. Wilcox of the 7th U.S. Infantry, warned his countrymen of an important caveat even as he promoted the possibilities of the rifle musket. In his book *Rifles and Rifle Practice* (1859), Wilcox warned that to truly exploit the increased range of the weapon, all soldiers had to be carefully trained to gauge distance and operate the sighting mechanism. The Minié ball traced a curved trajectory, sailing upward in a high arc before descending to the ground. In contrast to the flat trajectory of the smoothbore, this projectile curved over the heads of many men who stood in front of it. Sighted for a distance of 300 yards, anyone standing between 100 and 225 yards from the muzzle would be safe. Ironically, the initial 100-yard killing zone was about the same effective range as the smoothbore, and the other killing zone was only 75 yards deep. Moreover, the latter killing zone decreased if the rifle was sighted for longer distances. At 600 yards, for example, this killing zone was only 60 yards deep.[36]

This presented an enormous problem for the average soldier. He had to be able to see potential targets hundreds of yards away, accurately gauge the distance, adjust the sighting mechanism, and hope the enemy was within either of the two killing zones, near or far. Someone with a natural aptitude for weapons could learn to do this, but most recruits did not possess that ability. The British and French established musketry schools by the late 1850s to train soldiers how to estimate distance and work the sighting mechanism. The English School at Hyde was organized along carefully thought-out, scientific methods and had an international reputation.[37]

Despite Wilcox's plea, the U.S. Army did not create a course of rifle instruction before the Civil War. It encouraged subordinate officers to give rifle practice to their men but failed to provide funds to purchase ammunition. The army adopted a manual for rifle practice authored by Capt. Henry Heth of the 10th U.S. Infantry, which essentially duplicated the methods of the Hyde School, but it was never widely used.[38]

Because the army did not prepare its men to make the most of the new rifle musket, as well as several other equally important reasons, all predictions about its revolutionary potential on the battlefield remained academic. Wilcox thought the weapon could be "fourfold more destructive" compared to the older smoothbore musket if handled by trained men. Other writers tried to argue that even unaimed long-range fire could be deadly to large formations of infantry. Maj. Julius P. Garesché urged the War Department on the eve of the Civil War to train an elite corps of sharpshooters armed with breech-loading rifles and mount them on horses so they could move quickly from one part of a battlefield to another. Their role would be to pick off officers and fire explosive bullets into caissons. Garesché believed such a corps could rival the effect of field artillery on enemy personnel.[39]

Unlike Hardee's minor adjustment of the drill system, the French had been developing a quicker, more agile training regimen for skirmishers and for some line infantrymen to move troops faster on the battlefield. Raleigh E. Colston, among others, wanted the U.S. Army to adopt *chasseurs-à-pied* techniques and to give greater importance to skirmishing, for which the distinctive French tactics were well suited.[40]

A handful of volunteer military companies took up the call, most famously that commanded by Col. Elmer Ellsworth of Chicago. Ellsworth's U.S. Zouave Cadets

THE NORTH AMERICAN TACTICAL HERITAGE   33

excelled at the French tactics and demonstrated them in tours and competitions across the eastern states in 1860. He also wrote a drill manual to promote the chasseurs-à-pied method.[41]

But the Zouave tactics copied from the French were not suitable for training a national army of ordinary citizens. They were physically demanding, and only men with some agility, quickness of mind, and a high level of physical stamina could execute them. Zouave tactics were suited for specialty units, and skirmishing was a military specialty that not all line troops could perform equally well.[42]

Moreover, those observers who predicted the decline of the battle line in favor of the skirmish line in a new age dominated by rifle muskets were indulging only in theory. Until a large-scale war involving the rifle musket should take place, they could not truly know how combat might change on a rifle battlefield as compared to a smoothbore battlefield. Whether the linear system should be altered, scrapped entirely, or praised as the proper system to employ would depend on this experience.

☰ 3 ☰

Tactical Manuals and the Management of Men

Volunteers who became frustrated with the technical jargon that filled tactical manuals had to keep in mind that the ultimate purpose of the book was to instruct officers how to manage their men both on and off the battlefield. They contained detailed information about the organization of companies and regiments, taught individual soldiers how to behave under arms, and guided commanders in the process of moving hundreds of troops in coherent fashion. The manuals were far more than dry recitations of old maneuvers that seemed irrelevant to citizen-soldiers; they were much closer to military guidebooks covering many aspects of war on several different levels. Their value became apparent to anyone who viewed soldiering in a serious light.

Officers scrambled in the early part of the Civil War to obtain copies of manuals and begin learning their craft. They had several from which to choose. Scott's book was still viable in the eyes of many. It was used by the state forces of Vermont in May 1861 and continued to be read by Confederate officers such as Brig. Gen. William R. Scurry in early 1864.[1]

Hardee's manual, though, tended to be more popular and more readily available among Southerners than Scott's book. A man ignorant of military matters organized a company of the 2nd Mississippi and lined up his men "against a plank fence in single file," according to Samuel W. Hankins. "This was done in order to get as straight a line as possible." The captain then used Scott's manual to drill them. When the regiment assembled and moved to Harpers Ferry, Virginia, the officers began to use Hardee's manual.[2]

Col. John W. Love, a veteran of the Mexican War and of the interwar militia, used "old time army tactics—that were followed, I supposed, during the Revolutionary War," thought John Johnston of the 6th Tennessee. For example, Love had each platoon advance, fire, then fall back to the rear to reload. "This would have seemed worse than ludicrous a few months afterwards but we thought it all right then." Capt. John Ingram of Company K took over the training of the 6th Tennessee from Love. He had studied at a military school in Kentucky and "was every inch a soldier." Ingram used Hardee's manual, "and it was not many days before we could step like real soldiers, and enjoyed going through the beautiful evolutions of the new tactics. The people, old and young, would generally turn out to see us drill."[3]

Ironically, many Federal commanders used Hardee's tactics as well. Robert McAllister lost his baggage, which included a copy of the Confederate general's book, during the First Bull Run Campaign. "We drilled in Hardee's tactics," recalled Edwin Bryant of the 3rd Wisconsin, "then thought to be the perfection of simple, direct evolution." John Pope thought Hardee was "a great improvement upon the old tactics in use theretofore."[4]

Early in the war, Col. Ulysses S. Grant took his 21st Illinois only up to company drill due to lack of time and opportunity. Once settled into occupation duty in Missouri, he wanted to conduct battalion-level drills. While Grant had studied Scott's manual at West Point, his ranking in tactics as a cadet was "near the foot of the class." He claimed to have never seen a battalion drill even during the Mexican War. Once across the Mississippi, Grant acquired a copy of Hardee's manual and studied it enough to realize that it "was nothing more than common sense and the progress of the age applied to Scott's system. The commands were abbreviated and the movement expedited. Under the old tactics almost every change in the order of march was preceded by a 'halt,' then came the change, and then the 'Forward march.' With the new tactics all these changes could be made while in motion. I found no trouble in giving commands that would take my regiment where I wanted it to go and carry it around all obstacles."[5]

Hardee ran into copyright and royalty trouble because of his allegiance to the Southern cause. The 1855 edition of his manual was published by Lippincott, Granbo, and Company of Philadelphia, which sold 18,000 copies to the government for one dollar each; Hardee received royalties only on copies not sold to the government. While the Lippincott firm paid him what he earned until the outbreak of the war, it did not file a copyright on the book. The publisher reasoned that, with so many plates, it was unlikely anyone would try to reproduce the work, especially in peacetime.[6]

But the outbreak of war caused a huge demand for the manual. It was republished in "immense quantities" in the North, and Hardee had no share in the

Fig. 3.1. Silas Casey, who was given the task of compiling a new tactical manual to replace Hardee's book. It was adopted by the U.S. Army in 1862. (LC-DIG-cwpb-05572)

royalties. Lippincott refused to sell the book in the South, so Hardee made slight changes in his work and contracted with S. H. Goetzel of Alabama to come out with an improved edition by late May 1861. Goetzel's product went through nine editions by late 1863, with Hardee receiving twenty cents per copy. But at least four other Southern publishers came out with editions of their own, most of them based on the older Lippincott edition. Hardee and Goetzel filed several lawsuits against booksellers in Richmond, Mobile, and Memphis to stop this practice. When the case involving the seller in Mobile was concluded in July 1863, the judge ruled in favor of the seller, saying that his book was based on the original 1855 edition for which there was no copyright. The plaintiffs presented a memorial to the Confederate Congress in December 1863 asking for a special copyright that could be applicable to the Southern market. Lawmakers responded by granting such a copyright for the Goetzel edition in February 1864.[7]

The war ended the association of Hardee's book with the U.S. Army. Because he became a prominent Confederate general, Union authorities wanted a new drill manual. Brig. Gen. Silas Casey was given the charge to write that book for the Federal army. He based it largely on Scott's manual as well as on the French regulations of 1831 and 1845, though also to a degree on Hardee's work. Casey produced a three-volume set that remained the official drill manual for the U.S. Army from 1862 to 1867.[8]

Casey was the right choice for the assignment, having been a member of the board that approved Hardee's manual in 1855. He dated his preface January 1, 1862, indicating that he worked up his book in quick order. Formal War Department approval did not take place until August 11, 1862. In adopting the work, the department altered two aspects. It rejected Casey's adherence to the tradition of detaching two designated companies from each regiment to skirmish, preferring to rely on all companies at any given time to perform that duty, and his slight alteration of assigning place to each company within the regimental battle line according to seniority, preferring to retain Hardee's formula. Casey did a far better job than Hardee in explaining complicated maneuvers, inserting suggestions on how and when to use particular movements and defining many technical terms. The biggest difference between Hardee and Casey was the latter's full discussion of evolution-of-the-line formations and maneuvers at the brigade, division, and corps levels.[9]

Casey's first volume is filled with the School of the Soldier, the School of the Company, and "Instructions for Skirmishers and Music." The second volume deals exclusively with the School of the Battalion, while the third volume covers the evolutions of the line. More so than either Scott or Hardee, Casey tried to insert advice and direction on larger issues than teaching men how to drill. He argued that improvements in small arms and artillery made it necessary to drop the slow process of moving within range of the enemy. He also noted that European theorists since the French Revolution had widely rejected processional methods of deployment in favor of faster perpendicular methods of changing from column to line. Casey's aim was "to increase the rapidity of the gait; to increase the intervals between the battalions and brigades; to make, in the evolutions, the brigade the tactical unit; to hold the troops, when in manoeuvre in presence of the enemy, in closer order and well in hand; and as a general rule, to insist upon deployments upon the heads of columns, as the safest and most rapid means of forming line of battle." While Scott offered instructions to accommodate either two or three ranks and Hardee ignored the use of three ranks, Casey mandated the use of two ranks.[10]

Far from a quick derivative from either Hardee's or Scott's work, Casey produced a major drill manual on the same level as Scott's massive compilation of 1835. In fact, it was better than Scott's product because Casey provided much more grand-tactical advice than either previous author. Casey noted in his preface that he had been thinking about tactics ever since his assignment to the board to evaluate Hardee's work in 1854. Thus, he was ready to write his manual in quick order when given the task to do so.[11]

Casey's new drill manual was eagerly awaited by many officers of Brig. Gen. Clinton B. Fisk's command at Helena, Arkansas, in late 1862, and Col. Samuel A. Rice requisitioned forty-two copies of it for the 33rd Iowa. The commander of the 15th New Hampshire established a school for his subordinates to study Casey's tactics at Camp Parapet near New Orleans in May 1863; the school was taught by the major and met twice each week. Casey's book became the required reading for training clerks, workmen, and laborers of the Quartermaster's Department when it was necessary to place them in the defenses of Washington, D.C., in the summer of 1864.[12]

ORGANIZATION OF THE REGIMENT

Despite Pope's and Grant's comments that Hardee's tactics were an improvement over Scott's, the truth is that the majority of information in all manuals of the day was largely the same. It matters little whether one read Scott, Hardee, or Casey, for they consistently instructed officers how to give their commands and organize their companies and regiments. Hardee may have streamlined some of the maneuvers and the method of issuing orders, but that was not a major change from tradition.

According to Hardee, line officers were to give their commands in three stages. The command of caution consisted of the word *attention* given "at the top of the voice, dwelling on the last syllable." The preparatory command warned the men what was to come. If the third part, the command of execution, consisted of a phrase too long to be easily heard, the officer was to divide it into parts, "with an ascending progression in the tone of command." The command of execution set the men in motion. Overall, wrote Hardee, "the tone of command should be animated, distinct, and of a loudness proportioned to the number of men under instruction."[13]

Within ranks, enlisted men were to keep tight formations at all times. Hardee instructed them to "touch lightly the elbow towards the side of the guide" and "yield to pressure coming from the side of the guide, and resist that coming from the opposite side." If the touch of elbow broke for any reason, the men were to recover it "by insensible degrees."[14]

Americans encountered some confusion in the use of the words *regiment* and *battalion*. Scott's manual was taken from the French army, whose regiments actually were divided into battalions that often operated independently. The U.S. Army regiments that served in the Civil War also did this, but volunteer regiments rarely

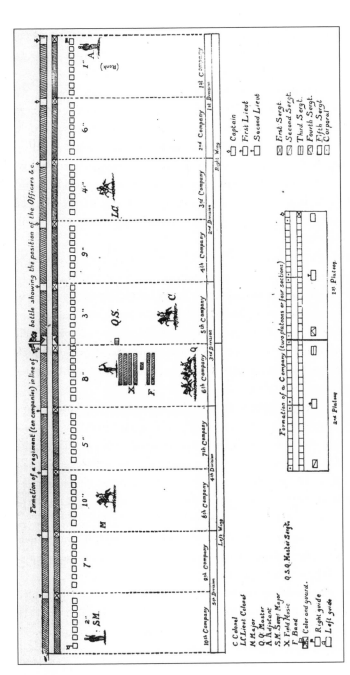

Fig. 3.2. Formation of a Regiment. The complex task of organizing a regimental formation in line is detailed in this sketch, which indicates the placement of companies and the positions of officers and noncommissioned officers. Each bar represents one rank. (From Copp, *Reminiscences*, 22–23)

subdivided into smaller operational units. As far as volunteer officers were concerned, the word *battalion* as used in the drill manuals simply was a substitute for *regiment*.[15]

Scott's manual, dating to 1835, continued to designate the right company of a regiment as a grenadier company and the left company as a light-infantry company. In theory, grenadiers were soldiers armed with grenades, a concept dating back to the seventeenth century, while the light infantry provided the designated skirmishers of the regiment. By the 1860s the concept of arming line infantry with grenades had long since disappeared. The idea that one or two companies would be armed with rifles (while the rest would be armed with smoothbores), and therefore be designated skirmishers, largely had passed as well due to the more general availability of rifle muskets.[16]

Scott and the other manual writers specified the arrangement of companies within the regimental battle line. Borrowed from Europe, it was based on the idea that the senior captain commanded Company A, the next senior led Company B, and so on. The arrangement was planned so that the senior captain and his men would be on the right flank and the next captain in seniority would hold the left flank to ably protect both ends of the line. While all drill writers agreed on which companies should hold the flanks, they differed in the arrangement of the other eight companies between them.[17]

This scheme was best worked out consistently in a standing army during peacetime, for in active service company commanders could change so often as to wreck its complexity. Moreover, the state of Wisconsin required by law that relative rank of its volunteer officers be determined by the date of their election by the men, not by the date affixed on the commission issued by the state government. This caused nothing but confusion in Halbert E. Paine's 4th Wisconsin, necessitating the drawing of lots by the officers to determine their seniority. The commander of the 23rd Kentucky had a novel idea: rather than rely on seniority, he held drill competitions to see which of his captains deserved to place their company in one of the honored spots on the flanks of the regimental line.[18]

Scott and the others indicated that the company should be subdivided as needed into two wings (or called platoons, if preferred), and each two companies could be considered a division. Hardee further organized each platoon into two sections. All drill manuals recognized yet a further subdivision, that of the section containing two squads each. While officers often detailed squads of men to perform a variety of duties in camp, squads were rarely used in actual operations on the battlefield.[19]

In fact, the various subdivisions of the company rarely appear in the official battle reports at all, indicating that they were not often used in operations. The commander of the 1st Michigan deployed his men "in column by platoon" at First Bull Run, while Lt. Col. Hagerman Tripp sent the first platoons of his Company A and Company B, 6th Indiana to skirmish at Stones River. Two other references to platoons being deployed as skirmishers by Federal commanders can be found in the *Official Records*, but it is striking that no more such references are readily available.[20]

The smallest subdivision of the company consisted of "comrades in battle"—four men adjacent to each other in the regimental line. According to Hardee, the "odd and even files, numbered as one, two, in the company, from right to left," constituted the group of four comrades in battle. Hardee did not elaborate on what this grouping could do other than to facilitate the deployment of skirmish lines. Emory Upton would develop the concept much further in his tactical manual, which was adopted by the U.S. Army soon after the Civil War. It was not his idea, but he deserves credit for making much more of it than any previous author.[21]

Scott called for a battle line consisting of two ranks if average company strength was low, three if it was high. He prescribed a distance of thirteen inches between ranks, defined as "from the breasts of the centre or rear rank men to the backs" of the men in front, or to their knapsacks if they wore them. Hardee wrote only of formations with two ranks, while Casey explicitly mandated nothing more than a two-rank line.[22]

Alignment and guiding were absolutely essential to the effective management of a regiment. Scott designated the color company in the center of the line as the habitual company of direction. That meant that companies to its right had to guide left while those to its left had to guide right. This enabled the regimental line to move forward lightly pressing toward the center, a compact method of maintaining command and control. The color guard was large in part to draw attention to this beacon of direction and morale. In addition to the color bearer, according to Scott, the guard consisted of five to eight corporals.[23]

Scott also allowed for two men to serve as general guides for each regiment. The colonel was to select them from among the regiment's sergeants based on "the most distinguished for carriage under arms, and accuracy in marching." One guide was to take his position in line with the file closers on the right flank, the other in the same place on the left flank. The file closers, who spread out in a line just behind the regiment, should not consider themselves "a mere ornament to the rear of the company," as Scott sarcastically put it. "They will be more particularly held

responsible for the alignment of the center and rear ranks, of which they will judge
by the squareness of shoulders and the touch of elbows. In battle, the arms of file
closers are often well employed in preventing the ranks from breaking to the rear."
George W. Squier of the 44th Indiana acted as a file closer and described his duties
as "to assist in giving orders, to keep the ranks well dressed, & c. I am not allowed
to fire." Cpl. Cornelius DuBois took pride in his role as left guide of Company C,
33rd Illinois. Emerging from a ravine during Grant's May 22 attack on the Vicksburg
defenses, DuBois "sprang to the front, aligning myself with the colors, our company
distance away, and pressed forward on this line, keeping my eyes on the flags."[24]

Because of his meticulous personality, and because he was writing a comprehensive drill manual for the peacetime army establishment, Scott devoted a good
deal of attention to precise alignment, orderly instruction, and show. He spent
three pages detailing how to form a regiment; marking and numbering ranks, files,
and platoons; and instructing the enlisted men to remember their numbers so they
could quickly find their places in a consistent fashion. Scott wanted the taller men
placed to the right or to the rear (the latter if it was a three-rank formation), which
comported with European practice. He also devoted a good deal of time discussing
how regiments could operate in two versus three ranks, forming and reforming
to go from one of those options to the other. Emphasis on showy appearance and
discussions of the outdated three-rank system contributed to the impression among
Civil War contemporaries that Scott's manual was out of date.[25]

The frontage of a regiment depended, of course, on the number of men formed
in its two-rank line. When engineer officer James St. Clair Morton testified before
the Buell Court of Inquiry, members of the board asked him how far a regiment
of 475 men would stretch out. He posited a formula: "A battalion will occupy, in
line of battle, as many paces as it has files, less one-fifth: 475 men in two ranks will
occupy 188 paces or 140 yards." A regiment this size was considerably less than full
strength but close to typical for most in both the Union and Confederate armies by
1862. A regimental commander had to exert personal direction and control over his
line, and it became easier to do that as the number of men declined due to disease,
combat losses, and detached duty.[26]

Maj. Gen. William T. Sherman believed that a brigade of 3,000 men should
occupy a sector of one mile; if a commander wanted a stronger line, he could pack
5,000 men into that mile sector. If arrayed in two battle lines, a division could be
assigned to that mile sector, making for an even stronger position. The frontage
of any unit larger than a regiment could be enlarged if the prescribed intervals

between regiments were maintained. Scott indicated that twenty-two paces was the normal interval between regiments within a brigade battle line or between brigades within a division battle line. Indications are, however, that Civil War officers rarely maintained intervals at all in actual practice.[27]

Many situational circumstances could influence commanders and their subordinates to mass their men more closely or string them out as needed. In late July 1864 Brig. Gen. Daniel Harris Reynolds's Arkansas brigade in the Army of Tennessee held a section of the Confederate defensive line around Atlanta. One of his men paced off the length of that section and found it was "216 yards or steps." While Reynolds did not indicate how many troops he had in the brigade, its numbers hovered around 500 by this stage of the Atlanta Campaign.[28]

Maj. Gen. Joseph Hooker ordered a detailed examination of his Twentieth Corps's position in early June 1864, during the New Hope Church phase of the Atlanta Campaign. He found that his command, consisting of 16,601 men, held a front of 4,150 yards (about 2.5 miles). But each of the three divisions were not holding a sector that was commensurate with their strength. The First Division actually held 1,000 yards but should have been covering 1,280 yards, while the Second Division actually occupied 1,250 yards rather than the 1,306 yards the general's staff thought it should, and the Third Division covered more ground, 1,900 yards, than its allotted 1,564 yards. Hooker therefore issued orders for the first two divisions to increase their frontage and the third to shrink its sector.[29]

Frontage depended on the size of the regiment, which also had an effect on command and control. There certainly was a limit to the number of men a unit commander could influence on the battlefield by his personal presence and the range of his voice. One of the reasons that Europeans tended to rely on the battalion as the level of basic command rather than the regiment was to improve the commander's ability to control the movement and cohesion of his men. Civil War observers often noted that a regiment at full strength was too large for one man to assuredly control. But steady attrition of manpower over the months, combined with the absence of an effective system of troop replacement, whittled the volunteer regiment down so that on average it had but 300 men by the midpoint of the war. Arthur L. Wagner, a postwar officer and influential military theorist, called these midwar units "flexible, well-seasoned, small battalions, easily handled." He further expressed his opinion on the topic of operational effectiveness in the Civil War. "On our greatest battle-fields the best work was done by these small regiments, which were, in fact, excellent small units."[30]

Civil War literature has many examples of commanders altering the organization of regiments in the field to either decrease or increase the size of operational units. Lt. Col. Reuben C. Benton's 1st Vermont Heavy Artillery, which saw its first combat during the Overland Campaign, was "larger than any other brigade in the division" when it joined the Sixth Corps of the Army of the Potomac on May 14, 1864. The solution to this excess size was to divide the regiment into three battalions, "each battalion serving as a full infantry regiment of eight platoon companies. This made it virtually a brigade command."[31]

Far more often, commanders had to deal with the problem of decreasing numbers rather than too many troops. When the 35th Alabama was reduced to only 185 men by sickness, Col. J. W. Robertson consolidated it into four companies before entering combat at Baton Rouge in August 1862. Lt. Col. Joseph B. Curtis temporarily distributed the men in Companies I and K, 4th Rhode Island to make eight companies after the regiment's losses at Antietam. Some Federal regiments, such as the 39th Indiana and 49th Ohio, were temporarily consolidated after the Battle of Stones River to make more viable operational units.[32]

No one spent more time studying the problem of keeping existing regiments up to strength than did General Sherman. He often bemoaned the lack of an efficient replacement system to blend new recruits into experienced regiments. He also criticized the habit of raising entirely new regiments to fill successive presidential calls for troops rather than distributing those new men into existing units. "The regiment is the family," Sherman wrote after the war, it "should never be subdivided, but should always be maintained entire." He also saw the company as "the true unit of discipline." Sherman admitted, however, that a "ten-company organization is awkward in practice" and preferred a regiment of twelve companies that could be divided into three battalions of four companies each for operational purposes. That was generally done in the cavalry but rarely in the infantry arm during the Civil War. Unable to maintain high levels of troop strength, Sherman toyed with the idea of consolidating several woefully understrength regiments into a single regiment, but that would have violated a number of things, including unit pride.[33]

Overall, Civil War commanders had to accept attrition that brought the average strength of some regiments down to about one hundred men by the end of the conflict. They added more regiments to brigade organizations to compensate for this. Most efforts to adjust the size of the basic regiment by consolidating small units were only temporary measures. But an important point needs reiteration: the reduction in size of the full regiment actually enhanced unit effectiveness by bringing the command down to a level more consistent with European battalions. There really was no reason why the volunteer army could not have organized its regiments in this way from the start, though reduced size would have rendered the battalion miniscule, forcing commanders to abandon that system anyway.[34]

BASIC MANEUVERS

Controlling the regiment as hundreds of men moved across a cluttered landscape was the essence of infantry tactics in the Civil War. This demanded not only a thorough knowledge of the maneuvers outlined in the tactical manuals but also, just as importantly, a sense of self-confidence among officers and an ability to judge what needed to be done before it became necessary to do it. Scott called this ill-defined art *coup d'oeil*, or "the faculty of determining, with correctness, distances, numbers, heights, and directions by a glance of the eye." The general referred not only to the commander's ability to quickly evaluate his men and their formations but the elements of the landscape as well. He wanted officers to "acquire accuracy and facility in judging the line of direction, and of conducting battalions on every sort of ground with the address and intelligence necessary to prevent faults, or promptly to correct them." The coup d'oeil could be acquired only through "persevering exercise."[35]

But first, everyone from the colonel down to the lowest private had to understand how to move forward and how fast to go. Scott indicated that common-time marching consisted of taking a step of twenty-eight inches (measured from heel to heel) 90 times per minute. Quick time involved taking that twenty-eight-inch step 110 times per minute. If faster speed was required, for wheeling or to cross the last few yards of an attack against a difficult position, Scott allowed the soldier to go at a run, which he defined as more than 140 steps per minute. But Scott warned that soldiers could not keep up a fast pace for long without disarranging their formation, so he advised all training to take place at no more than 110 steps per minute.[36]

Hardee agreed on the length of the step and the speed of common and quick time, but he indicated that double quick (which Scott did not address) involved a step of thirty-three inches at the rate of 160 steps per minute. If increased to 180 steps per minute, it theoretically would allow a regiment to cross 4,000 yards in twenty-five minutes. Hardee described a run as moving at the same rate as double quick but with "a greater degree of swiftness." He also urged commanders to tell their men to breathe through their nose rather than through their mouth for greater stamina.[37]

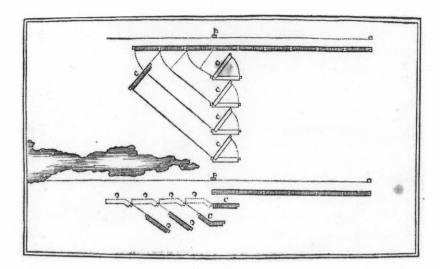

Fig. 3.3. Passing Obstacles. A line of troops negotiated obstacles in its path by breaking subunits away from the formation to shorten the line temporarily, restoring the frontage as soon as the obstacle was passed. In this case the four left companies of a regiment break away to allow the line to pass a water obstacle before moving obliquely to the left to regain their place in line. Each bar represents one line, not one rank. (From *Abstract of Infantry Tactics* [1830], 142, plate 20)

Both Scott and Hardee allowed for training in a backward step, but Scott thought it should rarely be used. Moving backward obviously could disarrange formations, and Scott thought that any such movement should never extend for more than fifteen or twenty steps. Hardee was more liberal in his manual, urging instructors to train men in backward stepping but never at more than quick time.[38]

Consistency in all matters of simple marching was vitally important. "It is by the uniformity of step," Scott wrote, "that the different battalions can alone maintain themselves without effort, abreast, or nearly so, with each other."[39]

Even a simple forward movement by a regiment had to have a designated guide, normally the color guard or color company. That guide, "being regarded as infallible by all the others," as Scott put it, "and having thus the greatest influence on them, its march will be superintended with the utmost care." Any deviation from the guide would cause jamming of files on one side of the regimental line and loosening of files on the other. Also, "the march of the battalion in line will be floating, unsteady, and disconnected." Scott warned officers to correct any problems as soon as possible "calmly, with few words, and without bustle or noise."[40]

If the regimental line met an obstacle such as a building during its advance, individual companies were to ploy into columns to the rear of the neighboring companies (but always toward the center of the regiment) to allow the moving line to pass the obstacle. They would then deploy back into line. If the line had to move farther toward the right or left while advancing, though maintaining what Scott called its "primitive direction" (the original direction), then the oblique step was required. It involved each man keeping his head and shoulders facing straight ahead but placing their right or left foot twenty-six inches in whichever direction was ordered. The other foot was to be placed eighteen inches behind the leading foot. This allowed the line to retain its original orientation while moving diagonally. When the men moved enough to right or left, they resumed placing their feet straight forward.[41]

If a brigade or division was formed in multiple lines, there would be need for understanding how to move one line past the other on the battlefield. Passage of lines was difficult and complex. Scott clearly spelled out how to do so if the first line maintained intervals of twenty-two paces between battalions while the second line ployed into columns placed directly behind the intervals. This made it comparatively easy because the retreating first line could ploy just a few companies into column to bypass the second line, just as it would do if meeting a barn during its advance. Likewise, the second line could pass its columns through the intervals of the first line and then deploy into line as well. Ironically, in actual practice this was not often done during the Civil War. Commanders preferred to connect their unit's line with that of the neighboring unit rather than maintain intervals. But there were few other ways to move one formation through another. As Benjamin Scribner of Indiana put it after the war: "The passage of lines is another incongruity. I never saw it done on the field as laid down in the books." (How this was accomplished under actual battlefield conditions is discussed in a subsequent chapter.)[42]

CHANGING FRONT

Advancing straight ahead was comparatively simple; far more complex were the maneuvers that allowed an officer to change the direction his regiment faced. One of the most basic ways to accomplish that goal was wheeling. As Scott expressed it, there were two fundamental forms of wheeling: on a fixed pivot and on the move. The former was done from a halt, with one end of the line remaining stationary while the other end moved. The second was done while the entire line continued to march; the man on one end of the line moved in nine-inch steps while the man on the far end continued to move in twenty-eight inch steps.[43]

"No infantry movement is more difficult than the wheel," commented Wilbur F. Hinman of the 65th Ohio after the war. "None is more graceful when executed with precision, nor more ungraceful when badly done. A perfect wheel, preserving the alignment, can only be accomplished after long practice."[44]

Wheeling was not the only way to change a regiment's front. If at a halt and the desire was to form so as to face right at a right angle to the original line, a complex maneuver called "changing front forward on the right company" was employed. As Scott explained, the commander had to move the right company to the new line, then order "Change front forward on (such) company. By company, right half wheel. Quick—MARCH." Each company then, in turn, executed the half wheel. This maneuver took a bit of time to execute, but it could be done forward toward the left and toward the rear either right or left as well. It was useful in order to meet an expected threat to either flank.[45]

Another maneuver designed to change front toward either right or left flank, but one that was faster than changing front forward on a company, was the left or right turn. While a line was moving forward, the guide at one end or the other was ordered to turn and face toward the right or left while marching and go in the new direction. The entire line was then to do the same in quick time so as to catch up with the guide, "turn the head and eyes to the side of the guide, and retake the touch of elbow on that side, . . . and then resume the direct position of the head and eyes. Each man will thus arrive successively on the alignment of the guide."[46]

The right or left turn did not involve wheeling. Rather than the entire line maintaining the touch of elbow as it wheeled, turning involved individuals rushing from one line to another while still maintaining a roughly linear formation without touch of elbow. It could look startling to an observer who was familiar only with the regimented maneuvers of linear tactics. When the 20th Massachusetts performed it in April 1864, Theodore Lyman was fascinated. He had just joined Maj. Gen. George Meade's staff and thus was new to military matters. He called it "a new drill of running in disorder and rallying, each man in his place, on a line established by the color & two guidons."[47]

By far the easiest way to move a battle line was by the flank. This involved each man turning either right or left in place and then the whole moved off in that direction looking like a long column of two men abreast. The tactical manuals, however, did not define this as a column but a line moving by the flank. It was one of the most common maneuvers to be seen on Civil War battlefields because it was simple, easy to manage, and flexible for negotiating obstacles on the field. Of course it could not deliver fire at the enemy and therefore was a maneuver designed only for movement and not for fighting. For this reason, Casey expressed the opinion that "marching by the flank in the presence of the enemy is a very objectionable movement, it will not be executed except for the purpose of moving the battalion to the left or right for a short distance, or when the narrowness of the way will not permit a company front." But Civil War commanders ignored this advice and marched their lines by the flank a great deal on the battlefield. Brigade and division commander William B. Hazen referred in his memoirs to "marching by the flank, as we generally did."[48]

In the two-rank battle line, it was considered important to keep the first rank always in front of the second. This concern is difficult to understand today, but it suffuses the drill-manual literature. Each man had his place in line and learned the maneuvers in that place: it was thought he could operate best if he stayed there under actual combat conditions. Scott used the term "direct order" to denote the proper placement of the two ranks and "inversion" to refer to circumstances wherein the front rank wound up behind the second rank when facing the enemy. This could easily happen if commanders mistakenly made the wrong turn when going from marching column to battle line; in many cases they had no choice but to do this to meet unexpected circumstances on the battlefield.[49]

Forming line en echelon led to only a few units being detached a short distance to protect the flank. Scott allowed for this deployment either parallel or obliquely to the battle line and offered much latitude to commanders to determine the distance from the line as well as the intervals between those units making up the echelon formation.[50]

COLUMNS AND SQUARES

All drill manuals devoted a good deal of attention to the formation of columns, and Civil War commanders widely used them for a variety of purposes other than assault. All columns consisted of battle lines stacked one behind another. Simple regimental columns consisted of each company's battle line placed behind the next. In

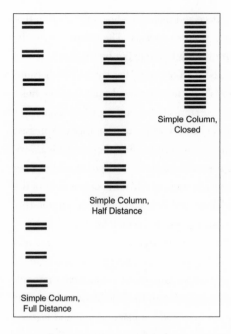

Simple Column,
Closed

Simple Column,
Half Distance

Simple Column,
Full Distance

Fig. 3.4. Simple Column at Full, Half, and Closed Distance. This diagram illustrates what a simple column (in this case a regimental column of companies) looked like. The distances refer to the space between ranks within the column. Each bar represents one rank.

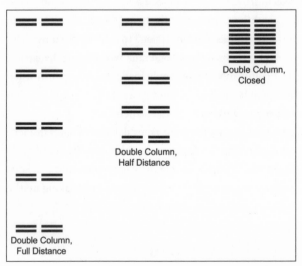

Double Column,
Closed

Double Column,
Half Distance

Double Column,
Full Distance

Fig. 3.5. Double Column at Full, Half, and Closed Distance. The double column widened the frontage and shortened the depth of the formation. It tended to be more popular among Civil War commanders than the simple column. Each bar represents one rank.

short, it consisted of one company front and ten battle lines. The distance between those ten battle lines varied. Closed en masse meant they were only eighteen inches apart, the same distance that existed between ranks within the battle line. The other two distances were referred to as full distance and half distance, but manual writers did not designate the number of paces for either of them. The reason for that omission was because full distance was as far as necessary for a company to wheel from column into line. This therefore depended on the number of men in the company, which determined how long its line would be. Half distance was exactly what the term implies, half the distance between closed en masse and full distance, also depending on the size of the company. Civil War soldiers often used the term *company distance* interchangeably with *full distance* because of these circumstances. Creating distance between ranks in column also was necessary when moving troops at route step, which involved the men freely swinging their legs at will.[51]

The manuals also allowed for the use of a double column, a formation that tended to be the most common column actually employed on Civil War battlefields. A regimental column doubled on the center consisted of two stacks of company battle lines, one next to the other. The two center companies remained in place and thus constituted the head of both stacks, while the companies to the right formed behind the right-center company and the companies to the left formed behind the left-center company. Each stack could form closed en masse, at half distance, or at full distance according to need.[52]

Yet a third kind of column, called division columns, appears never to have been used in the Civil War. Given that every two companies were referred to as a division, the division column consisted of the odd-numbered companies of the right wing and the even-numbered companies of the left wing moving behind the companies that remained in place in their respective wings. The regimental line remained intact except for alternating gaps; between the gaps were two companies, one stacked behind the other.[53]

The procedure for moving from line to column and back again called for some discussion in the manuals. Scott thought it should be done by companies acting as a whole to preserve proper alignment (the right flank remaining on the right and the first rank remaining first). He allowed it could be done by division too (two companies at a time) and by platoon, while Casey described how it could be done by files as well. Scott thought breaking to the rear to form a column, rather than breaking to the front, was "the most prompt and regular" way to do it.[54]

Scott and Casey devoted a good deal of space to the process of forming infantry squares, useful against cavalry attacks. "The formation of the square being often necessary in war," wrote Casey, "and being the most complicated of the manoeuvres, it will be as frequently repeated as the supposed necessity may require." Despite this opinion, forming squares was seldom practiced by volunteer regiments in the Civil War and rarely used on the battlefield. Reading the many pages in Scott and Casey that explain how this was done reveals why its use was so infrequent—it was the most difficult of all maneuvers in linear tactics. Another reason was that cavalry rarely attacked infantry, at least on major Civil War battlefields.[55]

Whether forming lines, columns, or squares, much depended on the process of moving groups of men from one spot to another. The many subdivisions of the regiment (companies, divisions, platoons, files, and ranks) could be utilized, but rarely were wings used to facilitate moving from one formation to another. William Hazen studied this process a great deal and came to the conclusion that moving troops by regimental wings was more efficient than doing so by smaller increments, especially when the size of regiments shrank as the war progressed. His motive for using wings as the default method of making formations in his brigade and division was "to simplify the movement of troops as much as possible." He did this by "folding . . . the two wings, as if by a hinge in the centre; the color-guard, which remains faced to the front, being the hinge. By this movement my command with ease and rapidity formed line of battle, moved into column, and disposed itself in

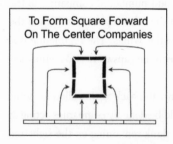

Fig. 3.6. Forming a Square. This simplified diagram shows how a regiment of eight companies could move forward and form in a way to achieve protection from threats in all directions. It was useful against cavalry but rarely employed, in part because of the complexity of the formation and because cavalry rarely attacked infantry on Civil War battlefields. Each bar represents one line, not one rank. (Based on Casey, *Infantry Tactics*, 2:248–49, plate 33)

camp after the day's march. The regiment can be formed for action in any direction by a single command." Hazen estimated he saved half the time needed to change from one formation to another by this method.[56]

EVOLUTIONS OF THE LINE

Scott, Hardee, and Casey devoted much time to describing basic maneuvers at the company and regimental level. That was, in fact, the most fundamental level to understand them. These maneuvers could be applied fairly easily to larger units such as brigades, divisions, and corps—and were referred to as the evolutions of the line. Hardee did not include these evolutions in his book, but Scott and Casey discussed them. They explained in detail where commanders were to stand and how they were to give their orders. For example, the proper place for a major general was 110 paces behind the center of his division; the general in command of the army could go anywhere he pleased, sending couriers with messages to his subordinates. Casey wanted intervals of 22 paces between regiments in a brigade and 150 paces between brigades. He preferred that all units be arranged in the line from right to left according to their numbers, something Civil War commanders rarely bothered to do.[57]

But officers often deployed their units in two or more lines on the battlefield, and Casey offered sound advice about multiple lines. He argued against deploying a brigade with four or less regiments in a double line. If more than four regiments filled a brigade, Casey advised that the first formation consist either of a line or columns at half distance. The second formation should always be in columns, "either simple or double, at half distance or closed in mass," and 150 paces behind the first line. He allowed for greater or lesser distance between lines depending on the circumstances of the terrain.[58]

SKIRMISHING

All tactical manuals of the Civil War era detailed how to deploy a skirmish line, but Casey insisted that two companies of each regiment be designated to perform this task. He suggested they be selected based on the men's skill as marksmen. Secretary of War Edwin M. Stanton, however, cancelled this provision when issuing Casey's book as the official manual of the Union army. The Federals rarely used designated skirmishers, preferring to rely on all units to perform this essential task as needed.[59]

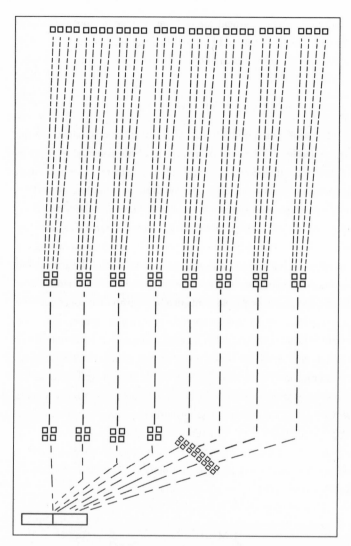

Fig. 3.7. Forming Skirmishers. This diagram illustrates the process of moving troops from a close-order formation to an open-order formation. During the Civil War, open order was used only for skirmishing. The process involved moving groups of four men forward to the skirmish line, where they operated as a team in conjunction with neighboring groups. While this may sound much like the modern fire-team concept, Civil War skirmishers operated in linear formations, though with intervals of five paces between each man in the group of four, and twenty to forty paces between each group. (Based on Casey, *Infantry Tactics*, 1:184–85, plate 26)

Casey spelled out the method for deploying skirmishers very clearly in his manual. A company could deploy forward from the regimental battle line or by the flank, if the skirmish line was to take position to cover the flank of the regiment. One platoon of the company, upon the order to deploy forward, moved in groups of four and spaced out so that a five-pace interval separated each man when they reached the spot where the skirmish line was supposed to appear. The other platoon moved up and took position behind the first as a reserve. Skirmish formation was the only real use of the fours concept; Casey argued it was important because on the skirmish line the men had to know, trust, and support each other more intimately than on the battle line. While each man maintained a five-pace interval with his neighbor, Casey advised that twenty to forty paces separate each group of four on the skirmish line.[60]

Once deployed, the skirmishers could maneuver like a battle line, employing wheels, moving by the flank, and moving at quick or double-quick time. Casey allowed the men to carry their weapons in any way that was comfortable, carefully pointing out that there was no need for precision in their movements. Officers were to "see that the men economize their strength, keep cool, and profit by all the advantages which the ground may offer for cover." While the skirmishers should maintain a line, they also could sacrifice regularity in order to take advantage of ground cover. The reserve troops should adjust their movements to the skirmish line and keep 150 paces to its rear. If both should move forward so far ahead of the battle line as to make support difficult, a second reserve should be created 400 paces behind the skirmish line.[61]

MARCHING

The tactical manuals also provided detailed instructions for marching. Scott and Casey noted that a marching column, or as they put it a "column in route" as opposed to a "column in manoeuvre," should be formed by the company. To pass over bridges too narrow for its frontage, files, sections, or platoons could break off temporarily. Even on the march, there was a need for men to serve as guides to maintain the formation and set the correct pace of marching. If the column had to change direction, Scott recommended that a man be placed at the spot where it was to turn to serve as a marker. The commander should order the change in direction when the head of the column was four paces from the marker. Scott also insisted that any changes in direction should be done so as to maintain proper frontage—

the normal right flank and first rank should be maintained so that if moved from column into line, the regiment would be ready for action.[62]

Maj. Gen. Don Carlos Buell tried to follow many of these marching directions with his Army of the Ohio, but Benjamin Scribner, at least, did not appreciate the effort. Buell had issued an order that mandated "section and platoon formation" and prohibited moving by the flank in marching columns. Scribner thought it "was very absurd when the narrow and obstructed roads are considered."[63]

Route step was used while marching. According to Scott, this was at the same pace as common time, ninety steps per minute. But route step did not involve cadenced marching; the men swung their legs individually. Casey recommended quick time, at 110 paces per minute, on good roads. If greater speed was required, the men could go to double-quick time but for no more than fifteen minutes, then down to route step and back to double quick again. Casey thought that if the situation called for it, the men could keep up the double quick for at least two miles.[64]

Hardee postulated that a marching column moving on the double quick (160 steps per minute) could cover five miles in one hour, while Scott estimated that moving at common time (90 steps per minute) would cover three miles in an hour. But these were merely estimates. Actual marching time during the Civil War varied a good deal. Maj. Gen. Gordon Granger once timed a column of 7,000 men in 1862, moving along a "pretty good road and marching well." The column had no wagon trains but carried along fifteen ambulances and two batteries of four guns each. Granger found it took two hours for the rear of the column to reach the starting point of the van. Near the end of the war, Brig. Gen. Romeyn Ayres noted that the Fifth Corps, which had about 9,000 men in it, normally took "two hours to pass any given point." On the march toward Five Forks, Virginia, his small division was the tail of the Fifth Corps column. Negotiating muddy roads with cavalry and wagon trains in the way, he could make only a mile per hour.[65]

The length of a marching column became an item of great interest to some officers. Sherman pondered this issue in his memoirs, noting that a marching column in "'good order'" should have had about 5,000 men in one mile. Based on that assumption, a corps of 30,000 troops would occupy six miles of roadway. But Sherman recognized that actual experience often varied. With wagon trains and artillery, "the probabilities are that it would draw out to ten miles."[66]

Members of the Buell Court of Inquiry posed an interesting question to Granger—what was the shortest space along a single road that an army of 40,000 men would occupy? They spelled out the details—seven divisions with three brigades each, four regiments per brigade. There would be no cavalry, but it would include three batteries of five guns each and a train of one hundred wagons for every division. Granger worked on the problem overnight and gave his answer the next day. Such a column, he figured, would stretch for sixteen miles along a roadway. He calculated it with intervals of twenty-two paces between units, each man needing twenty-two inches of space. Granger also reasoned that every gun and wagon would need fourteen yards of space.[67]

When asked if the column could maintain this length over the course of a long march, Granger answered emphatically in the negative. Even good troops on an average road would lengthen the column over time. After marching ten miles, the column would stretch from twenty-four to thirty-two miles instead of sixteen miles. As far as speed of marching, Granger thought that even with good management by officers over excellent roads, the column could only make about two miles per hour. If the roads were worse, then one and a half miles per hour over a time period of eight to ten hours would be a reasonable expectation.[68]

Commanders often issued orders regulating the march of their columns during the Civil War. Sherman laid down directions for a two-day move by his division before the Battle of Shiloh that would take it ten miles toward Corinth. He mandated progress at about two miles per hour and wanted brigade leaders to call frequent rests and keep the men in good order. "Troops marching thus make a better impression than when they straggle on the road." Buell issued orders in June 1862 mandating a marching column to be formed by section or platoon at half distance, lengthened to full distance if the road was dusty and there were no enemy troops nearby.[69]

Maj. Gen. George B. McClellan issued orders for the Army of the Potomac early in the Peninsula Campaign that established regulations for marching. He emphasized the need for maintaining proper intervals between units, authorized a halt of no more than ten minutes every hour, and wanted a stop of no more than sixty minutes at midday. When it became necessary to close up the column because of laggard marching, the order was to be given at the head of a unit and relayed back along its column. If a defile or obstacle was met necessitating delay, the rear of a unit was to mass close to the head until the entire command had passed through, after which it was to lengthen again and resume route step.[70]

More care was required if marching along roads within striking distance of the enemy. Granger believed that striking distance meant if an enemy was anywhere from eight to ten miles away. If this were the case, then the column should close up in tighter formation and be ready to deploy into line at a moment's notice. March-

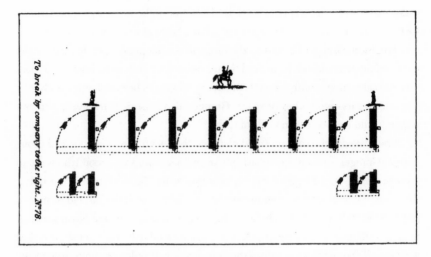

Fig. 3.8. Breaking by Company to the Right. In this diagram a regimental line of eight companies is breaking by companies to the right in order to form a marching column. Each bar represents one line, not one rank. (From Casey, *Infantry Tactics*, 2:18–19, plate 1)

ing orders in Hooker's Twentieth Corps during the Atlanta Campaign and in Maj. Gen. Horatio Wright's Sixth Corps at the close of the war bear testimony to the universal need to keep the men of a marching column well closed up and in hand while moving near the enemy.[71]

Marching at night posed unusual problems for soldiers and their officers. Maj. Gen. Gouverneur K. Warren reported that his Fifth Corps troops, while moving during the night at Cold Harbor, had a strong tendency to hesitate when they sensed the roadbed was descending. "It is unavoidable," he wrote, "the inclination to feel before planting the foot, and the frequent tumbles they get off of banks and other places makes them do it in spite of every effort of their officers." Warren summed up the problems by writing that soldiers who marched in the dark fared only "a little better than the crowd that walks the streets, as far as organization is concerned."[72]

The process of moving from a line to a marching column and back again was complex, but Civil War commanders tried to simplify it. "Theoretically, a marching column should preserve such order that by simply halting and facing to the right or left, it would be in line of battle," wrote Sherman after the war. But he admitted that this simple process usually did not happen. More often, each unit in the marching column had to be led forward by the flank to the right or the left to form the line. Sherman mentioned the two basic methods of going from marching column into line that had been developed by the eighteenth century. The first he mentioned was the processional method, an age-old process that was simple and effective but exposed the flank of the column to fire if conducted within range of the enemy. The second was the perpendicular method, one more commonly used, Sherman thought, by Civil War commanders.[73]

Scott and Casey laid out both methods in their tactical manuals, but they paid more attention to the perpendicular, probably because it was more complex rather than because they preferred it. The perpendicular method also was more flexible, allowing a commander to form line either ahead of his marching column or to the right or left of it. He also could form line on the lead regiment or on one that was halfway along the marching column (although the latter was far more complex than forming forward). Whether using the processional or the perpendicular method, Casey advised commanders to move entire regiments at a time, not subdivisions. This enabled the commander to keep his men better formed in as large a unit as convenient for the movement and be more prepared to respond to an enemy threat. But it also took longer to complete the transformation of a marching column into a battle line if officers relied on larger units such as the regiment as the basic unit of maneuver.[74]

The ultimate purpose of linear tactics was to enhance command and control of troops, resulting in many obvious benefits on the march and on the battlefield. Union and Confederate officers agreed with Lt. Otis Moody of the 51st Illinois, who wrote, "I believe those regiments suffer the least who keep together the best." The appearance of a well-ordered infantry advance could be awe inspiring, even if the soldiers wore the uniform of the opposing army. When Pickett's Division advanced against the Union center at Gettysburg on July 3, 1863, Col. Norman J. Hall was impressed by the sight. "The perfect order and steady but rapid advance of the enemy called forth praise from our troops, but gave their line an appearance of being fearfully irresistible."[75]

Soon after Gen. Robert E. Lee became general in chief of the Confederate army in 1865, he issued a circular stressing the importance of discipline and cohesion on the battlefield. "The appearance of a steady unbroken line is more formidable to the enemy and renders his aim less accurate and his fire less effective," Lee wrote. "Orders can be readily transmitted, advantage can be promptly taken of every opportunity, and all efforts being directed to a common end, the contest will be briefer and success more certain." To that end the general mandated that there be a file closer for every ten men in the battle line. He should move two paces to the rear of the rear rank of his ten-man squad, let none of them leave the ranks, and even fire on stragglers if needed. "The experience of every officer shows that those troops suffer least who attack most vigorously, and that a few men, retaining their organization and acting in concert, accomplish far more, with smaller loss, than a larger number scattered and disorganized."[76]

The three manuals available to Civil War officers—Scott's, Hardee's, and Casey's—provided readers with the most fundamental information they needed to transform volunteers into effective soldiers. They conveyed not just the details of formations and maneuvers but also advice about controlling large masses of men. By studying these books intently, officers gained the technical knowledge they needed to handle their regiments. They also largely imparted to the rank and file a respect for the linear system, which was the only and the best tactical system available to Civil War armies.

4

Training

There was no standardized system of training available to the Civil War soldier except the instructions contained in the drill manuals written by Scott, Hardee, and Casey. But it would be a mistake to disparage the lack of a comprehensive system of basic training in the 1860s. Most regimental officers pursued drilling in the linear system with relentless determination to make their units proficient in the craft of forming and maneuvering in ranks and files. The result was the best training yet to be seen in America's military history, applied to a far larger mass of armed men than ever before in North America. It was uneven, to be sure—some officers were less diligent and conscientious than others. But the standardized training regimens of World War I and World War II failed to produce uniformly high performance on the battlefield as well. Training married to repeated experience in combat produced effective soldiers; the longer the war lasted, the better the chances they would emerge as warriors capable of winning the conflict.

But first the men had to learn the often arcane nature of terms found in the tactical manuals. The overwhelming majority of Civil War officers and enlisted men had comparatively little formal education, particularly in technical subjects. Therefore, linear tactics seemed like a different world to them, filled with technical jargon that had to be learned as if it were a different language and understandable only to the initiated. As Charles McGregor of the 15th New Hampshire put it after the war, "None but those who have thus served can realize the extent of the military art and the marvelous intricacy of its movements, and the prodigious labor in acquiring the trade of a soldier."[1]

Volunteers who took training seriously understood its nature and its value. "Independent and individual effort is utterly futile and amounts to nothing," continued McGregor, "the whole must act as a unit and drill till they anticipate the order and move as though by instinct." Many other men saw that the primary purpose of drill was to instill a sense of self-discipline, conformity, and trust in officers. The troops had to reach a point where they performed "without forethought," as Benjamin Scribner put it. "You cannot drill your men too much," advised Col. R. R. Livingston of the 1st Nebraska Cavalry to one of his officers.[2]

Drilling not only addressed the problem of controlling the rank and file but also enabled officers to reach a high level of articulation on the battlefield. The military historian Paddy Griffith has defined articulation as "the ability to move large numbers of men quickly and without fuss from one place to another, in conformity with the terrain and the demands of the battle." This went to the heart of any system of tactics; it was the ultimate purpose of drill and training. The commander who understood which maneuver to use for a difficult situation his regiment encountered and could count on his men to execute it without hesitation or mistake had achieved a high level of combat effectiveness. Smart officers, therefore, put their men through regular rounds of drilling. Col. William R. Morrison referred to this point when praising the performance of the 17th Illinois at Fort Donelson. He had great confidence in the regiment because of its "power for efficiency in an assault," acquired from experience, skillful use of weapons, and its superior use of "evolutions and movements in the field."[3]

New regiments often went through an intense period of learning before they were ready to campaign. "We were put to drill at once," recalled Edwin Bryant of the 3rd Wisconsin, "and toes and heels were soon sore from the treading of the men before and the kicks of those behind, as we marched by file, by flank and in line." Bryant's colleagues were taught to align their little fingers on the seams of their trouser legs and to keep in step with each other. The 3rd Wisconsin held squad drill at 7:30 A.M. and battalion drill at 11:00 A.M. and again at 2:00 P.M. "We formed line, advanced and retreated; changed front forward and to rear; we marched in close column, formed square; we charged at double-quick, and retreated slowly, as if yielding the field inch by inch; and we kept the little finger on the seam of the trousers, though the sweat tickled our faces, and the flies tortured our noses."[4]

Nearly 8,000 Confederates gathered at Harpers Ferry by late May 1861, mostly Virginia units but parts of regiments from Alabama and Mississippi as well. They were "all raw and inexperienced," reported Lt. Col. George Deas, "wanting even in the first elements of the school of the soldier and there is a great scarcity of proper instructors." But two days later Deas reported that much progress had been made. Helped by men who had attended classes at the Virginia Military Institute, the troops already were becoming proficient in the Schools of the Soldier and the Company. Deas reported that there was a lack of suitable ground for drilling in larger formations and that the men still were hampered by "a lamentable want of knowledge of the first principles of formation into line and the changes of front and breaking into column."[5]

As Deas indicated, acquiring essential battalion-level skills was only a matter of time and opportunity. Once drilled repeatedly in them, most recruits learned their lessons well. Henry Morton Stanley of the 6th Arkansas recalled in his memoirs that "after a few drills, we could not even go to draw rations without the practice of the martial step, and crying out 'Guide centre,' or 'Right wheel,' or some other order we had learned."[6]

A number of Federal regiments raised in the summer of 1862 demonstrated the perils of being rushed into field service before they had a chance to drill. Col. Joseph Knipe's brigade of the Twelfth Corps received three new Pennsylvania regiments, constituting half the brigade, just before the Battle of Antietam. When the 128th Pennsylvania was ordered to go from column into line within seventy yards of the enemy, it could not do so. The five-week-old regiment had not been trained in this maneuver, which would have been difficult for even experienced troops to do so close to the enemy. Its colonel was killed immediately after giving the order, and despite the efforts of its major, the regiment collapsed. Brig. Gen. Alpheus Williams saw what happened to the 128th and other new regiments in his division. They tried, but "in attempting to move them forward or back or to make any maneuver they fell into inextricable confusion and fell to the rear." Williams noted that the soldiers rallied and then fought well when not required to make any movement. But "neither officers nor men knew anything, and there was an absence of the mutual confidence which drill begets."[7]

Schedules set by commanders indicate that the first and most intense phase of a Civil War soldier's training focused on the lower levels—squad drills, company drills, and battalion drills. For the 3rd New Hampshire, the education started at 5:30 A.M. and ended with dress parade at 5:30 P.M., with four drill periods filling in the middle part of the soldier's day and making a total of six intense drillings or parading.[8]

For some battalions, lower-level drill was followed by brigade- and division-level training. Alpheus Williams described for his daughter the intense activity in training camps in Maryland during the late fall of 1861. The units underwent instruction "in all kinds of drill, some by battalion, some by companies, some skirmishing, some forming squares, [and] some charging in lines of battle." By the latter part of the month, they were doing brigade drills, which Williams termed "'evolutions de luxe.'" After mastering the lower levels, the men went through brigade drills with precision and ease, "closing up into mass, then deploying into line of battle, then moving rapidly to the front in 'echelons' forming squares all in one grand oblong parallelogram, then separating into squares of single regiments, oblique and direct." As Williams indicated, there was a considerable amount of brigade- and even division-level training among Union regiments in the Virginia theater. The 123rd New York, a newly raised regiment, was drilled in brigade formations by Silas Casey himself at Arlington, Virginia.[9]

A correspondent for the New York Tribune who visited both the Army of the Potomac and the Army of the Ohio early in 1862 reported that Buell's western troops were three months behind the training of McClellan's eastern regiments. He concluded that four-fifths of Buell's regiments only went up to battalion-level drill, though many had not proceeded beyond the company level. Sometimes western regiments were not even well versed in the most basic level of training because of poor officers or the episodic need to rush them into field service soon after organization. James A. Garfield noted that the 27th Ohio had been sent to Missouri from Camp Chase after only two days of drilling. Later, when commanding troops in eastern Kentucky, he was shocked by the condition of the 14th Kentucky (U.S.). "Very few of its members have been drilled in the school of the soldier, much less that of the company and battalion. It can be considered but little better than a well-disposed, Union-loving mob."[10]

With enough time and good officers to lead them, regiments could achieve high levels of proficiency. Brig. Gen. John W. Phelps was known as a consummate drillmaster, putting several regiments through their paces on Ship Island, Mississippi. "It is a fine sight to see the brigade in his hands," commented John William DeForest of the 12th Connecticut. "[T]he five great regiments moving together, like an enormous machine; folding into column, forming square, recovering column, deploying into line, everything going at once in a sublimely smooth, sure, massive fashion." This level of intense drilling served the men well. When the 12th Connecticut was transferred to Brig. Gen. Godfrey Weitzel's command, Weitzel tried to embarrass it by requiring "a long series of double-quick movements, . . . doubled column, then into square, then into column again, then into line, and so on for half an hour as fast as the men could trot." When the 12th performed magnificently, the general was happy to have it in his brigade.[11]

Training on the brigade level seems to have been rare among Confederate regiments in the West. Hardee's manual, the most readily available to Southerners, did not go beyond battalion-level training, and Casey's new manual, which like Scott's went all the way up to corps level, was unobtainable.[12]

In the case of the 3rd Tennessee, an old regiment that spent many months in prison after the fall of Fort Donelson, everything had to be relearned when the men were exchanged and ordered to the field again. Flavel C. Barber resumed command of his company and instructed the men in squad drill for a week before he "'met with some success." After that the regiment concentrated on company training, with sporadic attempts at battalion and brigade drill. After a while Barber was ordered to conduct the regiment in a battalion drill. "I found it not so difficult a task as I had supposed—only made one blunder."[13]

OFFICERS

It became quickly apparent to all observers that the quality of officers (who were the primary drill instructors) was essential to success. That is why Scott in his manual emphasized the need of "joining theory to practice" and establishing schools of instruction so that battalion field officers and company leaders could be indoctrinated into the complex language and concepts of linear tactics first, before they tried to instruct their men.[14]

Col. William Hazen put Scott's advice into practice at Camp Wickliffe in western Kentucky during the month of January 1862. He established schools of instruction for the commissioned and noncommissioned officers of three new regiments in his brigade. Instructors were told to drill these officers in addition to requiring them to read lessons of twenty-five pages each from Scott's *Infantry Tactics* and recite before the instructor. Hazen required a record of attendance in addition to weekly reports on progress. Whether officers took to this sort of regimen well or poorly depended, of course, on their scholarly aptitude as well as on their sense of duty. Peter Wilson of the 14th Iowa forced himself to study tactical manuals while doing garrison duty at Columbus, Kentucky. "The fact is I don't like to study and never can hope to overcome the dislike I have to any kind of study," he admitted to his sister. But Wilson was willing to read Hardee's book, at least, because he knew he had to in order to perform his duties.[15]

Officers often began their military careers with mistakes on the drill field. John Henry Otto, a veteran of the Prussian army, reported that the colonel of the 21st Wisconsin made a mess of his first attempt to drill the regiment. Otto thought he should have assigned the noncommissioned officers to conduct squad- and company-level drill before the colonel attempted a battalion-level exercise. Capt. George Stanton of the 16th U.S. Infantry made a mistake on his first showing by forgetting to order shoulder arms before instructing the line to face right. The troops did not move. When Stanton asked the sergeant why, he said, "'the company does not obey a wrong command,'" then explained what the captain should have ordered. Stanton admitted he had forgotten, but he also forgot another important command later in the drill. At that point the battalion commander ordered Stanton to his tent to "study your tactics."[16]

Some officers never completely mastered the technical language of the linear system but managed to get by anyway. John Beatty recalled that Indiana colonel Solomon Meredith phrased commands to his regiment thusly, "'Battalion, right or left face, as the case may be, march!" It could be that Meredith merely memorized the language of the manuals, for they were written in similar fashion. George Herr of the 59th Illinois reported that many officers failed to use the exact language prescribed in the drill manuals for some maneuvers, though not necessarily due to ignorance. He heard "on many battle-fields orders that would shock the dignity of the purely tactician. The framing of those orders was frequently suggested by the emergency." Herr gave one example at Stones River, when the order was to "'fall back to the rail fence at the edge of the timber.'" William H. Gibson recalled that one of his sergeants could not recall what maneuver was needed to get a squad of only sixteen men in line through a gate and desperately shouted "'Boys, turn round and come out the way you came in! One at a time, forward!'"[17]

Confederate veterans also remembered stories about officers who found the technical jargon of the drill manual too difficult to readily absorb. When a lieutenant of the 4th Kentucky was asked in a school of instruction how he would deal with an enemy who suddenly appeared to the right, he replied, "I would move the regiment stauchendiciler to the front." A captain in the same regiment was more honest when asked a similar question: "Well, major, I can't answer that according to the books, but I would risk myself with the Trigg county boys, and go in on main strength and awkwardness."[18]

For conscientious officers freshly commissioned, learning the drill often involved an intense course of reading. "I study military tactics and drill all the time," moaned Robert McAllister of the 11th New Jersey. "There is so much to learn and so much to do." Arthur W. Hyatt of the Confederate Guards Response Battalion wrote by hand a small booklet of forty-four pages in which he condensed the commands for executing a number of formations and maneuvers. This crib book covered a wide array of topics, including evolutions of the line. Hyatt devoted more space to forming squares than to any other formation. John Calvin Hartzell of the 105th Ohio had great difficulty understanding the maneuvers on paper. Only when he saw a movement executed on the drill ground did it become clear.[19]

Making the officer's plight worse was the fact that sometimes his men knew more about drilling than expected. Irving Bronson enlisted as a corporal in the 107th New York, but he "was no greenhorn in military matters and . . . had the Manual of Arms and School of the Company down pat." Elbridge Copp reported to Company B, 3rd New Hampshire as a second lieutenant but immediately took command of the men because the captain was already under arrest and the first lieutenant was detailed to other duty. The soldiers felt superior to the new officer, who had never drilled troops before, and they planned to make it difficult for him. But Copp outmaneuvered them. On learning that the company had done little in the way of skirmish training, he studied those pages of the manual very hard and then put the company through two hours of tough drill, loudly pointing out their mistakes along the way. Copp never had trouble with his men after having established his authority on the drill ground. Other officers at times became the object of ridicule among their troops, even if it was meant as harmless fun. The only enjoyable part of drilling, according to L. W. Day of the 101st Ohio, "was to see the officers who drilled us, step into holes and fall over logs as they backed around in order to watch us, and then get mad and charge the whole thing to our mistakes."[20]

Col. Winchester Hall demonstrated how an intelligent and careful officer could still make mistakes on the drill field. His newly raised regiment, the 26th Louisiana, used Hardee's manual in the early spring of 1862. Hall instructed three of his captains to begin the process of training the regiment in battalion drill before he gave it a try. "I studied at first a few simple moves, took out the regiment and put it through so far as I had gone. I would then study a few more moves, add these to the drill, and so on." But he became so confident that he overstepped his ability one day and got the regiment into an "unseemly mob." Hall had to call on a more experienced captain to untangle the mess and "retire from the field with a wounded and subdued vanity."[21]

No officer could have been more conscientious than Halbert Eleazer Paine when he took command of the 4th Wisconsin. Paine had some experience in a militia company and knew "a smattering of tactics" on the squad level but nothing else. He studied Hardee's manual intently but still made mistakes on the drill ground. Once, he forgot to order shoulder arms before sending the 4th wheeling into columns. "But not a man moved. Instead an audible snicker ran up and down the line." Paine realized his mistake and felt embarrassed. "If I could have found a hole big enough for an ass of my size to hide in, I would have crawled into it."[22]

Paine continued his assiduous work when the 4th Wisconsin was transported to Ship Island in March 1862. He established a school of instruction for noncommissioned officers, writing a list of eighteen topics for study and testing them one day. As the men sat on the sand, Paine read several questions for them to write down and then gave the group three hours to compose answers. Apparently, the results of this test determined the order of companies in the regimental line. Paine ignored the traditional order of assigning the best captain to the right of the line, the second best to the left, and so on, and instead placed the company with the best noncommissioned officers in what he thought was the most important place.[23]

Even experienced officers sometimes made mistakes on the drill ground or on the battlefield, forgetting maneuvers or the proper way to order them. Thomas W. Hyde, after years of experience in the army, took command of a brigade in the Sixth Corps following the Battle of Cedar Creek. "I knew the tactics well enough and got along finely at first, but at length I got them by inversion and could not think how to get them out." The adjutant either refused or could not recall how to do this and remained silent as Hyde broke out "in a cold perspiration." His only recourse was to march the men aimlessly for fifteen minutes until "the right order came to mind." Col. Hugh T. Reid tried to drill his 15th Iowa one day in March 1863 but could not understand why unwanted intervals appeared in the line when he wheeled them from columns. Someone finally explained to him that the companies were of uneven strength.[24]

There are examples of officers late in the war having bad days and messing up a maneuver that they probably knew well. But if this happened on the battlefield, it was far more serious than merely disrupting a drill. Col. Jason Marsh handled his 74th Illinois in the Fourth Corps of the Army of the Cumberland very poorly on May 17, 1864. He insisted on exposing the men to artillery fire when it was unnecessary, wanted them to move slowly rather than double quick under fire, and insisted on stopping in vulnerable positions to dress line. The officers, especially Capt. Frederick W. Stegner of Company I, often took it upon themselves to disobey his orders or to issue contradictory instructions of their own. Marsh "could not give an inteligable command," as Stegner put it in a letter to his wife, and even came close to firing on the 79th Ohio until that regiment's major rode up to warn him that friendly troops were in his front. The officers reported Marsh's conduct the next day at brigade headquarters, but the colonel remained in command for nearly a month before leaving the regiment due to illness.[25]

Hazen believed that the schools of instruction he created at Camp Wickliffe early in 1862 paid off in the performance of his men at Stones River a year later. His brigade played a pivotal role in holding an area known as the Round Forest while nearly the entire Union line to his right was forced back in a fighting retreat. Hazen praised his regimental commanders for their "manly co-operation in bringing this brigade to its present high state of efficiency and discipline, through constant care, labor, and study." But he could not offer such lavish praise for other units. "I saw upon the field company officers of over a year's standing who neither had the power to or knowledge how to form their men in two ranks." The entire Army of the Cumberland needed to weed out incompetents and make way for young men of proven merit to take their place on the company level, Hazen thought. Even nearing the midpoint of the war, there seemed to be some officers who had not yet learned drill maneuvers properly.[26]

DRILL, DRILL, DRILL

Civil War soldiers underwent the most intense schooling of their lives when they entered the army and were compelled to learn linear formations and movements, which could only be accomplished by repeated practice. Of course, some units drilled far less than others, but the majority underwent considerable exercise in wheeling, breaking from line into column and back, advancing, falling back, and many other movements. Regiments drilled incessantly until the men were sick of it, then drilled some more. Also, the soldiers found that learning the drill early in their career was not enough; there was a need for repeated training literally until the end of the war, even for hardened veterans.

Interestingly, the overwhelming majority of soldiers North and South trained in the traditional linear tactics as laid down by Scott, Hardee, and Casey rather than in the relatively new Zouave tactics developed by the French army. It is ironic that Zouave training, inspired by the widespread adoption of the rifle musket, should have fallen into disfavor by 1861 even though most recruits in America wanted the most advanced weapon. Even the French, who initially tried to teach Zouave tactics to their entire army, soon gave that up as impractical well before the onset of the American war. With its quick movement and athletic demands, this training was wasted on the average soldier and was more suited to elite units.[27]

There was only limited interest in Zouave training early in the Civil War. Elmer

Ellsworth's Chicago-based militia unit became the exemplar of this fad, but only the 8th Missouri and 11th Indiana appear to have been trained from their organization in this manner. Eugene F. Ware had belonged to a prewar Zouave militia company that became Company E, 1st Iowa (a three-month regiment). "We were drilled running all over the country, jumping ditches and climbing fences. . . . Although the drill was hard, it was exciting." There is no evidence of any other volunteer or regular regiments in either the Union or Confederate army undergoing Zouave training.[28]

For the great majority of soldiers, the traditional tactical system was the order of the day. Within that paradigm, they received less instruction in skirmish formations than in line movements. Bayonet practice also was limited, according to most accounts. Regular regiments tended to drill in all kinds of weather on the correct assumption that fighting could take place under any conditions. Massachusetts troops on the way to Baltimore and Washington, D.C., in late April 1861 were required to continue drilling even on board ship.[29]

Efforts to simulate combat conditions by staging mock battles occurred sporadically but never became common. The 40th New York divided into wings, with one entering a patch of woods to be approached by the other. Everyone in the regiment was armed with blank cartridges. The resulting firefight came relatively close to simulating combat, and it also resulted in minor injuries among the men. The Army of Tennessee engaged in large-scale mock battles while rebuilding itself at Dalton, Georgia, in the early months of 1864, and the Army of the Cumberland staged sham assaults on enemy fortifications while recuperating at Murfreesboro following Stones River.[30]

A handful of commanders thought it was useful to perform drill even on the battlefield. James Garfield, "for the sake of brass and audacity," ordered a battalion drill that involved forming squares and wheeling into column to distract waiting Confederates at the Battle of Middle Creek in January 1862. It took a while for the rest of his command to close up, and Garfield wanted to inspire awe as well as to occupy the enemy's attention in the meantime.[31]

The 26th Louisiana entered its first combat at Chickasaw Bluffs in late December 1862, and Winchester Hall remembered how patiently the men had endured drilling the past several months. Yet some of them fired without orders, so Hall put the regiment "through the manual of arms, in plain view and entirely exposed to the enemy" less than four hundred yards away, to instill a greater degree of discipline.[32]

At Chickamauga the 89th Illinois participated in an attack that threw the three right companies into confusion. Brigade leader August Willich stood before the men as bullets continued to fly overhead and "calmed their excitement, instructed them how to advance firing and maintain their alignment, and after dressing them and drilling them in the manual of arms for a short time, ordered them to advance about 30 paces to the edge of an open space."[33]

In general, training was mostly effective in creating viable military organizations out of raw volunteers, but some recruits were smart enough to recognize that their drilling was inadequate. When Isaiah Harlan joined the Confederate army at Galveston, Texas, in the fall of 1861, he noted, "We drill a little every day." What Harlan meant was, "we form, right and left flank and file[,] mark time[,] countermarch[,] and right about a few times and then dismiss. We are learning next to nothing. We are altogether unprepared for the yankeys." Other recruits had similar feelings of inadequacy. Sgt. William Pitt Chambers of the 46th Mississippi confessed, "I guess that Gen. Hardee himself would have been puzzled to explain some of the maneuvers we executed" while training.[34]

One of the worst case studies of bad training involved the 11th U.S. Colored Heavy Artillery late in the war. An inspector wrote a damning report on the kind of drilling this unit performed. The problem started with officers who "were grossly unmilitary, and exhibited ignorance of primary principles. Swearing at the men seemed to be an approved mode of imparting instructions." The officers palmed off drill to their sergeants, who instructed the troops "in a manner more than useless, confirming the men in irregularities." There was little to be expected of this regiment if it was forced to participate in combat, given the shoddy training it had suffered at the hands of lazy white officers and ill-trained black sergeants.[35]

There was, of course, an intermediate category between the two extremes of well-drilled and badly trained units. Many regiments learned the essentials but not the more glossy aspects of linear formations and maneuvers. Edwin Metcalf's 3rd Rhode Island performed on the drill ground in a sloppy manner that was unsatisfactory to him. Even in the presence of the enemy, its movements were not "altogether precise. I have seen them more handsomely executed by home guards." The regiment did not regularly post guides or form in proper alignment, but company officers could give the necessary commands and their men more or less obeyed. The 3rd Rhode Island, in Metcalf's view, was good enough to get by on the battlefield.[36]

The 3rd Rhode Island was not necessarily unusual among Civil War regiments. Inspector reports and candid commentary by officers and enlisted men reveal that many units were good in some aspects of the complex system of tactics they had to learn and poor in others. An officer who evaluated the 2nd Texas, a regiment that had seen hard service during the siege of Vicksburg but had not drilled much in late 1864 due to an epidemic of yellow fever at Galveston, rated it deficient in company drill and badly deficient in battalion drill. The men were good at the manual of arms but did not handle their weapons "with proper life and vigor." An inspection of the regiments in Brig. Gen. James J. Pettigrew's North Carolina brigade in early 1863 revealed that they were good in company formations and movements but poor at skirmishing; in addition, the officers were not as proficient in the regulations regarding outpost duty as they should have been.[37]

"My regiment is not well drilled," candidly admitted Col. C. L. Dawson of the 19th Arkansas in June 1862. He blamed this deficiency on the need to perform a great deal of fatigue duty on fortifications and on illnesses that ran through the ranks, all of which interrupted training schedules. "The men, however, have some experience and good ideas of drill, and can, in two or three weeks' attention to drilling, be made quite efficient. They are all willing, which is 'half the battle.'" Older regiments that experienced an infusion of recruits had to take the time to drill them separately or suffer the consequences. When the 22nd U.S. Colored Troops (USCT) entered battle on October 27, 1864, near Petersburg, the recruits excitedly fired their weapons against orders and then broke and ran, "causing the worst of confusion."[38]

The uneven proficiency in drilling to be seen in many regiments justified what might be considered continuing education in linear tactics throughout the war. In other words, older, experienced units often needed refresher courses to maintain high levels of effectiveness. Within the Army of the Potomac, this need was institutionalized in a series of orders that required continued training over the years. "The intervals between active operations should be used" to train the men, according to an order Joseph Hooker issued to the army in June 1863. "All officers are expected to maintain a high state of drill, discipline, and efficiency within their respective commands." Hooker wanted brigade drills at least twice per week and division drills at least once per week. These sessions had to include forming columns as well as lines and, given his recent experience in the Wilderness, moving through woods and thickets and over ravines.[39]

In September 1864 Gouverneur Warren sought to "re-establish . . . the tone and condition" of his Fifth Corps by requiring brigade drills every day. He included a list of maneuvers. "To face by the rear rank, to face by the front rank; to march to the front in line of battle; to march to the rear in line of battle; to change front to rear on the right or left battalion; to change front forward on the right or left battalion; to come by right or left by file into line." If a brigade commander could not accomplish this to the satisfaction of inspectors, he was to be brought "before a board of examination." Warren's list included most of the basic maneuvers in the drill books even though his regiments had experienced many campaigns.[40]

In the dull winter of 1864–65, the Second Corps went through an intense period of drill while holding trenches at Petersburg. "Regular recitations in tactics and regulations should now be had," read a general order. "A systematic effort should be made by division, brigade, and regimental commanders to bring their troops to the highest practicable state of discipline." All evidence indicates that corps commander Andrew A. Humphries's edict was taken seriously and put into execution.[41]

The need for continuing education was recognized in regiments serving in the West as well. As the commander of the 78th Pennsylvania put it, "If troops are not improving they are losing what they already know." He mandated company and battalion drill two hours every day except Sunday in April 1862. Nearly two years later, Richard W. Johnson ordered squad drills for all recruits as well as company, battalion, and brigade drills for everyone else in the First Division, Fourteenth Corps. He especially emphasized skirmish drill with a bugler sounding the orders.[42]

The men in Col. Dan McCook's brigade of the Army of the Cumberland endured regular rounds of training throughout their service. In December 1862 Mc-Cook required each regimental commander to hold two recitations in tactics each week for his subordinate officers and sergeants who would be assigned to drill the men. Interestingly, McCook stipulated the use of Hardee's book for battalion drill and either Scott or Casey for evolutions of the line (brigade and higher maneuvers). By August 1863 he required regimental officers to recite for their commanders three times per week.[43]

The Army of the Cumberland's six-month stay at Murfreesboro following Stones River afforded unit commanders much time to train their troops. Brig. Gen. William P. Carlin's brigade used Casey's manual, while the 42nd Illinois intensely drilled not only on the battalion level but held many brigade level drills as well. Some of these exercises excited the interest of the participants. Merritt James Simonds noted that several of them were "interesting," but he did not explain why an experienced soldier would find something novel in a brigade training exercise.[44]

No one demanded more of his troops than William Hazen, who drilled them in company, battalion, brigade, and skirmish exercises near Manchester, Tennessee, right after the Tullahoma campaign.. He required ten-minute breaks every half hour and wanted the manual to be "implicitly followed." Hazen also trained his men in bayonet use and allowed them target practice three days each week.[45]

The Federals about to embark on the Atlanta Campaign intensely prepared during the early months of 1864. Fourth Corps troops drilled four hours each day, the 84th Illinois staging a "mimic skirmish fight" for two hours one morning followed by a brigade drill in the afternoon. The 98th Ohio in Col. John G. Mitchell's brigade of the Fourteenth Corps not only engaged in target practice but also "Battalion drill, Company Drill and every other kind of drill," according to Philip R. Ward. After Atlanta fell, the training continued. Col. James S. Robinson put his Twentieth Corps brigade through daily drills on the company and battalion level, "under which exercise the troops seemed to be rapidly improving in discipline and efficiency." At the same time, Maj. Gen. John M. Schofield ordered daily training on the battalion, brigade, and division level in the Twenty-Third Corps, with dress parades, weekly inspections, and instruction in picket and guard duty.[46]

While African American regiments in the Union army seem to have generally taken to drill as well as white units, many Native American regiments apparently did not. Col. William A. Phillips initially had a good deal of success training Indian troops, but when he took charge of a brigade consisting of Creeks and Cherokees, he had trouble bringing the units up to par. "My orders to drill are disregarded," he reported. Phillips requested two companies of regular infantry to demonstrate the proper manner of drilling as an example for the troops. "Indians are imitative," he informed his superior, "and I think, frankly, that some volunteers would be benefited by it."[47]

To some degree, constant drilling throughout the war was necessitated by the infusion of new men into old regiments. Michael K. Lawler in the Thirteenth Corps found it necessary to do continual rounds of company, battalion, and brigade drills because of the "large numbers of new recruits in the different regiments."[48]

But it is important to keep in mind that most of the justification for constant drilling throughout the war was to reinforce (or relearn) basic maneuvers in the minds of old veterans. There were no efforts to introduce innovations to the preexisting tactical system. The training periods were refresher courses that seemed to never end, yet they were necessary. Whether the problem lay with officers who refused to take their jobs seriously (as with Phillips's Native American units) or in enlisted men who tended to forget the maneuvers after a few months of inactivity, forcing the troops to toe the line in training usually paid off in terms of combat readiness.

Yet necessary as it was, the constant drilling often wore on the men, especially those who knew the routine very well and did not need additional training. "To the infantryman, down in the dust and stubble of old cotton and corn-fields, seeing nothing but the monotonous wheels and half-wheels, rights and lefts into line, facings and halts, it is indescribably dull and tiresome," asserted Robert J. Burdette of the 47th Illinois. When Lt. Col. Judson Bishop put the 2nd Minnesota through its paces while it was idle, many men groaned. "I hope to gracious we will leave here before long or we will all be killed[;] the boys sware that the Colonel has got the drill fever and that he raves about it in his sleep." With so many men absent, Daniel Wait Howe could not perform battalion drill with the 79th Indiana. He frankly admitted in his diary that "the men don't take any interest in Co. drill, so we usually stack arms" and do something else.[49]

The Army of Tennessee went through three periods of intense drilling between campaigns throughout its history. Hardee, who commanded a corps in the army, was put in charge of instruction at Tupelo, Mississippi, after the evacuation of Corinth. He used his own manual and required four hours of drilling every day, five to six days per week, focusing on company- and battalion- rather than brigade-level exercises. His own book did not go beyond the battalion level. The other two periods of intense drilling for the army occurred during the early months of 1863 at Shelbyville and Tullahoma, Tennessee, and in early 1864 at Dalton.[50]

There seems to have been a real deficiency among units in the Army of Tennessee in the evolution of the line (that is, brigade level and up). But then some regiments were even deficient in battalion drill. When Lt. Col. Theodore Gillard Trimmier returned to the 41st Alabama soon after Stones River, he found that "the Regt had been drilling very little, and every thing going on loosely, and if continued would, in a short time longer, have greatly impaired the Regt." He instituted a rigid schedule of training that brought the unit up to par with other regiments within a few weeks. Increasingly, in 1863 and 1864, the Army of Tennessee added brigade-level exercises to its drill routine, although it never reached the level of training in the evolutions of the line that other field armies North and South attained.[51]

Native American troops in the Confederate army also needed additional attention. Maj. Gen. Samuel B. Maxey instituted a program to improve the drill proficiency of the Native American units in his District of the Indian Territory as late as September 1864, appointing drillmasters on the district, division, and brigade levels. This was highly unusual, for at most a handful of regiments might have had a specially appointed drillmaster only for a brief time early in their war service. "It is unnecessary at this late day to point out the great advantage of thorough drill,"

Maxey lectured in general orders. "Every officer and soldier knows it, and the men will willingly learn, as it is to their interest to do so, if they have the chance."[52]

Like their counterparts in blue, Confederate veterans sometimes complained about excessive drilling. Edwin H. Rennolds of the 5th Tennessee, an old hand at maneuvers, griped about brigade drills in the Army of Tennessee as early as May 1863. "I see no good to be derived from it. We are learning nothing [new], and as to hardening us we are hard enough now."[53]

Bored veterans like Rennolds might take more interest in drill if there was a prize to win. When Hardee took charge of the Department of Mississippi and East Louisiana in the late summer of 1863, he went out to watch the 3rd Kentucky drill. Col. A. P. Thompson persuaded him to lead the regiment in maneuvers. According to Henry Ewell Hord, Hardee initially was reluctant, apparently afraid he might overtax the men's ability, but upon seeing how well they performed the spirit of the drillmaster took hold of him. He put the Kentuckians through their paces for an hour in the hot sun and could not "tangle us up," in Hord's words. Hardee praised the men highly, and the incident led to a drill competition between the 3rd Kentucky and the 15th Mississippi. Ladies in Canton, Mississippi, sent to Memphis for material to make a special flag as a prize (smuggling it through the opposing lines). The 15th Mississippi had many more men than the 3rd Kentucky, so it weeded out some members while the 3rd borrowed men from other Kentucky regiments in its brigade. A large crowd of soldiers and civilians gathered to watch the competition in the manual of arms and various maneuvers. In the end, the panel of judges (which included Hardee) chose the 15th Mississippi. A member of the 35th Alabama blamed local prejudice for the decision. "Kentuckians & Alabamians cant stand much show in Miss.," he wrote home.[54]

Some commanders in the Army of Tennessee also experimented with drill competitions to instill a greater degree of interest in continuous training. Brig. Gen. Edward C. Walthall offered a prize of $100 in his brigade in June 1863. The 27th Mississippi won the prize because it excelled in skirmish drill.[55]

The biggest and most successful drill competition of the war took place within the ranks of the Seventeenth Corps in early 1864. The troops largely were doing occupation duty at Vicksburg, Natchez, and along the Big Black River and understandably became somewhat lazy. Brig. Gen. Mortimer D. Leggett decided to inspire them by offering a special flag to the winner of a drill competition. His objective was to be certain that all men were "conversant with the tactics to maneuver correctly a company or battalion." The flag would be inscribed in silver letters, "Third

Division, Seventeenth Army Corps, Excelsior." The regiment winning it had to give the color up when another unit won the next contest. Leggett mentioned the general deportment of the regiment in camp and discipline as additional qualities that would be taken into account, noting that he retained the right to take the flag away from any regiment if he deemed its future conduct warranted it.[56]

Leggett's regiments drilled intently for more than a month in preparation, conducting competitions on the brigade level. On January 22, 1864, the 124th Illinois beat out all other regiments in its brigade, even though more than half of Charles Henry Snedeker's company had been put on extra duty for missing battalion drill a month earlier. The next day the 124th went up against the 17th Illinois and 78th Ohio from other brigades for the division flag. This competition was held two miles south of Vicksburg on the Mississippi River bottomland, with nearly the entire population of Vicksburg as spectators. Each regiment drilled for forty minutes and listened to a speech by corps commander Maj. Gen. James B. McPherson. The 124th Illinois won the "Excelsior" flag and was known thereafter as the "Banner Regiment." There was some disappointment among members of regiments raised early in the war that a newer unit, raised in 1862, had taken the prize. The 124th Illinois gave up the color on April 5, 1864, because it was transferred to a different division.[57]

There is no evidence that drill competitions took place in the eastern theater, but the spirit of rivalry ran high at times in Virginia. During the intense drilling of the Second Corps in early 1865, Robert McAllister caught that mood as he strove to make his brigade shine above others in maneuvers. "My officers and men all go into their drills with a spirit, and they are determined not to be outdone by any other brigade."[58]

The hard work paid off in battlefield performance. Thomas E. G. Ransom noted that his troops "moved as coolly and obeyed orders with the same promptness and alacrity under fire as in ordinary drill." Marcus M. Spiegel, who commanded the 120th Ohio in the Thirteenth Corps, understood that the essential goal of battlefield leadership was "to lead your men carefully into dangerous places and do the most damage to the Enemy and least to yourself." Spiegel felt by the start of the Vicksburg siege that he had learned that lesson and was able to execute it well. "My boys will follow me anywhere. I have it so now that I can go in as cool as on Battalion Drill; everything must be learned and I really think I had a good School." Reports and personal letters are replete with expressions of pride in the conduct of the rank and file of a well-drilled regiment, noting that the men acted "as unconcerned and self-confident while under one of the hottest fires as while on drill," as Nelson A. Miles reported. The historians of the 55th Illinois firmly believed that "unremitting practice" on the drill field produced a strong sense of steadiness under pressure among the men and "forever after made the regiment practically panic proof."[59]

Drilling continued even after it became apparent that the fighting was over and the volunteer regiments would soon be mustered out. The primary reason for this was that it occupied the men's attention during idle periods and continued to reinforce the awareness that they were still in the army. Even as demobilization neared, officers needed to control their men and maintain discipline. While occupying Mobile, regimental commanders in the Second Division, Thirteenth Corps had their orders clearly laid out in late June 1865: drill the men at least one and a half hours per day. As their commander put it, "much can be done to improve the accuracy and elegance of the manual of arms." He wanted them to pay attention to every detail in the drill manual and to train until the men were able to move their hands exactly at the same time. "The moral effect of superior soldiership in our troops in this part of the country will be great. It is also worth [the] painstaking [effort] for each regiment to appear thorough when it returns home."[60]

REVIEWS

Reviews and dress parades were a significant part of training throughout the Civil War. It was, in a sense, a test of the men's progress through the drill manual. Large reviews also became showcases capable of instilling pride in the larger unit the regiment shared with other troops. The reviews also involved marching past high-level officers and visiting dignitaries in column formation. In a Second Corps review in late March 1865, the pace was at quick time until each unit passed the reviewing party, then it was to move at double quick to leave the field. A stake was driven in the ground at the point where the men were supposed to quicken their step and staff officers were posted to make sure everything went smoothly.[61]

The Grand Review of the Army of the Potomac and Sherman's army group along Pennsylvania Avenue on May 23–24 was the biggest and best known of all reviews associated with the Civil War. Orders indicated that the marching rate was mostly route step to keep the massive procession going at a brisk pace, but for a couple of blocks the cadence step was mandated. Because the reviewing party, which included Pres. Andrew Johnson, was on the left, the guide in marching was on the left. Within the Ninth Corps, at least, the prescribed column was by company front. But for the sake of passing narrow parts of the street uniformly, the column was to be limited to a width of twenty files.[62]

Marching orders in the Grand Review were more detailed for the Second Corps than in any other unit. The choke point of the procession was the two-block segment between Fifteenth Street and Seventeenth Street, where the pace was slow and cadenced. A staff officer was posted at Eighteenth Street to ensure that every unit moved at route step. Another staff officer was posted at Fifteenth Street to stop any unit for a while if the previous one was slow or delayed for any reason. In order to pass the bridge over Rock Creek, the columns were to break in half, and each part march behind the other along K Street. If any pileup of troops occurred, units should move into side streets, mass, and wait for orders.[63]

It was well to prepare for the worst since this was by far the largest review in American history. But all went well, and commentary on the Grand Review tended to focus on the impressive sight of thousands of hardened warriors moving with discipline in massed formations. Sherman praised his own troops for the "steadiness and firmness of the tread, the careful dress on the guides, [and] the uniform intervals between the companies, all eyes directly to the front." He felt that many critics had tended to portray the western troops as little more than an armed mob bereft of true discipline. The Grand Review, in his mind, proved "that it was an army in the proper sense, well organized, well commanded and disciplined; and there was no wonder that it had swept through the South like a tornado."[64]

The Sixth Corps missed the Grand Review in Washington but held its own review on May 24 along the streets of Richmond. Its formation also was by company front at full distance, guide left. The corps held a later review along Pennsylvania Avenue in Washington on June 8, again in company front. The frontage was not to be more than twenty files, and if any company had a wider front than that, it was to form a column of platoons instead. Guiding left, the units were to maintain intervals long enough to allow wheeling of companies into line.[65]

The Fourth Corps also missed the Grand Review but held its own show on May 9 near Nashville, with Maj. Gen. George H. Thomas and a group of civilians as the reviewing party. The formation was by companies as well, with bayonets fixed. Brigade leader Emerson Opdycke was greatly impressed by the sight, and his description emphasized the beauty of linear formations and the discipline of these veterans who knew them so well. "It was a magnificent display of organization of order and power. Each regiment had the appearance of a solid cube protected by projecting steel. The step was in perfect unison and gave the same motion to the whole living moving mass leaving the impression that it breathed from one pair of great lungs and moved with one sett of immense muscles."[66]

Opdycke's commentary on the Fourth Corps review vividly expressed the ultimate purpose of drill in the Civil War: to create an automatic response to orders from large masses of men who acted upon those orders as one. Command and control, articulation, discipline, and cooperation were all wrapped up in the effective learning of linear tactics. Such a body of men was a true army, although made up of citizen-soldiers, and a mighty force on the battlefield.

5

Moving Forward and the Art of Skirmishing

Intensive drilling was but one element of a two-part combination for small-unit effectiveness. Matching the lessons learned with hard experience on the battlefield was essential, and most Civil War regiments took that second step in their first engagement. Some of them performed well, while others barely survived their test of combat. Intensive training minimized the difficulties encountered when executing formations and maneuvers on the battlefield, but it did not eliminate them. Even the best of regiments could make mistakes or suffer from misunderstood orders.

GUIDES

The all-important task of moving masses of troops in coherent fashion involved the use of guides, but the linear system produced two meanings of the term. One referred to individual soldiers assigned to stand as markers for a regiment to form a new line. Battle reports contain only a handful of references to using such guides under fire. It is possible experienced commanders felt little need of doing so, or perhaps guides were used often but commanders did not consider it necessary to mention them. Col. A. Van Horne Ellis referred to using guides to re-form his 124th New York after moving through the thick woods near Chancellorsville, and Lt. Col. W. H. Blake utilized guides to mark the position of his 9th Indiana while it formed a new line under artillery fire at Stones River. In fact, Blake made a deliberate show of coolness under duress; observers felt it was because he wanted to erase the stigma attached to Indiana troops who had done poorly in the Mexican War. Brig. Gen. John M. Palmer prepared for a dangerous reconnaissance at Stones River with great deliberation in order to inspire his men's confidence. The commanders of the 31st Indiana and 90th Ohio sent guides to mark "the proper direction for the

Fig. 5.1. Company E, 5th New York. Photographer George Stacy exposed this stereograph at Camp Butler near Fortress Monroe. It illustrates a Civil War company in line. Note that the formation is small enough to be readily handled by one man. Also note that the troops are dressed in Zouave uniforms. (LC-DIG-stereo-1s01792)

line," in addition to fixing bayonets. Col. Charles H. T. Collis also placed guides in addition to planting colors in order to re-form his 114th Pennsylvania at Chancellorsville. The fact that some officers placed guides in order to make an impression seems to imply that they did not normally use them in battlefield conditions.[1]

The other, more important meaning of the term *guide* in linear tactics referred to the focal point of movement within regiments and larger units. Battle reports contain many references to maintaining cohesion by guiding to the center, right, or left. As mentioned previously, a regiment invited trouble if it could not maintain proper ranks and files, and it could maintain them only by having a point against which to incline as it moved forward. The standard instruction, according to the manuals, was for each wing to guide on the center of the battle line, but officers could give other directions as well.

If the regiment was acting independently, it mattered little whether it guided to the center or to the flanks. But if it acted in concert with other units, it was more practicable to guide toward either flank. The experience of Godfrey Weitzel's brigade at the battle of Georgia Landing, near Labadieville, Louisiana, illustrates this point. He placed the 8th New Hampshire on the left and the 12th Connecticut on the right, but both regiments advanced toward the enemy while guiding on their

Fig. 5.2. 110th Pennsylvania. Photographer Andrew J. Russell exposed this photograph at Falmouth, Virginia, on April 24, 1863. Comparing the frontage of this regimental formation with that of a single company gives some understanding of the higher level of difficulty in commanding a regiment of hundreds of men compared to a single company only one-tenth as large. (LC-DIG-ppmsca-07268)

center. The trouble was that the color guards of both units "moved in different lines of direction," and the two regiments became separated. Weitzel compensated for this by advancing the 13th Connecticut between the two to fill out his brigade line.[2]

Incidentally, both regiments that began the advance failed to maintain internal cohesion as they went forward because they were experiencing their first combat at Georgia Landing. The center companies of the 12th Connecticut heard someone yell for them to lie down, which the men did, but the rest of the regiment continued forward. Realizing their mistake, the prone troops jumped up and ran so fast to catch up that the center companies outpaced the left and right wings. The 12th thus advanced toward the enemy in three segments, each firing as it went. In the center segment the troops tended to press against the colors, squeezing the smaller men out of line who then formed a third rank to the rear. Meanwhile, to the left of the 12th, the commander of the 8th New Hampshire apparently did not know how to deploy his men from column to line, and the regiment became terribly "tangled up."[3]

What the 12th Connecticut did at Georgia Landing was not regulation tactics, but it worked; the Confederates evacuated their position as the Federals advanced. Lt. Col. S. E. Hunter also reported an unorthodox formation for his 4th Louisiana when it advanced on a Federal battery at the Battle of Baton Rouge on August 5, 1862. The regiment formed what Hunter called "a sort of a wedge shape, gradually assuming a line as it approached the battery." Perhaps this happened because the regiment had moved by the flank twice that day to traverse patches of woods and wound up at a right angle to the main Confederate line before setting out on its unsuccessful attack. The wedge shape described by Hunter implies that the regiment was guiding on the center.[4]

Brigade commanders paid special attention to guiding their commands in a forward advance. During Breckinridge's attack at Stones River on January 2, 1863, Brig. Gen. Gideon J. Pillow arranged with the commander of the brigade to his left so that it would "dress upon my left, and the left of my line to dress upon his right, to guard against a separation of the line." Col. Thomas Kilby Smith used a road as the guide for the 55th Illinois, ordering the men to keep the regiment's right flank aligned along the roadway as it advanced in the May 19 attack at Vicksburg.[5]

The proper procedure was to give instructions as to the guide before an advance was made, but sometimes that was not done. Lt. Col. John G. Hall, who led the consolidated 51st and 52nd Tennessee in Wright's Brigade at Chickamauga, did not know how he was to guide before starting toward the enemy. "This embarrassed me somewhat in my movements," he admitted. During the advance, a gap developed between his unit and the 8th Tennessee to the right. "Learning that general commanding brigade was on my left, I determined to direct my movement" toward that flank. In contrast, everyone who entered the Battle of Peachtree Creek knew that they were to guide right as the Confederates advanced to attack the Army of the Cumberland. Partway through the movement, however, "some one gave the command 'guide left'" in Col. Edward A. O'Neal's brigade, and this created a gap that O'Neal had to fill with reserve units.[6]

In the movements at Mine Run, Brig. Gen. George H. Steuart's brigade formed to the left of the Stonewall Brigade in preparation for an advance. Steuart told Col. Stephen D. Thruston of the 3rd North Carolina to connect his right to the 37th Virginia, the left-most regiment in the Stonewall Brigade, and use it as the guide. But both the 37th Virginia to his right and the rest of Steuart's Brigade to his left began to move before Thruston was ready. He had to make a choice on the spot and decided to guide left so as to maintain touch with his parent unit, even though it opened a gap between the two brigades that was four hundred yards wide.[7]

It is worth stressing that even veteran units and their commanders often found it difficult to maintain strict alignment and guidance while advancing across difficult terrain under fire. Brig. Gen. S. A. M. Wood's brigade was the guide for Cleburne's Division during an attack at Chickamauga on September 19. While moving, Brig. Gen. Lucius Polk's brigade to Wood's right began to veer left; as a result, Polk's left wing got in front of Wood's right wing, covering his right two regiments. The third regiment in Wood's line, the 45th Alabama, also got ahead of his right two regiments. To the left, Brig. Gen. James Deshler's brigade pressed too closely against Wood's left flank because Deshler's line was "slightly oblique to mine," as Wood put it. Thus, the files in Wood's left regiment, the 33rd Alabama, became crowded. Descending darkness added to the confusion in Wood's command.[8]

In the case of Cleburne's Division on September 19, Wood failed to do his job as commander of the guiding unit only because other officers did not properly conform to his movement. At Jonesboro, Georgia, Brig. Gen. Hiram Granbury's brigade was designated as the guide for Cleburne's Division (temporarily led by Brig. Gen. Mark P. Lowery), but Granbury failed to fulfill his role. His brigade was positioned on the far left of the division line. In the Confederate attack on August 31, Granbury lost sight of his purpose and chased retreating Federals across Flint River instead of gradually wheeling to the right as clearly instructed by Lowery. The entire division line followed him, forcing another division to take its place in the advance toward the main Union position.[9]

One of the worst mistakes made in the Civil War concerning alignment and guiding occurred in the Ninth Corps on June 17, 1864, during the first Union offensive against Petersburg. Brig. Gen. John F. Hartranft's brigade formed in the head of a ravine under difficult circumstances; it was not easy to observe the Confederate trench line across open ground without dangerously exposing oneself. Hartranft formed exactly where John G. Parke, corps commander Ambrose Burnside's chief of staff, told him to assemble. Burnside's chief engineer, James St. Clair Morton, superintended the brigade's deployment and tried to gauge the enemy position and the exact line of advance by using a compass. He moved Hartranft's command farther to the right by a brigade front and then announced that the battalion of direction, the 2nd Michigan, was in the right place and at the correct angle relative to the enemy position.

But when the brigade set out across an open field of powdery topsoil, the men's feet and enfilading artillery fire created a huge dust cloud. The brigade wheeled right, exposing the left flank to rifle fire from the trenches. In short, instead of advancing forward, the brigade circled round in easy range of the enemy until it headed back to the Union line, crossed the position occupied by the Second Corps, and re-formed to the rear. Hartranft initially assumed that the artillery fire had caused his men to veer off course. The Confederates evacuated their position that night. Hartranft later examined the ground and came to the conclusion that Morton had erred in superintending the placement. His brigade line went forward at a severe oblique to the enemy position instead of straight forward. The men did veer away from both the artillery and rifle fire that devastated their exposed flank and essentially wheeled back toward the Union line. Morton was killed in this attack, and Hartranft lost 840 out of 1,890 men engaged.[10]

There were many pressures on Civil War battlefields that hindered a unit's ability to maintain formation and to move forward effectually. As we have seen, these emanated from failure to give proper instructions, failure to understand instructions properly given, misjudgments in aligning and positioning units, and the normal troubles associated with managing masses of men under fire.

Difficult as moving forward could be, officers strove to make sure their commands did it well. After two unsuccessful assaults on the defenses of Port Hudson, one of Maj. Gen. Nathaniel Banks's division commanders lectured his regimental leaders on the necessity of controlling their men. "No soldiers can march to an assault who fail to preserve their formation strictly," he wrote. Proper intervals were necessary to prevent uncontrolled massing. "When regiments are crowded, they are inefficient, and sometimes uselessly exposed."[11]

Many references to officers who tried to maintain strict control of their commands under fire by dressing the ranks can be found in battle reports. Unit cohesion and the ability to manage men were considered so important that it was worth stopping an advance and exposing the troops to further losses. The major of the 30th Maine was wounded while doing so during the Battle of Mansfield in the Red River Campaign. At Malvern Hill the 13th Mississippi stopped under "a most withering fire" to dress its line before resuming the advance. Maintaining the cohesion of its formation stood the 1st Maryland (C.S.) well at the Battle of Gaines's Mill. Met by retreating Rebels, the Marylanders steeled their nerves, "taking the touch of elbows and dressing on the alignment with the precision of a parade." The men thus prevented their comrades from breaking their regimental line as it swept forward.[12]

The cohesion of a unit could be broken by mistake as well. While advancing through woods at Malvern Hill, Col. Charles A. Ronald wanted to stop his 4th Virginia to dress its formation, but some other officers shouted a command to continue moving. Ronald tried to stop the men, but they were cheering and many failed to hear him. As a result, the regiment separated into two parts for the rest of the day.[13]

With the 4th Virginia, a mistake by an officer and the difficulty of hearing orders caused the regiment to split. With the 34th Massachusetts, fighting its first battle at New Market on May 15, 1864, it was excitement that led to an apparent inability to hear or understand orders. No matter how loudly Col. George D. Wells shouted, he could not compel the regiment to halt during an advance. As he reported, Wells had to run toward the flag, "seizing the color bearer by the shoulder, [and] hold him fast as the only way of stopping the regiment." The two wings went farther forward than the center, but the men soon realized what was happening and halted. Later the line officers heard the colonel's order and repeated it; even the enlisted men helped communicate these instructions by repeating them along the line. But Wells again had to physically grab the color bearer and head him to the rear in order to get the regiment to move off the field at the end of the battle.[14]

There is no explanation why company officers in the 22nd USCT failed to understand their orders to guide left while advancing against the Confederate line north of the James River on October 27, 1864, during the sixth Union offensive against Petersburg. The 1st USCT to their right understood orders and advanced successfully, but it had an open field to move through; the 22nd had to advance through woods. Col. Joseph B. Kiddoo communicated the proper instructions to his right-flank company, and the right platoon of the next company in line also understood them. But confusion reigned in the regimental line from the left platoon of that company to the left flank. Kiddoo's lieutenant colonel reported that he heard no order indicating what the regiment was supposed to do. When he tried to conform to what the right flank was doing, the entire regiment suddenly "charged as it was, and therefore accomplished nothing."[15]

OBSTACLES

Failure to communicate was a problem affecting any army in war, no matter what tactical system might be used. But physical obstacles posed a special problem for linear tactics given the sweep of compact lines and columns across the battlefield. Unit commanders had several alternatives in dealing with obstructions that barred the progress of their men. When the 3rd North Carolina confronted a burning building while advancing on the right of its brigade line at Antietam, Colonel Thruston moved it by the right flank far enough to clear the structure and then moved by the left flank to regain his position in line. Brig. Gen. Roger Hanson's Orphan Brigade encountered a pond during the Confederate attack at Stones River on January 2. The Kentuckians had always taken drill seriously and now proudly conducted a maneuver to avoid the obstacle and regain their position in line. The pond fronted only two companies of the 4th Kentucky, whose commander ordered "a movement by the right of companies to the front for a short distance." Lot Dudley Young, a lieutenant in one of the affected companies, wrote that the pond "was cleared in a manner that was perfectly charming."[16]

Fences were a more common obstruction on Civil War battlefields than buildings, and they could stretch for hundreds of yards across the landscape. As Maj. Gen. Winfield S. Hancock explained about the attack of his division at Fredericksburg, several "substantial fences" stood in the way. "Each of these fences destroyed the unity of at least one brigade. These obstacles naturally caused brigades and regiments to lose somewhat their solidity of organization for an assault." The normal practice was for men to tear them down. If time and opportunity presented, a special detail did so before an advance began. If not, whole regiments did so literally during the advance. The men of the 82nd New York had to contend with "fences and garden palings" at Fair Oaks, "which they tore down before them, . . . still preserving their line as well as possible."[17]

Other linear impediments on the battlefield included watercourses, and units often found them as disruptive as fences. Col. Silas Colgrove's 27th Indiana crossed "a small stream, with very deep and steep banks" at Cedar Mountain. The men got over it quickly, but the process completely broke up the ordered ranks and files. Colgrove called a halt on the other side to dress the line before moving on.[18]

Still another linear obstacle could be found in road cuts, although they normally did not extend very far. But if a battle line encountered one, it could be as disruptive as creeks or fences. Brig. Gen. Stephen Ramseur's brigade of North Carolinians foundered on a deep cut along the Mummasburg Road on July 1 at Gettysburg. Advancing against Brig. Gen. Gabriel Paul's Federal brigade, Ramseur formed in two lines, with three regiments in the first and two in the second. The Confederates started from a point six hundred yards from Paul's position and made it halfway before Ramseur could get a "full view" of the Federals, at which time he realized that they were positioned behind a stone fence. Even before reaching the

Mummasburg Road, Ramseur adjusted his formation a bit because the left wing was advancing faster than the right, causing some "momentary confusion." But the deep road cut angling across his path caused much more than confusion in the ranks. Ramseur's first line dropped into it with little hesitation. Capt. James I. Harris walked part way into the cut before he realized that formations were breaking up and mingling in confusion inside the excavation. He therefore called for his Company I, 30th North Carolina to get out before they merged into this mess, taking them sixty yards farther on. By now the Federals had abandoned their position and were in retreat, but the Confederates could not pursue because of the confused state of things inside the road cut. "For a minute whole regiments seemed mixed up without any regularity or order among any of them," Harris recalled. "It was not a panic—for no one appeared excited—the enemy was running, but it was created simply because the line was not preserved but a general massing at one point."[19]

A different type of obstacle lay in the presence of thick woods, which often filled half the ground of any given battlefield of the Civil War. In some engagements, such as Chancellorsville and the Wilderness, tangled vegetation dominated the landscape. Brig. Gen. Alexander R. Lawton pushed his Georgia brigade of 3,500 men through dense woods at Gaines's Mill. To keep the men going, he positioned himself just behind the center and sent staff officers to the right and left wings to press them forward. The brigade managed to penetrate the woods and more or less maintain cohesion, "the regiments occasionally disunited by the smoke, dust, and confusion of the battle-field, and then brought together again."[20]

For the 14th Michigan and 16th Illinois at Bentonville, thick woods posed a severe obstacle to forward progress. Ordered to advance on March 20, 1865, to see if the enemy still held their position in front, the two regiments moved forward at double quick without skirmishers. "The ground was exceedingly swampy and covered with a dense growth of underbrush and vines, fallen logs, &c." The Federals became "completely exhausted," and their line "was confused, broken, and disorganized. There was not even a semblance of a company organization." Yet the troops continued struggling forward until reaching a point thirty yards from the fortified Confederate line.[21]

George Steuart conducted a difficult maneuver through heavy woods at Mine Run on November 27, 1863, in an example cited earlier in this chapter. Forming to the left of a road, with the Stonewall Brigade to his right, he swung his line forward and to the right until it was nearly parallel to the road while maintaining connection with the left flank of the Stonewall Brigade. To do this, Steuart moved his left wing forward and obliquely to the right and told his right wing "to conform to the movement." It was "a slow and difficult" process; intervals developed between regiments and even between files within the regimental lines. The general also blamed "the extraordinary density of the thicket" for disrupting the "regularity and promptitude" with which his men conducted the maneuver. Soon "portions of my line . . . were little more than deployments of skirmishers," considering how many gaps appeared in the formation. Between the 37th Virginia and the 3rd North Carolina, "a large interval" had opened up because Colonel Thruston attempted to keep close to Steuart's Brigade rather than to the Stonewall Brigade. Within the 3rd North Carolina as well, "the files . . . were separated, so that it covered far more than its proper regimental front." The Federals took advantage of this and advanced between the two regiments, forcing both to retire and stopping Steuart's advance.[22]

Ironically, the formation of Evans's Brigade, led by Col. P. F. Stevens, was disrupted at Second Bull Run because the men left thick woods instead of entering them. The trees provided cover for the South Carolinians while advancing, but they were exposed to Federal fire upon emerging into the open. The 23rd South Carolina, on the far left of the brigade line, came out first and waited for the other regiments to appear. When the 17th and 18th South Carolina did so, they "almost instinctively inclined to the right still to keep under cover." The brigade line broke apart and massed on the far-right unit, the Holcomb Legion, until there were ten or twelve ranks on that part of the field. But Stevens had no time to reorganize and moved forward as best he could, the result being a confused and ineffectual advance.[23]

Admittedly, the second-growth timber around Chancellorsville was far worse than typical of battlefield vegetation. Rice C. Bull of the 123rd New York provided a telling commentary on the difficulties of moving through it when his regiment conducted a reconnaissance in force on May 1, 1863. His comrades "found the scrub pine so closely grown together with their branches extended out from the ground up and so interlocked we could not advance in company front. It was even difficult for a single man to move ahead in the thicket. We broke into columns marching by fours; even then we could not keep that formation. Then we went on as best we could in single file, breaking our way through the pine branches, many of them were dead and sharp as spears." The 123rd New York managed to go forward half a mile in this fashion before emerging into a field one mile from the main Confederate position. Bull noted that it took half an hour for the entire regiment to emerge from the woods and re-form a line. When the Army of the Potomac again operated in this area one year later at the start of the Overland Campaign, unit commanders often commented on what Capt. Thomas C. Thompson of the 7th New Jersey called "a dense jungle of scrub oak, which in a degree was almost impassable."[24]

At Chancellorsville and the Wilderness, the problem lay in vegetation, for the ground was relatively level. But on other Civil War fields scarred by erosion, the problem resided in the lay of the land. The engagement at Port Gibson, Grant's first battle east of the Mississippi during the Vicksburg Campaign, was a particularly good example of this problem. The battlefield was cut up by numerous deep ravines with steep slopes. In fact, the only decent ground for deployment lay on the roads that snaked along the narrow spines of ridges between the ravines. Brig. Gen. William E. Baldwin reported that his Confederate brigade could not form a true line. Even the 17th Louisiana within his brigade could not maintain a connected battle line because of the twisting contours of the ridge tops. Within the 17th Louisiana, "companies were compelled to act independently."[25]

In a fight at Liberty Gap, during the Tullahoma Campaign of June 1863, the problem lay in farmland recently plowed and saturated by heavy rain. Maj. J. McClelland Miller's 34th Illinois advanced across a cornfield on the double quick. No more than one hundred yards from the beginning, it encountered a fence, which caused "some confusion." The regiment re-formed on the other side and continued over "very mellow soil," as Miller phrased it. Heavy rain for the past two days converted the field into a loblolly. Miller himself fell so far behind his men in crossing the field that no one could hear his orders, so Capt. S. L. Patrick took charge of the 34th and managed to preserve a decent line despite the difficulties. Those problems included deepening mud as the regiment continued and dealing with two other Union regiments that met the 34th Illinois two-thirds of the way across the soggy cornfield as they retired to the rear. Add Confederate artillery and a burning sun to the mix, and one can get a sense of the experience of battle that afternoon. When the Illinoisans reached the fence on the other side of the field, they used it as shelter to fire at the enemy only one hundred yards away until the Confederates retired.[26]

RATE OF ADVANCE

The experience of the 34th Illinois at Liberty Gap points up the question of speed in forward movements. The purpose of Hardee's manual was to quicken the pace of advancing toward the enemy in an effort to compensate for the anticipated effect of rifle fire. It seems that Civil War commanders took that lesson to heart; references to quickened paces are fairly common in reports. Whether the men could sustain a fast step for long distance was a problem, but at least commanders tried to move troops quickly under fire.

One must divide this topic into two separate components, for commanders often called for quickened speed when moving to a field of battle to sustain comrades under fire as opposed to ordering a fast pace during an attack on the enemy. Of course, most commanders preferred to move at common time to preserve the strength of their men for the ultimate contest on the battlefield, but at times a sense of urgency called for fast movement to get reinforcements to the field. When Col. Oliver Otis Howard moved his brigade toward the scene of action at First Bull Run, orders came down from division headquarters to get there on the double quick. This compelled Howard to move his men nearly one mile at 160–180 steps per minute before he realized they could not keep up the pace. The tail of his brigade column had fallen back and become detached from the rest of his command. Howard slowed the pace to quick time for the next two miles, but still many of his men "dropped out and fainted from exhaustion."[27]

As troops gained experience and developed endurance, they could move quickly for long distances. The 100th Pennsylvania advanced for half a mile at double quick and by the flank to participate in the Battle of Secessionville in June 1862. A month later the 26th Georgia moved for a mile and a half on the double quick and under artillery fire to reach the field of Gaines's Mill. At Champion Hill, the climactic battle of the Vicksburg Campaign, Brig. Gen. Abraham Buford marched his brigade at double quick for two miles "under a scorching sun, through corn and rye fields, in about half an hour," to help Brig. Gen. John Bowen's division. Many reports of the fighting at Chickamauga make reference to rates of speed while marching to the scene of action. It was always on the double quick, and the distances noted include half a mile, one mile, and even two miles.[28]

Intense heat combined with distance to cause Lt. Col. Edwin A. Bowen to take caution while moving his 52nd Illinois to the scene of Sixteenth Corps fighting on July 22 east of Atlanta. His parent brigade had moved on before Bowen could retrieve all of his skirmishers, so he felt a sense of urgency in getting to the battlefield. "Tell Colonel Bowen to hurry up as fast as God will let him," was the order relayed by a staff officer, "the enemy are in our rear, and the brigade is fighting like hell." But Bowen knew that the heat was too great to go at double quick the entire distance, so he "ordered the battalion to move as fast as the men could walk." When the troops reached a point only three-fourths of a mile from the battlefield, an orderly brought word to double quick. "Notwithstanding the men were much exhausted from the pressure of heat, they moved forward to the scene of action with commendable zeal and celerity, and with ranks well closed."[29]

Battle reports indicate that advancing to attack the enemy also occurred at accelerated rates of speed. Both Union and Confederate commanders ordered the double quick for various regiments at Mechanicsville, Second Bull Run, and Fredericksburg. The 30th Arkansas advanced with its parent brigade at quick time for four hundred yards on December 31, 1862, at Stones River. At that point it came into full view of the Federal line and began to receive sporadic fire. The Arkansans continued another fifty yards at quick time under worsening fire and shifted to double-quick time when only one hundred yards from the enemy. Their attack was successful.[30]

Examples of using double-quick time to attack enemy positions abound in the Vicksburg Campaign and include engagements at Port Gibson, the Federal capture of Jackson in May 1863, and the fight at the Big Black River railroad bridge. On the second day at Chickamauga, Confederate troops arrayed in several lines under Lt. Gen. James Longstreet launched an assault against a sector of the Union position where a gap inadvertently developed. The Southerners started slowly and then "by degrees it became a quick step, and then a double-quick, and at length, a wild and impetuous rush," as William F. Perry put it. They passed through the gap in the Federal position and into a dense patch of woods. "Here the men lost their alignment, and soon the three lines were merged into an indiscriminate surging mass."[31]

The use of a quickened pace while attacking the enemy continued during the last year of the war. Normally, commanders ordered the quick step. At times, they merely reported that their men ran at the critical point of an advance as they closed within very short range of the enemy. When the 27th Iowa participated in the Federal attack on Fort DeRussy in March 1864, it was the first time the regiment had ever advanced on an enemy fortification. Col. James I. Gilbert ordered, "'Forward, double-quick, march!'" He admitted after the successful assault, however, that the regiment was "moving too rapidly at times for a long charge, but all the time under apparent good control."[32]

OBLIQUE MOVEMENT

The oblique movement was not a change of front, but rather it fell into the category of adjusting direction while moving forward. It was a bit complicated, requiring troops to face one way and walk slightly to the right or left so the line maintained its original orientation while moving diagonally. It was undertaken a fair number of times under fire on the battlefield. Col. Garrett Dyckman explained it well when he described the action of his 1st New York at Oak Grove during the start of the Seven Days' Battles. The regiment advanced "moving obliquely forward in line of battle to the right through the swamp." A month before at the Battle of Seven Pines, Maj. Bryan Grimes saw that a Federal redoubt lay a bit to the right of his regimental center. He therefore caused the 4th North Carolina "to right-oblique" in order to hit it more squarely. The 11th Pennsylvania Reserves performed a right oblique while formed "in close column by division" and advancing through woods at Antietam, a maneuver that demonstrated considerable skill.[33]

Examples of units conducting the oblique movement can also be found in western battles. Both Union and Confederate regimental commanders did so at Perryville and Prairie Grove. On the second day at Chickamauga, there was a good deal of jostling within Cleburne's Division just as had occurred in his attack the previous day. S. A. M. Wood advanced his brigade to the left of Lucius Polk's brigade. Wood obliqued to his left to make room as Polk crowded his right flank. Soon after, Polk suddenly obliqued to the right and opened a gap between the two brigades. Wood did the same, ordering an oblique movement to the right until he caught up with Polk. The next summer Quarles's Brigade also performed a left oblique at the Battle of Ezra Church to avoid passing across an open field under heavy fire. When Brig. Gen. John D. Kennedy moved his brigade obliquely to the left in order to bypass another Confederate unit at Bentonville, he was quite pleased with the result. "This oblique movement was performed very handsomely by the brigade under a terrific shelling," he reported.[34]

There are a few cases, however, in which commanders admitted that the oblique movement was not suited to a particular condition. Col. George C. Porter received an order on the first day at Chickamauga to conduct a right oblique across terrain that was heavily cluttered. His consolidated 6th and 9th Tennessee contended with ground that was "thickly covered with felled timber and piles of wood." Porter tried but "found it impossible to keep a correct line of battle. There were, unavoidably, gaps and groups along the whole line." After negotiating this terrain for 250 yards, Porter concluded it "was badly adapted to this move."[35]

Although an oblique movement was not ordered, Col. William S. H. Baylor of the 5th Virginia found himself conducting one during an advance at Gaines's Mill. He was told to maintain connection with the 2nd Virginia to his right. Because the entire brigade line was moving constantly to the right during the attack, he wound up obliquing in the gathering dusk of evening. Baylor often could not even see the left flank of the 2nd Virginia and had to gauge what to do as much by the cheering that erupted from its men as by the sight of the guiding regiment.[36]

Several unit commanders combined the oblique movement with other maneuvers on the battlefield. Col. James Keigwin crossed a ravine at Port Gibson by moving diagonally the right three companies of his 49th Indiana. But when he encountered a second ravine, he estimated that "the depth and roughness" was so great, "I would have to pass it without any order." Keigwin did not elaborate on how he did so, but his men crossed the ravine and reached the other side before reforming a line once more. Presumably, the Indianans simply broke up and passed through the ravine individually.[37]

Combining an oblique movement with a half wheel worked beautifully for at least two regiments on different battlefields. Capt. Edmund S. Read was told to deal with a squad of Federals off to the left of his line of advance against a Union battery at New Market on May 15, 1864. He ordered the left company of his 26th Virginia Battalion to oblique to the left, but many men failed to hear his command. Read led a portion of his unit to chase away the squad and then half wheeled to the right to fire on the battery and contribute to its capture. In the Union attack on Fort Gregg at Petersburg on April 2, 1865, Lt. Col. Andrew Potter led the 116th Ohio and 34th Massachusetts on a right oblique movement until he could conduct a left half wheel and front the Confederate fort to deliver fire on two of its faces simultaneously.[38]

Read and Potter demonstrated that the oblique movement could be combined with other maneuvers to change the front of a battle line. Doing this indicated a high level of articulation on the part of both the commanders and their men, demonstrated a superior level of thinking on the part of effective officers, and represented a potent element of success in difficult battlefield conditions.

SKIRMISHING

Skirmishing was in many ways a higher order of linear tactics than operating within the confines of a battle line. It demanded expertise in moving from close order to open order. A skirmish line was still a line, but one with extended intervals between each man within it. The art of skirmishing also called for a higher degree of individuality, personal skill at firing and taking cover, a greater degree of stamina and combativeness, and a firm sense of self-confidence among officers and men alike. The fact that inspection reports among both Union and Confederate units often indicated that most regiments did not seem to perform the skirmish drill very well indicates that commanders devoted less attention to this area of training than was wise. While some regiments excelled at skirmishing, others were poor at it, with the majority hovering somewhere in between.[39]

Good commanders understood the purpose of skirmishing and tried to perform it according to the manual. One of Maj. Gen. William S. Rosecrans's staff officers expressed its basic purpose in a nutshell, adding details on how to do it. He conveyed instructions to Col. George D. Wagner before the colonel's brigade set out to protect a foraging train near Murfreesboro in January 1863. Wagner was to "deploy a heavy line of skirmishers, at 5 paces intervals," and advance them double quick while deploying his brigade battle line "under cover of their advance." This instruction got to the essence of skirmishing, an action designed to protect and support the battle line rather than fulfilling an independent function on the battlefield.[40]

The tactical manuals provided detailed instructions about the process of forming skirmish lines. They recommended that two companies skirmish for the regimental front, and many commanders put this into practice. Col. Jesse Alexander initially placed Companies A and K, 59th Indiana on the skirmish line during one phase of the Vicksburg Campaign. Upon reaching a strong Confederate position, he sent the rest of his regiment forward until the skirmishers covered a front of 1,500 yards. When approaching the defenses of Jackson on May 14, Maj. Francis C. Deimling put Company A, 10th Missouri out as skirmishers, with five-pace intervals between each man. Then he placed Company D as the first reserve and Company I as the second reserve. Deimling then advanced as cover for the brigade column for two and a half miles toward the Confederate works, where the entire brigade deployed from column into line.[41]

There are examples of regimental commanders deploying only one company rather than two to skirmish duty. The 10th Missouri did so at the Battle of Iuka. The 34th Massachusetts deployed one company as skirmishers for the regimental front at New Market. Colonel Wells placed that company two hundred yards in front, "each man taking his exact interval and dressing to the right as steadily as on drill." But more typically, officers relied on the manual and sent forward two of their ten companies out to skirmish.[42]

On the brigade level, the length of skirmish lines and the number of men manning them varied according to circumstances and the judgment of commanders. Early in the war the tendency was to create skirmish lines for larger units that would have been considered thin by later standards. Gideon Pillow had 2,500 men in the five regiments constituting his brigade at the Battle of Belmont in November 1861. He deployed three companies to the skirmish line, drawn from three different regiments, and placed one of the regimental adjutants in charge. Pillow acted unusually not only by establishing a thin skirmish line but also by directing a staff member to command it. More typically, a line officer from the companies sent out to skirmish would have taken charge of the line.[43]

Col. Jacob Laumann deployed one regiment as skirmishers in front of his brigade column when attacking the outer defenses of Fort Donelson on February 15, 1862. Seven companies, however, constituted the skirmish line for Daniel E. Sickles's brigade at Oak Grove in June 1862, and the general placed those skirmishers three hundred yards in front of his main line. At South Mountain Colonel Thruston was instructed by his brigade commander to deploy only four companies of the 3rd North Carolina to skirmish for the brigade and at only two hundred yards distance.[44]

A more typical deployment involved sending an entire regiment out to skirmish for a brigade front. When told to do this, Col. Elliott W. Rice of the 7th Iowa sent out eight of his companies while keeping his "two center companies held as a reserve" during the Battle of Corinth. When Luther Bradley used his 51st Illinois on the skirmish line the day before the Battle of Stones River, he sent out alternate companies while holding the others as the skirmish reserve. Col. Daniel G. Bingham employed a different method when taking his 64th New York out to skirmish at Chancellorsville, deploying his right wing as skirmishers and placing his left wing in column to act as the skirmish reserve.[45]

The practice of deploying companies from different regiments to a brigade skirmish line, however, continued on many battlefields, even if it was not typical. During the Vicksburg Campaign, for example, it was often resorted to among Union and Confederate commanders alike. They consistently placed an officer from one of the parent units in charge of the combined line. There were advantages to this method as opposed to assigning an entire regiment to the task, for officers and men from different units in the brigade could mingle and get used to each other within the demanding combat environment of the skirmish line. Few commanders, however, bothered to estimate the number of men in any given skirmish force. In preparation for an advance at Cold Harbor, a brigade skirmish line in the Fifth Corps was doubled until it reached a total of 360 men and was supported by a reserve of four companies.[46]

An interesting example of mixing outpost duty with skirmish duty occurred during the Cedar Mountain Campaign of August 1862. Brig. Gen. George H.

Gordon instructed Silas Colgrove on how to place his 27th Indiana to cover the right and front of the brigade. Colgrove sent two companies to an advanced post three-quarters of a mile to the right and front to watch for the enemy. He also sent a portion of each company a quarter of a mile to his front as a brigade skirmish line and held half of each company as a reserve for the skirmishers.[47]

Once deployed, Civil War commanders made full use of skirmishers. One essential function of the skirmish line was to discover information about the opposing force, and there are many examples of such reconnoitering. The 19th Mississippi of Brig. Gen. Cadmus M. Wilcox's brigade sent two companies to skirmish at the Battle of Williamsburg. They advanced less than two hundred yards, fought heavily for fifteen minutes, and then retired to report the location and strength of the main Union position. Brig. Gen. Samuel Garland told Col. D. K. McRae to send fifty skirmishers from his 5th North Carolina into a "dense growth of small forest trees and mountain laurel" at South Mountain. McRae was instructed to let the skirmishers "go as far as possible and explore." They encountered Federal skirmishers only fifty yards into the tangled woods.[48]

A Fifth Corps directive on June 1, 1864, during the Cold Harbor phase of the Overland Campaign, set out the fundamental reconnoitering purpose of skirmishing. Corps commander Warren instructed his division leaders to "push your skirmish line along our front against that of the enemy, and make it of sufficient strength to force it back, and ascertain the position of the enemy's line of battle or strong intrenchments." Skirmishers from Brig. Gen. Lysander Cutler's division pushed ahead as ordered and advanced four hundred yards until they reached a point where they could see the Confederate earthworks located another two hundred to three hundred yards away across the flat, sandy landscape.[49]

In addition to gathering information, skirmishers fulfilled the fundamental role of fighting on the defense and the offense. The skirmish line was an advanced, thin line of battle, shadowing the main line and adjusting its movement to the needs of the main formation. The widespread use of skirmish lines has produced many examples of defense and attack by skirmishers in the official reports. The exposed position of these men wore on the nerves of many who preferred to remain in the relative security of the main line. Lt. Col. N. J. George of the 1st Tennessee (Turney's Regiment) complained of this problem while submitting his report on Chancellorsville. "I have been engaged with several bodies of skirmishers," he wrote, who "in general consider the individual responsibility too great; generally very cautious, and apt to start on trivial accounts—especially is this the case at night." George reassured his brigade commander that his men held firm and performed the perilous duties of skirmishing satisfactorily.[50]

For defensive purposes, skirmish lines were placed within shorter rather than longer range of the main line. Lieutenant Colonel George, for example, put his 1st Tennessee four hundred yards from both the Confederate main line and the opposing Federal main line at Chancellorsville. At Pleasant Hill Lt. Col. Thomas H. Hubbard positioned only one company as the skirmish line for his 30th Maine, with two other companies in reserve. That company performed well, firing three volleys at an advancing Rebel brigade before falling back on the reserve. Skirmishers could be useful in stemming the retreat of other units as happened on the evening of May 2 at Chancellorsville. Twelfth Corps skirmishers, deployed with very short intervals between each man, managed "in some measure" to slow down the Eleventh Corps's retreat.[51]

A Sixth Corps directive issued near the end of the war clearly spelled out instructions for skirmishers acting on the defensive and also differentiated between their role and that of pickets. While it was common in the Civil War to use those two terms interchangeably (especially among Union forces serving in the Atlanta Campaign), the purpose of the two differed markedly. Pickets made up a line of sentinels whose job it was to detect enemy activity and report as soon as possible. Much thinner than a skirmish line, there was little expectation that pickets could offer much resistance. The Sixth Corps created a force in front of its line on the night of April 1, 1865, that crossed the boundary between those two functions, necessitating instructions about what the men were expected to do. "They are to distinctly understand that while on picket they are not intended as camp guards to alarm and notify the troops of an enemy's approach, but they are placed in a carefully prepared and strong position as a fighting force." Staff officer George Clendenin Jr. further clarified their role in no uncertain terms: "Any attacking force less than a line of battle our pickets should destroy with ease."[52]

The placement of skirmish lines to serve as a defensive screen often was attended with extreme difficulty. The problems lay in tangled vegetation, darkness, and uncertainty about enemy positions. Three examples serve to illustrate these difficulties. They include the problems Col. Daniel G. Bingham encountered with his 64th New York at Chancellorsville (confusion about joining the flank of another skirmish line in the woods); Col. Peter Lyle's Fifth Corps brigade on August 18, 1864, during the Fourth Offensive at Petersburg (deploying a skirmish line to cover both his front and flank while forming his main line); and the immense difficulty experienced by Edward S. Bragg in deploying his brigade to cover a wide gap between the right of the Fifth Corps and the left of the Ninth Corps on August 19, 1864, during the Fourth Offensive at Petersburg (several staff officers produced different maps of the area, none of which were accurate, resulting in utter confusion about everything associated with the job).[53]

Civil War reports are filled with examples of aggressive skirmishing designed to take combat directly toward opposing skirmish lines and harass the enemy's main position. At times this was done primarily for defensive purposes. For example, brigade commander Col. William H. Irwin assigned Thomas W. Hyde's 7th Maine the task of pushing back Confederate skirmishers who were harassing Federal artillerymen at Antietam. Hyde formed the 7th in front of the brigade skirmish line, sent out part of his command as skirmishers, and advanced the rest of his regiment on the double quick with bayonets fixed, cheering all the way. He cleared the enemy from an orchard and outbuildings, but the Confederates reacted by moving more than three regiments against him. Hyde held on in the orchard until receiving fire from three sides, then fought his way out. He lost 88 out of 181 men engaged.[54]

Hyde failed because his lone regiment was not supported; only by holding the orchard could he have fulfilled his mission to protect the artillery. In contrast, Federal forces in the West mounted many successful skirmish efforts during the Jackson Campaign and the Atlanta Campaign because they acted in concert with other units. Col. Charles C. Walcutt praised his 46th Ohio for effective skirmishing on July 16, 1863: "On this day the regiment proved its real worth, the men exhibiting excellent judgment, coolness, and true bravery."[55]

Maj. Gen. William F. Smith formed large, dense skirmish lines to attack the fortifications of Petersburg on June 15, 1864, and coordinated the actions of skirmish units from different commands that participated in this operation. Joseph Kiddoo, for example, was told to have intervals of only one pace instead of the usual five paces in the skirmish line he formed with men from the 22nd USCT. There are many other examples of heavy skirmish lines pushing forward to test and if possible attack enemy positions in the last year of the war, demonstrating that both Union and Confederate commanders were learning how to use skirmishers more flexibly to fulfill their traditional role and expose their main line less often.[56]

In the West the four-month long Atlanta Campaign provided a wonderful venue for the skirmisher to shine. With years of experience behind them and extended contact with the enemy as Sherman drove deep into Georgia, Federal skirmishers normally dominated no-man's land. Officers often sent out reinforced skirmish lines, provided them with plenty of ammunition, and expected the men to come back with empty cartridge boxes. They aggressively pushed these heavy deployments forward to put pressure on the enemy and degrade their ability to resist. The sustained fighting along skirmish lines, increasing in intensity as the two armies settled into static and fortified positions near Atlanta during August 1864, amounted nearly to a small battle. Hazen's brigade skirmishers fired 5,000 rounds every day for three weeks at this stage of the campaign. On the opposing side, Manigault's Brigade maintained a skirmish line of 175 men who fired on average more than 6,000 rounds every day, amounting to 35 rounds per man. The wear and tear of intense skirmishing for long periods had an effect on troop morale and combat readiness. Civil War soldiers pushed the envelope in the art of skirmishing, taking it to its fullest development in Western military history. The work they did presaged the great emphasis to be placed on loose-order skirmish fighting in the decades to come as tactical theorists tried to reorder formations and maneuvers to better suit the expected effect of long-range fire from magazine weapons in the late nineteenth century.[57]

In the deceptively simple process of moving their regiments straight forward, Civil War commanders encountered many obstacles to their advance. From thick woods to fences, road cuts, and watercourses, impediments to an orderly movement of linear formations cropped up repeatedly. This was not unique to the American landscape, for such obstructions were readily found on European battlefields as well. But like their counterparts overseas, American officers learned how to deal with them. The linear system had built-in methods to move around any number of obstacles in the path of a regiment. Furthermore, as they gained more experience, both officers and men learned how to improvise within that linear system if a particular maneuver contained in the drill manuals did not seem to exactly fit the problem.

The tendency among historians has been to imply that the linear system was inadequate to meet the cluttered nature of the battlefield, but nothing could be further from the truth. As the numerous examples cited above indicate, obstacles provided challenges for the effective unit commander, but he normally overcame the difficulties and maintained forward movement or restored cohesion. A tactical system that flourished for two hundred years in Europe and North America could hardly have been so fragile as to have been stopped by a collection of trees, a fence, or a road cut.[58]

Civil War officers normally marched their men at faster rather than slower rates both in the movement toward combat and while actually attacking enemy positions. This had been the primary purpose behind the publication of Hardee's book. Commanders used more difficult maneuvers such as the oblique movement when necessary but preferred straightforward progress at all possible times. The fact that they were usually able to use the less favored and more difficult maneuvers means they had also learned how to conduct those movements on the drill ground, even if they chose not to use them very often on the battlefield.

Skirmishing had a much shorter history than the linear system that created it. Beginning in Europe only seventy years earlier, the art of skirmishing reached its apogee during the American Civil War. While some unit commanders gave skirmish training short shrift, many others took it more seriously. A number of Union and Confederate regiments practiced the art with commendable thoroughness and skill, and most units were able to skirmish with an acceptable degree of success.

In fact, the Civil War saw the best examples of effective skirmishing in Western military history. Many commanders came to rely on heavy skirmish lines not only to protect the main formation but also to seriously harass enemy skirmishers and mainline troops alike. A handful relied on skirmish lines to attack principal enemy formations. It was common to use skirmishers to develop opposing troop positions, occupy enemy attention, and thereby support offensive operations on the battle-field. Whether Americans had a better aptitude for skirmishing than Europeans is doubtful. Perhaps the extended nature of Civil War engagements (especially the continuous contact of the Atlanta, Overland, and Petersburg Campaigns) simply gave Americans more opportunity to gain experience at skirmishing than was typical of European operations.

☰ 6 ☰

Multiple Lines, Echelons, and Squares

Flexibility in tactical formations is quite evident in Civil War battle reports. Commanders did not slavishly concentrate on only a few formations nor did they totally ignore the more obscure ones. They utilized subunits of the company when needed, but that necessity only rarely presented itself on the battlefield.

SUBUNITS OF THE BATTLE LINE

Every officer regarded the two-rank battle line as the proper formation, but now and then someone split it in two, using one rank to perform a specialized task. Gouverneur K. Warren ordered two of his Fifth Corps division commanders to advance a single rank to reconnoiter at Spotsylvania on May 10, 1864, wanting to develop the Confederate position without exposing a full battle line to casualties. This was done successfully, and even the Sixth Corps commander did the same thing that day.[1]

William B. Hazen also used a formation of only one rank when his division attacked Fort McAllister near Savannah on December 13, 1864. He detailed three regiments from each of three brigades to form the assaulting force. Hazen wished to reduce casualties, thus the unusual formation of these nine regiments in one rank that resembled "a close line of skirmishers." The Federals lost 130 men in the successful advance, most due to Confederate torpedoes (landmines) planted just outside the fort and to the fierce hand-to-hand combat that erupted after they entered the work. Hazen's superior, Oliver Otis Howard, praised this formation in 1907 when writing, "Hazen acted very wisely when he gave instructions to do what all infantry commanders are now obliged to do: use thin lines."[2]

The use of one rank on the battlefield, however, was very rare in the Civil War.

It was possible for Hazen to do it because the garrison of Fort McAllister was very small compared to the numbers involved in the nine Federal regiments conducting the attack. In most other situations, advancing what amounted to a skirmish line to accomplish what a battle line ought to do would have been futile. Two ranks certainly provided more targets for defending infantrymen, but they also allowed the attacker to move more men against a well-defended position and have a better chance of success in the process.

All tactical manuals warned against inversion of ranks, a situation wherein the front rank became the second rank after a complicated maneuver took place. It was thought important to keep the regimental battle line intact at all times, with the proper placement of companies along its length for smoother operation. In general, this proved to be an important warning in the Civil War, for there are many cases of inversion of ranks leading to confusion among the men.

The 123rd Illinois underwent its first exposure to combat at the Battle of Perryville on October 8, 1862. The regiment led its brigade in moving forward by the flank until forming line only two hundred yards from the enemy, getting the ranks inverted in the process. This caused a good deal of confusion among the men, made worse by the fact that they were green and needed the comfort of known order to steady their nerves. The troops, however, managed to open fire and stand their ground. When Lt. Col. Enos P. Wood's 17th Illinois ran out of ammunition at Shiloh, he ordered the line to face to the rear and retire to a field. There he gave the order to move by the left flank, but his men became confused because the old left flank, when facing the enemy, was now the new right flank. Some began to face and move in one direction as others faced and moved in the opposite way. The 17th Illinois, as a result, was "thrown into some confusion" as Wood put it. He straightened out his regiment by moving the men farther away to the first convenient spot where he could reform ranks in the proper orientation.[3]

Yet there are many examples of regiments faring well even while fighting with inverted ranks. These examples all come from experienced units and took place under duress when there was no easy way to present the proper front to the enemy. As Brig. Gen. John Gibbon wrote of the first day at the Wilderness, "there was no time to change the formation," so the troops of his division went into action with inverted ranks and performed well. Col. Griffin A. Stedman was proud that the men of his 11th Connecticut managed to fall back through woods under fire with ranks inverted "without losing their formation or becoming confused," even though two-thirds of them were new recruits enduring their first battle.[4]

Combat operations on the squad level were rare indeed during the Civil War. In fact, as we have seen, the tactical manuals did not even recognize a permanent place for the squad in the regimental organization. When Confederate pressure compelled Federal regiments defending the heart of Corinth to break up into squads on October 4, 1862, they were able to continue fighting effectively. These squads were led by lieutenants and sergeants, and they managed to stop the disjointed enemy advance and save the town. "When the reaction came the men were easily brought back," reported their brigade commander.[5]

Movements by regimental wings were much more common. At times, this was done because of the force of circumstances rather than design. The 7th Connecticut encountered difficulties and wound up with its wings moving at different rates of speed while attacking Fort Lamar during the Battle of Secessionville. The 15th Ohio broke into two wings inadvertently while attacking at the Battle of Pickett's Mill during the Atlanta Campaign. The right wing (except one company) actually wound up moving diagonally and hitting the Confederate position to the left of the left wing, but the regiment gave a good account of itself despite this difficulty.[6]

Commanders often made a decision to operate in wings to meet circumstances as they cropped up on the battlefield. Maj. Andrew J. Weber found that his 11th Missouri had no support to right or left on the first day of the Battle of Corinth, so he told his right wing to fire right oblique and his left wing to fire left oblique at the approaching enemy. Lt. Col. Lucien Greathouse formed his 48th Illinois in columns of wings while approaching the skirmish line and before deploying into line at one point during the Jackson Campaign of mid-July 1863.[7]

Some officers learned how to use one wing to protect the other while advancing or retiring. Col. John E. Smith did so with the 45th Illinois at Fort Donelson after his men had been firing for one hour and thereafter found it necessary to retreat. He pulled back the right wing first while the left wing continued to fire, then withdrew the left. The Iron Brigade of the First Corps performed movements by regimental wings very effectively while advancing at the Battle of South Mountain. Col. Lucius Fairchild moved the right wing of the 2nd Wisconsin forward to obtain a better position from which to fire on the enemy. When that wing ran out of ammunition, it was replaced by the left wing, then by the 19th Indiana, also moving by wings. Lt. Col. Edward S. Bragg also used the 6th Wisconsin in this fashion, slowly advancing his regimental line by wings and firing all the time. He eventually maneuvered his left wing to outflank an enemy position while holding the Confederates in place with his right.[8]

The size of regiments was large enough so that it became expedient to use wings as if they were battalions, or subunits of the regiment, though officers never referred to wings as battalions. Likewise, it became common practice for regimental commanders to designate temporary wing commanders for a given engagement. This happened as early as the Battle of Williamsburg in May 1862, when Col. C. H. Mott placed Lt. Col. L. Z. C. Lamar in charge of the right wing of the 19th Mississippi; Mott retained control of the left wing. Lamar entered an area of "dense undergrowth and uneven ground," but he had Mott's authority to "operate . . . according to my own discretion." At the Battle of Ringgold the consolidated 6th, 10th, and 15th Texas occupied a position that placed its center exactly over the sharp crest of Taylor Ridge. The slope was so steep that neither flank could see the other. Capt. John R. Kennard therefore placed another captain in charge of the left wing while retaining control of the right. He also placed Asst. Adj. Gen. J. T. Hearne near the center of the line "so that the orders could be better observed and passed." William Hazen, as we have seen earlier, liked to maneuver by regimental wings near the end of the war. He found it superior in "simplicity and quickness" and thought it was well "adapted to all grounds."[9]

MULTIPLE LINES

The tactical manuals of the day discussed forming multiple lines as if it were so common as to be the normal formation on the battlefield, and Civil War commanders certainly employed multiple, or successive, lines very often. In fact, it was by and large the default arrangement in Civil War engagements as it had been during the long history of linear tactics in Europe and North America.

It is important to understand that multiple or successive lines *was not* a column formation. As the manual authors clearly indicated, a column consisted of a stack of battle lines placed very close behind each other—only a few feet to a few yards. Successive lines were placed much farther apart from each other—hundreds of yards in fact. In that way the multiple lines formation avoided the worst problem associated with columns, the strong tendency of each line to merge into and break the one in front, especially when the column hit an obstacle and slowed down or stopped, often leading to its collapse into a mass of disorganized manpower. In the multiple-line formation, each was far enough away from the other so that commanders had room to maneuver to avoid obstacles. They also were far enough apart to avoid the fire that descended on the previous line. Successive lines allowed

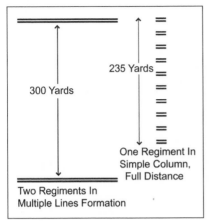

235 Yards

300 Yards

One Regiment In
Simple Column,
Full Distance

Two Regiments In
Multiple Lines Formation

Fig. 6.1. Comparing Multiple-Lines Formation and Simple Column at Full Distance.
Multiple or successive lines were so widely
used as to be the norm for Union and Confederate armies. But they represented a different formation than that of the column.
The key difference lay in the distance separating ranks and lines in the two formations.
The longer distances gave the multiple-lines
formation more flexibility than the short
distances in a column. Each bar represents
one rank.

for much more tactical flexibility than did columns. There was much to be gained
by organizing the available force in two or more battle lines, including depth in
defense and support for the first line in an attack. If nothing else, multiple lines
gave a sense of security and confidence to a harried commander who was worried
about the outcome of an engagement.

One of the most controversial examples of multiple lines is the attack plan of the
Confederate Army of the Mississippi at Shiloh. Gen. Albert S. Johnston intended
to align his three corps in one battle line with a reserve to the rear. But his second
in command, Gen. Pierre G. T. Beauregard, suggested a different arrangement,
which Johnston accepted. Beauregard drafted Orders No. 8, calling for a formation
of multiple lines. That was not the controversial feature of his plan, for many officers would form successive lines in later battles by assigning one corps or division
to a specific sector of the field and requiring unit commanders to place some of
their men in a second line behind their first in order to exploit any initial advantage. But Beauregard's scheme was to assign an entire corps to the first line and
another to the second, which meant that the supporting troops were commanded
by officers of a different corps than those in the first line, making coordination of
reserves extremely difficult. Johnston's army organized a front of three miles between Owl Creek and Lick Creek, with Hardee's Third Corps forming the first line.
Hardee was reinforced by a brigade from Maj. Gen. Braxton Bragg's Second Corps,
while the bulk of Bragg's command formed the second line one thousand yards
behind Hardee. Beauregard suggested that Bragg should, "if practicable," deploy

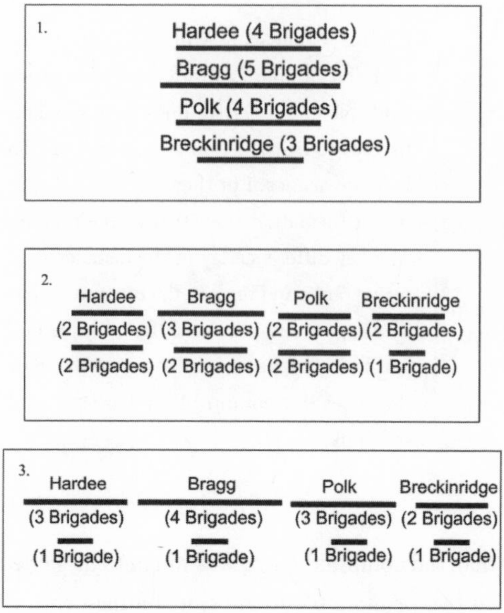

1.

Hardee (4 Brigades)

Bragg (5 Brigades)

Polk (4 Brigades)

Breckinridge (3 Brigades)

2.

Hardee	Bragg	Polk	Breckinridge
(2 Brigades)	(3 Brigades)	(2 Brigades)	(2 Brigades)
(2 Brigades)	(2 Brigades)	(2 Brigades)	(1 Brigade)

3.

Hardee	Bragg	Polk	Breckinridge
(3 Brigades)	(4 Brigades)	(3 Brigades)	(2 Brigades)
(1 Brigade)	(1 Brigade)	(1 Brigade)	(1 Brigade)

Fig. 6.2. Actual and Theoretical Confederate Deployments at Shiloh.

1. The actual formation used by the Confederate Army of the Mississippi at Shiloh, with each corps deployed in a line that matched the army's front. Corps leaders had less command and control over their troops and no reserve that they could directly command.

2. Theoretically, the Confederates could have assigned each corps a sector of the battlefield, packing each successive line as fully as possible with troops, but this would have led to a narrow front and great depth. This was not normal practice during the war.

3. What the Confederate deployment might have looked like had planners used the more typical arrangement for Civil War commanders, which included a front as wide as possible with a small reserve to the rear. The reserve also has more room to maneuver to threatened areas or to exploit success within the corps sector. Each bar represents one line, not one rank.

"with regiments in double columns at half distance" according to the demands of the terrain. Maj. Gen. Leonidas Polk's First Corps was placed eight hundred yards behind Bragg, either "in column or massed on the line of the Bark Road, according to the nature of the ground," while Brig. Gen. John C. Breckinridge's Reserve Corps was to be close behind Polk. Cavalry units screened both flanks.[10]

Beauregard's decision to arrange the army in this fashion produced chaos when the Confederates attacked the Federals at Pittsburg Landing on April 6, 1862.

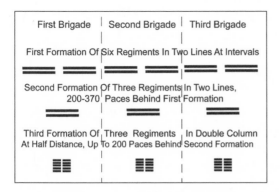

Fig. 6.3. Buell's Standard Division Formation. Soon after Shiloh, Don Carlos Buell mandated multiple lines as the habitual formation of his Army of the Ohio, with the first and second formations in lines and the third in column. Each bar represents one line, not one rank. (Based on General Order No. 8, Headquarters, Army of the Ohio, Apr. 15, 1862, *OR*, 52[1]:238–39)

Bragg's men could not be restrained from "closing up and mingling with the first line" during the advance. As long as Hardee's troops drove the enemy, this did not prove to be much of a problem, but when they hit resistance and stalled, most of Bragg's units moved up without orders and joined Hardee's formation. The Army of the Mississippi lost much of its cohesion as a result, becoming "greatly disarranged and scattered," in the words of Beauregard's staff officer Thomas Jordan. It remained a powerful force for pushing forward because most regiments and brigades managed to retain their formation, but Johnston lost the opportunity to articulate his command as an army and was relegated to being a well-placed cheerleader rather than a true commander.[11]

The lesson of Shiloh was clear: successive lines wherein each line was formed of a different unit presented a recipe for confusion. The proper way to form multiple lines was to assign sectors of the field to unit commanders and expect them to form successive lines with their own manpower. This allowed for greater command and control because the multiple lines all belonged to the same larger unit. This arrangement worked very well on hundreds of Civil War battlefields.

Maj. Gen. Don Carlos Buell, who led the Army of the Ohio at Shiloh, came away from the engagement with a desire to mandate a habitual order of battle for his troops. General Orders No. 8, issued on April 15, 1862, specified that each division should form three lines on the battlefield. The first line should consist of six regiments, two from each of the three brigades in the division, so that each brigade would have its own reserve. These six regiments were to deploy one or two of their companies as skirmishers. Buell wanted the interval between regiments on the first line to be maintained as required by the tactical manuals. The second line was to consist of three regiments, one from each brigade, placed "opposite the intervals between the regiments of the first line." He wanted the flanks of this second line to extend beyond the flanks of the first line so as to protect the formation with an echelon arrangement. The second line was to be placed 370 paces behind the first if the ground was open and level, but 200 paces if in wooded country. The third line, constituting the division reserve, was to consist of three regiments, again one from each brigade, and "formed in double column at half distance, each column placed opposite the interval between the two regiments of the first line of the brigade to which it belongs." The third line was to be placed 200 paces behind the second in favorable terrain, closer in "broken or wooded ground." This arrangement conforms closely to the suggestions laid down in all the tactical manuals available to Civil War commanders.[12]

Buell put into general orders what most officers chose to do anyway on battlefields throughout the war: use multiple lines in some way or another. The official reports are full of such examples, though they differed in the distance separating each line. At Chickasaw Bluffs, the Thirteenth Corps formed in two lines 100 yards apart, but Brig. Gen. Frank P. Blair placed his brigade's second line only 150 feet behind the first in preparation for a risky attack on a strong Rebel position. Hazen formed his brigade at Perryville with three regiments on the first line, one forming the second line 150 yards behind the first, and a reserve of one regiment 150 yards behind the second line. At Murfreesboro Braxton Bragg placed the second line of his Army of Tennessee 800 to 1,000 yards from the first while preparing to meet the oncoming Union army commanded by William Rosecrans. For his part, Rosecrans recommended that the Federals' second line be placed 300 yards behind the first. Federal brigades at Stones River consistently formed two lines of equal strength. For Charles Cruft's brigade, this meant a front of only six hundred men, but he had maximum depth in his formation as a result.[13]

When major campaigning began in Virginia early in 1862, Union and Confederate commanders also consistently formed two lines when entering battle. In fact, Maj. Gen. Fitz John Porter's corps formed five successive lines when attacking a strong Confederate position at Second Bull Run on August 30. In a rather typical

Fig. 6.4. Samuel Beatty's Brigade at Stones River on December 31, 1862. This illustration shows the successive-line formation typical of Civil War armies in action. The two lines of Beatty's Federal brigade appear much closer to each other than was usual, but the entire formation is evocatively depicted. (From *Battles and Leaders of the Civil War,* 3:622)

formation, Col. Alfred T. A. Torbert's brigade of the Sixth Corps formed two lines with two regiments each at South Mountain on September 14. The lines were from one hundred to three hundred paces apart "according to the nature of the ground." On another part of the Union line at South Mountain, Brig. Gen. John P. Hatch's division of the First Corps formed successive lines of brigades to advance up the slope. Brig. Gen. Marsena Patrick's brigade led the advance in line, while Col. Walter Phelps's brigade moved forward two hundred yards to its rear, followed by Brig. Gen. Abner Doubleday's brigade. Phelps and Doubleday formed "in columns of division at half distance, preserving the intervals of deployment." Part way up the slope, however, Phelps and Doubleday deployed into line to continue the advance.[14]

At Antietam the Federals tended to place their second line much closer than normal, perhaps because of the need to move masses of men across largely open country against the enemy. Phelps placed his brigade only fifty paces behind and in support of John Gibbon's brigade while advancing across Miller's cornfield. When Gibbon began to engage the enemy, Phelps closed the distance to only twenty-five paces and told his men to lie down and wait. The presence of a second line so close behind them must have encouraged the men on the first line, but there was a disadvantage to close support. Alpheus Williams noticed that when the Second Corps went into battle at Antietam, its second line was only forty paces behind the first, so close that it "suffered almost as much as the front line and yet could not fire without hitting our men. The colonel of a regiment in the second line told me he lost sixty men and came off without firing a gun." When Williams had a chance to command the Twelfth Corps for a few days during the Chancellorsville Campaign, he mandated by "personal order" a formation of two lines, with only two regiments in the first line and the rest of each brigade placed at a safe distance behind in reserve.[15]

Successive lines normally worked more effectively when each was placed a couple of hundred yards from the next. In this way the troops were more protected from enemy fire and were less likely to interfere with or share the same fate as those ahead. They also acted as true reserves and supports rather than as poorly placed segments of the initial attack formation.

Union and Confederate officers persisted in using successive lines during the intense campaigning that took place in the West during 1863. At the Battle of Port Gibson, the first of several battles during Grant's operations against Vicksburg east of the Mississippi River, Federal brigades typically formed two lines, with three regiments in the first and two regiments in the second, the latter acting as a reserve and placed two hundred yards to the rear of the first. This formation continued at Champion Hill and appears to have been a consistent policy in Grant's Army of the Tennessee, at least during 1863. On the second day at Chickamauga, John Palmer decided to form his division in successive lines supported by a column. His motive was "to avoid what seemed to me the common error of the day before (too extensive lines)." He placed Hazen's and Cruft's brigades in two lines, with Col. William Grose's brigade "in double column" as a reserve. The fighting that day demonstrated again the danger of placing successive lines too close to each other. Col. Fred Knefler's 79th Indiana was positioned "a few yards" from the first line and suffered for it when those units broke in confusion. Knefler's men "were literally trampled down and overrun by artillery. Had a sufficient space intervened, a stand could have been promptly made," the colonel complained.[16]

The use of multiple lines continued in both opposing armies throughout the Atlanta Campaign. Normally, brigade commanders divided their strength evenly between the two lines they formed. The distance mandated by superior officers typically was three hundred yards between lines, a safe distance enabling commanders to minimize losses, provide flexibility for maneuvers, and yet be within quick supporting distance of the front line.[17]

Official reports covering the intense operations in Virginia during 1864 also bear out the consistent use of multiple lines at all levels of command. But there tends to be less detailed information on how they were placed than exist in reports covering the western engagements. On the second day of the fighting at Nashville, for example, Col. Abel D. Streight formed his brigade of the Fourth Corps in three lines, each one 150 yards from the next. He placed two regiments each on the first and second lines but only one on the third line, a formation mandated by division headquarters. At the Battle of Bentonville, Brig. Gen. Edmund Pettus formed his brigade of the Army of Tennessee as a second line 250 yards behind the front line. His division commander told him to keep about 300 yards behind the troops ahead during an attack on the Federals.[18]

With so many formations assuming successive lines, the need to adjust positions to accommodate other units became constant. Commanders had to keep the placement of neighboring troops in mind when managing their own men. Sometimes they adjusted their position to let units from the rear line come forward and strengthen the front. For example, Lt. Col. William A. Olmsted moved his 2nd New York about six hundred feet to the right to make room for the 10th Massachusetts to come up and join the front line at Oak Grove, just before the onset of the Seven Days' Battles. There are many examples of one unit moving in front of another while advancing and masking the fire of part or even all of a regiment. Affected commanders, therefore, had to think of some maneuver to unmask their men and straighten out the formation. When intervals were maintained between the left flank of one regiment and the right flank of its neighbor, commanders often closed the space because they felt more secure within a solid line when facing the enemy.[19]

Multiple lines normally worked very well on Civil War battlefields as long as unit commanders maintained proper distance and retained control of their men. If they could not control them, the troops often disrupted operations. The colonel of the 59th New York allowed his troops to move forward from the second line of Maj. Gen. John Sedgwick's Second Corps division at Antietam while the first line was stationary and firing away at the enemy. The New Yorkers advanced nearly forty yards, even though no other regiment in the second line did so, and stopped a short distance behind the 15th Massachusetts. There they started to fire "through my left wing on the enemy," as Lt. Col. John W. Kimball reported. The Massachusetts men began to take casualties from this friendly fire. Kimball tried to get the 59th to stop but failed. Only when Maj. Gen. Edwin Sumner rode by and was informed did the corps commander manage to put an end to this insane firing.[20]

A breakdown of command and control accounted for another disastrous use of multiple lines when the Confederates launched a major attack during the Battle of Tupelo on July 14, 1864. It started with a formation of three lines, which "could be distinguished separately" by observers in the Union position. But this formation quickly began to collapse under the enthusiasm with which the Rebels conducted the charge. As Maj. Gen. Andrew J. Smith reported, the Confederates "lost all semblance of lines and the attack resembled a mob of huge magnitude. There was no skirmish line or main line or reserve, but seemed to be a foot race to see who should reach us first. They were allowed to approach, yelling and howling like Commanches, to within canister range" before Federal artillery opened. Although some Confederates managed to get within thirty yards of the Union line, the attack was repelled.[21]

PASSAGE OF LINES

A serious breakdown of discipline accounted for the confused attack with successive lines at Tupelo, something quite unusual on this scale compared to other Civil War engagements. But operating in multiple lines certainly did place a premium on knowing how to pass lines on the battlefield. Carefully explained in all tactical manuals, this was an essential maneuver in the Civil War. Scott explained it in pretty elaborate terms, though he assumed a first line supported by a second line arrayed in columns. As mentioned in chapter 3, the process of passing lines as Scott described rarely took place in actual practice. This was due to the fact that the supporting lines often were not arrayed in columns and that intervals were usually not maintained. As a result, commanders often improvised when faced with the need to quickly move their men through the line of another unit. Often it worked well, but at other times it caused much confusion.

A survey of examples stretching across East and West demonstrates that commanders had difficulty dealing with the problems associated with passage of lines. When the 1st Kansas retired at Wilson's Creek in 1861, it sliced through the line of the 1st Iowa, separating Companies A and F from the rest. Col. William H. Merritt shouted for his Iowans to retire and reform, but they could not hear him. He then led Companies A and F to the rear, regrouped them, and tried to return to the regiment. Two other companies that had been detailed to the skirmish line now joined them. Merritt eventually gave up hope of reuniting his regiment and sent his major back to take charge of these four companies while he controlled the other six for the rest of the battle.[22]

Several regiments at Shiloh managed to deal with interference from others quite effectively. Col. John A. Logan's 32nd Illinois reacted positively when a retiring regiment broke through its line. The men "closed up and continued the deadly strife" after the other unit passed through. The 15th Illinois did the same, even though its line was broken several times by retreating infantrymen, artillery pieces, and mules that had broken away from their handlers. Col. John A. Davis's 46th Illinois lay on the ground when another regiment marched through its ranks. "As soon as it passed my men rose, dressed their line, and immediately commenced pouring a destructive fire upon the enemy."[23]

Of course, maintaining the standard interval between units helped a great deal. Brig. Gen. Alexander R. Lawton moved his Georgia brigade of 3,500 men through the interval between two regiments to form line beyond them at Gaines's Mill. When there were no intervals, there was little choice but to go through or over the unit that lay in the way. Col. John Neff found a Georgia regiment lying on the ground in his path as he advanced the 33rd Virginia at Malvern Hill. His first thought was to pass through, but the Georgia commander "remonstrated against it," and Neff moved by the flank to bypass the prone men. When the 17th Georgia was cut in two by a passing regiment as it moved forward on that same field, marching by the left flank, Col. Henry L. Benning was unable to reunite his regiment until the next day.[24]

Very often regimental leaders became victims of other commanders who had lost control of their men or who took no care of units around them while moving their formations on a crowded battlefield. The 2nd Excelsior Regiment of New York "was almost carried away" when another regiment hit it while retiring during the Second Battle of Bull Run. In fact, the troops who did this were "perfectly panic-stricken, breaking and carrying away with them the left of my line," reported Col. Nelson Taylor. In the same engagement a regiment of volunteers cut into the line of the 1st Battalion, 17th U.S. Infantry. Maj. George L. Andrews tried to divert or stop them, but it was no use. After they passed, Andrews proudly reported that his men quickly re-formed even though many of them were recruits experiencing their first combat.[25]

The official reports covering the first half of the war indicate that most regimental commanders performed maneuvers to make the passing of lines easier.

Normally, the affected regiment, the one being passed through, had to take these precautions. Officers could do this only if they had timely warning and if their men had the requisite training. When these circumstances applied, the passing of lines not only worked effectively, but it also could be a thing of beauty to observe.

Many commanders merely reported that they opened ranks to let other units safely through their formations, without providing more details about exactly how it was done. But the 4th Michigan doubled its files to allow those of the 12th New York to pass through its ranks at Malvern Hill. Col. Samuel Beatty formed his brigade in two lines, two regiments each, at Stones River. Wanting to relieve the first line with the second, each regiment on the front "wheeled into column" to allow the other two units to pass through the intervals. "The whole movement was accomplished in fine order," reported Beatty, "under the very heavy fire of the enemy." Cruft's brigade performed a similar move at Stones River. Without explaining exactly how the two regiments of the second line moved through the first line, Col. Thomas D. Sedgewick nevertheless wrote that "the passage of lines by the advancing and retiring regiments was executed in the most perfect manner and in good order."[26]

The problems associated with passing lines continued during the last half of the Civil War. Retiring regiments often cut into other units to the rear while moving away from contact with the enemy, often because they had run out of ammunition and needed to find the ordnance train for resupply. When retreating Federals sliced into the 114th Pennsylvania at Chancellorsville, Col. Charles Collis was able to identify and reassemble his men more easily because they wore a distinctive Zouave uniform.[27]

In the woods at Chickamauga, the men of the 19th Ohio became "confused and scattered" when a retreating Federal battery broke through their formation. "I did not succeed in rallying them again in a body until evening," reported Lt. Col. Henry G. Stratton. "They rallied in squads, however, and remained on the field until dark, fighting with fragments of other regiments." The 58th Indiana was placed only five paces behind the caissons of the 8th Indiana Battery on that battle's first day, undoubtedly because of the heavy vegetation. The first Federal line was positioned only seventy-five paces in front of the 58th, making for a very compact and dense formation. Suddenly, the front line and the artillery retired in such haste as almost to be in a panic. The horses attached to the caissons "became frightened and unmanageable, and were directed toward this regiment and driven madly through the line, crushing several men and utterly destroying all line or order in the regiment, and cutting off three companies on the left of the regiment." In fact, several units suffered because of the hasty withdrawal of a first line as infantrymen ran over them.[28]

In the fierce fighting of the Overland Campaign, there occurred several examples of units retiring through others without taking proper care. Col. John W. Henagan endured a hasty retreat at the Wilderness that "created some confusion and some uneasiness on my part," for he feared that the panic might spread through his ranks. But "as soon as I could disentangle the brigade from those that were retiring," Henagan re-formed and advanced. On the same day but on another part of the battlefield, the 121st New York and 95th Pennsylvania of Emory Upton's brigade in the Sixth Corps were moving by the flank when other Federal troops ran through their formation. This interference "threw both regiments into unavoidable confusion." Efforts to compensate for this trouble were hampered by the fact that the thick vegetation had caused the files to increase their distance from each other while moving by the flank. Although portions of these two regiments were able to rally quickly, other segments had to reform farther away near Sixth Corps headquarters.[29]

The only thing the commander of a disrupted regiment could do was to pick up the pieces and continue, which happened many times on various battlefields of 1864–65. There are a few cases where one sees a regiment that took the time and effort to minimize disruption as it retired. At Jericho Mills during the North Anna phase of the Overland Campaign, a Fifth Corps brigade broke from the first line and retreated toward Col. J. William Hofmann's brigade 150 yards behind it on the second line. Fortunately for the colonel, the retreating troops "passed around our left flank," though only because Hofmann held the extreme left of the second line and the retiring soldiers took the effort to veer off and go around that flank rather than to pass through his line.[30]

Regimental and brigade commanders often reported that another unit disrupted their formations on the battlefield, though rarely lodged any official complaint. But Brig. Gen. Samuel Crawford did complain when Brig. Gen. Charles Griffin's Fifth Corps division passed through his own division one day during the early stages of the Petersburg Campaign. Griffin indicated to his colleague that he had authority to do so from corps headquarters, and General Warren thus had to accept responsibility for it. Warren explained that he was under a great deal of stress that day and misremembered Crawford's placement when he gave hasty orders to Griffin to hurry his division forward. He had not intended to disrupt Crawford's division, but he also gently chided his subordinate for complaining about it, telling him that "annoying occurrences of this kind must be met with mutual forebearance."[31]

Of course, there was no need for "mutual forebearance" if officers had the opportunity and presence of mind to conduct passage of lines in the prescribed fashion. The 2nd Rhode Island relieved another regiment on May 3 at Chancellorsville because the other unit ran out of ammunition. "Forming directly behind them," reported Col. Horatio Rogers Jr., "we let them fall through our ranks, opening fire as they passed." When Lt. Col. Henry V. N. Boynton's 35th Ohio was told to give way to an advancing brigade on the second day at Chickamauga, it was done with precision and grace. "The withdrawal was accomplished in regular order by the successive passage of lines to the rear," as Boynton reported. Lt. Col. Orson Moulton of the 25th Massachusetts broke his "three right companies to the rear into column" to allow the 9th New Jersey "to pass between my command" and the 27th Massachusetts during an early phase of the Bermuda Hundred Campaign.[32]

Now and then, as we have seen, some officers were successful at talking another commander out of passing through their lines. When Col. Paul Frank moved his brigade up behind Col. Robert McAllister's brigade on the second day at the Wilderness, he asked permission to pass through the formation. McAllister refused, saying he had a skirmish line out front and also understood that Frank was to align to his left. Frank claimed that he had authority to hit the Rebels wherever he deemed appropriate, but he refrained from disrupting McAllister's troops. Instead, Frank moved his command by the left flank until it could march around McAllister's flank, then moved back in front of it and advanced directly forward.[33]

The pervasive use of multiple or successive lines by both Union and Confederate armies created a battlefield that demanded expertise in passing lines backward and forward through other lines. Normally, that was done well if time and opportunity allowed, but it caused a great deal of disruption and confusion when conducted in a hurried or careless fashion. Most affected regiments were able to re-form fairly quickly when their ranks were torn apart by another regiment.

ECHELON FORMATIONS

The echelon formation was designed to protect an exposed flank against possible enemy threats or to more effectively outflank an opposing line. It consisted of units that were separated from the battle line on either flank, placed 200 or 300 yards to the right rear or left rear of the rest of the formation. In fact, an entire brigade or division could be deployed in this fashion to create a serrated formation. The key was that intervals separated the echeloned units from the others to create a forward- or rear-slanting shoulder.

Echelons were used quite often on many battlefields across the breadth of the war zone, from Pea Ridge in Arkansas to the battles in Virginia. When Daniel Sick-

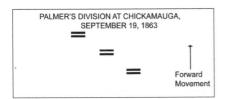

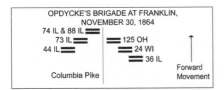

Fig. 6.5. Echelon Formations. The first diagram illustrates the theoretical use of echelons for defense of a friendly flank or for offense against an opposing flank. The other two illustrate actual uses of echelons on two battlefields. John Palmer formed his division in this formation to protect the flank of the unit to his left at Chickamauga, while Emerson Opdycke's brigade advanced in the shape of a chevron to seal a break in the Union line at Franklin. Each bar represents one rank.

les was told to deploy his Excelsior Brigade to protect a line of guns at Malvern Hill, he placed his left regiment to the left and rear of the left battery. The general arrayed his other regiments at intervals of twenty paces toward the right and rear of the preceding one. Col. Dandridge McRae formed his brigade at the Battle of Prairie Grove with each regiment en echelon and intervals of two hundred paces between them. The space separating units formed en echelon varied a great deal on Civil War battlefields. For example, Brig. Gen. Arthur M. Manigault maintained a distance of fifty yards between the regiments of his brigade at Stones River.[34]

Rosecrans made a personal suggestion that Palmer use the echelon formation when moving his division into action at Chickamauga on September 19. The army commander sent a note to that effect, believing that arraying Palmer's brigades en echelon with intervals of one hundred yards would protect his right flank as the troops moved through the woods. Palmer reported that it was "a most advantageous" formation for his purposes.[35]

The Confederate battle plan at Peachtree Creek incorporated an echelon formation for the entire attacking force, but it was not meant to protect an exposed flank. Gen. John Bell Hood wanted to hit the Army of the Cumberland as it crossed the stream on July 20, 1864, and roll it up toward the left. Therefore, Hardee's Corps was supposed to start the attack on the Confederate right, but each successive division in his corps, as well as those of Lt. Gen. Alexander P. Stewart, were to wait until the division to its right was two hundred yards ahead before they started their advance. This was to allow room for each division to swing left once it hit the Federal position. Commanders were told to be guided by the action of the division to their right, even though the object was to eventually swing left. It was an overly complicated plan that failed to achieve its purpose, in part because brigades on the left end of each division line approached the enemy position with no immediate support to their left and therefore received enfilade fire. Also, several commanders misunderstood the directive or were incapable of fulfilling it. The Confederate attack wound up being roughly a forward movement that failed to drive the Federals from the field.[36]

Hood's fault lay in trying to achieve too much with the echelon formation. Commanders successfully employed it on many battlefields, though on a small scale. In fact, Col. Emerson Opdycke used an echelon formation to seal the break in the Union line that opened up along Columbia Pike during the Battle of Franklin on November 30, 1864. His men happened to be in reserve some distance behind the position. As soon as Opdycke saw Federal troops retire from the works, he moved his brigade forward, deploying as it advanced, with three regiments to the left of the pike and three to the right. Each regiment spread out so that the brigade formation resembled a chevron, the two center regiments farther forward than the others. "I had to take them up in echelon," Opdycke informed his wife, "and the circumstances made this the best and most suitable of all possible movements, for the break commenced at the pike, and then kept increasing in both directions. I occupied the works at the pike first, and then the other regiments came up successively, just in the right time; as my last regiment occupied the works, the break was stopped."[37]

SQUARES

While echelons were fairly common on Civil War battlefields, the same cannot be said of squares. This complicated formation was learned by only a relatively small number of regiments, it appears from the evidence, and only rarely employed in actual operations. I have encountered only three examples, although there might well have been more instances where squares were used on the battlefield.

Col. Moses B. Walker held his brigade near George H. Thomas's headquarters

Fig. 6.6. The 139th Pennsylvania deployed in a square at its winter camp, vividly illustrating the all-around protection afforded by this complex formation. (LC-DIG-ppmsca-33189)

at the Battle of Stones River for a time, and when told that Confederate cavalry hovered nearby, he formed each of his regiments into a square, placing a section of artillery inside each. Col. John H. Holman ordered the 37th USCT to form a square when he feared that nearby Rebel cavalry might charge during operations north of the James River on October 27, 1864, during the Petersburg Campaign. And the 52nd North Carolina formed a square to protect itself against a small number of Federal cavalrymen during a major attack at Gettysburg on July 1.[38]

While squares were rarely used, echelon formations were more common on Civil War battlefields. Commanders sometimes utilized subunits of the regimental battle line, but they widely employed formations involving multiple lines. The tactical manuals described many elements of the linear system available to officers, and the evidence presented here indicates that most of those elements were taken seriously, even if not used very often. Naturally, commanders found some formations and maneuvers more useful than others.

Of the formations described above, multiple or successive lines constitutes the most important because it was so widely used by both Union and Confederate commanders. This offered depth to formations, which comforted officers because it created a layered defense and placed substantial troop strength within easy supporting distance of a forward line while conducting an attack. Arraying troops in multiple lines offered options to the brigade or division commander, and thus their preference for it is understandable. The tactical manuals recommended this as a default formation, and that advice was widely followed. Only when circumstances demanded a longer first line did commanders dispense with successive lines by necessity rather than by choice. It is important to keep in mind that these were not columns, the key difference being the distance between battle lines within each formation.

Multiple lines placed a premium on knowing how to pass one line through another. The tactical manuals also provided for that by maintaining intervals between units in each line. But Civil War commanders widely preferred to close intervals and achieve a continuous, touch-of-elbow line for greater security. This compelled them to improvise when it became necessary to pass lines. The process of improvisation often resulted in the disruption and shattering of formations, but at other times officers managed to work out a way to smoothly move one line through another.

= 7 =

Changing Front

While moving a regiment straight forward had its difficulties, changing its front or direction of march proved to be more complicated. This involved maneuvering the regiment so that it faced to the right or left, often to meet an unexpected threat from the enemy. A range of maneuvers existed in the drill manuals to achieve this change of front. Performing them well constituted a deeper test of proficiency for officers, and a more profound challenge to the emotional stamina of the men, than almost any other movement.

Brig. Gen. Samuel Garland's North Carolina brigade had been surprised and devastated by a raking fire at the Battle of South Mountain. Its survivors also participated in the engagement at Antietam three days later, and much of their mental composure had returned by then. Division commander Daniel Harvey Hill reported they fought well on September 17 until a cry arose from Capt. T. P. Thomson of the 5th North Carolina, "'They are flanking us.' This cry spread like an electric shock along the ranks, bringing up vivid recollections of the flank fire at South Mountain. In a moment they broke and fell to the rear."[1]

Garland's troops were good soldiers who had suffered a bad experience on the battlefield; if not for that experience, they might have been able to change front to meet the new threat from the flank and continue holding their position at Antietam. Hundreds of regiments and brigades successfully did this during the four-year course of the war.

REFUSING A FLANK

The fastest and easiest way to deal with a threat to the flank was to refuse part of the regiment to face it. This involved placing several companies of a regimental wing at an angle compared to the main line. Unlike the echelon formation, these companies maintained touch-of-elbow with the line they protected. The 52nd New York bent the three companies on its left flank to do this during the Battle of Fair Oaks on June 1, 1862. Lt. Col. Lewis A. Grant refused two or three companies of his 5th Vermont to face a developing crossfire at the Battle of Savage's Station in the Seven Days' Battles, an operation he termed a "hazardous movement."[2]

Col. Samuel B. Hayman refused more than half of the 37th New York to meet a Confederate attempt to flank his left at Williamsburg. Hayman placed six companies in an extended line a bit less "than a right angle" to the rest of his regiment. Further examples of regimental commanders refusing half their units (that is, wings) can be found with the 2nd Massachusetts at Antietam, the 118th Pennsylvania at Gettysburg on July 2, and the famous example of Col. Joshua L. Chamberlain's 20th Maine at Little Round Top. Faced with a major flanking threat to his left, Chamberlain extended the front occupied by his right wing, creating intervals of three to five paces between each man, so the right wing could cover the entire regimental front. Then he refused the left wing to meet the new threat. In this way Chamberlain lost no ground that was originally occupied by his regiment, a circumstance that naturally would occur if a commander refused a wing in the normal fashion by bending back half his regiment.[3]

Brig. Gen. William Grose was able to refuse the flank of his brigade at the Battle of Resaca without losing ground as well. He used his second line to create a perpendicular extension from the left flank of his first line. "It was formed and ready for action, with skirmishers out, in less than ten minutes," Grose reported.[4]

CHANGING FRONT FORWARD ON A SUBUNIT

Far more complicated than refusing a flank was changing front forward on a subunit of the regiment or brigade, but many commanders did it well. Col. W. H. Wallace responded to an order from his brigade commander "to change front forward on first company and advance, with the view of taking a column of the enemy in flank," at the Battle of South Mountain. He gave the necessary orders and watched as the 18th South Carolina performed the movement. Other examples can be found with the 3rd South Carolina at Antietam, the 10th Missouri (U.S.) at Iuka, the 43rd Ohio at Corinth, and the 26th Ohio, 51st Illinois, and 13th Tennessee at Stones River.[5]

Changing front forward on a subunit inspired praise when done properly. The

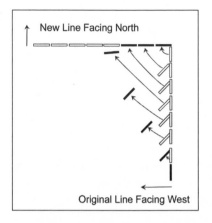

New Line Facing North

Original Line Facing West

Fig. 7.1. Changing Front Forward on a Sub-unit. This diagram indicates how a regimental line of eight companies could change its direction from west to north by moving one company at a time to the new line. The process resembles moving from column to line by the perpendicular method except that it starts with a line and ends with a line. Each bar represents one line, not one rank. (Based on Casey, *Infantry Tactics*, 2:186–87, plate 25)

2nd Battalion, 18th U.S. Infantry executed this maneuver "as if at ordinary battalion drill" before moving through a cedar thicket at Stones River. Brig. Gen. William P. Benton ordered the movement at the Battle of Port Gibson and marveled at his men's performance. It was "accomplished most handsomely, at a double-quick, over the most difficult ground," he reported. "So promptly and splendidly was the movement executed, under a galling fire of shell and musketry, that I was at a loss which most to admire, their valor or the efficiency of their drill."[6]

But sometimes troops attempted and fouled up the change of front on a subunit, or they were unable to make it work because of conditions beyond their control. Abner Doubleday gave orders for his brigade to deploy forward using the 95th New York as a pivot, but it failed. John Hatch simultaneously told the two right companies of the regiment to move away and support a battery without telling Doubleday. Those two companies were the pivot for this movement, and thus it fell apart when Doubleday tried to execute it. At the Battle of Corinth, Maj. John W. Jefferson wanted to change front to the rear on the first company of the 8th Wisconsin to meet a Confederate flanking move. But the 47th Illinois had come too close behind his line to allow him room to do it. Instead of changing front, Jefferson felt compelled to retreat because the 47th was in his way. At Stones River the 1st Ohio and 93rd Ohio got tangled up with the 6th Indiana when the latter attempted to change front forward on its first company to meet a Confederate flanking maneuver. Confusion was unavoidable in some battlefield situations, preventing men who knew the drill from executing maneuvers properly.[7]

Changing front to the rear on a subunit was a bit more difficult than changing front forward. Col. Albert M. Blackman's 49th Ohio successfully executed this maneuver twice at Shiloh, its first combat experience. When the Confederates placed men in a ravine to his left rear, Blackman changed front "to the rear on first company" and fired into the ravine to drive them out. His brigade commander then ordered him to change "front forward on first company, resuming my former place in line." Later advancing to another position, Blackman again changed front to the rear when once more threatened in that direction.[8]

Accounts are filled with references to well-executed changes of front to the rear on subunits. A perusal of the official reports for Stones River, including those for the 9th Indiana, 10th Wisconsin, and 27th Illinois, reveals that many regiments performed the move to meet constantly flanking Confederates. Capt. Francis Adams Donaldson recalled that the 118th Pennsylvania performed the maneuver "as upon parade" at Gettysburg. During the Battle of Atlanta on July 22, 1864, the 54th Ohio "changed front to rear on right company" when Confederate troops broke through the Union line to its left. At Third Winchester the 49th Pennsylvania and 119th Pennsylvania, both in the Sixth Corps, performed the maneuver without a hitch.[9]

Col. Van H. Manning tried to get his 3rd Arkansas to perform the change of front to the rear on a subunit during Longstreet's attack at Gettysburg on July 2. He was prompted to try it when he noticed Yankee troops trying to get past his left flank. Because Manning anchored the left of Brig. Gen. Jerome Robertson's brigade, he ordered his men to change front "to the rear on first company, but the noise consequent upon the heavy firing then going on swallowed up my command." Manning had no choice but to let the regiment work its way to meet this threat in any fashion company commanders chose. "I contented myself with the irregular drawing back of the left wing," he reported, which fired well and stopped the Federals.[10]

Lt. Col. James W. Langley managed to retain command and control over the 125th Illinois under very trying circumstances in the initial stages of the Confederate attack at Bentonville. Supporting troops to his right fell back, so Langley changed front to the rear by moving two companies at a time to the new line. "This movement was not executed by the entire regiment at once nor after the approved system of battalion drill," he admitted in his report. Langley did this to maintain firing to the front even while changing his position. It worked very well, allowing him to keep his men together while conducting a fighting retreat.[11]

Langley's example, and that of hundreds of other officers during the war, demonstrated that the men need not worry too much about enemy flanking columns. Division commander William B. Bate in the Army of Tennessee wanted his men to understand that point. Addressing an order to the subject just before the onset of the Atlanta Campaign, Bate felt that "too much apprehension has been felt among our troops in reference to being flanked in an engagement by the enemy, which movement can easily be met by 'change of front' of a brigade or regiment, as the case may require, with a prompt notification of the fact to the brigade or division commander."[12]

MOVING BY THE FLANK

Of all the maneuvers explained in Scott, Hardee, and Casey, the most commonly executed on Civil War battlefields was moving by the flank. It was a movement of simplicity and ease, designed to shift a line laterally, to left or right, with minimal fuss and bother. The maneuver involved each man turning to right or left in place and moving on, and the regimental battle line had the appearance (but not the reality) of being formed in a long column of two men abreast. But commanders often used it as an easy way to move their regiments forward or backward as well as laterally, and it could also be used to change the front of the unit. The file at the lead of the movement could turn in any way and expect the rest to follow. Its ease of execution, simplicity, and versatility made moving by the flank a pervasive maneuver in the Union and Confederate armies.

To note all the examples of moving by the flank in the official reports would be to compile a chronicle of every battle in the Civil War. At Baton Rouge, Antietam, Raymond, Gettysburg, Chickamauga, and throughout the Atlanta Campaign, the movement was used to close intervals between regiments, to adjust position within the larger battle line, to avoid obstacles, and to change position when enemy intentions became clear. At Champion Hill, for example, Maj. Gen. Carter L. Stevenson's division moved left several hundred yards after forming line to compensate for Union movements against its position. The division not only moved left by the flank but also bent its line while doing so at nearly a right angle. It was a complicated maneuver demanding close supervision by brigade leaders.[13]

Contributing to the pervasive use of this maneuver was the cluttered nature of most Civil War battlefields. At Belmont Col. Henry Dougherty led his brigade "through almost impenetrable woods, climbing over felled trees and filing around tree-tops." He did so by the flank until halting "to form a line." Regimental com-

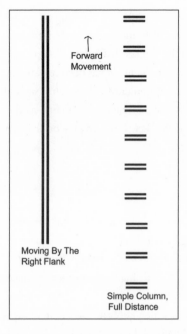

Fig. 7.2. Comparing Movement by the Flank and Simple Column at Full Distance. Moving by the flank was very common on Civil War battlefields. The men turned right or left in place and moved forward in two long lines that resembled a column. It was not a column, however, as defined by the tactical manuals. This diagram illustrates the differing appearance of both formations. Each bar represents one rank.

manders at Williamsburg and Seven Pines found vegetation so dense that the only way they could maneuver was by the flank. When Lt. Col. William P. Davis's 23rd Indiana moved forward in line at the Battle of Raymond, it hit the edge of a dense forest. Davis halted for a while until his brigade commander issued orders "to move by the right flank into the timber." After the regiment passed through the trees, it formed back into line and kept advancng.[14]

Participating in a counterattack during Grant's Fifth Offensive at Petersburg, Maj. Robert B. Fauntleroy moved his 55th Virginia by the flank over "difficult and boggy ground, tangled with brush and strong, matted undergrowth." His men emerged from this mass of vegetation and formed line but soon encountered terrain that was still "intractable," as Fauntleroy put it. Brigade commander William McComb told him to go by the flank again and redirect forward when he got through it. As Fauntleroy reported, "the difficulties of ground still increasing, we were compelled to move by flank to extricate us from the almost impassable jungle of tangled briers, grape-vines, and alder bushes."[15]

Moving by the flank proved useful for crossing linear barriers on the battlefield as well. Many regimental and brigade officers ordered it when they encountered

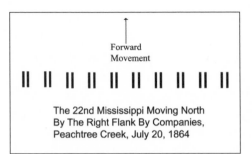

Fig. 7.3. Moving by the Flank by Companies. A comparatively rare method of moving troops through dense vegetation involved individual companies moving by the flank. The Confederates did so when approaching the Federals at the Battle of Peachtree Creek. This diagram illustrates what the formation looked like as the 22nd Mississippi moved through the woods. Note that upon reaching open ground, the companies redirected toward the front to form a regimental line. Each bar represents one rank.

a stream while advancing in line. Examples of this can be found at Hanover Court House, Fredericksburg, and Prairie Grove. Fences also could be dealt with by moving units through them by the flank, although a more typical mode was simply for the battle line to close up on the fence and tear it down before moving on. Yet Col. Thomas B. Smith decided to confront a picket fence that stood in the way of his 20th Tennessee at Stones River with the following order: "By the right flank, tear down that picket fence, *March!*" As some men tore a small hole in the fence, the regiment faced right and marched through the gap, formed line again on the other side, and continued the advance.[16]

Unit commanders also employed a variant on the movement by the flank to deal with tangled terrain features. Rather than move an entire regiment through the undergrowth by the flank, they moved with each company marching by the flank, creating ten small formations that looked like columns. This movement more or less preserved the regimental frontage and allowed for each company to form line again as needed in relatively quick fashion. It placed a premium, however, on company officers and their ability to conduct a semi-independent movement through rough terrain. Evidence of this maneuver appears more often in the last half of the Civil War, suggesting it was resorted to only after experience had hardened commanders and men alike.

The movement forward by companies marching by the flank appears by the time of Stones River and Chancellorsville. The 8th Illinois used it to negotiate "a dense canebrake" at Port Gibson, while the 51st Ohio and 8th Kentucky moved in this way for nearly a mile across the tangled battlefield of Chickamauga. A Sixteenth Corps brigade commander used the maneuver at Bayou De Glaize in Louisiana, though only with "much difficulty" because of "a dense briar thicket." Several Confederate brigades advanced through tangled vegetation during the initial phase of Hood's attack at Peachtree Creek. The brigade commanders chose to move by the flank of companies and imparted these instructions to regimental officers. As Maj. Martin A. Oatis of the 22nd Mississippi described it, the terrain included "overhanging and exuberant growth of vines and brambles, and fences covered with briers so dense as to form an almost impenetrable jungle." Oatis was barely able to move his Mississippians through this mass, but he of course lost sight of regiments to right and left. Only when emerging into relatively open ground after passing through this vegetation for nearly half a mile was it possible to form a line. While the movement forward by the flank of companies normally took place in tangled terrain, the 12th Connecticut utilized the maneuver to advance across relatively open but rolling ground, "here and there wooded," at Fisher's Hill.[17]

Like almost every maneuver in Scott, Hardee, and Casey, movement by the flank could be used to retreat as well as to advance. In many cases unit commanders used it to extricate their men from enemy attempts to bypass their position, especially if the battlefield was cut up by ravines or covered with tangled vegetation. Lt. Col. John A. McLaughlin held his 47th Indiana in a forward position during the Battle of Port Gibson and fired at the 3rd and 5th Missouri (C.S.) for half an hour before he noticed that the Confederates were approaching his right flank. His regiment then "changed position, retiring by the left flank along the ravine through which we had gained the summit of the hill, and formed in line of battle at right angles with our former position." Here the Federals held for two hours. The rugged terrain at Port Gibson produced many examples of unit commanders moving their regiments by the flank toward the rear, but others can also be found at Corinth, Chancellorsville, and Spotsylvania.[18]

Well-drilled troops could perform a retreat by moving by the flank and elicit admiring remarks from observers at the same time. The 1st and 2nd Battalions, 16th U.S. Infantry did so through a cedar forest at Stones River, retiring "by the right of companies." "The men performed this movement with the same order and regularity they would in an ordinary drill," wrote Capt. Robert E. A. Crofton. The regulars fell back one hundred paces and then re-formed to fire a while before retiring another one hundred paces by the right of companies. "The manner in which they fell back showed them to be well drilled soldiers," wrote a member of the Confederate brigade advancing against them.[19]

Troops of the famed Iron Brigade conducted a similar retreat in the face of a strong attack by Brig. Gen. James J. Pettigrew's North Carolina brigade on the first day at Gettysburg. Pressured in front, the 2nd and 7th Wisconsin retired "by the right of companies to the rear some 150 or 200 yards, halted, and wheeled into line again to support the other regiments in retiring." The Wisconsin men performed this maneuver several times until ordered to give up the field, doing so "by the right of companies to the rear, through the orchard over [Seminary] ridge, and then by the right flank by file left into column," according to William W. Robinson.[20]

Moving by the flank could lead to an inversion of ranks. The 33rd New York was suddenly fired on while moving by the flank at Antietam, and Lt. Col. Joseph W. Corning faced the threat as fast as possible. There was no time to reform in a way to face the enemy with his front rank, so Corning presented his rear rank to the Confederates. A Ninth Corps brigade commander was well aware of this problem when planning how to cover the rear of Meade's Army of the Potomac in the move from the Wilderness to Spotsylvania. The 50th Pennsylvania marched by the right flank as the 20th Michigan marched by the left flank to its right, both regiments bringing up the end of the column. In this way both units could redirect quickly and present their front rank to the enemy.[21]

Given the pervasive use of movement by the flank, there are a few examples to indicate that it sometimes did not work very well. The causes include too much noise for the men to hear the commands properly and intense enemy fire disrupting the movement. When Col. Thomas W. White was told to move his 9th Mississippi by the flank to another spot on the battlefield of Munfordville on September 14, 1862, he gave the command but could only watch as his men failed to execute it. "As the noise was great and the order given on our right flank the regiment did not get off in good order, some leaving in advance of others as the word was passed along the line." The 9th Mississippi managed to reach the new position but without the proper order or cohesion usually associated with this maneuver.[22]

Lt. Col. Frederick J. Hurlbut tried to move his 57th Illinois to the right to support other Union troops who were falling back on the second day at Corinth. He received a heavy fire from the front as he moved his regiment by the right flank. In fact, it was "a galling fire . . . , which was impossible to pass through." Hurlbut told his regiment "to half front and open fire," but the left wing fell back rather than stand its ground, and he told the right wing to fall back too. "I sincerely regret the last two movements of my command while under fire," Hurlbut reported, especially the movement by the flank. "I had the men well formed" before executing that maneuver, yet the regiment broke apart and retired from the fight while trying to put it into effect. These examples simply mean that, like any battlefield maneuver, moving by the flank sometimes was not the best choice for a given situation.[23]

Students of tactics must also keep in mind that terminology can trip up our understanding of the movement by the flank. In other words, determining exactly what type of maneuver was used sometimes involves careful consideration of the language employed by regimental commanders in their reports. "Moving by the right or left flank" could loosely refer either to the textbook definition (facing the men right or left and moving in what appeared to be a column of two men abreast) or guiding a regiment on either the right or left flank as it advanced in battle line.

Some unit commanders were careful in their use of terminology and have provided examples to illustrate the difference between these two meanings of moving with reference to a flank. Col. A. T. Hawthorn led his Arkansas regiment in the Confederate attack against the Union garrison of Helena, Arkansas, on July 4, 1863, moving it by the right flank along a ridge parallel to the enemy line. As soon as his left flank (or the end of his formation) cleared a road that ran perpendicular to the Federal position, Hawthorn stopped and redirected to face the enemy, then "moved by the left flank in line of battle." Brig. Gen. Alfred Iverson used similar language to describe his brigade's advance at Chancellorsville, moving "forward by the right flank in line of battle." Col. J. Warren Keifer carefully instructed his regimental commanders how to advance at Mine Run while getting around another Union brigade that was positioned in their way. Keifer told his subordinates to move by the left flank until the two first regiments (the 110th and 122nd Ohio) cleared the left flank of the other brigade. Then they were "to move by the right flank, in line of battle," toward the enemy. Examples of language such as this can be found in other battle reports too (for example, at Bristoe Station in October 1863).[24]

Even accounting for confusing language, it is clear that moving by the flank was a common way for Union and Confederate units to shift laterally, forward, or backward. Regimental commanders very often made a point of stating that orders to move by the flank came from brigade leaders. As Brig. Gen. Paul J. Semmes put it when reporting his part in the Chancellorsville Campaign, "Marching by the right flank, the most rapid mode of forming . . . , was executed."[25]

Regimental commanders often moved by the flank more than once during the course of a single battle, as did the 25th Tennessee at Perryville; the 5th Virginia at Chancellorsville; the 2nd Battalion, 15th U.S. Infantry at Jonesboro; and the 123rd Ohio at Third Winchester. In a little-known engagement at Bayou De Glaize, Louisiana, Col. James Gilbert moved his 27th Iowa forward by the right flank for one mile, then formed line and advanced another half mile before stopping five hundred yards behind the first Union line in the formation. Gilbert held his men here for two hours under Confederate artillery fire. Then at 3:00 P.M., he was ordered to move double quick for five hundred yards by the left flank and take position perpendicular to his first line. The 27th Iowa helped repel an enemy attack before moving by the right flank again "and filing right" into a third position. It stayed there half an hour before advancing one thousand yards into heavy timber, retiring only because of intense artillery fire into an open field. Gilbert held his regiment in this field for half an hour and then fell back by moving by the flank for half a mile. He performed the movement by flank four times during the course of the day's action.[26]

WHEELING

The last maneuver designed to change a regiment's front was wheeling a line to the right or left. Wheeling was difficult enough on the parade ground, doubly so under battlefield conditions. Col. Archibald C. Godwin, writing about his North Carolina brigade's wheel at Gettysburg on July 2, declared that it was "a movement which none but the steadiest veterans could have executed under such circumstances." His men crossed three stone fences and traversed ground that was "rocky and uneven" to close on the Yankees.[27]

Yet veterans of both sides often conducted wheeling movements under difficult circumstances. The 2nd New Jersey did so near the crest of South Mountain, and the 3rd South Carolina wheeled to the left "in gallant style" during Longstreet's July 2 attack at Gettysburg. Rough ground did not prevent the 22nd Alabama from conducting a right wheel on the second day at Chickamauga. Experienced troops were capable of wheeling despite the difficulty of keeping the line intact while one flank either remained stationary or moved slowly and the other flank moved at a faster rate of speed over rocks, uneven ground, or through tree cover.[28]

Unit commanders often mentioned conducting either a full or complete wheel as opposed to a quarter or half wheel. This terminology does not appear in Scott, Hardee, or Casey, but Emory Upton included it in his tactical manual adopted by the U.S. Army in 1867. Upton defined a full wheel as a movement that put the line

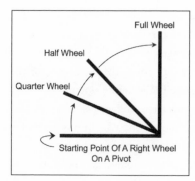

Fig. 7.4. Full Wheel, Half Wheel, and Quarter Wheel. Upton defined a full wheel as taking the line to rest at an angle of 90 degrees compared to its start. Logic may imply that a full wheel involved a turn of 360 degrees rather than 90 degrees, but that would face the regiment in exactly the same direction from which it started the maneuver. Each bar represents one line, not one rank. (Based on Casey, *Infantry Tactics*, 2:162–63, plate 21)

"at right angles to its original position, or changed ninety degrees." A half wheel was therefore a movement in which the line ended up at a forty-five-degree angle to the original line, while a quarter wheel brought the line to a twenty-two-degree angle compared to the original line. A wheel of 180 degrees (which Upton called an "about") brought the line facing in the opposite direction compared to its start. Drill manuals mention the utility of training a squad of men in wheeling by taking them in a complete circle of 360 degrees until they fully understood the principle, but this was unnecessary for larger units or experienced troops.[29]

Examples of regiments conducting a partial wheel include the 23rd Indiana at Champion Hill, which was ordered by its brigade leader to make a "one fourth wheel" to the right before becoming engaged with the enemy. Col. James Wood Jr. responded to corps commander Oliver Otis Howard's instruction during the Chattanooga battles to "swing round my line of battle to the left, making a left-quarter wheel upon the left of the regiment as a pivot."[30]

Civil War officers could detect the difference between a quarter wheel and a half wheel even when conducted by the enemy. Capt. Peter C. Olson of the 36th Illinois watched as a Rebel regiment moved across open ground at Stones River to hit his men. It initially approached at an angle, then conducted "a left half-wheel and came up directly in front of us." Other examples of regiments that conducted a half wheel include the 124th New York at Chancellorsville, the 5th Texas and 28th Alabama at Chickamauga, and the 20th Maine at Cold Harbor. Maj. Samuel F. Gray's 49th Ohio held the left flank of his brigade on the second day at Chickamauga when he detected Confederate troops trying to flank the line. Gray "immediately faced by the rear rank" before conducting a half wheel to the right to deliver fire on them. In this case Gray inverted the ranks in the process, but his men were able to half wheel with success anyway. On the first day at Chickamauga, Col. Allen Buckner's 79th Illinois "doubled its column at half distance" to wait as a reserve. Later the regiment moved a bit and "made a half right wheel, advanced about 200 yards and made a left quarter wheel, then deployed into line of battle." Buckner's men conducted these wheeling movements in column.[31]

Perhaps the largest wheeling movement of the war was conducted by Bragg's Army of Tennessee at Stones River on December 31, 1862. The general wheeled his left wing by using the right flank of Maj. Gen. Jones M. Withers's division as the pivot. Including Withers, a total of four Confederate divisions took part in this grand wheeling movement, arrayed at the start in two lines of battle. Instructions were to guide right "in order that the line may be unbroken."[32]

Of course, it proved impossible for these divisions to advance wheeling over terrain cluttered with farm houses, outbuildings, limestone outcroppings, and thick cedar brakes without breaking contact with each other. In fact, cohesion tended to break down even within each division line as brigades veered off in semi-independent actions only loosely coordinated with each other. Brig. Gen. Evander McNair's brigade of Maj. Gen. John P. McCown's division, which was on the far end of the wheeling movement, advanced half a mile before hitting the Union line and then drove the Federals one mile. By then it had completely broken contact with other brigades of the division, so it fell back 150 yards, changed direction to the right, and advanced half a mile to a fence. There it stopped, then moved by the right flank and then by the left flank to get on the right end of a Union line that was opposing another Confederate brigade. McNair's men attacked and drove the enemy, but they had to perform other adjustments to their line of advance (including moving by the oblique) to more or less keep up the wheeling movement until reaching a point about three miles from the start of the attack.[33]

Col. H. G. Bunn, who commanded the 4th Arkansas in McNair's Brigade, estimated the location of a line he temporarily held during the course of this wheeling movement by its reference to the original line from which he began the attack that morning. At one point Bunn believed his regiment had swung around enough "so as to make an angle of 40° with our line in the last engagement, and make an angle of nearly 60° with our first line in the morning." A private in Maj. Gen. Benjamin F. Cheatham's division at one point in the day estimated that his regimental line was "at right angles to the position we had occupied at daylight."[34]

Maj. Gen. Patrick R. Cleburne provided the most detailed report of how one division conducted the Confederate attack at Stones River. He started four hundred to five hundred yards behind McCown's Division early on the morning of December 31, "swinging to the right as I moved forward, . . . stepping short upon the right and full upon the left, so as to swing round my left as directed." Cleburne found it impossible to maintain contact with Cheatham's Division to his right, partly because Cheatham started later than he did and partly because his own men tended to incline to the left as they moved on. Corps commander Hardee pushed forward S. A. M. Wood's brigade to fill the resulting gap.[35]

Cleburne's left flank advanced less than half a mile before his men heard the sound of "heavy firing" to the front, indicating that McCown had become engaged. Then Federal skirmishers appeared on Cleburne's right and left center, indicating that McCown had veered left in the tangled landscape and uncovered at least two-thirds of Cleburne's Division. Not yet having deployed skirmishers, Cleburne now sent them forward and "pressed on, continuing the difficult wheel under fire, through a country cut up with numerous fences and thickets. There was a great deal of crowding and improper opening out in the center of my line. [Lucius] Polk's and [Bushrod R.] Johnson's brigades had to be moved by the flank more than once to regain their true positions."[36]

Nevertheless, Cleburne's line steadily drove the Federal skirmishers until he hit the Union main line about three-quarters of a mile from the starting point of his advance. His troops drove the Yankees away in a frontal attack, though suffering heavy losses. Continuing the advance, Cleburne encountered stiff resistance along the Wilkinson Pike. Johnson's Tennessee brigade had suffered so many casualties during the previous encounter that he found it hard to keep a solid line. "The space between the Forty-fourth and Seventeenth . . . was then too long for so few men," reported Lt. Col. Samuel Davis. But the Confederates "took advantage of the good room they had and went forward like skirmishers." The 17th Tennessee surged ahead faster than the rest of the brigade and opened an oblique fire on the defending Federals to help the 44th Tennessee advance.[37]

After chasing the enemy from the Wilkinson Pike, Cleburne paused to regroup. He had lost all contact with Cheatham, McCown, and Withers, although Alfred Vaughan's brigade of Cheatham's Division came into his sector and encountered Johnson's Brigade. The two units found that their battle lines were perpendicular to each other, which caused some delay. Vaughan finally moved through Johnson's line, changed his front, and continued his advance.[38]

Cleburne also resumed his advance after a while but encountered even worse obstacles. Enfilading fire from lurking Federal units often forced his division to stop, face right and drive them off before continuing the wheeling movement. Johnson's Brigade ran out of ammunition once, and Woods's men ran out twice, forcing them to drop out of the advance to replenish their supply and hurry to rejoin the division. Brig. Gen. St. John Liddell veered far to the left in the woods instead of inclining to the right. By the time Cleburne reached the Nashville Pike, Liddell was on the far left flank of Bragg's army, separated from the division by a gap three-quarters of a mile wide. Cleburne moved Polk and Johnson to the left and sent a message for Liddell to move to the right to close this gap. Vaughan's Brigade was available to him, so he placed it between Polk and Johnson.[39]

When Cleburne pushed on after reforming his division line, Liddell encountered a pocket of heavy resistance only one hundred yards away and fought another fierce engagement. He forced the defenders out of the woods by firing at ranges as close as twenty-five yards, but this delayed his advance. Cleburne allowed his other three brigades to continue. They advanced obliquely to the left to threaten Liddell's opponents with encirclement, a move that worked. Liddell followed up the Federal retreat by forming one hundred yards to the rear and left of Johnson.[40]

Cleburne attempted one last attack to gain the Nashville Pike in the late afternoon, but it failed miserably. He later explained that his men had advanced three miles across rugged terrain and had had little if any rest the night before because of the need to reposition the division before the attack. The troops had been fighting since dawn "without relief, food, or water," and their ammunition was nearly exhausted. Rumors flew among the ranks that the Federals were flanking them on the right, and suddenly heavy artillery fire caught them on that flank. A panic suddenly developed in Vaughan's Brigade, communicated to Polk's and Johnson's troops, and all three commands fell back in haste. Cleburne re-formed them four hundred yards to the rear, although some men ran all the way back to the Wilkinson Pike. Liddell's Brigade was immune to this near panic and retired in order.[41]

Cleburne maintained division-level cohesion better than any other Confederate officer on the field that day, and yet his detailed report indicates the extreme difficulties involved in accomplishing that feat. Bragg's plan to conduct a massive wheeling movement of four divisions for three miles across a landscape filled with serious obstacles to linear movements made sense on the surface, but it was impossible to execute as planned. As W. D. Pickett, Hardee's assistant inspector general, put it after the war, the wheeling movement "was not and could not be carried in practice on the field." That is true, but it is also in one way irrelevant, because those four divisions managed to succeed in driving the Union right and center back to the Nashville Pike. They did not perform a true wheel because they lost connection with neighboring units, but they did accomplish an essential objective of the battle plan. The Confederates took the Federals by surprise, drove them across the countryside, inflicted heavy losses in manpower and material, and held possession of the battlefield. Brigade commanders were capable of controlling their men across this rugged terrain and managed to loosely coordinate their actions with often dimly seen neighbors so as to achieve a brilliant tactical victory on December 31.[42]

A portion of the Army of Tennessee was called on to conduct another wheeling movement at the Battle of Resaca on May 15, 1864, when Maj. Gen. Alexander Stewart's division attempted to hit the Union left flank. Stewart placed Henry D. Clayton's brigade on the left of his first line and Marcellus A. Stovall's brigade on the right. He instructed both commanders "to make a half wheel to the left to place them in the proper direction" but also told them "to continue inclining by a slight wheel to the left" after that point as well. Clayton reported that Stewart gave "very particular instructions" on how to move, and the brigadier general relayed those orders "with the same particularity" to his regimental commanders. "I ordered the regiments to move out successively, beginning on the right, and advance with a left half-wheel, guiding to the left," Clayton was careful to report. "To make the matter doubly sure, I moved out" the 18th Alabama "on the right," then directed the consolidated 32nd and 58th Alabama as it executed "a left half-wheel, [and] halted them in that position." Clayton then sent one of his staff officers to get the other two regiments up to his new brigade line, now facing toward the left. Col. Bushrod Jones reported that his 32nd and 58th Alabama rested in this position with its right flank two hundred yards from the start point of the movement and its left flank only one hundred yards from it.[43]

The attack proved to be an utter failure. Ironically, Stewart started the advance a few minutes before orders arrived to cancel it. Not knowing this, Clayton personally took position just behind the center of his brigade and advanced up to three hundred yards toward the entrenched Federal line. He gave his regimental commanders the order, "Forward, guide left, march," in order to fulfill Stewart's directive to wheel slightly as they advanced. Bushrod Jones thought the 32nd and 58th Alabama never moved forward better than on any drill ground, but Clayton reported that his brigade alignment became "somewhat confused" by the terrain, so he ordered a halt to re-form. Clayton then advanced another fifty yards but soon realized that there was no support to his right or left. Jones reported that his consolidated regiment managed to get as close as twenty yards from the enemy and held there long enough to fire five rounds before retiring.[44]

Ironically, Clayton did not exactly fulfill Stewart's orders during this abortive flank attack. He did not wheel his brigade but moved the regiments to the end point of that projected wheel in stages. Clayton's action implies that he did not have confidence in his brigade to conduct a wheel as a continuous, connected line.

There certainly were battlefield situations where wheeling was counterproductive. Col. Rutherford B. Hayes's brigade was ordered to wheel gradually to the right during the Second Battle of Kernstown on July 24, 1864. After he began the wheel, Confederate troops suddenly appeared to his left and fired on the flank and rear of his formation. Hayes tried to change front to face this new threat, but "the left was doubled back in confusion on the right of brigade." He was compelled to fall back to a stone fence and re-form. If not caught in the act of wheeling away from the enemy, Hayes probably could have adjusted his line quickly enough to maintain his position and the cohesion of his command as well.[45]

But the other examples discussed above demonstrate that wheeling was a rather common maneuver for both the Union and Confederate armies and normally executed effectively. It also was quite useful in the passage of lines. The 12th Connecticut, for example, "wheeled into column of companies to give passage" to other units moving forward or backward at the Third Battle of Winchester. Obviously, some units understood the maneuver better than others, but in general most regiments and brigades could execute the wheel even under difficult circumstances.[46]

In fact, complex maneuvers to change front were learned well by most regimental officers in the Civil War and utilized from start to finish. Only in a few cases, as with moving companies by the flank through difficult terrain, was a particular maneuver not used early in the war but suddenly appeared halfway through it.

Changing front by refusing a flank, forming forward or backward on a subunit, moving by the flank, and wheeling were essential tools of the Civil War tactician. They enabled commands to move forward or to retreat more effectively and offered handy ways to deal with unexpected developments on the battlefield. Learning these formations and maneuvers took regimental leaders to a new, more sophisticated level of small-unit effectiveness. All these formations and maneuvers were key components of the existing linear system; they did not need to be improvised or altered to fit battlefield experience.

Columns

The two basic formations of Civil War units were line and column. While there was no argument over the utility of columns for a wide range of functions in military life, observers often discussed the wisdom of using them to attack a strongly held position. Most officers preferred to attack in line, while some believed in the value of columns for this dangerous task. But the benefit of columns for everything from reviewing troops to holding units ready for action on or near the battlefield was unquestioned. As a result, this became the default formation for many purposes in both armies.

The advantage of a column was that officers could better control their men because the troops were massed in a tight, compact group. They could better observe and speak to them than in an extended line stretching across the countryside.

The disadvantage of a column was that it proved to be less flexible than a line. If any rank stumbled and fell, it caused every other rank to the rear to do the same, resulting in the collapse of the formation. A line could deal with obstacles more easily because any disruption in it was limited to only a few men who had the elbow room to recover quickly. Another basic disadvantage of the column, and a prime reason why it was normally not used to attack the enemy, was that only the men in the first two ranks could fire their weapons. Those ranks, in turn, masked and nullified the fire of everyone behind them.

While the column proved to be of limited use in attacking enemy positions, it possessed great utility for many other purposes. For example, an inspection of Brig. Gen. Alexander W. Reynolds's brigade in the Army of Tennessee early in 1864 began with the regiments formed in columns of companies. Afterward, the regiments formed a brigade line to be presented to Reynolds, then formed again into columns of companies to pass in review. Moreover, even when not conduct-

Fig. 8.1. The 26th New York formed in a simple column at Fort Lyon, part of the defenses of Washington, D.C. This photograph vividly illustrates the narrow front and long length of this formation. (LC-USZ62-46924)

ing a formal inspection or review, commanders typically formed a column if they simply wanted to make an announcement. Brig. Gen. James D. Morgan drew up his brigade, "massed in column by division," to read a congratulatory order from President Lincoln commending them for the fall of Atlanta.[1]

SIZE OF COLUMNS

It was possible to form columns of all sizes because they were made of subunits within a larger unit. Formed in a simple column, a regiment presented a company front and extended ten lines (or twenty ranks) deep. A brigade of four regiments formed in a column presented a regimental front and extended four lines (or eight ranks) deep. References to a simple column like these can be found in many official reports.[2]

A double column looked quite different. A regiment thus formed presented a front of two companies and extended five lines (or ten ranks) deep. There are so many references to forming double column in battle reports that one is tempted to conclude it was more popular than the simple column during the war. It short-ened the length of a formation and widened it as well, representing a compromise

Fig. 8.2. The 2nd Rhode Island formed in a double column at Camp Jameson. This photograph well illustrates the extended front and the shorter depth of this formation. The Sibley tents with stockade walls indicate that this was a winter camp early in the war. (LC-DIG-ppmsca-33197)

between the long extended line and the deep but narrow simple column. Unit commanders probably found it more easy to maneuver than the simple column, and they could articulate a double column in a more facile way.[3]

Whether simple or double column, commanders understood that it was an effective formation in which to maneuver around the battlefield. There are a few references to retiring from an advancing foe while in column, although these regimental and brigade leaders failed to note whether they were in one or two columns at the time.[4]

Also rare are references to columns formed of units smaller than a regiment. Col. William Baldwin's Mississippi brigade formed a simple column among its regiments at Fort Donelson on February 15, 1862. Later in the day it also formed a column of platoons within those regiments. Company A, 45th Massachusetts approached a Confederate position by advancing along the railroad near New Berne, North Carolina, in April 1863 while formed in column of platoons with bayonets fixed. The company even delivered fire by platoons, with the members of the first platoon "stooping down" after they fired to allow the men of the second to fire over their heads.[5]

When Maj. Gen. James G. Blunt approached the enemy during the Battle of Honey Springs in the Indian Territory, he formed his entire command in columns. While the infantry regiments made columns of companies, the cavalry formed columns of platoons, and the artillery formed columns by section (two guns each). Everyone was "closed in mass so as to deceive the enemy in regard to the strength of my force," Blunt explained. He deployed his command when a quarter mile from the Confederates and proudly reported that his troops formed a line long enough to cover the enemy front in only five minutes.[6]

Late in the Virginia campaigns, Second Corps commander Andrew Humphreys believed his men could form a column of fours to approach the Crow House Redoubt along the bank of Hatcher's Run in order to avoid the worst part of the abatis the Confederates had erected. His suggestion was shelved because Grant favored a different operational plan that would avoid this redoubt altogether. Humphreys, however, made reference to the concept of fours that was written into every tactical manual from Scott to Hardee to Casey but which was rarely used in regimental field operations.[7]

FROM COLUMN INTO LINE

The foregoing examples show that commanders relied heavily on columns as an effective formation with which to approach an enemy position, but they typically deployed into line in order to attack. There are dozens of examples in the official reports to demonstrate the universality of this mode of operations.

In the East, deploying from column into line can be seen as early as First Bull Run. After marching eight hours in a column formation, the 27th New York "formed in line of battle by the left flank" and advanced without halting to drive the Confederates it encountered. John Gibbon's Iron Brigade of the First Corps, Army of the Potomac, deployed from column to line about 300 yards from the Confederate position at Antietam, while the 26th New York deployed when 350 yards from the enemy during the same engagement. Most unit commanders, however, did not estimate the exact distance at which they changed formation. "When near enough we deployed into line of battle," Lt. Col. John Clark reported of the 3rd Pennsylvania Reserves at Antietam. Brigade leaders had to keep in mind that, when ployed in column, their regiments needed to maintain proper distances from each other in order to deploy into line. Brig. Gen. George H. Gordon received an order to go to Joseph Hooker's assistance at Antietam. "I moved accordingly my ployed masses by the flank at double quick, gradually gaining deployment distance, thus throwing forward in line of battle" his Massachusetts, Wisconsin, and Indiana regiments.[8]

In fact, the Army of the Potomac used columns a great deal to approach Lee's position at Antietam. Perhaps this was because the battlefield consisted of unusually open, rolling terrain, and commanders felt the need to mass troops in order to move them quickly through the zone of Confederate artillery fire. The Second Division, Second Corps formed a column of three brigades one and a half miles from the battlefield and then moved forward at the double quick. It passed through woods and got "considerably crowded." Col. James A. Suiter of the 34th New York estimated that there were no more than forty paces between the left flank of the lead brigade and the right flank of the last brigade in the division column. The 7th Michigan encroached on Suiter's regiment, "causing considerable confusion." The division deployed into line as soon as it reached an open field and continued to advance at the double quick.[9]

Maj. Gen. Joseph K. F. Mansfield was obsessive about forming his Twelfth Corps in columns to approach the enemy at Antietam. A West Point graduate and career officer, Mansfield had little faith in several newly raised volunteer regiments assigned to his command. In fact, Mansfield had only recently been given the Twelfth Corps before the battle and had relatively little experience in the field thus far in the war. He therefore insisted that his troops approach the battlefield in columns. Alpheus Williams, who led a division under Mansfield, admitted that his green troops had great difficulty in ploying because of inadequate training. Nevertheless, he obeyed orders and formed his division in simple regimental columns. Williams explained this formation to his daughters as a company front, each line "closed up to within six paces" of the one in front so that "a regiment looks like a solid mass." Once formed in this fashion, Mansfield hoped the green troops would be more easily controlled under fire. But the problem was that an artillery round could rip a column like this to shreds; "dozens of men would have been killed by a single shot," as Williams complained. He "begged" Mansfield to let him deploy, but the corps commander feared the new troops "would run away."[10]

Samuel Crawford, who commanded another division of the Twelfth Corps, initially formed his men in columns according to Mansfield's order. At the van of the corps in its approach to the scene of action, Crawford emerged from the woods and entered a field. An order came to halt and deploy "without delay," but while doing so Mansfield showed up and told him to stop. The corps leader wanted Crawford's division to go back into column even though "the command was then exposed to an artillery fire." After Mansfield rode away, one of Williams's staff officers brought Crawford instructions to deploy into line and advance. It seems as if Williams, at least, was doing his best to bypass Mansfield and use formations that would be less wasteful of manpower under the circumstances at that time.[11]

Columns were used less often in the tangled vegetation of the Chancellorsville battlefield, although there are references to them in the official reports. At Gettysburg, a far more open battlefield than the Wilderness surrounding Chancellorsville, officers again used columns quite often. The Iron Brigade seamlessly moved from a marching column to a battle line when approaching the scene of combat west of town on July 1. The next day a Third Corps brigade shifted from column to line on its approach to the fighting as soon as it began to receive Rebel artillery fire.[12]

When Nineteenth Corps troops moved from the Department of the Gulf, where they had relatively limited combat experience, to the heavy fighting in Virginia, they soon learned to go from column to line under duress. George L. Beal's brigade formed a column of regiments behind another brigade at the Third Battle of Winchester. When the first line broke under pressure, Beal quickly deployed his men even though "small bodies" of the first line penetrated his formation.[13]

Commanders in the West used columns as frequently as did their counterparts in the East. Maj. W. L. Doss formed his 14th Mississippi behind the Confederate outer line of works at Fort Donelson in preparation for an attack on the encircling Federals. His orders were to capture a Union battery four hundred yards away, so Doss crossed the fortifications and deployed into line before beginning the advance. As part of the Confederate effort to break out of Fort Donelson, the 3rd Tennessee formed in double column, with a front of two companies. Flavel C. Barber commanded the last two companies, designated the fifth division of the regiment for the purpose of this formation. When advancing toward the Federals, the first division (or first two companies) broke and fled to the rear, disrupting the formation of the other four divisions so that the 3rd Tennessee had to fall back and re-form.[14]

Union and Confederate reports relating to the Battle of Chickamauga are replete with references to moving columns across the field and then deploying into line when near the enemy. In fact, Brig. Gen. Samuel Beatty's brigade formed a double column at half distance while waiting and then moved forward to find a spot in the developing line. After deploying, Beatty discovered that there was no place for his troops and retired to the starting point of his move, going back into column. When ordered forward a second time, the general still could not find a place in the line. He deployed once more and then moved by the left flank until he discovered an empty spot. Brig. Gen. Archibald Gracie's Confederate brigade advanced in column toward the scene of action for one mile on September 19 before forming line to the left of another brigade. Later, when ordered to a different part of the front, Gracie pulled away and formed column again to lead his men "by a circuitous route" to their new assignment.[15]

Many Union soldiers were treated to a grand sight at the battle of Marksville, Louisiana, on May 16, 1864. The Nineteenth Corps, Thirteenth Corps, and detachments of the Sixteenth and Seventeenth Corps all approached the Confederate position arrayed in columns across three miles of open prairie. "It was a splendid sight," proclaimed Maj. John C. Becht of the 5th Minnesota. "In the rear of and following us was a long column of regiments, the numerous banners glistening in the clear morning sunlight, and seeming to wave defiance to the foe." The columns transformed into battle lines when within range of the enemy.[16]

On the first day of fighting at Nashville, December 15, 1864, Col. Lucius F. Hubbard's brigade advanced on the right flank of its parent division. Hubbard approached the fortified Confederate line in column of regiments and "in order of echelon by battalion, the formation being made on the left." He advanced about one mile in this fashion before his division leader ordered him to form two lines (of two regiments each) to attack a battery. Hubbard did so and captured the guns.[17]

MIX OF LINE AND COLUMN

Civil War armies very often operated in a combination of lines and columns. The French and the Prussians had experimented with this mixture in the 1700s. By the Napoleonic era, it was known as the ordre mixte, which referred to placing a unit in column next to another unit in line within the same formation. While the ordre mixte was rare in the Civil War, it was very common for Union and Confederate commanders to mix line and column in other ways that were also consistent with European practices. They typically formed the forward unit in line, with the supporting units in columns. This scenario can be found in reports emanating from eastern battles such as Fair Oaks, Second Bull Run, Gettysburg, Kelly's Ford, and Petersburg. Col. A. T. A. Torbert, for example, organized his brigade of six New Jersey regiments at Fredericksburg in two formations. The first consisted of two

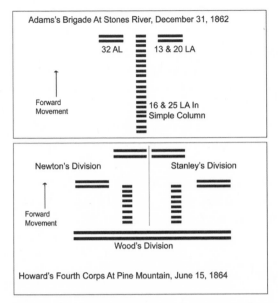

Fig. 8.3. Mix of Line and Column at Stones River and Pine Mountain. Daniel Adams temporarily formed a true example of the ordre mixte by placing one consolidated regiment of his brigade in column while keeping the rest in line at Stones River on December 31, 1862. In this diagram each bar represents one rank. Oliver Howard formed a mix of line and column more typical of Civil War formations. His forward units were in line, while the supports formed in columns when his corps conducted a large reconnaissance in force at Pine Mountain on June 15, 1864. In this diagram each bar represents one rank, although it is not known how many regiments comprised the brigades arrayed in column.

units in line, with the other four regiments forming his support "in line of masses 100 yards in rear."[18]

In the western theater Confederate forces combined line and column as early as Shiloh. As mentioned earlier, Beauregard devised a complex formation for the Army of the Mississippi in which he advised Bragg, who held the second line in a three-line formation, to form his corps by "regiments in double columns," if possible, "at half distance, disposed as advantageously as the nature of the ground will admit, and with a view to facility of deployment." Buell mandated the habitual deployment of his Army of the Ohio so that the third line would be formed in columns.[19]

At Stones River Brig. Gen. Daniel W. Adams experimented with a mix of line and column in order to bypass the burned ruins of the Cowan House and its out-buildings, which stood near his line of attack against the Union center. Adams ordered the consolidated 16th and 25th Louisiana to form "into column of compa-nies" while retaining lines in the rest of his brigade. This column did not constitute the second line of his formation (he had none). Adams displayed one of the rare examples of the true ordre mixte in the Civil War, using lines and columns in one formation. The 16th and 25th Louisiana advanced in column for nearly a quarter of a mile before deploying back into line to lessen casualties in the face of increasingly heavy Union fire.[20]

Combinations of line and column continued to appear in many other engage-ments. At Rocky Face Ridge Col. Frederick Knefler placed four regiments of his brigade in line, with three others behind them "in columns doubled on the center in readiness to deploy, should it become necessary." When told to conduct a mas-sive reconnaissance in force to see where the Confederates went after evacuating Pine Mountain during the Atlanta Campaign, Oliver O. Howard arrayed his Fourth Corps with two divisions in the lead. Brig. Gen. John Newton formed his division on the left, with two brigades in front (deployed in lines, with one brigade placed en echelon to the other) and one brigade in column as their support. Maj. Gen. David S. Stanley formed his division to Newton's right in similar fashion. Brig. Gen. Thomas J. Wood's division came up to the rear of these as their support. At Nash-ville, Col. Abel D. Streight's brigade formed with two regiments in line supported by three regiments to the rear, which were "in double column at half distance within supporting distance of the front line." Those three regiments maintained half distance so they could more readily deploy into line, something impossible to do if they were closed en masse.[21]

COLUMN OF MANEUVER

The pervasive use of columns on Civil War battlefields led to a variety of uses. Although columns were always formed in the same way (by stacking lines one be-hind the other), it is useful to classify them based on their purpose. The column of maneuver, for example, was used to move a unit into the fringes of the combat zone in order to reach a point where it might be called on to go into action. For ex-ample, Col. Joseph B. Palmer shifted his 18th Tennessee toward the zone of action during the attempted Confederate breakout from Fort Donelson on February 15. He crossed the Rebel outer line of works and moved through wooded countryside in a double column. Palmer managed to move in quick time through "the timber and denseness of the undergrowth, on which the snow was thickly depositing and melting somewhat rapidly," and formed line before going into action.[22]

There are many examples like that of Palmer's regiment on other battlefields in the West. Col. James C. Veatch's brigade formed columns to move on the double quick through deserted Union camps and thick woods "in pursuit of the retreating enemy" at the end of the fighting at Shiloh on April 7. When the Confederates attacked Helena, Arkansas, on July 4, 1863, they approached with brigades formed in columns. As soon as Brig. Gen. M. Monroe Parsons encountered the Federal skirmish line, he stopped and ordered his subordinates to increase the distance between regimental lines within his brigade column to half distance to make it easier to deploy into line when they closed on the enemy works.[23]

COLUMN OF WAITING

Once near the scene of action, unit commanders often waited in column formation before receiving orders to enter the fray. Examples of the column of waiting can be seen in many battle reports, often when an infantry unit was ordered to support an artillery battery as it fired on the enemy. In the early stages of the Yorktown campaign, when the Federals were gingerly going forward to develop the Confederate line, Col. Jesse A. Gove held his 22nd Massachusetts in column while waiting for pioneers to repair a bridge. The next day he supported artillery "in close column of companies right in front," and later his regiment moved to a point 1,500 yards from the Rebel trenches and waited for further orders while the 2nd Maine did the same in column to the rear. Willis A. Gorman brought his brigade to the field of Fair Oaks on May 31 and went into column of regiments to wait instructions. Lt. Col. Alexander D. Adams waited for half an hour in column at Gaines's Mill before orders came for his 27th New York to deploy and close in on the scene of battle.[24]

Columns of waiting can be found on the fields of Malvern Hill, Fredericksburg, Gettysburg, Petersburg, and Third Winchester. While holding units within range of enemy artillery, casualties often resulted. This was the case especially when infantry supported artillery batteries that were engaging enemy cannon. Moreover, some units remained in a column of waiting for very long periods during an engagement. Capt. John Thompson's 7th Connecticut held position thusly all day during the Second Battle of Deep Bottom.[25]

Numerous examples of columns of waiting appear in reports of western battles.

At Corinth William S. Rosecrans advised Maj. John W. Jefferson to form his 8th Wisconsin in double column rather than simple column while the unit waited for orders so as to facilitate Jefferson's ability to move the regiment to another place or to deploy into line when needed. The 29th Iowa also formed double column while waiting in reserve during two days of action at Prairie D'Ane during Maj. Gen. Frederick Steele's advance toward Camden, Arkansas. Frederick Schaefer's brigade of Philip Sheridan's division paid dearly for using the column formation while waiting under fire on the evening of December 31 at Stones River. The brigade formed "in close column of regiments" and lost twenty men killed "by round shot" as a result. Federal columns of waiting can be seen in the Atlanta Campaign. When Cleburne's Division came up to support Hood's line near Pickett's Mill on May 27, 1864, Hood instructed Cleburne to deploy his men "in a column of brigades, in the rear of my immediate right." The division was to wait until Federal moves demonstrated whether it would be necessary to extend Hood's line to meet flanking attempts.[26]

COLUMN OF ATTACK

The tactical manuals advised caution when using columns to attack the enemy. While Scott, Hardee, and Casey thought columns might be useful when striking a particularly strong position, such as one protected by fortifications, there were many disadvantages to the column of attack. As already noted, they easily collapsed when the front ranks hit any obstacle or resistance. Columns also prevented unit commanders from fully using their own firepower against the enemy. Lines were more flexible and allowed complete freedom for all men in a regiment to fire at the enemy. While the column of attack had the appearance of a hammer, capable of smashing whatever it encountered, that appearance was more elusive than real. The only true advantage was that unit commanders could better control the movement of their men, but only as long as the column remained intact.

Nevertheless, some commanders failed to understand this reality and continued to believe in columns as a proper mode of assault. In fact, General Howard wrote in his memoirs of Edwin Sumner's fascination with columns. In Howard's words, columns were Sumner's "favorite method" of advancing on the foe. Sumner directed his division commanders at Fredericksburg to form "a column of brigades," with intervals of 150 yards between each brigade. The formation did not serve the Federals well in this perilous assault.[27]

Col. Samuel V. Fulkerson's small Virginia brigade assailed a Union battery at the First Battle of Kernstown "in close column by division." The men maintained their cohesion well, at least according to some observers, but they failed to capture the guns. In the same engagement Col. E. B. Tyler attacked the Confederates with five brigades, all "advancing in column of divisions," and they managed to drive the enemy from behind a stone wall. On the second day at Chickamauga, Col. Bernard Laiboldt rested his brigade "in column of regiments at company distance" until the Union line collapsed in confusion. Laiboldt received orders to charge bayonets and did so while still in column, wheeling on the way in a vain effort to stem the rout that engulfed the Army of the Cumberland in the wake of James Longstreet's breakthrough.[28]

Attack columns were comparatively rare on Civil War battlefields, despite the examples cited above. In a survey of seventy-two engagements from the beginning to the end of the conflict and covering all theaters of operations, attack columns appeared in only fourteen (or 19.4 percent) of those battles. But even that low figure gives an inflated view of how often they were used. Although a total of 406 Union and Confederate regiments participated in the Battle of Chancellorsville, only 6 of them (1.4 percent) attacked in column. A total of sixty-six Union and Confederate brigades participated in the Battle of Chickamauga; only one of them (1.5 percent) attacked in column. The conclusion can only be that Union and Confederate commanders avoided attack columns in the overwhelming majority of unit actions throughout the war.

What follows are detailed discussions of the use of attack columns on particular battlefields. Historians devote little attention to the details of how these formations were used for all purposes in Civil War military operations. The following extended discussions hopefully will rectify that weakness in the historiography and further demonstrate that columns had only a muddled record of success, at best, when used to attack enemy positions.

Corinth, October 4, 1862

Maj. Gen. Earl Van Dorn launched a vigorous attempt to capture Corinth on the morning of October 4 as a follow up to his tactical success in pushing Federal forces into the inner line of defenses guarding that important town the previous day. His Army of the West had often used columns even in its attacks on October 3, and most Confederate units seem to have gone into the assault on the fourth in the same formation.[29]

Because of a paucity of detailed reports, much of our understanding of those formations actually comes from Union observers. Col. John W. Fuller, whose brigade protected Battery Robinette, saw "four close columns" of enemy troops moving to attack the work. All four belonged to Brig. Gen. C. W. Phifer's brigade. One regimental column (the 6th Texas Cavalry [Dismounted]) moved along a road directly toward the battery, while the 9th Texas Cavalry (Dismounted) formed a column west of the road and two Arkansas units (3rd Arkansas Cavalry [Dismounted] and Stirman's Sharpshooters) formed the other two columns east of the road. The 6th Texas made faster headway along the road than the other three units, and the 63rd Ohio fired on it at a range of one hundred yards. "The head of the column almost instantly disappeared and the rear recoiled rapidly to the edge of the woods," Fuller reported. This was a fairly typical result when using columns of attack. The Confederates re-formed at the woods' edge and advanced again, although Fuller did not report what formation they used . This time the Rebels delivered such a killing fire as to riddle the ranks of the 63rd Ohio, which suggests they were now in line rather than column. The Ohioans were forced to retire as the 11th Missouri advanced to drive the Rebels away. The 27th Ohio repelled the 9th Texas to the left of the position held by the 63rd, and the 43rd Ohio repelled the two Arkansas units east of the road.[30]

"It was a terribly beautiful sight to see the enemy's columns advance," reported Col. Thomas W. Sweeny. Most other units along Van Dorn's line duplicated the attack by regimental columns that Phifer's Brigade attempted. One column that approached Brig. Gen. Charles Hamilton's division deployed into battle line, fronted by "a cloud of skirmishers," to press home its assault.[31]

Chancellorsville, May 3, 1863

Seven months after Corinth, Maj. Gen. John Sedgwick formed assaulting columns to take Marye's Heights at Fredericksburg as part of the Battle of Chancellorsville. To relieve pressure on the rest of the Army of the Potomac several miles west of Fredericksburg, Sedgwick hedged his bets by forming two columns of assault combined with a battle line to advance along the Plank Road. The right column, led by Col. George C. Spear, consisted of the 61st Pennsylvania in the lead, followed by the 43rd New York, the 67th New York, and the 82nd Pennsylvania. The left column consisted of the 7th Massachusetts and the 36th New York. All these regiments formed columns of companies and moved forward along the Plank Road and to its right. The line consisted of the 5th Wisconsin ahead as skirmishers, followed by the 6th Maine, 31st New York, and 23rd Pennsylvania in one line of battle. This force advanced to the left of the Plank Road.[32]

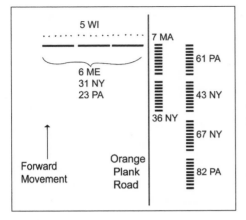

Fig. 8.4. Mix of Line and Column at Chancellorsville. John Sedgwick organized an assault against the heights west of Fredericksburg with three regiments in line and six regiments in column. This formation succeeded in taking the objective on May 3, 1863. Each bar represents one line, not one rank.

Sedgwick's attack succeeded but mostly because the Confederate position on and at the foot of Marye's Heights was thinly held. The 61st Pennsylvania was supposed to deploy into line at an appropriate time but received heavy artillery fire before it could do so and suffered many casualties. The unexpected fire "caused the regiment to waver for a few moments," but it rallied and continued advancing. Sedgwick's battle line to the left of the Plank Road hit the famous stone wall at the foot of the heights, the same position that had caused Ambrose Burnside so much grief on December 13, 1862. This time it was held by only eight companies of the 18th Mississippi and a few men of the 21st Mississippi. The Federals this day took the wall, and the Confederate position west of Fredericksburg collapsed. Union casualties amounted to 1,100 men, while the Confederates lost 475 troops, more than a third of the number engaged.[33]

Vicksburg, May 22, 1863

Less than three weeks later and hundreds of miles away in Mississippi, Maj. Gen. Ulysses Grant prepared to launch a major attack against the line of Confederate works protecting Vicksburg. He had closed in on the city at the end of a stunning campaign of maneuver in May 1863. After establishing his line and making a partial attack on May 19, Grant issued orders for a general assault. He mandated that all infantry forces, except for the skirmishers and reserves, should be formed "in Column of plattoons" or move by the flank "if the ground over which they may have to pass will not admit of a greater front." He wanted the men to go in light with fixed bayonets and begin the advance at quick time. "If prosecuted with vigor," Grant urged, "it is confidently believed this course will carry Vicksburg in a very short time, and with much less loss than would be sustained by delay."[34]

There is no evidence that any of Grant's subordinates formed a column of platoons, which would have stretched out a brigade in an impossibly long formation. They did form the normal simple column and double column, however, and also moved by the flank on May 22. Observing the landscape, broken up by deep ravines, Brig. Gen. Peter J. Osterhaus ordered his Ninth Division, Thirteenth Corps to form "columns of divisions at half distance . . . in order to have the necessary pressure and connections on the point of attack, without the danger of the lines being broken, which deployed lines in this terrain could not have avoided." His right column consisted of two regiments, the center column of three regiments, and the left column of two regiments. Osterhaus had one regiment out to skirmish and another to screen his left flank during the advance because he was on the far left of Grant's line. Other Thirteenth Corps units formed lines and then moved forward by the flank.[35]

In the Fifteenth Corps, positioned on Grant's right, Col. Lucius F. Hubbard of the 5th Minnesota reported that the "broken nature of the country and inaccessible character of the position made it necessary that the storming column should move by the flank." Hubbard's regiment was on the left of the brigade line, so it was at the rear when the brigade moved forward by the right flank. The head of this formation hit an open area close to the Rebel works and "was met and literally melted down by a terrific fire of musketry and artillery." The brigade lost two hundred men "probably in the space of a minute." Other Fifteenth Corps officers chose to move forward in a column of regiments.[36]

The Seventeenth Corps was positioned in the center of Grant's line. Commanders there chose different formations according to their own judgment. Brig. Gen. John D. Stevenson formed his brigade in two columns, with two regiments to the left and three to the right. Brig. Gen. John E. Smith moved his brigade two hundred yards forward by the flank and then filed the men into line when they were one hundred yards from the Rebel works, but a "deep ravine" and abatis barred their further progress. T. E. G. Ransom's brigade advanced by the flank and then formed columns closed en masse under the cover of a ridge one hundred yards from the enemy. Each regimental column was placed next to the other in a line with sufficient intervals to deploy, if necessary. Here the brigade waited until midafternoon but never advanced farther. When George Boomer's brigade of the

Seventeenth Corps was ordered to go to the Thirteenth Corps sector, it formed two lines of two regiments each for its unsuccessful assault.[37]

None of the formations and maneuvers used by the Federals on May 22—simple and double columns, moving by the flank, and multiple lines—succeeded in breaking the Confederate position. But all of them were effective at moving units across difficult terrain to a point where they were within short range of the enemy. The Rebel works were not particularly well made, but they were well placed on commanding ground and resolutely held by the defending troops.

Fort Wagner, July 18, 1863

Two months later on the Atlantic coast, a major attack took place on Morris Island at the entrance to Charleston Harbor. Headed by the 54th Massachusetts, Brig. Gen. George C. Strong's brigade advanced along a narrow space of sand near the ocean's edge toward Fort Wagner on July 18. While most regiments of the brigade made simple columns, Col. Robert G. Shaw formed his 54th Massachusetts into two wings, one behind the other. He therefore presented a front of five companies, while the regiments behind him presented a front of only one company. Although many of Shaw's men entered a corner of the fort, many others retreated, "striking the head of the column" of Col. Sabine Emery's 9th Maine. Emery had to untangle the confusion caused by this retrograde movement before he could continue.[38]

Col. Haldimand S. Putnam's brigade came up to support Strong. It had started the approach with each regiment in a column of companies, closed en masse to navigate obstructions. Putnam then ordered a brigade column to be formed, each regiment deploying into line, one stacked behind the other, and again closed up en masse. As Putnam neared the scene of action, retreating men from Strong's brigade severely disrupted his formation; in fact, the 100th New York line was broken by the fleeing refugees. Pulling his brigade forward, Putnam met many members of Strong's brigade lying down near the glacis of the fort who joined in his attempt to take the work. Only a limited penetration was possible before the Federals gave up and fell back.[39]

Orchard Knob, November 23, 1863

The narrow approach to Fort Wagner compelled most units to form columns, but the relatively open terrain around Chattanooga also became a venue for their use,

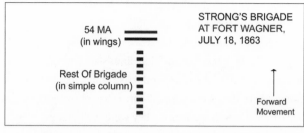

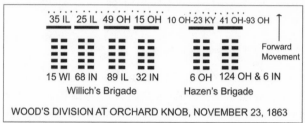

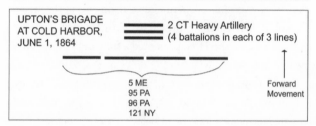

Fig. 8.5. Mix of Line and Column at Fort Wagner, Orchard Knob, and Cold Harbor. These three examples illustrate the variety of combinations actually used on Civil War battlefields. Generally, lines were placed forward and columns were placed behind to support the first formation, but Upton (third example) decided to lead his attack with a column at Cold Harbor on June 1, 1864. Each bar represents one line, not one rank.

indicating that the column was a versatile formation adaptable to different topography. The opening move of Grant's efforts to drive Bragg's Army of Tennessee from its "siege" of the city was a limited effort to secure Orchard Knob, a conical hill that lay between the Union and Confederate lines east of town. Thomas Wood's division of the Fourth Corps conducted the attack with support from Sheridan's division of the same corps and Brig. Gen. Adolph von Steinwehr's division of the Eleventh Corps.[40]

In Wood's division Brig. Gen. August Willich's brigade constituted the left wing and William B. Hazen's brigade formed the right. Both officers organized their brigades in two formations, the first in line and the second "in double column closed *en masse.*" Willich placed four regiments in his first formation and ployed the other four regiments in column to the rear. Hazen temporarily organized his nine regiments into five battalions for operational purposes during this attack. He formed his first line with two battalions and placed two others in his second formation in column, sending one battalion to skirmish.[41]

The Federals formed on a broad slope south of Fort Wood. When they moved forward, visible to friend and foe alike, "troops in line and column checkered the broad plain of Chattanooga," and Wood reported that "not one straggler lagged behind to sully the magnificence and perfectness of the grand battle array." The attack was a complete success, capturing Orchard Knob with minimal loss.[42]

Cold Harbor, June 1, 1864

Near the end of Grant's Overland Campaign, the opposing armies settled in for three weeks of confrontation on the wooded, level terrain near Cold Harbor. Commanders continued to utilize column formations during the course of the heavy fighting. In fact, during just one day of battle, the careful observer can detect numerous instances of column use. For example, Col. Lawrence Keitt approached Union cavalry holding the area around Old Cold Harbor early on June 1 with his South Carolina brigade formed in regimental columns of companies. The Federals easily stopped this advance.[43]

On another part of the Cold Harbor battlefield, along the developing Union line, Maj. Gen. William F. Smith's Eighteenth Corps tried to fill a space between the Sixth Corps on the left and the Fifth Corps on the right. Smith also had to prepare for a major attack on Lee's line, but he did not have enough troops to cover that gap and support the Sixth Corps advance at the same time. He placed two divisions on his left, connecting to the right flank of the Sixth Corps, and formed them in two lines. But his third division, under Brig. Gen. John H. Martindale, was compelled to protect its own right flank because it could not extend far enough to the Fifth Corps position. Martindale therefore organized several units in column. Brig. Gen. George Stannard placed his brigade with one regiment in line and three others in simple column closed en masse in echelon formation toward the right.[44]

Horatio Wright's Sixth Corps used columns at least to a limited degree on June 1. Emory Upton had received the 2nd Connecticut Heavy Artillery as an addition to his brigade in late May. Like most of the heavy artillery units that were added to the Army of the Potomac, it was organized into twelve companies and had many more men than the typical regiment. Upton therefore formed the 2nd Connecticut into a column of battalions (consisting of three lines of four battalions each) and placed the other four regiments of his brigade into a single line behind the Connecticut men.[45]

Kennesaw Mountain, June 27, 1864

Shortly after the seemingly stalemated operations at Cold Harbor played themselves out, William T. Sherman temporarily broke his normal mode of operations during the Atlanta Campaign in Georgia. Setting aside for the time his tendency to flank strongly fortified Rebel positions, he ordered a major assault on Gen. Joseph E. Johnston's line centered on Kennesaw Mountain on June 27. Three attack formations were organized, one by the Fifteenth Corps, one by the Fourth Corps, and the other by the Fourteenth Corps. The Fourteenth and Fifteenth Corps aimed at high ground, while the Fourth targeted low ground. Corps and division commanders had the option of choosing their own formations. Fifteenth Corps officers chose multiple lines for the three brigades involved in their attack on Pigeon Hill and an open field to its south. In the Fourth and Fourteenth Corps, columns became the preferred formation.[46]

Oliver Howard decided to use columns of regiments in each of the three brigades of the Fourth Corps he planned to throw at the enemy. Those brigades would maintain intervals of one hundred yards. While Brig. Gen. George Wagner's and Brig. Gen. Nathan Kimball's brigades organized simple columns, Brig. Gen. Charles Harker formed his command in double columns after temporarily reorganizing each regiment into eight companies. Supporting brigades from another division also formed columns of waiting in case they were called on to assist.[47]

Brig. Gen. Jefferson C. Davis also ordered the two brigades of his Fourteenth Corps division to form in simple columns for the attack. They had to cross a valley before ascending a moderately high hill upon which the Confederates had dug a sharp angle in their line of works. Col. Daniel McCook's brigade formed on the left while Col. John Mitchell's brigade was on the right. Mitchell altered his formation slightly because he was told to deploy his regiments into line to the right as soon as he closed on the enemy works. To facilitate that maneuver, Mitchell directed Col. Henry Banning to place his 121st Ohio, the second regiment in the brigade column, farther to the right so that the right flank of his third company from the right would be exactly behind the right flank of the 113th Ohio, the regiment just in front of Banning's command. To do this, Banning instructed his two right companies to guide left in the advance and the rest to guide right, making the right flank of his third company the guide for the entire regiment. Mitchell hoped that this would enable Banning to move swiftly to the right under close-range fire from the enemy, with every regiment behind him doing the same. The brigade column thus appeared to be approaching the Confederates in an echelon formation. Nevertheless, the Federal attack failed to dent the Confederate line.[48]

EVALUATING THE USE OF COLUMNS

In fact, most assaults in column ended in a repulse of the attacking force. Yet that does not mean that columns were useless in Civil War military operations. In fact, as we have seen, they were commonly used on the battlefield for a number of purposes other than assault. The tactical manuals devoted a great deal of space to forming columns and emphasized their usefulness for managing large groups of men.

Columns were the preferred formation in both the Union and Confederate armies when commanders held units in waiting to go into action or moved them around on the battlefield from one point to another. In the West Rosecrans's chief of staff instructed subordinate commanders in the Army of the Cumberland during the Tullahoma Campaign: "Troops will be habitually maneuvered in double column, closed *en masse*; especially the second and third lines should be held in column, and posted in sheltered positions; the lines should habitually bivouac in column, with proper distances for deployment." In the East a staff officer in Maj. Gen. John Pope's Army of Virginia lectured a division commander: "As a general thing, which will admit of few exceptions, brigades should be drawn up in two lines, the second line being in double column at half distance, so as to best enable them to take advantage of the undulations of the ground to screen the men from the enemy's fire."[49]

Despite problems attending the use of attack columns, some commanders remained convinced they were effective. Theodore Lyman, one of Meade's staff officers, talked to Brig. Gen. Francis C. Barlow, who "discoursed on . . . the advantages of the assault in column." It is true that column formations allowed Barlow to bring a huge number of men onto a small target (the tip of the Muleshoe Salient) on May 12 at Spotsylvania. But he ignored the fact that once there, the salient became a scene of utter confusion as thousands of Federals broke their formation and milled about instead of exploiting their brief advantage. The result was but a partial success as far as breaking Lee's line and achieving any real advantage. Even Meade seems to have tended to think of columns rather than lines for attacking. During Grant's Second Offensive at Petersburg on June 23, 1864, Meade instructed Sixth Corps commander Wright: "Your line of battle is the formation to attack in. I know there is no time to form columns."[50]

Oliver Howard went to some length to explain why he chose the column formation for Newton's attack against the strong earthworks at Kennesaw Mountain. "That formation seemed best for the situation," he wrote in his memoirs, "first, to keep the men concealed as well as possible beforehand and during the first third of the distance, the ground being favorable for this; second, to make as narrow a front as he could, so as to make a sudden rush with numbers over their works." Once the line was broken, Howard hoped to follow through with advances by supporting troops deployed into lines rather than columns.[51]

But the bloody repulse of Newton's men resonated with the survivors of June 27. Arthur L. Wagner, a postwar U.S. Army officer, was interested in the use of columns versus dispersed lines and collected testimony from Newton's subordinates about the attack at Kennesaw. Luther P. Bradley, who took over Harker's brigade after the general was mortally wounded, stated that the entire operation had been a disaster. "The assault on Kenesaw was a bad affair, badly planned and badly timed, and the formation of our column was about the worst possible for assault on a fortified line—a column of regiments, each regiment in column of divisions."[52]

Kimball also wrote a letter to Wagner damning the column formation. "Harker and I were at Newton's headquarters when we received our orders. We condemned the formation at the time. Newton said that such were the orders, and of course we obeyed and did the best we could. Such formations have only the *appearance* of strength, but are really suicidal in their weakness."[53]

Criticisms of the column formation for attacking came from other sources as well. Jacob Cox, who commanded a division in the Twenty-Third Corps of Sherman's army group, wrote after the war that fascination with attack columns was largely a holdover from pre–Civil War French tactical theory. Even during the Peninsular War of the Napoleonic era, according to Cox, Wellington was able to defeat French attack columns with concentrated firepower. Their continued use in the American Civil War was tragic. "So hard it is to free ourselves from the trammels of old customs and a mistaken practice!" Cox lamented.[54]

Ironically, even Howard criticized Hooker's decision to approach the Confederate position at New Hope Church on May 25 in columns of attack. He felt that the defender could deliver more fire on the formation than those in the column could return. This occurred a month before Howard himself decided to use attack columns at Kennesaw Mountain. An anonymous member of Wagner's brigade, who survived the attack of June 27, was quoted by a newspaper correspondent as blaming the formation for the failure of the onslaught. "Damn these assaults in column, they make a man more afraid of being trampled to death by the rear lines than he is of the enemy."[55]

Columns offered a higher degree of control over large numbers of men, but in their own way they were fragile formations. Regiments found it difficult to deal with obstacles in their path when so formed, and enemy resistance often proved too much for this formation to handle. But the facility with which they enhanced officer control of movements ensured that columns were widely used for a large number of purposes in military life, from reviews to holding units ready to enter battle.

Civil War commanders took the advice contained in Scott, Hardee, and Casey to heart. They only sparingly used columns to attack enemy positions, and even when they did, they tended to use them only in the approach phase. Most of the time, officers ordered their men to deploy into lines for the final closing on the target.

Exactly what was a column and what was not has confused students of the Civil War. The key lay in the distance separating lines within the formation. Within columns, the distance was measured in a handful of yards; within multiple-line formations, it was hundreds of yards. Grady McWhiney and Perry Jamieson refer to Longstreet's assault at Chickamauga and Upton's assault on the Muleshoe Salient as column attacks, but they were really advances by successive lines as Wayne Weisiang Hsieh has correctly noted of Upton's formation. McWhiney and Jamieson properly identify Jackson's flank attack at Chancellorsville on May 3 as taking place in "close successive lines" but incorrectly say the same about the formation adopted by Sedgwick's division at Antietam, which actually was a formation of columns. The difference between multiple lines and columns is not just academic; the two formations were very different in their purpose and usefulness. It is important to recognize those differences.[56]

Multiple Maneuvers

Most Civil War commanders took seriously the task of learning various tactical formations and maneuvers well enough to handle their commands without incurring disaster on the battlefield. Overwhelmingly, long-serving officers accomplished that task very well. There were certainly different levels of proficiency; some regiments could outperform others on the drill ground and on the battlefield alike. The official reports provide ample evidence that many regimental leaders were capable of using different formations and maneuvers during the course of a single engagement, choosing from among their tactical options the right ones to deal with new situations arising from the fog of battle. When a commander utilized multiple maneuvers in a single engagement, he not only provided a showcase of small-unit articulation but also imposed battle force on the enemy in potentially winning ways.

Multiple maneuvers normally appeared after a regimental commander and his men had gained a certain level of experience in battle. Early in the war, Col. William E. Baldwin complained that the troops of his brigade seemed skittish when threatened with flanking fire during the Confederate attempt to break out of Grant's cordon around Fort Donelson. Baldwin concluded that "any other than forward movements are extremely dangerous with volunteers."[1]

There was at least some truth to Baldwin's statement. Early battles tended to display simple articulation, if one may coin such a term, meaning the use of only one or two basic maneuvers self-consciously conducted by green troops. As their experience level and self-confidence rose, many soldiers North and South were able to throw themselves with little hesitation into a series of different maneuvers like an accomplished artist playing an instrument. This was certainly not done for show but for practical purposes: to meet developing threats and rapidly changing circumstances and to take advantage of tactical opportunities that suddenly appeared. Regimental commanders who ordered their men to conduct multiple maneuvers with confidence were dangerous opponents on the battlefield.

FIFTY CASE STUDIES

Following is a discussion of fifty case studies found in the official reports of Union and Confederate commanders selected because they display evidence of a significant number of maneuvers performed by units, mostly on the regimental level. Virtually every major maneuver described by Scott, Hardee, and Casey (and discussed in earlier chapters) are represented in these examples. It is interesting to see how often particular formations or maneuvers were used compared to others, shedding light on the choices made by small-unit leaders under the duress and changing circumstances of combat.

These fifty examples are representative of the varied experiences to be seen in the Civil War. Thirty-eight (or 76 percent) are of Federal units, while the rest represent Confederate activity. Exactly half of the case studies took place in the eastern theater, while 46 percent took place in the West; the remaining examples occurred in the Trans-Mississippi. Thirty-eight were of regimental-level articulation, eleven of them (or 22 percent) took place on the brigade level, and one occurred on the division level.

Formations

Of course, battle lines were the most common formation for units when within danger of enemy action, appearing in all fifty case studies. But columns appear in 42 percent of the examples, indicating the widespread use of this formation. Multiple lines were used in 40 percent, testifying to the common use of this formation.

Unit commanders found it necessary to refuse their flanks in 28 percent of the case studies. In short, one can assume that there was nearly one chance out of three that an officer would find his flank threatened in battle. The echelon formation was adopted in 26 percent, a surprisingly high rate considering the relatively limited usefulness of this formation, but it is another testament to the need for flank protection on Civil War battlefields.

Officers wound up inverting their two-rank battle lines in 20 percent of the cases. In other words, there was one chance out of five that a commander would place his regiment out of its traditional order, either by choice or accident. But choosing to use one rank instead of two was very rare, appearing in only 4 percent of the examples.

Maneuvers

By far the most common maneuver was movement by the flank. In 72 percent of the examples, one can see unit commanders ordering their men to turn either right or left in line and move in an extended formation that looked like a column of two men abreast. It was by far the easiest way to shift a battle line from one place to another (except directly forward or backward), which accounts for its prevalence.

The second-most-common movement to be found in the case studies, occurring in 58 percent of the examples, involved moving a unit to the rear or facing it to the rear. This was made necessary by failed advances, the appearance of enemy troops in unexpected quarters, and by adjustments in the positioning of units within a larger line.

Wheeling appears in 36 percent of these samples. More than one-third of the time, unit commanders chose to wheel in order to change the front of their formation right or left. Officers also chose to change front forward or backward on a sub-unit nearly as often as they chose to wheel. One can see this interesting maneuver taking place in 34 percent of the examples.

Moving by subunits of the larger command in any direction included the movement by files, which took place in 30 percent of the case studies. Movement by wings also took place in exactly 30 percent of the examples. Officers involved in these cases did not move their units by other subdivisions, such as platoons, squads, or fours. The common practice was to move units by the larger subdivisions, not the smaller ones.

The difficult task of passing one line through another took place in nearly one-third of the samples. In 28 percent of them, unit commanders either carefully tried to get through a neighboring command or more likely than not simply smashed into it and let the chips fall where they may. An officer had to consider that he had nearly one chance out of three of having to face the problem of picking up those chips and putting his regiment back together again.

Moving through heavily entangled terrain in battle line presented enormous difficulties. But regimental commanders only rarely ordered their company leaders to go into the morass by the right or left flank. This maneuver occurred in only 2 percent of the case studies.

Confirming that Civil War officers felt it useful to move their men quickly across deadly space, commanders ordered the double-quick march in 52 percent of the examples. In contrast, officers resorted to quick time in only 2 percent of them.

Finally, the famous bayonet charge appears in only 12 percent of the fifty examples. The overwhelming majority of those attempts to meet the enemy with cold steel did not turn out that way. Mostly, the opponent fell back before contact was made, or the attack was repulsed by rifle and artillery fire. Hand-to-hand combat occurred in only 6 percent of these examples.

Admittedly, fifty case studies represent a relatively small sample of a very large war. The overwhelming majority of small-unit experience on Civil War battlefields is not represented here. We also should not take it for granted that even the best report contains literally all the information about formations and maneuvers that took place in a regiment's battle experience. For instance, these case studies reveal that in 52 percent of them, unit commanders utilized the double quick in moving their commands (and in 2 percent they used quick time). But this does not prove that officers in the other 46 percent failed to do so. It is possible they did move quickly but simply did not mention it in their reports. Historians are limited by existing documentation and can make conclusions based only on what they read, not on what they assume in order to fill in the gaps. But an examination of these fifty case studies at least is a start toward understanding the frequency with which particular formations and maneuvers were used in actual practice on the battlefield.

A detailed look at seven of the case studies follows to demonstrate the flow of battlefield events leading unit commanders to adopt various formations and maneuvers as needed. Only one Confederate example appears below; this is not by design, and it does not imply that Confederate regimental leaders were less able than their blue-clad counterparts. Confederate battle reports often are less detailed and fulsome than Union reports.

32nd Indiana at Shiloh, April 7, 1862

Col. August Willich had served as a captain in the Prussian army before immigrating to the United States following the failed liberal revolutions of 1848. A strict disciplinarian who demanded a great deal of his volunteers, the colonel took them into their first battle on the second day at Shiloh. He advanced the 32nd Indiana in double column, but the enemy retired before they made contact. Willich then "deployed into line of battle, to give him the benefit of all our rifles." The regiment advanced in this formation for a while before he reverted it to a double column and sent two companies ahead to skirmish. Due to what he termed "bad management in our squeezed-up position," the skirmisher companies received friendly fire and broke. The men disrupted the rest of the 32nd when falling back to the regiment, so Willich pulled the whole unit back to a nearby ravine and re-formed it in double column. Upon resuming the advance, he again deployed into battle line to fire at the enemy and check their counterattack, then reverted to double column, this time sending four companies to skirmish. Conducting his last advance of the day, Willich became dissatisfied with the fact that his men were firing "at too great a distance." His solution was to order a cease fire, after which he "practiced them in the manual of arms, which they executed as if on the parade ground, and then reopened deliberate and effective fire."[2]

Willich had ably gone from column to line and back again twice during the course of the day, ploying and deploying the 32nd Indiana on four different occasions. Few other regimental commanders had the audacity to stop the fire of their men and drill them on the battlefield before letting them resume their work. He pushed ahead toward enemy formations using both line and column as he felt the situation demanded and left no indication that he was dissatisfied with his men, except for their somewhat undisciplined firing.

83rd Pennsylvania at Gaines's Mill, June 27, 1862

Two and a half months after Shiloh and hundreds of miles to the east, Lee's Army of Northern Virginia gained one of its most important tactical victories at the Battle of Gaines's Mill on June 27. This engagement turned the tide in his Seven Days offensive against McClellan's Army of the Potomac. Massive Confederate attacks on a semicircular line north of the Chickahominy River produced a decisive breakthrough and chaos in the Union position.

Col. John W. McLane noticed that regiments to the right of his 83rd Pennsylvania gave way suddenly and Confederate troops began to head toward the rear of his intact unit. In the words of Lt. Col. Hugh S. Campbell, McLane gave the order "to face by the rear rank and wheel obliquely to quarter circle on the proper right, then become the left." In other words, the 83rd faced to the rear, inverting ranks, and then wheeled left until the line was at an angle to its original orientation. The regiment, in short, pivoted on its current left flank (which was the original right flank before inverting ranks by facing to the rear). The men conducted this difficult maneuver "rapidly," as Campbell put it, but McLane was killed in the process.

Also, the major of the regiment was mortally wounded during the course of this wheeling movement.[3]

Campbell now took charge of the 83rd Pennsylvania. His men fired toward the front and drove the Confederates away. But the enemy did not disappear; they re-formed a line somewhere nearly opposite the current right flank of the regiment. At this point Maj. Ernest von Vegesack of Brig. Gen. Daniel Butterfield's staff rode up, took in the situation, and advised Campbell "to face by the right flank, advance, half face to the left, thereby still keeping the rear rank in front, . . . and again face the foe." Campbell tried to do this as best he could. The 83rd Pennsylvania managed the maneuver, which was designed to bring it to a new position facing the Confederates.[4]

The Rebels, according to Campbell, seemed to be struck with awe while watching the Pennsylvanians perform this movement only one hundred yards away from their line. Astonishingly, the Confederate commander raised a flag of truce, and Campbell sent one of his officers to see what they wanted. He brought back a message encouraging the Federals to surrender. This news "caused indignant mirth among us," Campbell reported, and he sent back a refusal. The Confederates resumed firing even before the Federal officer returned to the 83rd Pennsylvania after delivering the reply. For the rest of the evening, the opposing regiments slugged it out in a stationary firefight until dusk put an end to the fighting that day.[5]

61st and 64th New York at Antietam, September 17, 1862

Lee's victory in the Seven Days, followed by his spectacular success at Second Bull Run, set up the conditions for an invasion of Maryland. The Army of the Potomac met the Army of Northern Virginia in battle at Antietam on September 17. Edwin Sumner's Second Corps launched a massive attack against the center of Lee's line, largely targeting the area near the famous Sunken Road, in which part of the Confederate line had taken shelter. Col. Francis C. Barlow directed the movements of the temporarily consolidated 61st and 64th New York that day, moving for twenty minutes on the left of Brig. Gen. Thomas F. Meagher's Irish Brigade. Then Barlow left his position and moved by the right flank toward the rear and to the right of Meagher's line. He then faced his men toward the front and advanced, crossing the crest of a rise and coming on the Confederates in the Sunken Road, breaking their position.[6]

Barlow saw an opportunity to exploit his advantage by, in the words of Lt. Col. Nelson A. Miles of the 61st New York, "changing front forward on first company,

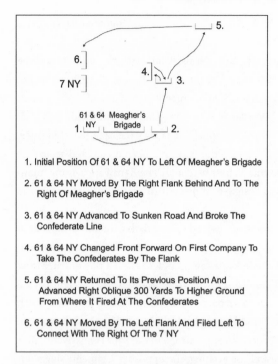

1. Initial Position Of 61 & 64 NY To Left Of Meagher's Brigade

2. 61 & 64 NY Moved By The Right Flank Behind And To The
   Right Of Meagher's Brigade

3. 61 & 64 NY Advanced To Sunken Road And Broke The
   Confederate Line

4. 61 & 64 NY Changed Front Forward On First Company To
   Take The Confederates By The Flank

5. 61 & 64 NY Returned To Its Previous Position And
   Advanced Right Oblique 300 Yards To Higher Ground
   From Where It Fired At The Confederates

6. 61 & 64 NY Moved By The Left Flank And Filed Left To
   Connect With The Right Of The 7 NY

Fig. 9.1. Multiple Maneuvers at Antietam. Francis Barlow adroitly maneuvered the consolidated 61st and 64th New York across the battlefield of Antietam on September 17, 1862. Each
bar represents one line, not one rank.

thereby flanking the rest of their line." Acting quickly before the enemy could retire, his men nabbed three hundred prisoners. In the meantime, Barlow noticed
a large force of Confederates attempting to move around his right. He resumed
the position held before changing front forward on the first company and gave an
order to move right oblique three hundred yards until reaching a rise of ground.
There the New Yorkers opened fire, expending twenty rounds per man before the
Confederate force broke and retired.[7]

Soon after this small victory, Barlow heard the sound of firing off toward the
left of his current location and in front of the position he had formerly held near
the Sunken Road. He moved his combined regiments to the area by the left flank
and filed left in order to connect to the right flank of the 7th New York. After facing forward, Barlow's troops moved ahead and entered a cornfield. Here he was
wounded, and Miles took charge of the consolidated regiments. Barlow survived

his wound and soon rose to division command in both the Eleventh and Second Corps before war's end.[8]

Barlow's performance at Antietam was a superb demonstration of how to break and exploit an enemy line on the battlefield. He saw opportunities and seized them without hesitation, knowing exactly what maneuver to perform to achieve his goals. Moving by the flank and changing front forward on a subunit were the chief tools he utilized on September 17. Combined with a quick eye and a confident demeanor, Barlow inflicted more damage on the enemy than one small battalion normally did in Civil War combat. Moreover, with a high level of articulation, he maneuvered his command across a considerable space of ground to fight several small actions. It was an impressive performance.

63rd New York at Fredericksburg, December 13, 1862

Antietam ended Lee's incursion into Maryland, but the Army of Northern Virginia fought a defensive battle at Fredericksburg on December 13. In Ambrose Burnside's offensive, many Federal units were compelled to advance through areas littered with obstacles. First there was the town of Fredericksburg itself, plopped in the path of those units assigned to Burnside's right wing. After traversing its streets, these Federals hit a canal just west of town, then ascended a gradual and open slope dotted with houses and fences to reach the position of James Longstreet's men behind a stone wall at the foot of Marye's Heights. The ground offered every advantage to the Confederates and few to the attacking Federals. Regimental leaders had to exercise considerable skill just to get within range of the enemy on this part of the battlefield.

Maj. Joseph O'Neill's 63rd New York was placed at the rear of Meagher's brigade column as it formed along the first major street that ran parallel to the Rappahannock River, near the center of Fredericksburg. When the brigade left for the battleground west of town, it moved by the right flank and also by the left flank to negotiate six streets before reaching the western edge of Fredericksburg. It was, in a way, easier going from there. Meagher moved the brigade by the right flank toward the canal, but it began to receive scattered fire as it continued. There were only three planks stretched across the canal near the point where the brigade intended to cross. Many of the men hurried over the planks but a great many others broke ranks and splashed through the shallow water wherever they could find a convenient place to go down and then up its banks.[9]

Meagher re-formed his broken ranks on the west side of the canal before pushing on another fifty yards. The men stopped to rest a bit and then continued to advance. But the 63rd New York was compelled, due to its position in the brigade line, to cross the men of Maj. Gen. William H. French's division, who were lying prone. During this passage of lines, O'Neill was hit by a bullet and relinquished command of the regiment to Capt. Patrick J. Condon.[10]

Condon soon encountered many difficulties. Only "a few paces" away from French's prone men, the 63rd New York came to a building in the center of the regimental line. Condon ordered the right wing to oblique right and the left wing to oblique left to bypass this obstacle. After moving past the building, the captain personally took charge of the left wing so as to march it obliquely to the right and close on the right wing. He obviously felt this was easier and more efficient than marching both wings obliquely toward each other, which could have resulted in a collision of two moving lines.[11]

Soon after that maneuver, the brigade came close enough to engage the enemy, stopped, and began firing. Condon's men spent forty-five minutes "kneeling and lying" during this firefight. Then Brig. Gen. John C. Caldwell led his Second Corps brigade forward to Meagher's right to support the line, but Caldwell did not bring up his troops to align properly with Meagher. Condon's 63rd New York was posted on Meagher's right flank, and two of Caldwell's regiments came up behind his line instead of to the right. A few of Caldwell's men "lay down amongst our thinned ranks and commenced firing over our heads," reported Condon. This posed a danger to the New Yorkers, who told Caldwell's troops "to cross over our line." They did so but fell back again in less than two minutes. The wavering became troublesome, and Condon caught sight of Caldwell "about 4 paces in my rear, ineffectually endeavoring to rally his brigade." Before long, the Union line was compelled to give way; there was no possibility of advancing farther, and losses were mounting while in the stationary position.[12]

Condon provided evidence of many formations and maneuvers utilized in a particularly difficult environment at Fredericksburg. Column, line, moving by the flank, extemporizing the crossing of a watercourse, the passage of lines, oblique marching to avoid an obstacle, and mingling and unmingling battle lines are all apparent in the experience of the 63rd New York in this engagement. O'Neill (who Condon praised as a highly effective officer) and Condon himself kept firm control of the regiment during all the trials of December 13. Condon even offered a snide comment on Caldwell's inability to control his men at one point in the battle as a way to emphasize his own success in controlling troops. Self-confident officers leading disciplined troops in an impressive demonstration of small-unit articulation, as well as command and control, can be seen in the experience of the 63rd New York at Fredericksburg.

19th Ohio at Stones River, December 31, 1862

Only two weeks after Burnside's tragic failure, Rosecrans's Fourteenth Corps (later designated the Army of the Cumberland) engaged Bragg's Army of Tennessee in one of the war's bloodiest battles outside Murfreesboro, Tennessee. Bragg launched a massive surprise attack on the last day of 1862. The resulting battle threw the Federals on the defensive at a severe disadvantage, scrambling to maintain a viable line in the face of repeated flanking movements, harassed by Rebel cavalry tearing into their flanks, and impeded by a cluttered field dotted with dense cedar brakes and limestone outcroppings. It was a day of magnificent tactical success for the Confederates, near disaster for the Federals, and a heavy toll of death and wounds among the men of both armies.

Maj. Charles F. Manderson's 19th Ohio was not initially caught up in the maelstrom that morning. As part of Col. Samuel Beatty's brigade of Brig. Gen. Horatio Van Cleve's division, Manderson's regiment initially took part in Rosecrans's planned offensive against Bragg on the Union left. Van Cleve was told to push his division across Stones River and advance on Murfreesboro. Manderson formed his 19th Ohio in double column at the start of this movement, occupying the extreme right of the division's first line. When word arrived to start, Manderson deployed into line and ordered his men to load their weapons, then moved them by the right flank and crossed Stones River. On the other side, the 19th Ohio refaced in the correct direction and sent two companies out to skirmish.[13]

But that was as far as Manderson went in the planned Union offensive toward Murfreesboro. Indications of trouble began to appear on the far Federal right. This caused Rosecrans to hold Van Cleve where he was for a time until developments became clear. Finally, at 10:00 A.M. orders arrived to recross Stones River and head toward the right to support the reeling Union troops. After splashing over the stream again, Manderson moved the 19th Ohio by the right flank until halting for a time in position just west of the Nashville Pike. Later he moved the regiment by the left flank back across the pike and across the Nashville and Chattanooga Railroad, which ran parallel to and east of the road. After staying here a while, Manderson moved the 19th by the right flank to another position, where he met and repelled a Confederate advance. He followed up that success by counterattacking for a quarter of a mile.[14]

When that counterattack came to a halt, Manderson discovered that his men were low on ammunition. He reported this to Beatty, who ordered the second-line unit behind Manderson to advance past the 19th Ohio and take its place. Manderson wheeled his regiment into a column to let the 79th Indiana pass. Deploying back into line, the 19th Ohio now followed the 79th Indiana as Beatty advanced three-fourths of a mile through the woods.[15]

At this point the Confederates mounted an effective counterattack on Beatty's brigade. The supporting troops to Beatty's right gave way, and Manderson was exposed to a flanking fire. He sent word twice to Beatty to inform him of this development but received no instructions, so he had to protect the flank as best he could. With Rebel troops only fifty yards away "and in position to destroy us, I ordered a change of front to the right and rear." Manderson did not indicate exactly what maneuver he chose to effect this change of front, but he reported that refugees from units to the right of Beatty's position now began to retire hastily through his formation. This movement caused "temporary disorder," but the 19th Ohio quickly re-formed "an excellent line in good position, and fired with such precision" that the Confederates were checked. By now the regiment had fired off what was left of its ammunition and even began receiving misdirected rounds from Union artillery. It moved by the right flank into a patch of woods to join other Federal units and later was relieved and retired to the rear. Manderson lost eighty-two men during the course of this grueling day. He praised the "cool, manly daring" of his officers and the "utmost bravery and coolness" of the rank and file for the regiment's survival.[16]

Like the 63rd New York at Fredericksburg, the 19th Ohio encountered battlefield obstacles ranging from a river to thick vegetation at Stones River. The Ohio men also encountered a very fluid combat environment, demanding cool judgment and well-ordered ranks for quick reaction to shifting conditions. The regiment utilized column, line, moving by the flank, wheeling to effect passage of lines, and an effective maneuver to face a developing enemy threat to right and rear during the battle. Manderson had cause to be proud of his officers and enlisted men for what they did on December 31.

23rd Tennessee at Chickamauga, September 18, 1863

The next battle between the Army of the Cumberland and the Army of Tennessee took place nine months after Stones River. Col. R. H. Keeble's 23rd Tennessee was involved in operations taking place near Chickamauga Creek on September 18, 1863, when the opposing armies were still seeking each other in the tangled vegetation of northwestern Georgia. Keeble provides the only Confederate case study in this array of tactical examples of articulation. His regiment advanced ahead of its brigade to clear a bridge over Chickamauga Creek, crossing by the left flank. Keeble then formed a battle line on the other side based on his left company, while the 25th Tennessee formed to his right. At that point Col. John S. Fulton moved the brigade line to the right for three hundred or four hundred yards by the flank. The troops stopped and then refaced to the front. Fulton ordered the brigade to move forward and to the left four hundred yards, which the 23rd Tennessee did by making "a left wheel over the crest of a hill" with the other regiments.[17]

The wheeling movement took place to meet an anticipated Union advance on the other side of the crest. But when Fulton's men arrived, they found no enemy in sight. Sometime later the brigade moved a full three miles by the left flank. After conducting this long movement, word arrived of a possible Yankee advance, so Keeble moved the 23rd Tennessee three hundred yards to the right by the right flank along with the rest of Fulton's Brigade. Again there was no enemy to be found. By now dusk was near, so Fulton placed his command in bivouac for the night in a battle-ready formation. In Keeble's words his unit "changed front forward upon left battalion." The brigade formed a new front aligned with the 17th Tennessee, Fulton's left regiment, and settled down for the night.[18]

Keeble's men performed at least seven maneuvers during the course of the day, including movement by the flank, wheeling, and changing front forward on a subunit. The ground they traversed was cluttered with thick vegetation, and the elusive enemy seemed hidden somewhere in the confusing landscape. The 23rd Tennessee had to perform these maneuvers with the understanding that danger could burst upon the scene at any moment, yet they did so with precision and courage. Ironically, the men of the 23rd Tennessee never fired a shot that day.

12th New Jersey at Burgess's Mill, October 27, 1864

More than a year after Chickamauga, the long Petersburg Campaign dominated military operations in Virginia. Grant conducted several offensives during the campaign in an effort to flank Lee's line, stretching his position ever westward until he could force the Confederates to overextend and break. In the Sixth Offensive on October 27, 1864, however, Grant expected too much of a small force.

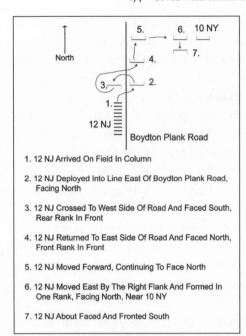

1. 12 NJ Arrived On Field In Column

2. 12 NJ Deployed Into Line East Of Boydton Plank Road,
   Facing North

3. 12 NJ Crossed To West Side Of Road And Faced South,
   Rear Rank In Front

4. 12 NJ Returned To East Side Of Road And Faced North,
   Front Rank In Front

5. 12 NJ Moved Forward, Continuing To Face North

6. 12 NJ Moved East By The Right Flank And Formed In
   One Rank, Facing North, Near 10 NY

7. 12 NJ About Faced And Fronted South

Fig. 9.2. Multiple Maneuvers at Burgess's Mill. Henry Chew maneuvered the 12th New Jersey from one formation to another and across the battlefield at Burgess's Mill during the Sixth Union Offensive at Petersburg on October 27, 1864. Each bar represents one line, not one rank.

Winfield Hancock's Second Corps moved without hindrance across the Virginia countryside and lodged astride the Boydton Plank Road just south of its crossing over Hatcher's Run and near Burgess's Mill. With further progress, Hancock could have threatened to turn the Rebel flank, so the Confederates reacted quickly. Utilizing a little-known crossing point farther downstream than the plank road, two brigades of Confederate troops launched a surprise attack on the right flank of Hancock's position. The Second Corps was isolated, detached several miles from the main Union line of fortifications, and waiting for Fifth Corps troops who failed to arrive. The result was a pitched battle fought in an open field with many threats appearing from different directions.

Initially, Capt. Henry F. Chew's 12th New Jersey went from a marching column west of the Boydton Plank Road to a battle line east of and at a right angle to the road. Chew did this by "changing front forward on first company" and faced his men north. Later in the day he moved his regiment to the west side of the road and formed it facing south, with the rear rank now in front. Still later the 12th New Jersey returned to the east side of Boydton Plank Road, now with its usual first rank in front. Chew advanced the men forward for a while, then stopped and moved them by the right flank toward the east. Still later he received orders to form the regiment in one rank only, covering the Union right flank. The 10th New York was positioned next to the 12th New Jersey, also in one rank. Near the end of the regiment's movements that day, Chew found that Confederate forces were approaching from the rear. He ordered his men to face about and confront them.[19]

Although Hancock's corps repelled all Confederate attacks and maintained its tenuous hold on the Boydton Plank Road, the Union high command realized his position was untenable. Hancock evacuated the area that night and returned to the main Union line.

Chew moved his 12th New Jersey about with aplomb to meet developing threats on a fluid battlefield. He employed changing front on a subunit, inversion of ranks, moving by the flank, and deploying in one rank rather than two to cover as much ground as possible. The latter formation was quite unusual in Civil War military operations, and it appeared only when dire necessity demanded it.

CONCLUSION

Unit commanders who ordered a multiplicity of formations and maneuvers in a single engagement demonstrated a number of positive things about linear tactics in the Civil War. These case studies illustrate the facility of complex maneuvers under difficult circumstances when executed by proficient officers and men. All those dreary hours of drill paid off handsomely in such instances. These maneuvers were not mere parade-ground show; they were vital components of survival and success in actual warfare. The case studies discussed above are not only showcases of small-unit articulation, they are also showcases of small-unit effectiveness. The linear tactical system used by Civil War armies was far from outdated—it was a vital foundation of success for Civil War commanders and their units.

≡ 10 ≡

Large Formations

Of the three tactical manuals in use by Civil War armies, only those written by Scott and Casey detailed the evolutions of the line. That term was defined as formations and maneuvers by brigades, divisions, and corps—units larger than the regiment. Hardee did not include that long section in his manual. Evolutions of the line were essentially like those of the company and the battalion with minor exceptions, such as where officers were supposed to stand and the size of intervals between subunits of a brigade, division, or corps. But the evolutions of the line also were more complex than the maneuvers of a regiment because of the larger size of units. While a regiment had about 300 men by 1863, the corps that it belonged to consisted of 10,000–20,000 troops. That fact alone inhibited coordinated maneuvers by larger units. Increased numbers of men created longer lines, which in turn created more problems of command and control. Many volunteer officers could muster up the skill to maneuver 300 troops, but far fewer had the ability to maneuver 20,000 men, and still fewer had what it took to handle 100,000 men.

The following discussion deals with formations and maneuvers on the higher level of organization in Civil War armies, that of the evolutions of the line, specifically examining how well commanders organized large formations above the brigade level. Brigades were part of the category of formations and maneuvers that tacticians called the evolutions of the line, but they are excluded here because their commanders generally achieved a high degree of articulation, especially by the midpoint of the war. Articulation on the division and corps levels was much more uneven than on the regimental and brigade levels. Previous chapters have detailed this thoroughly, but we must consider that command and control began to weaken the higher up the order of battle one looks.

Training plus experience were essential if officers hoped to execute the movements of large formations. All three drill manuals started with the School of the Soldier (the manual of arms) and progressed to the School of the Company and then the School of the Battalion. As Gerald Prokopowicz has shown within the ranks of the Army of the Ohio, training concentrated on company and regimental levels for the first year of the war. It progressed with time to include brigade-level drills and even division- and corps-level training by the end of the conflict. This was true of all Civil War field armies.[1]

But the intensity of training in all field commands always was fixed more strongly on the lower levels than on the higher levels. This was necessary, for battalion maneuvers were the basic foundation of command and control. A large military force cannot function if its basic units are poorly trained and badly handled. Given the limitations inherent in Civil War military forces (filled with citizen-soldiers and with no institutional apparatus for uniform training), officers were well advised to concentrate heavily on battalion- and brigade-level practice.

There was a very strong tendency for commanders to conduct attacks by single regiments or brigades during the first two years of the war. Capt. William W. Chamberlaine, a Confederate artillery officer, blamed "the impetuosity and lack of experience of the high ranking officers" for this tendency. "Many attacks were made by single Brigades and even single Regiments, which were repulsed with great loss." Chamberlaine also cited greed for glory among officers, lack of sufficient staff officers to communicate information, and a breakdown of command and control for this situation. "As time passed General Officers became more proficient and their men became veterans."[2]

But the increasing proficiency that Chamberlaine noted did not necessarily lead to larger formations. Subordinate commanders often received orders from their superiors to conduct small-scale operations on a large battlefield. Given the nature of the terrain and the swirling course of the first day's fighting at Stones River, Rosecrans instructed Hazen to "fight by brigades" on December 31.[3]

There are many examples of Civil War armies conducting large attacks by throwing small units forward in uncoordinated fashion. The Federals moved seventeen brigades against the stone wall protecting the approach to Marye's Heights at Fredericksburg on December 13, all of them moving forward with little if any support to right or left. One can see, however, increasing examples of coordinated advances by division commanders who managed to handle all their brigades in good order by 1863. Maj. Gen. George E. Pickett's attack on July 3 at Gettysburg is a good example of this. By 1864 and 1865, far more large-scale assaults organized on the corps level took place than one can find in the early part of the conflict. Hancock's formation of the Second Corps in the attack on the Muleshoe Salient at Spotsylvania is a good example.[4]

But large formations were not uniformly successful even late in the war. The ability of officers to exert command and control on the division and corps level remained spotty, and it varied from field army to field army as well. The Confederate Army of the Mississippi, which was renamed the Army of Tennessee in November 1862, had the worst record of success in evolutions of the line. Limited space prohibits a full discussion of the many problems associated with the performance of this famed army, which carried the main burden of defending the western Confederacy with woefully inadequate resources. But a quick overview of its campaigns reveals that the army rarely was able to mount coordinated attacks above the brigade level. One of the few instances occurred during the Battle of Franklin, where Hood managed to advance 18,000 troops across mostly open, ascending ground. But this was, after all, a general advance by a long line over favorable terrain, which was not a severe test of articulation on the army level. Instead, at Shiloh, Stones River, Chickamauga, Peachtree Creek, Atlanta on July 22, Ezra Church, and Jonesboro, the Army of Tennessee conducted the most basic maneuvers imaginable with varied degrees of coordination between brigades, divisions, and corps. There can be no doubt that on many battlefields this limited higher level of articulation hurt the army's ability to achieve its tactical goals.[5]

The Federal Army of the Tennessee produced a record of proficiency in evolutions of the line that was not much higher than its counterpart in gray. Nevertheless, the army that Grant organized, Sherman commanded, and Howard led for nearly the last year of the war was one of the most successful field forces of the war. The Army of the Tennessee won its victories mostly through successful campaigning. It had the ability to fight doggedly but rarely mounted large-scale attacks. Mostly, the troops fought on the defensive, as they did at Shiloh, Atlanta, and Ezra Church. Or, as on May 22 at Vicksburg, they assaulted in small-scale increments arrayed along an extended battle line. That attack occurred primarily on the brigade level; there were no coordinated division-level assaults that day. Sherman crafted a pretty impressive large-scale formation for his attack on Tunnel Hill during the Chattanooga Campaign, but that assault was bluntly repulsed by essentially one division of Confederate troops mounted on good defensive ground.[6]

The Army of the Ohio (which became the Army of the Cumberland by early 1863), contained a number of highly gifted regular and volunteer officers who helped transform that force into what was arguably the most professional field army of the war. Buell, Rosecrans, and Thomas, its only commanders, set a good example, and men like Hazen, Harker, Daniel McCook, and Opdycke followed through with vigorous efforts to transform their brigades and divisions into models of efficiency.

And yet the Army of the Cumberland only rarely mounted impressive large formations. More often than not, its tactical situation led commanders to string out a long line across the countryside and attack by segments rather than massing division or corps strength. Its famous assault at Missionary Ridge saw interesting formations on the division level, and each division moved forward roughly in coordination with the others. It was a well-conducted traditional attack for Civil War armies, a sign of success in achieving articulation on the corps level. But at Pickett's Mill, Howard threw one brigade at a time into an uncertain contest without coordinating their efforts in a reversion to the sloppy articulation seen early in the war. More often than not, the Army of the Cumberland found itself fighting on the tactical defensive, as it did at Perryville, Stones River, Chickamauga, and Peachtree Creek. It did not consistently put together well-coordinated operations on the division and corps level during the war.[7]

Much the same can be said about the Army of Northern Virginia. Created by Joseph E. Johnston and Beauregard and brought to a high level of success by Lee, the army exhibited many examples of poor articulation on the division and corps level early in the war. At Seven Pines and again at Malvern Hill, it could achieve coordination only on the brigade level at best. With battlefield success and confidence in Lee's leadership, officers managed to achieve far greater articulation as the war progressed—Longstreet's attack at Second Bull Run and the assault of Pickett's Division at Gettysburg are two good examples. But the army continued to do poorly on other fields. It conducted the attack on May 3 at Chancellorsville with a good deal of confusion, caused not only by the tangled vegetation of the Wilderness but also by poor handling on the part of division commanders.

Lee's army was thrown mostly on the defensive in the heavy fighting of 1864–65, and its counterattacks show that high-level articulation almost ceased entirely. At the Wilderness Lee's men mounted several local counterattacks with small forces, doing the same on May 12 at Spotsylvania. At Petersburg the Army of Northern Virginia continued to react to Union offensives with small counterattacks. One Rebel brigade at a time was thrown onto the contested ground at the Battle of the Crater on July 30. Maj. Gen. John B. Gordon mounted an admirable corps-level formation for the attack on Fort Stedman on March 25, 1865, but that attack foundered on many obstacles that the formation could not overcome. Overall, the Army of Northern Virginia was unable to maintain a high degree of articulation on the division and corps level after 1863.[8]

But the Army of the Potomac developed an impressive degree of articulation in evolutions of the line. In fact, it was the only Civil War field army to do so in a consistent and important way. Created by George McClellan, led by a succession of commanders who either failed or put in a muddled record of success, and ultimately guided by Grant's unyielding hand, that army suffered but triumphed in the last year of the Civil War. Forced by Lee's defensive strategy to adopt the tactical as well as the strategic offensive in 1864, its leaders were compelled to learn how to conduct large-scale attacks to bring its weight to bear on the enemy. At Spotsylvania on May 12, at Five Forks, and at Petersburg on April 2, the Army of the Potomac turned in the best examples of large-scale formations to be seen in the Civil War. They were among the most successful examples of articulation on the corps level as well.[9]

What follows is a series of case studies illustrating the problems and successes of organizing coordinated attacks at the corps level. They show that Civil War commanders had a mixed record in organizing large formations and using them on the battlefield. The focus is on large formations designed for offensive action because that is where the true test lies. Defending a position was comparatively easy; capturing it was not. Excluded are examples where the commanders simply had to take care of a sector of the field as they saw fit, with minimal cooperation from neighboring units. Instead, the focus is on the assembling of an entire corps in a specially designed formation with the objective of advancing on a single point. This process demonstrates a high level of articulation on the upper levels of organization in an army. The five examples that follow display a mix of formations and varied degrees of success.

CHANCELLORSVILLE, MAY 2, 1863

Lt. Gen. Thomas J. "Stonewall" Jackson was given a unique assignment by Lee. Entrusted with 21,500 troops, he moved them all day of May 2 to gain a position from which he could turn and attack Joseph Hooker's right flank, hanging without adequate protection in the dense woods of the Wilderness near Chancellorsville.[10]

Once near the enemy, Jackson organized a compact formation using the Orange Turnpike as the axis of his advance. Brig. Gen. Robert E. Rodes's division formed the first line with two brigades under Alfred Iverson and Edward O'Neal to the left of the road. Two other brigades, under Brig. Gens. George Doles and Alfred H.

Colquitt, formed to the right of the road. Brig. Gen. Stephen D. Ramseur's brigade took position one hundred yards to the rear of Colquitt's line but farther right so as to overlap Colquitt by one regiment and provide support for his flank.[11]

Rodes gave each of his brigade leaders clear directions to use the turnpike as their guide. As instructions filtered down the chain of command, Iverson told the commander of his left regiment to cover the left flank of Jackson's large formation by forming perpendicularly to the brigade line, and to move by the right flank so as to keep pace with the division. Rodes also placed a skirmish line four hundred yards ahead of his command. Brig. Gen. Raleigh E. Colston's division formed the second line. He placed his men two hundred yards behind Rodes. Maj. Gen. A. P. Hill's division formed the third line behind Colston.[12]

When the Confederates began their advance at 5:15 P.M., the tangled terrain immediately began to interfere with the regularity of the formation. The skirmish line slowed down so much that Rodes's main line caught up with it, and he had to instruct the skirmishers to push forward and try to maintain a reasonable distance ahead. The Confederates continued to advance but encountered trouble in maintaining their formation when hitting resistance near Melzi Chancellor's house. Colston's Division began to close up to Rodes's Division and "mingled together in inextricable confusion" with the men of the first line. Col. Daniel H. Christie of the 23rd North Carolina in Iverson's Brigade complained that this was done "before there was the least necessity for their assistance. The consequence was, that no officer could handle a distinct command without halting and reforming."[13]

Colston defended his troops by reporting that Rodes advanced too slowly. His men, Colston argued, were "already within a few steps of" Rodes and "in some places mixed up with" his troops even before the Confederates hit the Federals. Colston claimed that two of his brigades actually "pushed on with and through the first line" and were the first to hit the Union position at Melzi Chancellor's. One of his regimental commanders reported that this was done upon Rodes's request for help. Colston's chief engineer suggested that Rodes's men "apparently faltered and were overrun by our division, owing, first, to the eagerness of the men, and, secondly, to the probable fact of General Jackson's having ordered the attack to be vigorous." Colston admitted that by the end of the action, "the formation of the troops had become very much confused, and different regiments, brigades, and divisions were mixed up together."[14]

To the astonished Federals who met Jackson's attack, the Confederates seemed to present "a heavy, solid mass" of troops moving through the tangled vegetation. Some of those Rebel units were able to maintain their formation well despite the difficulties. Edward O'Neal praised the regimental commanders in his Alabama brigade for "the order, regularity, and precision with which [they] moved and handled their commands through this charge." Even though he advanced the units "through a dense and tangled forest for a mile, all the regiments were connected and moved in a regular, unbroken line."[15]

O'Neal indicated that unit cohesion was good on the brigade level, but coordinating the movements of one division closely stacked behind the other resulted in confusion. No one blamed the tangled vegetation for the fact that Colston blundered into Rodes's line, citing poor management instead. Colston refused to admit responsibility for merging his division with Rodes's, blaming it rather on Rodes's men for moving too slowly. The confusion certainly inhibited Jackson's ability to take advantage of his tactical success.

SPOTSYLVANIA, MAY 12, 1864

A little more than a year after Chancellorsville, Federal efforts to reduce a huge bulge in Lee's line at Spotsylvania resulted in assaults by large formations organized by Meade's Army of the Potomac. The Mule Shoe Salient had been constructed to take in slightly higher ground that Lee's engineers deemed significant when the Army of Northern Virginia assumed its position at Spotsylvania. It was about 1,800 yards wide at the base and about 1,320 yards deep from the tip to the base. The works were constructed on the night of May 8–9, with improvements made over the next several days.[16]

On the evening of May 10, the Federals made their first serious strike at the salient. Emory Upton organized a formation of twelve Sixth Corps regiments, totaling 5,000 men, to hit the west side of the bulge at a place called Doles's Salient. He formed them into four lines of three regiments each and assigned a specific task to each line in order to exploit the initial break in the enemy position. An open field two hundred yards deep had to be crossed before the Federals reached the first fortified line, which was supported by a second fortified line one hundred yards behind it. To help the men cross this open space, Upton told his officers "to repeat the command 'Forward' constantly, from the commencement of the charge till the works were carried." He also mandated that the troops in his first line load and place a detonation cap on their muskets, whereas those in the other lines were to load but not cap their weapons; all were to fix bayonets.[17]

Upton achieved limited success. After setting out at 6:35 P.M. on May 10, his

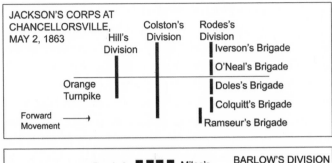

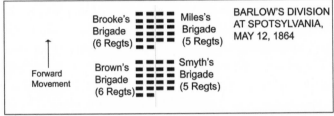

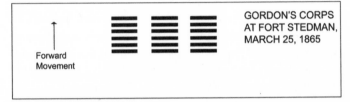

Fig. 10.1. Large Formations at Chancellorsville, Spotsylvania, and Fort Stedman. These two Confederate examples and one Union example indicate the combination of line and column used in large formations during the Civil War. Each bar represents one line, not one rank.

first line broke the Confederate position and took a section of its first fortified line, but the Federals were unable to exploit their advantage. In part, this was due to effective maneuvering by reserve Confederate units to contain the breach. In addition, a Second Corps division that was supposed to support Upton failed to go forward. Yet a third reason lay in the fact that the second, third, and fourth lines of the Union formation could not fulfill their missions due to the fact that the first line became stalled without breaking through the enemy position. The Federals were compelled to retire with losses of about 1,000 men, but they had inflicted casualties of about 1,300 men on their opponent.[18]

Grant was encouraged by the partial success and resolved to hit the tip of the salient with a massive force. Hancock's Second Corps was given the assignment, with support from other corps to the right and left. In effect, the Federals would make their major attack on the tip, but nearly the entire perimeter of the salient would be pressed as well. The attack was scheduled to take place at dawn of May 12, giving Hancock little time to position and prepare his troops.[19]

The Second Corps began to move toward its assembly point at 10:00 P.M. on May 11. Hancock organized a massive formation of nearly 20,000 men in the woods just north of the salient. Francis Barlow's division would lead the attack, but Barlow was frustrated that his superiors could not tell him much about the lay of the land or even the exact distance to be covered before reaching the enemy works. It was already too dark for him to examine the ground personally. "Then I assume the authority to form my division as I please, and that will be in two lines of masses," he told Hancock. Barlow had a tendency to trust columns, and when Hancock objected to this formation, he explained why he wanted it. "If I am to lead this assault I propose to have men enough, when I reach the objective point, to charge through Hell itself and capture all the artillery they can mass in my front." As one of Barlow's staff officers put it, "After an extended controversy he carried his point."[20]

While Hancock assembled his units 1,200 yards from the target, his staff members used a compass to establish a line of advance toward "a large white house known to be inside the enemy's works." Barlow formed each of his four brigades in a column of division, each regiment in a double column. He placed two brigades side by side in his first formation and the other two behind them, with intervals of only five paces between regiments and ten paces between brigades. The twenty-three regiments of the division therefore composed "a solid square" in the words of staff officer John D. Black. Brigade leader Nelson Miles assigned a staff officer to move behind his left wing and another to do the same behind his right, while telling yet a third staff member to stick close to him as he moved behind the center of the brigade, all of this to better control the movement of the men. Barlow also placed a skirmish line in his front. The skirmishers took intervals of only one pace and were told to run and capture the enemy pickets before they could give an alarm.[21]

Edwin C. Mason, an officer in Maj. Gen. David Birney's division of the Second Corps, believed that Barlow's formation was the best adapted to the terrain and the objective of Grant's attack. It "gave a compact mass of . . . regiments that could be hurled against the works like a battering ram, and handled with ease and rapidity in the thickets through which the attack must be made." To a large degree Mason was correct, but this massed formation also presented a wonderful target to Confederate artillery. Barlow adopted it because the attack would go in at dawn and hopefully would be a surprise, and he counted on being able to get into the salient and capture the guns before they could deal with his exposed infantrymen. Under other circumstances, such a formation could have been torn to shreds by artillery fire. The two Second Corps divisions to the right and left of Barlow's formation formed lines rather than columns.[22]

Hancock's command was able to cross the deadly ground in front of the salient quickly when the attack began at first light on May 12, but the Federals were lucky that the Confederates were indeed taken by surprise. Moreover, Lee had pulled his artillery out of the salient hours before, mistakenly believing that Grant was disengaging from the lines at Spotsylvania, only to shove them back again during the night when he realized his mistake. As a result the guns were in the salient but not ready for immediate action.[23]

The Federals advanced in tight formation for the first half of their journey across no-man's land but then began to loosen their alignment. As Hancock put it, they "broke into a tremendous cheer, and spontaneously taking the double-quick, they rolled like an irresistible wave into the enemy's works." The Federals engulfed the tip of the Mule Shoe Salient, capturing 3,000 men and twenty-four guns. But then all formation evaporated, and the Federals became mixed up in a jumble as 20,000 men jammed into the constricted space of the tip. As a result, Hancock was unable to quickly exploit his success. Lee thus had opportunity to move fresh troops to the threatened sector and hold the base of the salient against tentative Union efforts to advance farther. When the Confederates launched counterattacks, the Federals held on to the tip for many hours to come, pelted by rain and often protected from close-range fire only by the width of the parapet. By dawn of May 13, Lee constructed a new line across the base of the salient and retired to it, leaving a gory field in Union hands. The Federals suffered 9,000 casualties, while the Confederates lost about 8,000 men in all the fighting that took place on May 12.[24]

With the benefit of hindsight, Black argued that Barlow had been wise to organize his command in such a tightly packed formation of columns. According to Black, "we had men enough in the captured works to repulse any attack that might be made against them." That was an odd conclusion, revealing a desperate effort to justify his commander's preference for columns while ignoring the fact that the Federals should not have had to act on the defensive at all. Fewer men arrayed in multiple lines probably would have worked better. Division and brigade leaders needed more room and flexibility to maintain command and control. The large number of men and the use of columns by Barlow contributed to the confusion inside the tip of the salient, which in turn contributed to Hancock's inability to make more of his initial success. E. Porter Alexander fully understood the basic vulnerability of columns when attacking a position armed with artillery: "It would be very instructive to know what 20 well served guns could do with such a column [as Barlow's] even within the space of 150 yards. And this column was heard coming at least 400 yards."[25]

FORT STEDMAN, MARCH 25, 1865

The bloody combat of May 12 was followed by weeks of tough campaigning as the Army of the Potomac continued to fight and maneuver toward Richmond. By mid-June 1864 Grant's long drive from the Wilderness landed the army at Petersburg, where the confrontation between the opposing forces extended into the longest campaign of the war. Sometimes the Confederates were able to counter Federal efforts to extend their line westward with limited counterattacks, often by single brigades. The only time Lee mounted a large offensive by a cohesive formation was at Fort Stedman on March 25, 1865. Second Corps commander John Gordon initiated the plan, believing he could mass his men and break through two Union lines. He might then be able to threaten Grant's logistical base at City Point and force the Federals to contract their position. Lee endorsed the plan and saw strategic benefits in it. If Grant was forced to constrict his posture outside Petersburg, Lee might be able to hold his trenches with fewer men and send a mobile column to North Carolina to oppose Sherman, who was bringing 60,000 western veterans to help Grant. In the end, of course, the Confederates failed to accomplish the larger goals of the operation, but they did manage to break one Union line and cause a good deal of frenzied activity in the enemy camp.[26]

Gordon pinpointed a spot where the opposing lines were as close as 204 yards from each other, with picket lines only 145 yards apart. He meant to strike with three divisions, necessitating a major effort to form the men behind the Confederate fortified line. The Rebels quietly left their assigned sectors after dark of March 24 and assembled well behind the line near Colquitt's Salient, which lay opposite Fort Stedman. Finding relatively open ground, the three divisions formed in mass, although Confederate accounts fail to indicate exactly how they did so. Brig. Gen. James A. Walker mentioned that the three divisions formed "their separate columns," which implies that each made columns of brigades and were aligned abreast of each other. Walker's division was on the left and had the assignment of hitting Fort Stedman squarely, while the other two divisions were positioned to his right. Gordon assembled nearly 11,000 men and then moved the columns toward Colquitt's Salient so as to have the head of their formations poised to cross the line at the signal to attack. Each column was preceded by a storming party of 100 troops while another group of 50 men carried axes to cut through obstructions fronting the Union works. Each division was "to follow closely behind the storming party, marching by the right flank," according to Walker.[27]

Close attention to detail in planning and organizing, striking before dawn, and taking the enemy by surprise spelled success for Gordon's men in the initial stage of their attack. Actually, the storming party seems to have captured Fort Stedman without much assistance from the division column behind it. Walker noted that it took him more than one hour to move his division forward after his advance party took the fort. In the interim he sent skirmishers toward the second Union position three-quarters of a mile away while he worked to form the bulk of his division in line beyond Fort Stedman. Meanwhile, the Federals in the works to both sides of Stedman held fast, and reinforcements soon arrived. The second Union line was too strong for the Rebel skirmishers to take by themselves. Before long, the initial Confederate success was contained, and Union counterattacks drove the enemy out of the breach by about eight o'clock that morning. Gordon lost 2,681 men compared to Federal casualties of 1,044 troops.[28]

Gordon's attack at Fort Stedman was a comparatively rare example of Lee's army forming an assault force larger than one brigade to hit a single target late in the war. A paucity of Confederate accounts hinders our ability to understand in detail how that force was formed and how it fared in trying to accomplish its task. But the evidence suggests that the troops were unable to accomplish much because of the constricted area of the battlefield, effective Union fortifications flanking Fort Stedman, and the difficulties of maneuvering massed columns across extensive Confederate and Union trench systems. The break in the first Union line was largely accomplished by the advanced parties, numbering only three hundred men, while the bulk of the three divisions behind them struggled to come onto the field with little opportunity to use the full weight of their numbers.[29]

FIVE FORKS, APRIL 1, 1865

Only a week after the failed Confederate attack at Fort Stedman, the Army of the Potomac fought a pivotal battle to turn Lee's extended line at Petersburg. It had managed to assemble several impressive massed formations on the corps level during the last year of the Civil War, with Hancock's grouping for the May 12 attack at Spotsylvania constituting the first. Now Gouverneur Warren formed his Fifth Corps in a tightly packed formation to attack the Confederates who held a key road junction called Five Forks on April 1, 1865, achieving an important victory in Grant's ten-month-long effort to pry Lee out of his fortified lines. Because Philip Sheridan, who was in charge of the Union forces operating against Five Forks, relieved Warren of his command during the battle, a court of inquiry was held fifteen years later that cleared Warren's name. In the process, many officers gave testimony about the Fifth Corps operations that included formation and alignment. In fact, because of this lengthy and precise testimony, we have far more details on the Fifth Corps at Five Forks, and on how the units were handled by their officers, than for any other sizeable formation in either the Union or Confederate armies during the Civil War.[30]

Warren had about 12,000 men available against George Pickett's Confederate force of 9,200 men holding Five Forks. The Fifth Corps struggled to move across muddy roads on April 1, marching in the wrong direction for a time and redirecting its approach to the designated assembly area. Warren began to form his troops in a slight ravine straddling Gravelly Run Church Road, facing north, at 1:00 P.M. Sheridan told him that the left flank of Pickett's fortified line ended at the intersection of this road with White Oak Road, due north of the assembly area, although Warren could not see the Rebel position because of the lay of the land and the tree cover.[31]

The Formation

Sheridan ordained the general formation—two divisions in front and the third behind as a reserve, the right front division to be slightly advanced compared to the left to facilitate a left wheel when the corps should hit the end of Pickett's line. But Sheridan left the details of deployment to Warren, who decided to place two brigades (each deployed in two lines of battle) on the front line of the two divisions that would lead the advance. Each of these divisions, commanded by Romeyn B. Ayres on the left of the road and Samuel Crawford on the right, would also have a brigade in the rear and center of their front line. The reserve brigade would also be deployed in two lines of battle. The third division, led by Charles Griffin, was "posted in column of battalions in mass" behind Crawford. When Ayres realized it would be difficult to form one of his brigades in two lines, he organized it in three lines instead. The front of the Fifth Corps formation was one thousand yards wide.[32]

Well before Warren completed the formation of his corps at 4:00 P.M., he carefully prepared a sketch map of the terrain and instructions to go with it. Warren told his division leaders "to keep closed to the left and to preserve their direction in the woods, by keeping the sun, then shining brightly, in the same position over their left shoulders." They were to move a thousand yards north until closing on White Oak Road, then wheel left so as to hit and engulf the left wing of Pickett's position, forming line perpendicular to White Oak Road. Warren believed Crawford would hit the angle of the enemy line, where the extreme left of the Rebel position was refused, with the center of his division formation. Warren prepared meticulously for the assault. While Sheridan explained his intentions by drawing in the dirt with the tip of his sword, Warren personally drew the sketch map and made multiple copies by using "manifold paper," a kind of tracing paper. "I wanted to see that the line of markers for the line were put in the right direction," Warren testified at his court of inquiry. "I had to consult with division commanders as to the strength of their regiments. We had to modify for every little particular case. I recollect telling, especially in Crawford's division, what the commanders should do."[33]

Ayres's Division

Each of the three brigades in Ayres's division consisted of a little more than eight hundred men. The two brigades in his first line were deployed in two battle lines rather than one; each brigade thus had a front of only two hundred men. Ayres estimated the combined front of the two brigades occupied a line only eight hundred feet (or 266 yards) long. That placed a combined front of four hundred men in a sector of eight hundred feet, or two feet per man, a comfortable but compact deployment for the troops. His reserve brigade was deployed in three lines 150 yards to the rear of his first formation. While Ayres's right flank was nearly on Gravelly Run Church Road, there was an interval (he estimated it as the length of the room in which the court of inquiry was meeting) between his right and Crawford's left.[34]

Crawford's Division

Within Crawford's division, brigade commanders worked to make sure that the two lines they deployed were roughly equal in strength. Richard Coulter, whose brigade held the right wing of Crawford's first line, temporarily consolidated the 56th and 88th Pennsylvania into a battalion of 323 men and did the same with the

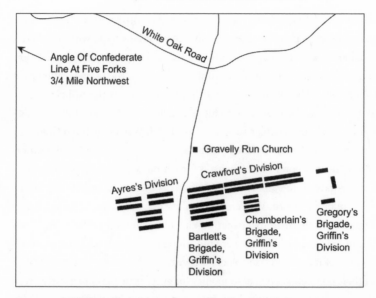

Fig. 10.2. Fifth Corps Formation at Five Forks. Gouverneur Warren's corps organized for a major assault on Confederate forces holding Five Forks on April 1, 1865, using a combination of lines and columns. Each bar represents one line, not one rank.

121st and 142nd Pennsylvania to form a battalion of 210 men. The strength of his other regiments ranged from 94 men in the 95th New York to 327 men in the 14th New York. Coulter was able to roughly equalize his brigade into two battle lines with 546 men in the first and 631 men in the second line.[35]

Griffin's Division

Griffin formed his division behind Crawford and apparently allowed his brigade commanders much latitude in determining the exact formation. Joseph J. Bartlett formed his brigade on the left in three lines with two regiments in each line, one regiment as a reserve, and another on the skirmish line. Joshua L. Chamberlain formed his brigade to Bartlett's right, and Griffin gave Chamberlain the responsibility of directing Edgar M. Gregory's brigade as well. Chamberlain formed his own brigade in a column of four regiments, although he divided one of his regiments that had twelve companies into two battalions to equalize the column's width. He then "massed them up in order that I might handle them readily in any direction."

Chamberlain positioned Gregory's brigade to cover the right flank of the Fifth Corps formation, even though a cavalry division was assigned to screen that flank. Gregory put one regiment to the front as skirmishers, one facing right on the flank of the corps, and one held in reserve. Chamberlain reported that his orders "were to keep closed to the left on [Bartlett's brigade], and also to wheel to the left in moving."[36]

The Advance

Warren's careful planning for the attack at Five Forks was based on an erroneous assumption by Sheridan. The left of Pickett's line did not end at the junction of Gravelly Run Church Road and White Oak Road, but about 1,200 yards (or three-quarters of a mile) farther west of that spot. The Federal infantry would not realize this until they were nearly on White Oak Road, necessitating a quick change of plans and direction. Ayres's small division of only 2,600 men would therefore play a key role in the battle because it occupied Warren's left wing and had to respond first and fast to the change in circumstances. It would be the pivot upon which the entire Fifth Corps formation was to turn, but that would not be easy to do because of the terrain. As Bartlett testified, "it being a difficult wooded country there, and broken up by ravines a little, it was a little difficult to perform that with precision." Warren noted that in such conditions he sometimes "gave compass directions" to his subordinates to help them find their true line of advance. But in this case the sun was in the right position to serve as a ready guide. His men could keep it to the left as they advanced north and then when turning left have it before them as a beacon.[37]

Ayres's Division

As soon as Ayres's division reached White Oak Road, it became clear that the Confederate position was some distance to the west. Ayres knew what had to be done and struggled to change the direction of his division as fast as possible, but trouble had already developed. A Confederate skirmish line appeared directly in front of the division, and the commander of Ayres's Third Brigade, James Gwyn, ordered his men to move directly north against it on the double quick. Gwyn therefore became detached from the rest of the division, taking the right wing of the first line away from the rest, and Ayres had no chance to control the brigade. But Ayres took personal direction of the left wing of the first line, the Second Brigade, when its commander, Daniel L. Stanton, was shot. Rather than conduct a complicated wheeling movement, Ayres directed this small brigade as it "faced and filed . . . to the left, then faced . . . to the right to make this new front." The general estimated it took him five minutes to redirect the forward movement of Stanton's command. The reserve brigade, commanded by Frederick Winthrop in the second line, also changed front in similar fashion, while Gwynn eventually wheeled left some distance to the north to join elements of Griffin's division and participate in the battle.[38]

Ayres's superiors tried to understand exactly how the division leader had changed direction so quickly. Warren admitted in his testimony that it was not a wheeling movement. Ayres "made more of a left turn. Everything went around at a double quick or by a left flank movement." Sheridan engaged Warren in conversation about it. "He would not ask me to do it by a swing if I could do it by facing to the left," Warren recalled fifteen years later. "Our conversation was very direct on that point, to get to the support of the troops engaged at the earliest point in time."[39]

Crawford's Division

While Ayres handled his small division with aplomb, Crawford lost sight of the larger plan and allowed his division to drift off course. As soon as Ayres began to change direction, the interval between the two divisions widened quickly. Moreover, the line of Confederate skirmishers that had deflected Gwynn's brigade from Ayres's command also deflected the whole of Crawford's division from the Fifth Corps.[40]

Even before that moment arrived, members of Crawford's division recalled that there was much muddling of ranks during the short march northward from the assembly point. Col. J. Tarbell of the 91st New York testified that "a great deal of crowding right and left" occurred, but he also noted that this was typical of most attacks. The tendency was to drift right, and regimental and company officers had difficulty getting the men to guide left instead. Warren rode for a short time by Tarbell's side and chastised him for "giving instructions" instead of shouting strict orders for his men to "'right oblique' or 'left oblique,'" to relieve the pressure." There was so much shifting from the right as well as from the left that the "danger of companies being doubled up from crowding" was real.[41]

The veteran officers and men of Crawford's division managed to contain this shuffling on the approach march so that it did not impair their effort to move forward. But when it came time to turn left in support of Ayres, the division broke up into segments. Warren was able to personally direct Crawford's left brigade, commanded by John A. Kellogg, to wheel left toward the enemy. Kellogg did this quickly on a fixed pivot, but subordinates later testified that it was "a sort of swinging wheel to the left." Richard Coulter, who commanded Crawford's reserve brigade, saw what was happening and did the same. "I suppose it was more a change of front," Coulter recalled. "It was by no means a perfect wheel." Coulter further testified that it was best to call the maneuver a "change of direction because I would not like to designate it a wheel." Tarbell recalled that there was "no distinct command" from Kellogg "except the general direction that we were to incline towards the left."[42]

Warren glanced and saw that Kellogg completed his change of direction, no matter what term should be used to describe the exact movement. He also noticed that Kellogg established his brigade facing west or northwest by placing men as markers to designate the new position. Warren had told him to wait until the rest of Crawford's division had also completed this change of direction. But as Warren was issuing instructions to the rest of Crawford's command, George A. Forsyth of Sheridan's staff, without Warren's knowledge, told Kellogg to move forward and engage the enemy. When Warren next looked in that direction, Kellogg was gone. In a decision he regretted for the next fifteen years, Warren decided to stay where he was so as to be in better communication with Sheridan and with his own couriers. He hoped that the message he sent to Crawford would have an effect and bring the rest of that division into action.[43]

Griffin's Division

Warren lost control of Crawford's division and also was unable to influence the movements of Griffin's division. Griffin remained in the dark as to what was happening for some time. He continued to move northward, becoming alarmed when it was evident that the Confederate line was not where it was supposed to be, yet he continued past White Oak Road even though Ayres broke off to the west and Crawford's division split, part going west and the remainder going north. In fact, Griffin soon lost sight of his compatriots. Upon reaching the open expanse of the Sydney Farm, Griffin stopped his men and tried to gauge the situation. Musketry could be heard off to the left rear, and staff officers from Sheridan arrived who urged him to head toward it.[44]

To get the men redirected involved a sharp wheeling movement, which Bartlett's brigade began to do. Bartlett posted "a huge fellow" as a marker upon which to pivot. The man held his musket with the butt high in the air to provide a visible point upon which to wheel. The brigade swung around quickly as Bartlett rode on the moving flank, "his horse curvetting in fine style and he marking time with his saber," according to Augustus Buell, who served as one of Griffin's staff officers.[45]

But at least one unit, the 1st Maine Sharpshooters, lost connection with the rest of the brigade during this sharp wheeling movement. Positioned on Bartlett's far right, the sharpshooters were forced to run in a futile effort to keep pace with the rest of the brigade line. "We were caught swinging off the pivot," recalled Capt. Charles F. Sawyer, "so that it required all our efforts to keep them to the left. We had to keep the men running all the time." The men could not keep pace; "we were snapped off," Sawyer continued, "we lost our guiding point." The 1st Maine Sharpshooters had moved on the double quick during the short march from the assembly area up to the point where Bartlett began to wheel; they had kept up a fast run during the wheel but slowed to "a kind of a dog-trot" after losing connection with the brigade. Soon they began to realize they were alone and had no idea where to go.[46]

Bartlett was able to bring only three regiments to bear on the enemy in a concentrated fashion after completing his wheel. Those units "squared up their formation," wrote Buell, "and then it was, 'Forward, right oblique' (as they had to take ground to the right), and then 'Quick, march!' 'Double quick!!' and 'Charge!!!'" Bartlett connected with Gregory's brigade to conduct a successful advance on the Confederates.[47]

How Gregory changed direction to face the enemy is not known, but Chamberlain tried to explain how he maneuvered his own brigade to achieve that end. In his official report Chamberlain wrote that he "drew my brigade into the field by the left flank and formed them facing this fire." In his testimony before the Warren court of inquiry, Chamberlain explained, "our instructions were not to wheel to the left but to change direction to the left—neither a wheel nor a change of front, but the tactical expression would be change of direction to the left in marching." Exactly what was done is not clear, but it appears to have been a change of front forward by the left flank, with men moving on their own rather than by companies or any other subunit, a fast but potentially chaotic fashion of changing front. Nevertheless, it worked.[48]

Conclusion

The Federals managed to win a smashing victory at Five Forks, crushing Pickett's position and completely outflanking Lee's line at Petersburg. They had massed 12,000 men in a tight formation to do this, but mistaken ideas about the exact Rebel position contributed to the difficulty of moving that mass on the enemy.

More importantly, Crawford lost control of his division at a critical point in the attack, allowing one brigade to continue moving north rather than wheeling left and letting Warren control the movements of the rest of his division. Ayres handled his small command well to provide an essential foundation for success, and Griffin deserves great credit for managing his own division in a constructive way despite the problems inherent in rapidly wheeling Bartlett's brigade. The only issue upon which Sheridan based his decision to relieve Warren of command was that the general chose to stay put when seeing that Kellogg's brigade had moved on before the rest of Crawford's division could align with it. The actions of his subordinates saved the day after that point. The court of inquiry exonerated Warren of wrongdoing, but Sherman, now general in chief, disagreed with the court, castigating Warren for losing control of his command at a critical moment in the battle.[49]

PETERSBURG, APRIL 2, 1865

The long campaign at Petersburg finally came to an end the day after Five Forks, when Grant ordered frontal attacks against Lee on April 2. The Ninth Corps would advance along Jerusalem Plank Road into a system of fieldworks that had been carefully crafted for ten months and sported two lines of defense. The Sixth Corps would attack much farther west against a single line of works thinly held by the Confederates. The former achieved only limited success, while the latter made a clean break in Lee's line, both corps massing thousands of men in tightly packed formations to accomplish their goals.[50]

The Ninth Corps

John G. Parke used portions of five brigades belonging to the Ninth Corps, placing Robert Potter's division west of Jerusalem Plank Road and John Hartranft's division east of the road. All units formed columns of regiments for the assault. Potter headed his formation with three companies of the 31st Maine acting as a vanguard, followed by pioneers with axes to clear obstructions fronting the Confederate works. Parke marshaled a total of eighteen regiments in his strike force and planned to hit a sector of the enemy line held by three Confederate brigades, with four Rebel regiments stationed near enough to offer help if needed.[51]

The Ninth Corps troops initially captured a segment of the enemy lines but soon got stuck in it. Going in at 4:30 A.M., Potter's advance force took Battery 28 and a portion of Fort Mahone, while Hartranft's men captured Battery 25 and Battery 27. But the system of earthworks, held by tough veterans, contained the breach in Lee's line. For the rest of the day, bitter fighting took place at close range, the opponents often separated only by the width of a traverse. The Federals controlled only about five hundred yards of the Confederate first line of works when the fighting came to an end, losing 1,500 men in the process.[52]

The Sixth Corps

Horatio Wright, in contrast, delivered one of the rare examples of a fully successful attack on fortifications in the Civil War. He massed 14,000 Sixth Corps troops in a formation that fronted a little more than one mile to hit Confederate works held by about 2,800 men. Wright placed George Getty's division as the point of a triangular formation, with Frank Wheaton's division to Getty's right and rear. Truman Seymour's division took position to the left and rear of Getty. The troops assembled under cover of darkness on open ground between the main Union line and the Federal picket line. Wright issued detailed instructions: "the entire formation being by brigade, with regimental front, small regiments being consolidated so as not too much to extend the column."[53]

GETTY'S DIVISION

The troops of Getty's division organized columns for their assault on the fortified Confederate line. Lewis Grant's Vermont brigade took position on the left in column of regiments, while Thomas Hyde's brigade organized a similar column to Grant's right. James M. Warner formed his brigade in column to the right of Hyde's command. It was necessary to temporarily rearrange the units to equalize these columns. Hyde broke up a couple of regiments in order to make four lines with his six regiments. Warner divided his unusually large 93rd Pennsylvania into two lines and then formed a total of five lines in his brigade column. All columns were closed in mass for maximum control by their officers. Grant would serve as the guide not only for Getty's division but also for the entire corps as it advanced.[54]

WHEATON'S DIVISION

Wheaton positioned his division to the right and rear of Getty but in a formation that mixed multiple lines with columns. Oliver Edwards's brigade headed Whea-

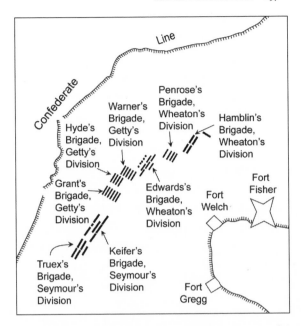

Fig. 10.3. Sixth Corps Formation on April 2. Horatio Wright's corps organized for a major assault on the Confederate line protecting Petersburg on April 2, 1865, using a combination of lines and columns. Each bar represents one line, not one rank.

ton's division and was placed some twenty-five paces to the right and rear of Warner's brigade in Getty's division. Deploying a skirmish line, Edwards then placed two regiments in his first line and three in his second line three hundred paces behind the first formation. The brigade's third line consisted of one regiment formed three hundred paces behind the second. Fifty paces behind and to the right of Edwards, William H. Penrose positioned his brigade in a column of regiments four lines deep. One hundred paces behind and to the right of Penrose, Joseph E. Hamblin placed his brigade in two lines of two regiments each. Hamblin also deployed one regiment to cover his right because there were no supports in that direction.[55]

Wheaton issued detailed instructions about the distances between his brigades and between lines within each brigade. "In the advance the brigade will preserve a sufficient distance to prevent the front line of one being mingled with the rear line of another. The lines in each brigade will be kept well apart, not less than fifty paces, and one line must not be permitted to crowd or touch another. The distance between lines may be increased to conform to the character of the advance we may be able to make, the nature of the ground, &c." Edwards was to be the guide for the division, and in turn he was to take his guide from Getty's division. Wheaton thought it best to uncap all muskets except for those men in the first line of each brigade to prevent friendly fire in this complex formation of column and multiple lines.[56]

SEYMOUR'S DIVISION

Seymour positioned his division to the left rear of Getty in a formation of multiple lines. J. Warren Keifer put two and a half regiments on his first line, the 9th New York Heavy Artillery on his second line, and three regiments making up the third. William S. Truex, the only other brigade under Seymour, took position to Keifer's left, with two regiments on his first line, two on his second line seventy-five yards behind the first, and only one regiment on the third line.[57]

THE ADVANCE

By the time Wright finished the deployment of his corps, dawn was about to break. In the meantime, the Confederates began to fire on Getty's division, which was placed only two hundred yards from the Rebel pickets and six hundred yards from the Confederate main line. "Everything will be ready," Wright had assured army headquarters the evening before. "The corps will go in solid, and I am sure will make the fur fly." Wright further predicted, "If the corps does half as well as I expect we will have broken through the rebel lines fifteen minutes from the word 'go.'"[58]

When the Federals started at 4:40 A.M. on April 2, they nearly fulfilled Wright's prediction to the letter. Individual units moved forward as planned, but Thomas Hyde advanced his brigade of Getty's division in an odd manner. Having formed a column of regiments that would have allowed him to move the men forward as a large group, he chose instead to send each line of the column forward in staggered fashion as if he had a formation of multiple lines and worried that one would interfere with another. Hyde told his second line to wait until the first had moved forward 100 yards before it set off, and the third line left after the second had gone 100 yards away. The fourth line waited until the third had advanced 250 yards before it left the starting point.[59]

In Wheaton's division, Elisha Hunt Rhodes adroitly maneuvered his 2nd Rhode Island through a gap in the Confederate abatis fronting the works. He found a hole in the obstruction the Rebels used to drive a wagon through to collect wood in no-man's land. "I gave the proper commands which caused the Regiment to go through by the flank and then come into line in front of the two gun Batteries."[60]

A combination of factors, including an overwhelming manpower advantage and effective formations and handling of troops contributed to a clean breakthrough by the Sixth Corps. Within half an hour of starting, Wright's men crushed a wide segment of Lee's line and were free to operate behind the enemy position and exploit their success. This compelled the Confederates to shift troops and fight desperately to hold on to the inner lines protecting Petersburg from the west until nightfall, when Lee ordered the evacuation of the city and of Richmond.[61]

In the Appomattox Campaign that followed the collapse of Lee's position at Petersburg, Wright's Sixth Corps continued to operate with a high degree of dexterity in the evolutions of the line. Most of the Army of the Potomac assembled near Amelia Court House by April 5, expecting to advance on Lee's position for a climactic battle. Wright was positioned to the right of the Fifth Corps, now commanded by Charles Griffin. Given the dense vegetation, Wright issued orders for Getty and Seymour to form in two lines, with each regiment or battalion moving forward by the right flank to better negotiate the terrain; when "it becomes proper to resume the formation of line of battle," they would re-form lines. The regiment on the extreme left would serve as the guide, and its commander was to "carefully preserve his original distance" from the right flank of the Fifth Corps. Wright enjoined all other regimental and battalion commanders to "carefully preserve their distances [from neighboring units] and keep the heads of their regiments well up to the front." Wheaton formed a reserve line three hundred yards to the rear of Getty and Seymour, but Wright allowed Wheaton to decide how to form his command. Upon advancing, the Federals discovered that Lee had already evacuated his position at Amelia Court House and had marched west.[62]

CONCLUSION

These five examples of large formations on the corps level during the last half of the Civil War exhibit a variety of elements. Jackson's corps at Chancellorsville was organized in a formation of multiple lines, while Gordon's corps at Fort Stedman formed wholly in columns. Hancock's Second Corps at Spotsylvania on May 12, Warren's Fifth Corps at Five Forks, and Wright's Sixth Corps on April 2 all displayed examples of the ordre mixte. Latitude allowed to division and even brigade commanders produced an interesting mixture of column and line within these three formations.

Why did some of these examples produce success on the battlefield and others did not? There are many factors that affect the outcome of any engagement; formations and maneuvers are but one. It is doubtful that Jackson could have been any more successful if he had used columns instead of multiple lines—most likely his attack would have been more troubled than facilitated in columns. Barlow's column formation helped him bring his division into the Confederate position but contributed greatly to the confusion that developed once the initial victory was accomplished, limiting the Federals' ability to follow up and achieve something greater from their effort. Gordon's use of columns at Fort Stedman probably was the only formation possible given the constricted nature of the battlefield, but he was unable to bring his force to bear properly on the target because of many factors beyond his control. Warren and his subordinates spent many hours forming a complex formation of columns and lines in order to better control their masses in a tricky maneuver. The detailed testimony from the court of inquiry clearly indicates that some of the officers fared better in accomplishing that task than others, saving the day for the Fifth Corps at Five Forks. Finally, Wright's equally complex formation of columns and lines on April 2 worked much more smoothly because it had to execute a simple straight-forward approach to the target and enjoyed a huge superiority of numbers over the defender.

The level of articulation within the ranks of the Army of the Potomac far exceeded that of any other field army by the end of the war. In part, this was because it was compelled to assume the tactical offensive from the initial confrontation of the Overland Campaign on May 5, 1864, until Lee's surrender at Appomattox on April 9, 1865. Army, corps, and division leaders accepted the responsibility of planning and executing dozens of tactical offensives during the course of eleven months of nearly continuous campaigning until they learned how to do it on a large scale and, oftentimes, very effectively.

But the success achieved by some corps leaders in the Army of the Potomac does not mask the fact that articulation on the division and corps level was, at best, uneven during the Civil War. One wonders if that made much difference. After all, a key component of warfare during the Napoleonic era was decentralization of battle control. Corps and even division commanders had considerable leeway to conduct action on their part of the field according to their own decisions as long as what they did comported with the army commander's overall plan for the engagement. Certainly, those officers able to organize large formations and handle them effectively had a better chance of success than those who could not. But these large formations were comparatively rare in the Civil War. Most battles were fought by extended lines of troops, and individual regiments and brigades were either successful or not in their immediate sector. The importance of achieving articulation on the larger level comes into play as a way to exploit that initial, local success. Most commanders' inability to achieve that higher degree of proficiency certainly limited, and at times neutralized, local success in many attacks conducted by both blue and gray during the conflict.

The question of how to exert battle force on enemy formations, break them up, and destroy a position is at the heart of combat effectiveness. Civil War commanders could often do that on one part of the battlefield but fail to take their performance to the next level of effectiveness by exploiting and following through with a massive defeat of the entire opposing army. Some reasons for that failure, which contributed to the length of the war and the seeming indecisiveness of combat, are discussed later. For now, it is worth noting that the difficulty of coordinating corps-level actions certainly was one of the factors that inhibited more militarily decisive action on the field.

≡ 11 ≡

Tactical Developments after the Civil War

In the 1850s, enthusiasts had predicted that the rifle musket would revolutionize military operations. The longer range of the weapon, five hundred yards compared to the one hundred yards of the smoothbore musket, could act upon advancing enemy troops throughout a deeper killing zone. This would increase casualties, make frontal attacks too costly, neutralize the effect of field artillery and cavalry in attacking infantry, and usher in a new era in weaponry.[1]

But these glowing predictions failed to come true in the Civil War. The rifle musket's only improvement over the smoothbore was its much-longer range; there is no evidence it was easier to load or necessarily more accurate, even at short range, than the previous weapon. Yet the evidence to be found in official reports and other sources is conclusive. Civil War infantry combat normally took place at short ranges that were consistent with the range of infantry fights conducted with smoothbore muskets.[2]

There were many reasons why infantry continued to fight at short range during the Civil War. The trajectory of the Minié ball fired from the rifle arced considerably when aimed at long range, making it very difficult to calculate how to deliver the projectile so as to hit a man far away, and the army failed to train its troops to deal with this problem. More importantly, there was a widespread feeling among enlisted men and officers alike that short-range combat was more effective than long-range firing. For the first one hundred yards or so, the trajectory of the rifle-musket ball was comparatively flat, like that of the smoothbore musket's projectile. It was far easier not only to see an enemy soldier at ranges less than one hundred yards but also to deliver the ball so as to hit him. Civil War soldiers naturally believed that close-range fighting was more decisive of results than long-range firing.

As a result, officers of all ranks urged their men to wait until the enemy moved as close as possible before opening fire.[3]

The long-range capabilities of the rifle were never realized by more than a few men in the Civil War. A small percentage of soldiers had a natural aptitude to use weapons effectively, and they were able to experiment with the rifle musket to get the best performance out of it. These men became expert skirmishers, good sharpshooters (the equivalent of modern-day snipers), and trusted gunmen. By the latter half of the war, many units came to rely on these gun-adept soldiers as comrades loaded muskets and passed them to these men for rapid firing when the enemy neared.[4]

But expert gunmen were in the minority during the war. For most troops, the best way to use their rifle muskets was to wait until the enemy was seventy-five, fifty, or even twenty-five yards away before opening fire. It is worth repeating a story regarding Confederate general Benjamin Cheatham. He reported that the overwhelming majority of dead and wounded Confederates at the Battle of Franklin lay within a space only fifty yards from the Union position, even though the battlefield was unusually open and undulating for a long distance. The Federals had every opportunity to fire long range with their rifles if they had wanted to do so at Franklin, but they did not.[5]

The short range at which Civil War combat normally took place was part of a consistent pattern in military history. Infantry combat continued to occur at short ranges throughout the rest of the nineteenth century and into the twentieth century. Even in World War II, Korea, and Vietnam, when American soldiers were armed with small arms that were far more advanced than the rifle musket, infantry fighting reportedly took place at ranges of one hundred yards or less. This fact was worked into the training of these infantrymen as well. Instructors advised them to wait as long as possible to allow the enemy to come within a very short killing zone before engaging them. It is ironic that, even though armed with weapons that had effective ranges of three hundred yards, most infantrymen in the twentieth century used them at ranges consistent with the capabilities of the smoothbore musket of the eighteenth century. Limitations of human sight, the cluttered nature of the battlefield, and the difficulties encountered by average soldiers in using their sophisticated weapons have shaped infantry fighting as close-range combat throughout the past three hundred years.[6]

Realizing this fact allows us to cast a different light on the tactical formations used in the Civil War. A shoulder-to-shoulder linear system was the best formation for armies using smoothbores, and it remained the best tactical system for armies using rifle muskets. In fact, the Civil War was the last conflict in American history in which traditional formations were useful; tactical theory and practice slowly developed after Appomattox toward dispersed order for main-line units.

Several veterans of the conflict wanted to alter the tactical system in order to improve it based on two major factors. First, they wanted to make the method of moving from one formation to another faster and easier, believing that Scott, Hardee, and Casey insisted on conducting those movements by units that were too large to make them efficient. Second, these veterans also wanted to take into account the destructive power that breech-loading and magazine weapons could have on a tightly packed line of troops. In other words, they worried about the possible effect that a heavy volume of fire—not long-range fire—would have on close-order formations. As a single-shot muzzle-loading weapon, the rifle musket could not revolutionize military affairs in terms of volume of fire. But a number of breech-loading and a few magazine-fed weapons were introduced during the Civil War without becoming widespread among Union or Confederate troops.[7]

There were some theorists in the late nineteenth century, such as Arthur Wagner, who remained fascinated with the possibilities of long-range firing and wrote about its potential. Wagner predicted that rifle fire could annoy the enemy at 2,500 yards, or about a mile and a half. He further thought that it could have a serious effect on opposing troops at one mile, become "really effective" at 1,000 yards, and prove "decisive" at 500 yards. But Wagner had not served in the Civil War, and his bloody predictions about massed rifle fire devastating enemy formations at long ranges never proved true. Tactical change instead was driven by the potential inherent in volume of fire.[8]

What follows is a brief survey of developments in tactical theory and practice after 1865. It begins with a discussion of changes proposed by three Civil War veterans in the immediate aftermath of the conflict. Those changes were comparatively slight and did not significantly alter the close-order nature of linear tactics. But by the 1880s, renewed interest in the effect of massed rifle fire on shoulder-to-shoulder formations spurred major efforts to disperse the battle line by creating intervals between soldiers. Thirty years later, World War I saw the end of linear attack formations. Instead, most armies decentralized their tactical formations until squads or platoons became the unit of maneuver. These were armed to the teeth with modern firepower and supported each other while trying to find weak spots in the enemy position. Infiltration tactics finally brought the end of the linear system. Such tactics were further developed in World War II until the fire-team concept that rules small-unit operations into the twenty-first century came into being after 1945.

THREE CIVIL WAR VETERANS AND THEIR VIEWS ON TACTICS

The men who fought the Civil War deserve to be heard when it comes to evaluating the effectiveness of their tactics. While there is no evidence that Confederate veterans offered revisions of the system, several Northern veterans were keenly interested in improving it. Despite the sometimes overblown interpretations accorded those efforts, they really were adjustments to an existing system rather than attempts to dramatically change the basic nature of linear formations and maneuvers.

William Hopkins Morris

A New York native, William Hopkins Morris was descended from two men who had signed the Declaration of Independence. He graduated from West Point in 1851 but later resigned to help his father edit the popular *Home Journal* magazine. The war propelled Morris into service again, as chief of staff to Brig. Gen. John J. Peck during the Peninsula Campaign. He also commanded the 135th New York, which was reorganized as the 6th New York Heavy Artillery by the fall of 1862. Morris was promoted brigadier general of volunteers and led brigades in the Third and Sixth Corps in 1863, only to be badly wounded at Spotsylvania.[9]

After his active service ended, Morris proposed revisions in the army's tactical system to improve what he considered defects. He worked for two years to develop his ideas and published them at his own expense in a book called *Field Tactics for Infantry* in 1864. Morris resigned from the army due to his Spotsylvania wound that August and in early 1865 lobbied Grant to consider his manual seriously. Morris argued that many of the details contained in Casey's manual were not suited to actual conditions on the battlefield. Hilly, wooded terrain so inhibited large formations that unit commanders adopted short cuts to more effectively maneuver in actual practice. "I do not seek to change the tactics," Morris assured Grant, "but I am trying to have a text-book . . . which will teach tactics as *they now are,* in order to ensure uniformity among old and new troops."[10]

In sending a copy of his book to Grant, Morris explained, "I have omitted all movements and explanations which are unimportant *for the field.*" Mostly, he emphasized movement by the flank as the best way to worm a regiment through a heavy forest. Morris also shortened the commands and further simplified the maneuvers so "that new troops can master the subject in half the time required to learn the intricate and impracticable movements of former systems."[11]

Morris forwarded recommendations from several generals and twenty state adjutant generals who favored his "simplified system of Infantry Tactics." Grant read the two-volume work carefully but was not overly impressed. In October 1865 he concluded that the changes were not important enough to justify the expense of throwing out Casey's manual and substituting Morris's work. "Our present tactics, tho' perhaps defective, have been sufficient during the maintenance of a large army, and are sufficient for our present organization," he concluded.[12]

Lewis Wallace

Soon after disposing of Morris's work, Grant considered a revision of the tactical system proposed by another Union general, Lewis Wallace. An Indiana lawyer and volunteer officer during the Mexican War, Wallace served as colonel of the 11th Indiana and commanded troops under Grant at Fort Donelson and Shiloh. He also delayed Lt. Gen. Jubal Early's drive toward Washington, D.C., long enough at the Battle of Monocacy Junction to possibly save the national capital from capture by Confederate forces.[13]

Wallace shared Morris's view that the tactical manuals were burdened with unnecessary commands and ceremonial display rather than practical advice for how to conduct men as they shifted from one maneuver to another. He worked out a revision so that basic maneuvers would be conducted by as small a unit as six soldiers rather than by companies. Wallace also advocated fighting in one rank instead of two but worked up a system to shift from one rank to two or even three if needed. The third major emphasis of his proposed tactics was to place more attention on skirmishing. He believed that Casey did not provide enough detail about that important operation and suggested "a complete and perfect system" to regulate it. In January 1866 Wallace assured Grant that his work posed no threat to the body of knowledge within the current tactical system. "The present *organization* is in no way disturbed by it."[14]

Grant took Wallace's work more seriously than Morris's because it contained some real innovations and significant changes compared to the accepted system. He recommended that a board of three officers examine Wallace's proposal. That board, however, rejected the changes as unnecessary. It found "little to recommend, either, in the deviations from the authorized System, or in the additions thereto." Grant endorsed its findings on April 5, 1866, and Wallace's attempt to replace Casey's manual failed.[15]

Emory Upton

Emory Upton proposed a change in the prevailing tactical system that found favor with the authorities. Born in upstate New York and a graduate of the West Point class of 1861, the young Upton became colonel of the 121st New York in October 1862. He commanded a brigade in the Sixth Corps and gained notice for carefully planning a formation of multiple lines to attack the shoulder of the Mule Shoe Salient at Spotsylvania on May 10, 1864. The attack was at best partially success-ful, but it inspired Grant to plan the massive Second Corps assault on the tip of the salient two days later. Upton went on to lead infantry in the Shenandoah Val-ley Campaign of 1864 and commanded a cavalry division in Brig. Gen. James H. Wilson's mounted raid through Alabama and Georgia at the end of the war. He was made lieutenant colonel of the 25th U.S. Infantry in 1866.[16]

By 1864 Upton had become interested in adjusting the prevailing tactics to prop-erly suit battlefield conditions. "Without being an iconoclast," wrote his colleague and friend Peter S. Michie, "he had no special reverence for established usages, simply because they had the authority of age. He preferred rather to test all things by the standard of utility." Upton concluded that the tactical system was "capable of great improvement." He drew up his ideas and tested them before a gathering of generals who encouraged his further work. "Tactics became the theme of his daily conversation," remembered Michie; it "engrossed his mind almost to the exclu-sion of everything else, and he drew from every battle-field its important lesson."[17]

Upton's reforms shared some of the ideas developed by Wallace. Rather than maneuvering on a small unit of six men, Upton wanted to maneuver on an even smaller unit of four men. He rightly ignored the implications of inverting ranks, for many regimental commanders had demonstrated during the Civil War that the second rank was capable of operating as the first rank if needed. He reduced the number of commands and simplified their wording. Upton also advocated the use of single-rank lines armed with the Spencer rifle, one of the more advanced magazine-fed weapons available by the end of the war. According to Michie, Upton thought one rank armed with the Spencer was equal to two ranks armed with the rifle musket. Moreover, Upton argued that maneuvering on a system of fours could easily work within a formation of either one or two ranks as needed.[18]

After obtaining permission to have his ideas studied by a board early in 1866,

Upton wrote a brief explanation of his work to William T. Sherman in an effort to enlist his support. "If you will take a front of twelve men, in two ranks, and call off by fours from the right you will have three sets of fours," Upton began. "If now you give the command fours right (or left), you will form a column of fours. . . . [T]his column can be formed in line, to the right by the command Fours right; to the left by the command Fours left; to the front by the command Right (or Left) front into line, and to the rear by the same commands, after having wheeled about by fours." Upton thought Sherman would endorse his use of one rank armed with a repeating rifle because, while the two happened to meet while traveling to Nashville, Sherman had told him that most of the fighting during the Atlanta Campaign was conducted by skirmish lines. Upton was thinking in terms of thinning the fighting ranks because, with magazine rifles like the Spencer, it now was possible to do so without diminishing firepower.[19]

The board examined Upton's proposal in 1866 and recommended that it be adopted as the official manual of the army early the following year. But opposition by a number of officers compelled authorities to appoint a second board in June 1867. This board included several high-ranking Union generals from the Civil War, including Grant himself. The primary objections to Upton came from former generals of the Federal army as well, including Thomas W. Sherman, Silas Casey, Morris, and Henry J. Hunt. Thomas Sherman's point was that the unit of four came entirely from the front rank, leaving the rear rank little to do. The second board witnessed demonstrations of Upton's tactics by cadets and engineer troops at West Point. Its members questioned Upton and examined all objections raised by the critics. Once completed, they recommended that the new manual replace Casey's book. It was officially adopted in August 1867. Six years later another board was appointed to adapt Upton's concepts to artillery and cavalry maneuvers.[20]

UPTON'S MANUAL

Upton's book was published in 1867 as *A New System of Infantry Tactics Double and Single Rank, Adapted to American Topography and Improved Fire-Arms.* The author made it clear that his system was based on a maneuver unit of four men, but he organized the manual in exactly the same way that Scott, Hardee, and Casey had organized their own books. It started with General Instruction, then progressed to the School of the Soldier, School of the Company, Instructions for Skirmishers, School of the Battalion, Evolutions of a Brigade, Evolutions of a Division, and

Evolutions of a Corps. Upton managed to pack all this into one volume instead of three (mostly by cutting down on what he considered extraneous wording and commands). He also included extracts from the report of the first board that had approved his manual in order to lend authority to his work.[21]

One need only compare Upton's manual with that of his predecessors to realize that his changes were comparatively small, retaining the linear system largely intact. This is not to minimize his significant alterations but to point out that his system was still a linear one, as he himself admitted. Upton did not change the basic organization of the regiment or interfere with the traditional method of arraying companies within the battalion. He even retained the old concept of placing men within the line according to height.[22]

The new aspects of Upton's system involved the use of fours and a flexible use of double- and single-rank formations. All maneuvers, including wheeling and moving by the flank, were to be undertaken by fours. His system made these maneuvers quicker and easier for soldiers to learn. Upton envisioned the continued use of multiple lines within a brigade formation, specifying that an interval of twenty-four paces should exist between the flanks of battalions within a brigade line. The distance between the first and second lines of a brigade would depend on circumstances and the terrain. He also advocated multiple lines within a division formation.[23]

Upton replicated the instructions for skirmishers to be found in previous manuals, but he added some thoughts that went beyond teaching formations and maneuvers. He urged officers to "impress each man with the idea of his individuality, and the responsibility that rests upon him." To be good skirmishers, soldiers had to develop "the feeling that they cannot be whipped, and that, when compelled to give ground, a new position will be rapidly gained from which the action will be renewed." No previous author except Casey attempted to write significant directions such as this in their manuals.[24]

Perhaps the board best summarized the advantages of Upton's new system, prompting the author to include its assessment in his book. The manual "dispenses with the manoeuvring by the rear rank, by inversion, and the counter-march, and substitutes therefore rapid and simple conversions of front, and changes from column into line. . . . [I]t increases the number of modes of passing from the order in column to the order in line, facing in any direction; diminishes the time required for these changes, and preserves always the front rank in front."[25]

Upton's manual found much wider acceptance than Morris's and Wallace's attempts to revise the standard tactics. Morris's changes were minor, while Wallace had the right idea (focusing on a smaller maneuver unit of six men) but failed to fully develop the potential of his concept. Officers from John Pope to Ulysses Grant became strong advocates of Upton's work. "I have seen the system applied to company and battalion drills," Grant wrote, "and am fully satisfied of its superior merits and adaptability to our service." But he inaccurately characterized the manual as "no translation but a purely American work." In reality, Upton retained most of the wording and commands from all previous manuals, which had been translations of French books. Upton's use of fours and of a single rank were new adaptations to the American situation, it is true, but that did not transform the entire work into an "American" system of tactics.[26]

William Sherman also supported Upton's work, believing the wider use of breech-loading weapons justified his innovations. Sherman credited him with being the first to exploit the advantages inherent in a small unit of maneuver such as the grouping of four men. "Upton's tactics is another result of experience," wrote Union volunteer officer Benjamin Scribner of Indiana. "The commands in battle of the old tactics were very complicated and impracticable." Upton simplified them greatly, in Scribner's view. It is true that a handful of veterans, including Casey and Morris, opposed the adoption of Upton's book, but the majority opinion seems to have been overwhelmingly positive.[27]

Modern scholarly opinion of Upton's manual tends to be heavily guided by the assumption that the rifle musket revolutionized warfare. Therefore historians who have written about tactical formations in the Civil War seem to look for any sign of modernization of the system to accommodate those supposedly revolutionary changes. They criticize commanders for not recognizing those changes and altering their tactics and praise Upton for his attempts to do so. At times this praise can be overblown; at other times historians criticize Upton for not modernizing enough. Henry Osterhoudt, in an unpublished dissertation about tactics in the American army, thought Upton should have eliminated the battle line altogether in 1867. Paddy Griffith, however, has been about the only historian to correctly point out that Upton's manual was not a revolutionary departure from the previous tactical system.[28]

To build further on Griffith's point, there was no need for Upton to revolutionize the old tactical system, for it worked perfectly well for the type of weapon generally used in the Civil War. Ironically, the breech-loading and magazine rifles that Upton's work was adapted to were not generally issued to the U.S. Army for decades after the war. The trap-door Springfield, an attempt to convert the muzzle-loading rifle musket of the Civil War to a breech-loading weapon, remained a single-shot rifle that lagged far behind many small arms available in the immediate postwar period. But this converted rifle musket remained standard issue for decades to come. Upton's manual was more directly relevant to such rifles as the Spencer, the Henry, or the Remington, all of them magazine weapons that could be reloaded much faster than the trap-door Springfield.[29]

TACTICAL DEVELOPMENTS, 1877–1914

By 1877, American tactical theorists became more alarmed about the possible range at which decisive battle could take place when they read reports of the Russo-Turkish War. Russian attacks on a fortified Turkish camp at Plevna seemed to portend the doom of close-order formations. Ottoman soldiers armed with Henry rifles reportedly devastated Russian formations at long range with small-arms fire.[30]

As a result, Upton began to revise his tactics and was largely finished with the work before his death on March 15, 1881. Peter Michie finished it for him. The revision consisted primarily of urging the government to reorganize the regiment into three battalions of four companies each. Infantry units would move toward the battlefield in traditional column formations but deploy before coming under enemy fire. Upton sought to eliminate the battle line altogether. He proposed that two companies of each battalion deploy in loose order to skirmish, detailing some of their manpower to act as supports and reserves for the skirmishers; the remaining two companies of each battalion would constitute the battalion reserve. Upton proposed a truly revolutionary change in this revision, deleting the main feature of linear tactical formations. As Michie put it, "the first importance is given to skirmishing" because the increased range of deadly fire now seemed to mandate a reliance on open order rather than the shoulder-to-shoulder formations of the old battle line.[31]

Morris also read the reports about Plevna and, like Upton, tried to revise his own book to accommodate longer-range fire. He adopted Upton's maneuver on a unit of four men, worked out a system of using two ranks to maneuver but only one to engage the enemy, and streamlined the language of command. His work was only a slight improvement on Upton's 1867 manual in that Morris gave far more significance to the rear rank. Morris did not attempt to completely alter the linear system and was still a step or two behind Upton in conceptualizing change in tactical formations, for he did not greatly emphasize loose-order formations or skirmishing.[32]

Ironically, neither Morris's work nor Upton's revisions were adopted by the army. Even though many theorists in America argued that loose-order formations were necessary to deal with the new small arms, those weapons still were not adopted by the government as general issue to the U.S. Army. The experience of fighting a highly mobile enemy during the Plains Indian Wars of the 1860s and 1870s also encouraged officers to favor loose-order formations, but weapons procurement continued to lag far behind developing doctrine.[33]

The army began to work on a completely new manual in 1888 by appointing a board that called for suggestions. It received twenty-one proposals from various people. The board's recommendations led to the official adoption of *The Infantry Drill Regulations, U.S. Army* in October 1891. It was a thoroughly different product compared to Scott, Hardee, Casey, and Upton. The new manual was not a translation of a foreign publication but a new kind of military book that recognized the difference between drill and battlefield tactics. Similar books were also produced for the artillery and cavalry, all of them called the Leavenworth manuals because the board met at Fort Leavenworth, Kansas.[34]

The tactical system adopted in 1891 followed through with current thinking, adapting to what was perceived as a major threat to close-order formations. It mandated a formation of three lines, the first being a skirmish line, the second a line of support for the skirmishers, and the third a reserve line. Commanders were allowed to choose between loose order and close order, depending on circumstances. The 1891 manual continued Upton's emphasis on the group of four as the essential unit of maneuver. It identified a squad consisting of two groups of four men each as the unit of maneuver and emphasized the increased responsibilities on lower-ranking company officers and noncommissioned officers to control their men. The 1891 manual also was the first drill regulation in American history to dispense with the shoulder-to-shoulder formation of a battle line, relying primarily on skirmishing to deal with the enemy. Moreover, skirmishers were enjoined to maneuver in short rushes, seeking cover where possible. The new manual also gave impetus for the reorganization of the regiment into three battalions of four companies each, though Congress hesitated to authorize this until 1898 because of the expense of creating two new companies for each of the twenty-five permanent regiments of the U.S. Army.[35]

No officer was more impressed by the possibility of long-range rifle fire than Arthur Wagner. A graduate of the West Point class of 1875, Wagner served on the plains in an infantry regiment and spent half a year observing European armies, especially the Germans, in 1888. He wrote a book on military operations entitled *Organization and Tactics,* which was published in 1895.[36]

Wagner understood the need to use loose-order formations to reduce casualties in the face of an increased volume of rifle fire, but he wanted to avoid opening up the order so much that formations were unable to deliver a heavy volume of fire in return. He noted that French and German formations retained the battle line but created intervals of a couple of paces between each man and longer distances between multiple lines of troops.[37]

Wagner also advised American officers to take long-range rifle fire seriously. He advocated opening concentrated fire when the enemy was 2,000 yards—more than a mile—away. But he never addressed the important issue of how one could see a man at that long distance, much less fire effectively at him. Presumably, the enemy would also be in loose order, making it even more difficult to detect him at that distance. Wagner urged commanders to send out a line of scouts 150 yards in front of the first line to find enemy positions and to snipe. He advised that the three lines laid down in the 1891 manual should be 600 yards behind each other on the battlefield and that the first line should advance in rushes of 30–50 yards. Wagner warned against a general frontal attack unaccompanied by a threat to the enemy's flank, believing that the combination of the two approaches would work best. He also warned against using complicated movements to change the direction of advance by a unit while under fire. It was acceptable to conduct such things as a half wheel before the heavy firing started, but "any movement except straight ahead or direct to the rear" was dangerous to cohesion under fire.[38]

Recent conflicts served as units of study for Wagner. Because the Franco-Prussian War of 1870–71 was fought by armies generally armed with magazine rifles, he sought any evidence that either side used loose-order formations and rushes to approach their enemy. He also found evidence that when traditional columns were used, the results included heavy losses and stalled offensives. Wagner viewed the Russo-Turkish War of 1877–78 in a similar light, noting that the Russians initially used close-order formations, often in column, and suffered for it. They adapted and experimented with loose-order formations in later battles.[39]

The Spanish-American War of 1898 offered the U.S. Army some opportunity to test its new tactics. By then it had adopted the Danish Krag-Jorgensen, a magazine-fed bolt-action rifle, as its standard-issue infantry weapon, although volunteer regiments still used black-powder Springfield single-shot and breech-loading arms. Wagner was a keen observer of operations during the campaign in Cuba. He believed the tactical doctrine and the training regimen that was in place worked well on these battlefields. Wagner was impressed that few commanders adhered slavishly to the doctrine but were ready to improvise as needed to meet unexpected problems. In practice, regular and volunteer regiments divided into battalions even though the army had not yet mandated the battalion organization. The only flaw in the doctrine he perceived was the reliance on squads as the basic unit of maneuver. At least as practiced by the 71st New York, it produced confusion that contributed to a panic among the members of that regiment. "I have long been of the opinion that the squad system has more defects than advantages," concluded Wagner, "and I think it would be advisable to have the Drill Regulations so revised as to admit of a simple and prompt deployment without attempting to use the squad system."[40]

But when the army revised its 1891 regulations in 1903–1904, it continued to emphasize the squad as the basic unit of maneuver. These revisions offered detailed information about how to advance toward an enemy position without overly exposing the troops while retaining enough command and control to deliver heavy fire on the target. Wagner's fantastic estimates of the extreme long range at which rifle fire would be effective were largely ignored. Skirmishers were to be deployed 1,200 yards from the enemy (in contrast to Wagner's argument that volley fire should be delivered when 2,000 yards from opposing troops). The regulations urged skirmishers to go forward in rushes of 50 yards when within 1,000 yards of the enemy and mandated intervals of three feet between each man on the skirmish line to avoid presenting a massed target. The new manual also offered guidance about how and when troops should fire while advancing, normally doing so by squads and platoons that remained stationary while other squads and platoons rushed forward.[41]

Yet another revision of the drill regulations took place in 1911, responding to critics who argued that the previous system was too rigid. As a result, the newly revised doctrine retained all the essentials of the old system but allowed unit commanders much more freedom to decide the details in the field. It also placed greater emphasis on taking advantage of cover on the battlefield to reduce losses.[42]

The American adoption of new tactical formations reflected developments in major European nations. In Germany theorists divided into camps supporting either loose-order formations or greater centralized control over the men. What drove this discussion, at least initially, was not the longer range of small-arms fire but the increased volume of it due to the widespread use of breech-loaders and magazine rifles. Advocates of loose-order formations eventually dominated the discussion and influenced the opening up of German tactical formations over time.[43]

The British tactical system emphasized the first line of an infantry formation loosening into a skirmish line, with the second line acting as the skirmish support and the third acting as the reserve for the whole. This dispersed manpower but in depth, not laterally, because of the difficulties officers would encounter in controlling a battalion that was too spread out. They anticipated receiving and delivering long-range rifle fire (up to 3,000 yards) on the battlefield. By 1893, British tactics included an advance toward the enemy by rushes of forty to fifty paces conducted by alternating sections within the company.[44]

Events during the infamous Black Week of December 10–17, 1899, during the Second Boer War in southern Africa, seemed to confirm the wisdom of greater dispersal on the battlefield. British troops massed in tightly packed columns suffered heavy casualties in the face of Boer rifle fire. At the Battle of Magersfontein Kopje, the Highland Brigade of 3,500 men was closed en masse within a space about 40 yards wide and 160 yards deep. This formation would have presented an inviting target to any defender, no matter what type of weapon he used. As a partial explanation for the British action, the advance toward the fortified Boer position was conducted at night and in the rain, and officers felt the need for maximum control of their men. Yet as a result, about 650 men were lost in the failed assault.[45]

WORLD WAR I

No matter how far Western armies had gone along the path toward dispersal of manpower, the Great War of 1914–18 upset all expectations about the nature of military operations in the modern era. It took place on a scale that dwarfed previous campaigns and involved huge armies made possible in part by an impressive growth of population in Europe and North America during the nineteenth century. The large armies made it possible to create continuous fronts along national frontiers. The western front stretched for upward of five hundred miles, making it impossible to find and turn the enemy flank. When troops dug into the earth for protection, massive field fortifications increased defensive power by a great deal. Moreover, previous fears that long-range rifle fire would shape infantry operations disappeared as modern artillery came into play. Important technical advances in many areas affecting field artillery, combined with massive production of pieces, allowed artillerists to dominate the western front. Breech-loading mechanisms, recoil systems, and high-explosive propellants revolutionized artillery practice. The longer range of the big guns, as much as 4,000 yards, represented a four-fold increase over the reach of Civil War rifled cannon. Whereas the rifle musket had inflicted at least 80 percent of the casualties in the Civil War, artillery now accounted for at least 80 percent of the losses suffered on the western front.[46]

Before the United States entered the war in 1917, European armies struggled to deal with the new tactical realities they encountered. The British used lines and columns to create multiple formations, or "waves," in their early offensive battles in 1915–16, as men moved forward in dispersed order with ample intervals between them. Some of these battles witnessed at least limited success by the attacking British troops, while others resulted in casualties that were seemingly too heavy to justify the gain.[47]

But the wellspring of new tactics emerged not so much from these large-scale attacks as in the small trench warfare that developed along the lines between major offensives. The British began to conduct trench raids with small units designed to harass the enemy, capture a bit of advantageous ground, or grab German prisoners for interrogation. This experience honed small-unit tactics and pointed the way toward their increased use in major offensives designed to break enemy lines. Gradually, the idea of letting battalion, squad, or platoon commanders have more latitude in conducting their operations and trusting to a more heavily armed small unit to find weak spots in the opposing position began to develop. Much had to be done to support this devolution of control and initiative within a larger tactical plan. Small units went forward protected by creeping barrages of friendly artillery fire, and thus the British had to accumulate enough good pieces with ample supplies of ammunition to support them. The small units also had to be armed with the latest weapons that could spew a heavy volume of fire and yet be portable enough so that one man could carry and use them.[48]

By the winter of 1917–18, nine months after the United States entered the war but before American troops were able to participate in the fighting, the development of infiltration tactics in the British army came to fruition. The platoon became "a complete and independent 'tactical unit,'" according to Paddy Griffith. Two British manuals spelled out the process, which included a creeping barrage, the platoon advancing in two waves with supports, and Lewis guns to increase individual firepower. Griffith believes this scheme was "still essentially linear" but rested responsibility on a small unit armed to the teeth. In fact, Griffith convincingly argues that dispersed lines were still important to the British even in the latter stages of the war. "Far from being the antithesis of infiltration, in fact, waves permitted the infiltrators to be systematically backed up and sustained within a short timescale, wherever they found an opening" in the enemy lines.[49]

Historians generally praise the British for honing infiltration tactics during the last hundred days of the war, when they conducted successful assaults. According to Griffith, they adopted units of maneuver smaller than the platoon. The blob system included small groups of men, each blob consisting of a section of nine troops and organized in a pattern compared to those next to them. In this way, four blobs could advance with maximum flexibility and initiative, supporting each other while penetrating less well defended ground between German strongpoints.[50]

The German army went through a similar process of developing infiltration tactics as the British. In the 1880s it still emphasized close-order formations, especially columns, so officers could better control their men. By 1914 the tactical doctrine became more open to dispersed order. Soon after the first major battles, the Germans quickly converted to open-order formations and began to experiment with infiltration tactics. Capt. Willy Martin Rohr developed a squad of storm troopers to replace skirmishers at the forefront of battle, armed with a variety of weapons and specially trained to break open enemy positions. Rohr set up a training camp to disseminate his ideas.[51]

The Germans did not rely on one man to develop infiltration tactics but took cues from every possible source. This included a pamphlet written by a young French officer named Andre Laffargue in 1916 that advocated infiltration units backed up by linear formations. Infiltration tactics had not become dominant in the German army at the time of the costly offensive at Verdun, but the lessons of that protracted battle included the need for "close coordination of heavy weapons at the lowest possible level and . . . squads capable of moving and fighting as independent units," in the words of historian Bruce Gudmundsson. Also, the great defensive battles fought by the Germans in 1916 led them to develop a system of defense in depth, thinning out the forward line and placing their main strength much farther back. This elastic defense in depth emphasized the need for all units to launch counterattacks on their own initiative whenever they saw an opportunity. Intensive German trench raiding between offensives also contributed its lessons to the development of small-unit tactics.[52]

The winter of 1917–18 witnessed the full development of German infiltration tactics at the same time that the concept jelled among British forces. Erich Ludendorff became a champion of the idea and more thoroughly trained German soldiers in these tactics than did the British. He designated 56 divisions as special storm-troop units and gave them priority in training, replacement personnel, and weapons. The other 136 divisions were designated as trench divisions and had to make do with older men and second-rate weapons. Battalion commanders were responsible for sending out squads to conduct infiltrations and coordinating artillery support for them. Commanders above the battalion level also coordinated resources but rarely spelled out in detail how squad leaders were to accomplish their goal. A remarkable degree of decentralization of command and control characterized German storm-troop tactics.[53]

The distribution of modern small arms was a key aspect of infiltration tactics. By the end of 1917, the idea of a company uniformly armed with bolt-action rifles had disappeared in the German army. "Every infantry unit down to the platoon was a combined arms force," according to Gudmundsson, "capable of supporting its maneuver with its own fire." They possessed "a greater variety as well as a greater quantity of firepower than ever before."[54]

The Russians, Austro-Hungarians, and Italians organized special-assault units, but the Germans developed infiltration tactics far more than any other belligerent. The American army was woefully behind the learning curve in this area, and many factors accounted for it. Gen. John J. Pershing was convinced that the Allies had committed a grave error in developing concepts of trench warfare. He held to a belief that rugged American soldiers well trained at rifle practice could break through the trenches and engage the Germans in open-field maneuvers to bring the war to an end quickly. But Pershing's view was unrealistic, even naive. When U.S. troops finally engaged in combat on the western front in the summer and fall of 1918, they advanced in dispersed lines as the British and Germans had done early in the conflict and suffered heavily for it. Pershing's headquarters staff analyzed American performance in September 1918 and concluded that commanders employed formations that were too dense and inflexible. Poor coordination of support arms, inadequate initiative by junior-level officers, and little use of fire-and-maneuver tactics also hampered operations. The training regimen established in France was inconsistent, with some units receiving instruction in fire and maneuver but not others. Although the American Expeditionary Force (AEF) had 1.4 million troops in Europe, it displayed a serious "lack of tactical acumen" in the words of historian Timothy K. Nenninger.[55]

These problems severely limited progress during the early phase of the Meuse-Argonne offensive that began in late September 1918. Rather than a war-winning breakthrough, this largest American offensive of the war bogged down in rugged terrain against a much smaller but far more experienced German force. But the Americans began to learn on the job. In late October a pause ensued in operations as officers tried to understand the problems and fix them. The AEF began to improve soon after. It more widely adopted fire-and-maneuver tactics and combined-arms operations among small units. Several American divisions performed well during the final stage of the offensive before the armistice ended the war on November 11. While Gudmundsson believes the Americans ignored infiltration tactics, the truth is that a handful of officers understood the concept and experimented with it before the end of hostilities. Col. Conrad Babcock in the 89th Division encouraged training of four-man teams armed with heavy weapons to move forward and exploit weaknesses in German positions.[56]

All historians agree that the short time of participation in large-scale operations was a key factor in the poor tactical performance of the AEF. With more experience the Americans began to show signs of learning the same lessons as the British and Germans. Mark Ethan Grotelueschen intensely studied the operations of the 1st, 2nd, 26th, and 77th Divisions and believes those units "experienced significant doctrinal adjustment and operational improvement" by the end of the war. Yet he warns that these four divisions were exceptional rather than typical. For the most part, the Americans pushed through the war employing "clumsy tactics," according to historian Edward Lengel. They never fully developed true infiltration tactics.[57]

But then again, infiltration tactics did not prove to be a war-winning innovation for the British or Germans. While their use was sometimes effective at breaking open enemy positions, supporting troops often could not exploit that advantage and achieve important strategic results. This fact is reminiscent of Civil War linear tactics. Historians describe many factors affecting this situation, but they tend to point to the rail-based logistical system supporting both sides of the western front. The defender could always shift reinforcements to threatened sectors in time to contain an initial breach of their trench system, and the attacker could rely only on foot power to move forward—the equation usually favored the defender. Therefore initial victories such as the German counterattack at Cambrai from November 30 to December 15, 1917, and the great German spring offensive of March 21–31, 1918, failed to pay the attacker larger dividends.[58]

Paddy Griffith has pointed out that the German storm-troop successes of World War I tended to be won against ill-prepared sectors of the British line. At Cambrai the British had only recently advanced and created a salient in the area by the effective use of tanks. They had not had time to consolidate their new ground before the Germans counterattacked. In the spring of 1918, the greatest German success occurred against a British force that was not in good shape. Griffith concludes that infiltration tactics worked "only when the enemy defences [were] crumbling or incomplete."[59]

Infiltration tactics certainly were no panacea for the problems of trench warfare, but they did point toward a new direction in tactical development. Dense formations were now a thing of the past. Devolution of command and control from the regiment down to platoons and squads, the arming of small units with a variety of modern weapons, and covering the infantry with heavy artillery support were among the lasting results of World War I. How far down the order of battle one emphasized fire-and-maneuver methods varied from army to army, but the old linear system was now a relic of the past as far as combat operations were concerned.

TACTICAL DEVELOPMENTS, 1919 TO THE PRESENT

In 1919 the U.S. Army assembled a board on tactics to evaluate the experience of World War I. The board came to the conclusion that the army needed to move farther toward fire-and-maneuver operations and lessen the use of lines and columns on the battlefield. The revised regulations were published in August of that year. With the development of effective automatic weapons small enough to be operated by one man (the barrage-assault rifle), a further reorganization of the basic infantry unit became necessary by the end of the 1930s. As Lt. Col. Walter R. Wheeler explained in his book *The Infantry Battalion in War*, the battalion consisted of three companies of troops, one machine-gun company, and one headquarters company. It was "the fundamental tactical unit of the infantry arm, . . . the largest unit whose chief can personally lead maneuver." At 824 men, the battalion was the size of a strong infantry regiment of the Civil War.[60]

Within the battalion, each infantry company consisted of three platoons. Company commanders normally kept one platoon in reserve while advancing the other two toward the objective. Each platoon consisted of two sections of six squads each. One man in each squad carried a barrage-assault rifle and was required to carry 480 rounds of ammunition. Each soldier armed with a bolt-action magazine rifle had to carry 100 rounds of ammunition into battle. As Wheeler proudly put it, the "infantry battalion is the keystone of the arch of the military structure."[61]

But the 1919 board and Wheeler's book indicate that the American army had not absorbed all the lessons of World War I. The basic unit of maneuver remained the battalion rather than the platoon or the squad. The distribution of weapons capable of a heavy volume of fire was very limited. In fact, according to Kenneth Finlayson, the U.S. Army continued to operate with an emphasis "on the primacy of the infantry rifleman and steadfastly clung to that idea" until the outbreak of World War II. While the interwar doctrine reduced dense formations, it did not fully develop anything like the German storm-troop tactics. It was a generic, all-purpose tactical system that continued to reflect a flawed concept from the days before the Great War despite three revisions of the regulations adopted in 1923, 1939, and 1941.[62]

The U.S. Army entered World War II still identifying the battalion as the basic unit of maneuver. The 1941 edition of Field Manual 100-5, *Field Service Regulations, Operations,* advised units to envelope the enemy rather than penetrate prepared positions. Two companies were to advance side by side, with the third company behind as the battalion reserve. The field manual stressed the importance of cooperation between all arms to make the advance work. It also recognized, as historian Michael Doubler noted, that "battalion-size attacks were usually nothing more than frontal assaults against enemy defenses."[63]

American tactics at the start of World War II were amenable to change. In fact, the great strength of the U.S. Army during that conflict was adaptation. In contrast to its experience in World War I, the army instituted a thorough system of learning from experience on a continual basis to change its doctrine to meet developing circumstances. While the AEF on the western front had mostly displayed "tactical ineptitude," American units deployed around the world in the 1940s might well have exceeded any other army in their ability to improve. It was an impressive example of tactical virtuosity.[64]

Ironically, the experience of combat in World War II and in subsequent conflicts continued to disprove the fears of nineteenth-century theorists that long-range rifle fire would dominate infantry combat. Short-range infantry fights continued to characterize operations. During the Korean War, the Defense Department commissioned the Operations Research Office of Johns Hopkins University to conduct a study of the current small arms used by the U.S. Army and make recommendations for change. As part of this study, Norman Hitchman conducted historical research, examined conditions in Korea, and arranged for target practice by soldiers rated as expert marksmen to cover all angles of the question.[65]

Hitchman's report confirmed the continuity of short-range fighting. He found that on the island of Bougainville during World War II, nearly all rifle-bullet hits on American wounded occurred at ranges less than seventy-five yards. Among wounded in the Turkish Brigade in Korea, the mean range of 108 rifle-bullet hits was a little more than one hundred yards. A survey of 602 American soldiers in Korea revealed that 80–90 percent of them said that at least 95 percent of their rifle fire took place at ranges less than three hundred yards. Hitchman conducted research on visibility in battle by studying topographical maps of a wide range of terrains. He concluded that in 70 percent of the cases, a prone rifleman could see an erect man only if the target was less than three hundred yards away. Hitchman concluded that "the infantry basic weapon is actually used, on the average, at shorter ranges than commonly believed."[66]

Another of Hitchman's conclusions related to the casualty rate of combat over time. He studied estimates of losses from engagements in ancient history to the twentieth century and decided "that battles are no more bloody now, despite vastly 'improved' weapons, than they were in the days of the short sword: the casualties incurred per number of men engaged per unit of time remains about constant. In fact, it may well be that the sword is much more lethal than conventional weapons because it can be directed with more control at the vulnerable areas." Hitchman thought the cause of this lay in the fact that modern weapons increased the zone of fire but failed to increase the effectiveness of fire because the bullets were greatly dispersed, making it a matter of mere chance that any of them hit a human target. Moreover, those human targets were now taking cover at every opportunity. Dispersed formations decreased concentration of manpower and thus lessened the number of vulnerable targets. Hitchman concluded that modern assault weapons were "little if any more effective" in terms of casualty rates than old-fashioned weapons.[67]

Hitchman also conducted tests of soldiers identified as "expert rifleman" (the army's highest rank of marksmanship) and "marksmen" (the lowest qualified grade). His conclusions must have disappointed many officers. Hitchman found that at ranges up to one hundred yards, these two grades of marksmen had a high probability of hitting the target. But from one hundred to three hundred yards, the hit probability sharply dropped; at five hundred yards it was unsatisfactory. The marksmanship of most experts failed to come close to the design capability of the weapons they used. Hitchman found one man, a Sergeant Justice, whose performance on the test range at Fort Benning actually came very close to fulfilling the capability of his weapon. But Justice told Hitchman that it would take nine years of training to reach his level of expertise. Hitchman himself estimated that it was doubtful if 10 percent of the average recruits in the army could ever hope to reach that level of capability even if they were given nine years to try.[68]

Hitchman contended that the army should recognize important facts about infantry combat. It will always be conducted at short ranges. Only the first round in a burst of automatic-rifle fire can be aimed at a specific target. Marksmanship training is wasted on all but a small handful of naturally apt men, and a smaller-caliber weapon probably would be just as effective as the .30-caliber small arms then in use. Moreover, smaller-caliber ammunition would be lighter to transport to the combat zone and easier for the soldier to carry.[69]

This is what came of the misplaced belief that long-range rifle fire would revolutionize conditions on the battlefield. Civil War officers were correct to urge their troops to wait until the enemy arrived within short range before opening fire, despite the five-hundred-yard range of their rifle muskets. Shoulder-to-shoulder linear tactics were the correct formations for Civil War armies using that rifle musket just as dispersed tactics became the correct formations to be used in the mid-twentieth century when the battlefield was dominated by artillery and automatic weapons. But the notion that the rifle musket exceeded the smoothbore in killing effect is wrong. Equally wrong is the notion that automatic weapons exceed the killing effect of the rifle musket. As Hitchman cogently pointed out, the killing effect of thrusting swords in ancient warfare probably was greater than that of automatic weapons in the twentieth century. The proposition that battlefield loss ratios have remained relatively constant over 2,000 years is fantastic, but the evidence points to its reality.[70]

From 1865 to the late twentieth century, great changes took place in the formations and maneuvers associated with infantry combat. Initially, the direction of change was toward dispersed linear order, creating intervals between men in battle. Then with World War I, the direction suddenly shifted toward decentralization and dispersal of troops. Small units such as the battalion, the platoon, and the squad became the key to infiltration tactics. Commanders sought ways to bypass enemy strongpoints and exploit weaknesses in order to penetrate and break a continuous front. It did not prove to be a decisive breakthrough in solving the tactical problems of the western front, but the war gave rise to decades of experimentation. For example, the Americans continued to focus on the battalion rather than the platoon or squad as the basic maneuver unit during the interwar period.

According to Bruce Gudmundsson, the modern fire-team concept "was not universally accepted until well after World War II." This refers to the smallest unit of maneuver developed in the long transition from linear tactics to the modern dispersed system of organizing men for combat. Fire teams consist normally of only four men each, reminiscent of Upton's use of fours as a basis for shifting from one formation to another in 1867. It is also reminiscent of the British blob system of World War I. Fully automatic small arms are one of the factors that make the four-man team feasible on the battlefield.[71]

The current tactical system is clearly spelled out in the army's Field Manual 3-21.8, adopted in March 2007 to replace Field Manual 7-8, which had been in use since 1992. *The Infantry Rifle Platoon and Squad* explains the fire-team concept in very simple and detailed language. There is plenty of jargon, but it is always defined and explained, in contrast to the Civil War–era drill manuals that retained clear understanding of technical terms for those few men who were experts in the tactical system. Moreover, another key difference in modern manuals is that there is no single book explaining the tactical system in several volumes, but a plethora of field manuals designed to cover specific aspects of it as applied to various levels in the army organization. The clarity and ease of understanding is remarkable compared to mid-nineteenth-century manuals.[72]

"The Infantry's primary role is close combat," proclaims Field Manual 3-21.8. It stresses the combination of firepower and maneuver working hand in hand to achieve battlefield success. The infantry fire team is the basis of this system, with each squad divided into two fire teams, each armed with a variety of weapons. The teams are arranged in formations, some of which are similar to those used in the Civil War. The primary formations are line, column, vee, box, wedge, diamond, and echelon.[73]

In the line formation, the fire teams are arrayed flank to flank for maximum firepower to the front, although the flanks are vulnerable. One of the teams is designated as the guide for the movement of the others. In the column formation, the teams have maximum firepower to the flanks but less to the front. The column is easier for platoon leaders to control than the line. The vee formation combines the assets of both line and column by placing two fire teams flank to flank in front with others in column behind them. The other formations—box, wedge, diamond, and echelon—also mix the arrangement so as to provide differing degrees of firepower to flank, front, and rear as needed. Within the fire teams, individual soldiers normally are placed ten yards apart in the same formations if advancing over open ground. In other words, the same seven formations (line, column, vee, box, wedge, diamond, and echelon) order the placement of individuals within the fire team as well as order the placement of fire teams to each other. The same formations order the placement of squads within the platoon.[74]

Modern armies thus continue to use formations similar to some aspects of the linear system in order to achieve command and control over the dispersed nature of small-unit action—to do otherwise would produce chaos. When it comes to marching troops outside the combat zone, training them, or conducting reviews and parades that remain important aspects of indoctrination and unit pride, the old linear system is used almost as it was during the Civil War. What really changed from 1865 to 2007 were the formations in which troops engaged in combat. Admittedly, that was an important and fundamental change in the tactics of battle, but there was no similar revolutionary change in the tactical formations used in noncombat functions within the army.

Linear tactics played an equally important role in the noncombat functions of the Civil War army as well. Today the marching rate tends to be a bit faster than was common in the 1860s. For example, quick time is defined as 112–120 steps per minute (with a step defined as thirty inches) compared to 110 steps per minute (at twenty-eight-inch steps) in the Civil War era. But the fact that this has to be defined today indicates the reliance modern armies still place on certain aspects of controlling and maneuvering troops through the old linear system, which has lasted for three hundred years.[75]

12

Comparison and Context

The troops raised by the Union and Confederate governments to fight the Civil War made up the largest, most effective citizen armies yet organized in North America. Close to three million volunteer soldiers served in blue and gray during America's worst internal conflict. The country called forth these men, gave them weapons and a drill manual, and expected them to learn how to be effective in the field without a standardized method of basic training. Despite these hurdles, most of them accomplished this fundamental goal of military mobilization. It was an impressive achievement.

Two key factors underlay this accomplishment. Civil War officers used an effective system of tactics. Most of them took the job of learning it seriously and imparted that earnestness to their men. Ironically, despite the lack of standardized training, Civil War soldiers trained more often and more intelligently than their counterparts had done in any previous American conflict.

Second, the Civil War proved to be a huge, protracted conflict. It provided many opportunities for soldiers to practice in combat what they had learned on the drill field. The link between intensive training and repeated experience on the battlefield transformed raw recruits into seasoned and reliable soldiers. The only other conflict that has equaled or exceeded the Civil War in terms of size and duration has been World War II. In that globe-girdling conflict, U.S. troops received basic training as well as advanced training and learned how to adjust their tactics to suit developing circumstances.

In the Civil War, battlefield success started from the ground up. Small-unit tactics were the foundation. It is theoretically possible to win without solid proficiency on the primary tactical level if other factors strongly influence the course of battle. But if both sides are equally well trained and using similar weapons, performance on the primary tactical level becomes ever more important in sustaining repeated efforts on the battlefield.

Historian Wayne Wei-siang Hsieh believes Civil War volunteers gained their knowledge of unit formations and maneuvers "in an astonishingly short period of time considering the circumstances." He credits much of that swift attainment of proficiency to West Pointers who knew more of such matters than of the higher level of tactics. While Hsieh's first point is certainly valid, his second is questionable, given that the overwhelming majority of volunteer units were drilled by their own volunteer officers. In the sense that West Pointers maintained a good system of tactics and promulgated it in drill manuals, they provided the foundation for volunteers to train themselves during the Civil War.[1]

Much credit must be given to the state governments as well, for they were responsible for raising the volunteer regiments. As Jerry Cooper has pointed out, the states did a far more impressive job of mobilizing soldiers in the Civil War than in any previous or subsequent conflict in American history. Their mobilization efforts were better funded and better supported by enlarged state-level staff departments. The growth of modern transportation facilities in the form of railroad networks also facilitated the rapid mobilization of volunteers during the Civil War, in contrast to the chaos that characterized state volunteer mobilization during the Mexican War only fifteen years before the firing on Fort Sumter.[2]

THE CIVIL WAR AND THE CITIZEN-SOLDIER TRADITION

The Civil War was the only conflict in which the nation relied heavily on state volunteers to carry the overwhelming burden of battle. It was the culmination of a long, hallowed tradition of reliance on voluntary military service in American history. Beginning in the seventeenth and early eighteenth centuries, when the colonial militia was almost the only defense for settlers, Americans had preferred to trust the willingness of citizens to offer themselves for military duty.

In the American Revolution the Continental Army was created by the Second Continental Congress, the de facto central government of the former colonies that now called themselves states. Without a constitution to lend it authority, Congress had to rely on the state governments to supply manpower. The Continental Army consisted of regiments raised by the states that were then loaned to the central government. State governments relied mostly on volunteers to create those units, although they offered bounties to recruits. The men elected their officers, but state

governments retained the power to commission them. Many of these characteristics applied to volunteers of the Civil War as well, although most Continental
enlistments were for only one year. Beginning with the intensive drilling supplied
by Baron von Steuben midway through the Revolution, some Continental units
achieved a level of proficiency equal to that of the British regulars they opposed.
But the quality of performance remained uneven among American units. The many
state-militia units raised, mostly for short terms of service and with precious little
training, generally exhibited a lower level of competency in executing maneuvers
on the battlefield.[3]

The Militia Act of 1792 relegated almost complete control of the militia system
to state governments. As a result, the central government had to experiment with
alternate ways to supplement the tiny U.S. Army created by the Confederation
government after the Revolution. While George Washington and John Adams
experimented with federal volunteer enlistments (men organized for short-term
service directly by the central government), Thomas Jefferson and James Madison
experimented with calling up state volunteers. This represented a link with the
mobilization method that had created the Continental Army and set a precedent
for future conflicts. In fact, the Civil War saw not only deep reliance on state volunteers but mobilization of Federal volunteers as well, most notably in the form of
138 regiments of black troops.[4]

During the War of 1812, the government avoided calling up state volunteers
and relied on an expanded U.S. Army of about 70,000 men. In contrast, a total of
458,463 militiamen served during that conflict, with results far from creditable to
the militia system. Even the regulars, swelled by raw recruits, turned in normally
dismal performances in the field. The most impressive levels of proficiency came
about because of the intensive training accorded Jacob Brown's small army of regulars and militiamen that operated along the Niagara frontier in 1814.[5]

A mix of regulars, state volunteers, and state militia contributed to the forces
engaged in the Second Seminole War of 1835–42. A little over 10,000 regulars
participated along with about 30,000 citizen-soldiers. While statistics differentiat-
ing the two categories of citizen-soldiers (militia and volunteers) are not available,
troop strength in Florida at the end of 1837 included 4,636 regulars and 4,078 state
volunteers. In March 1841 all citizen-soldiers—militia and volunteers alike—were
sent home, and the war was carried on solely by the U.S. Army.[6]

Since the Revolution, no conflict had given the state volunteer system the opportunity to play a large role in determining the outcome of war. But Pres. James
K. Polk called up 73,000 state volunteers to supplement 27,000 regulars during the

Mexican War of 1846–48. The relative contribution of these two forces was starkly uneven. The regulars provided the staying power and the tactical proficiency for success on the battlefield. The U.S. Army began to come of age by midcentury, and it won literally every battle and ended the conflict with Mexico in a relatively short time. The volunteers gained a well-deserved reputation for lacking discipline, marauding, committing atrocities against helpless Mexicans, and running away from battlefield dangers.[7]

This background makes the success of Civil War volunteer armies seem like a miracle by comparison. While 67,000 men served in the U.S. Army during that conflict, more than 2.7 million Northerners and Southerners served as state volunteers. Abraham Lincoln also authorized the organization of a wide array of U.S. Federal volunteers, and Jefferson Davis sanctioned the creation of a very small contingent of C.S. national volunteers. Bolstered by high motivation, subject to intense training, and willing to endure almost anything to succeed, the core of committed volunteers in blue and gray made the Civil War a long and bloody contest. The fate of the Union and the future of 4 million slaves hung in the balance as citizen-soldiers decided which direction their country would take in its future development.[8]

There was no point during the war at which the tactical performance of Union and Confederate units suddenly improved. Baron von Steuben's training regimen at Valley Forge proved to be the pivot upon which the effectiveness of many Continental regiments dramatically increased. Likewise, the intensive training in the camp at Buffalo early in 1814 proved to be crucial in the performance of Brown's army along the Niagara frontier. In contrast, the proficiency level of Civil War regiments rose gradually from the start of the conflict and more rapidly and steadily after their first couple of engagements. One can see more-complicated maneuvers, such as moving by the flank by companies, in the latter part of the war. The most successful skirmishing took place in the last half of the conflict as well. But training combined with experience worked more smoothly than one had a reason to expect, given that the overwhelming majority of Union and Confederate soldiers were new to military life when they enlisted.

No subsequent conflict has offered state volunteers the opportunity to affect their country so much as the Civil War. In the Spanish-American War of 1898, 75,000 regulars and federal volunteers participated in a conflict that lasted only four months. In contrast to these numbers, the states fielded a volunteer force of 200,000 troops. While commissioned and noncommissioned officers from the National Guard tended to lead volunteer units, the rank and file came directly from civilian life. The state volunteers played only a limited role in the war. William

Shafter's army of some 17,000 men, which conquered Cuba after a month of campaigning, contained only two volunteer regiments. Nelson Miles relied on eight volunteer regiments and only two regular regiments to take Puerto Rico, while fifteen volunteer regiments provided a significant contribution to the American forces operating in the Pacific theater. Most of them participated in the first few months of the Philippine War of 1899–1902 before they were sent home for mustering out. Given its short duration and its often low-intensity nature, the Spanish-American War was not a demanding test of the state volunteer system.[9]

In fact, the Spanish-American War turned out to be the last conflict involving state volunteers. Army reforms took place in its wake so that the United States mobilized manpower in a dramatically different way when it went to war against Germany in 1917. Gone were the state volunteers in favor of a modern draft system administered by the federal government. About two million men still volunteered for service, but an additional three million were drafted and served in the armed forces. Even with standardized training on the basic and advanced levels, the American Expeditionary Force remained behind the learning curve throughout its brief experience of heavy combat during the last two months of the war. It lagged far behind the British, French, and German armies in developing new tactics to meet the realities of the western front. This was not due to ineptitude, for many American divisions improved dramatically in performance by the end of the Meuse-Argonne Offensive. But the training regimen was hampered by a belated realization that trench warfare had imposed enormous limitations on the possibility of conducting open-field operations. The short duration of the offensive also denied American units the extended combat experience necessary to innovate and practice new tactical doctrine.[10]

The limitations of the AEF in 1918 were not duplicated by the U.S. Army during World War II. Fielding a force of ten million men, it entered the conflict with a sound tactical system that needed only to be altered to meet particular battlefield conditions in Europe and the Pacific. Michael Doubler has shown that the army did an impressive job of adjusting its methods on a regular basis to suit "terrain, weather, and novel German defensive tactics" in the European theater. It was done in a decentralized fashion on many levels of the deployed forces and without strict adherence to doctrine compared to the Germans and the Soviets. Doubler believes the Americans were especially good at adjusting the operations of their combat teams to gain advantages over the Germans. In the Pacific, American analysts studied the Japanese with equal discernment and also concluded that fundamental changes in the tactical system were unnecessary. They emphasized fire and maneuver and the effective coordination of supporting arms even in heavy jungle terrain.[11]

Although consisting mostly of draftees, the American army of World War II was in fact a citizen army. Its size dwarfed the number of men who fought in the Civil War, and there was far more evaluation of tactics on an ongoing basis in the 1940s than ever took place in the 1860s. But in both conflicts a very large war was fought with a basically sound tactical system that needed little in the way of innovation, in contrast to the boiling kettle of tactical change that took place during World War I among the British, French, and Germans.

Large citizen armies newly raised to fight a major war had to undergo intense training before they could fight effectively, but the same was largely true even of standing professional forces. The British army did not undergo a huge increase in size when the periodic wars of the eighteenth century broke out. Its ranks were increased with new recruits, but on average they represented only about 27 percent of regimental strength. Yet those regiments had to undergo intensive training at the start of each war because there was so little time for drilling during peacetime. The army's peacetime obligations (including the need to deal with smugglers and suppress domestic rioting) were so demanding that the troops received minimal training only on the basic levels of the drill manual. Upon the outbreak of war, more-intense training in the basics and the introduction of advanced drilling in the evolutions of the line took place. Even during peacetime, it took two to three years for a regiment that had degraded to the point of ineffectiveness to train itself up to be "fit for service." This same process had to be done much more quickly in wartime. As John A. Houlding has stated, "it was always at the eleventh hour that the best training was done in the British Army." And yet regiments had to endure two or three campaigns before they could wed experience with that intensive training and become formidable. "Initial inadequacy followed by intensive practice was a general pattern . . . wherever the enemy was militarily competent."[12]

The basis of success in the eighteenth-century British army reflects on the experience of Union and Confederate regiments. Houlding sees little tactical innovation among British units as they put their training into practice on the battlefield. He concludes that the linear system as explained in the drill regulations was adequate to meet their needs and praises the army administration for it. The British had "successive sets of drill regulations, carefully prepared and kept up to date by an informed and competent authority." Such a statement could easily apply to the American situation as well. In addition, the British maintained a system of annual inspection and review of its units during peacetime, and many officers wrote thoughtful treatises on their art to produce a thriving military literature that promoted the professionalization of the officer corps.[13]

In short, the problems associated with getting a newly raised citizen army ready for war were not so different from those associated with preparing a standing professional army for intense conflict. The key in both cases was maintaining a viable tactical system that could be adjusted if needed to meet the demands of war. Taking that system seriously by intensively learning its details, then learning from experience how to make it work, were fundamental keys to military effectiveness no matter what type of defense force a national government preferred to maintain.

The fundamental adequacy of the linear system is an important theme. For some reason, historians of tactics are eager to see change and innovation in every war. This seems to go beyond their normal training to gauge change over time. Nearly every historian of Civil War tactics cited in this book has searched for evidence of change in linear tactics during that conflict. This overtone appears even in conversations and correspondence on the subject with Civil War enthusiasts and various other people who have communicated with me.

This seems mostly driven by the standard interpretation of the rifle musket's effect on Civil War battlefield conditions. Historians believing in that interpretation assume the rifle changed the tactical scene and want to find evidence that somebody in the 1860s recognized it and tried to find an innovative solution (such as Zouave tactics) to the killing. If we drop that interpretation, we also can drop the imperative to find innovation. In fact, after a nearly exhaustive survey of battle reports, I can see very little innovation of any kind during the war and believe it was not really needed. The quirky alterations one sees, such as using one rank instead of two, are not startling changes that lie outside the existing linear system. One can see far more consistency with the existing tenets of the drill manuals than deviation from them in battle reports. There are far more examples of successful use of the standard formations and maneuvers than there are examples of failure to do so. The war that truly embodied rapid and varied innovation in tactical theory and doctrine was fought from 1914 to 1918, and the U.S. Army was well behind nearly every other belligerent in the learning process that took place in Europe during those years.

THE CIVIL WAR AND THE EUROPEAN AND NORTH AMERICAN TACTICAL HERITAGE

It is far more valuable to view Civil War tactics from the perspective of the past than to see it as the harbinger of something to come in the future. Arguments over the modern aspects of warfare in the 1860s need not concern us here, only to note

COMPARISON AND CONTEXT   233

that many historians rightly see the Civil War as one of the last Napoleonic conflicts in Western history. The composition of the armies, the handling of the troops on campaign and on the battlefield, and the results of numerous combats could hardly have surprised one of Napoleon's field marshals in 1815. They would have seemed hopelessly antiquated, however, to a division commander of the AEF in 1918.[14]

In fact, one can see many parallels between the armies of the Civil War and those of the French Revolutionary government in the early 1790s. That decade marked the true beginning of what many writers refer to as Napoleonic tactics. It saw the creation of huge volunteer armies mixed with some degree of conscripted men. It also witnessed the beginning of modern skirmishing as practiced during the Civil War. Revolutionary armies relied heavily on the voluntary commitment of the troops to the cause and yet also instituted surprisingly rigorous and continuous training regimens to impart the modified linear system of the day, replete with a mixture of lines, columns, and the same array of formations and maneuvers familiar to soldiers of the 1860s.

John A. Lynn, who has studied the Armée du Nord, the largest field force raised by the French Revolutionary government, portrays its composition in a way highly familiar to students of the Civil War. "They represented the entire range of French society, not just its losers," Lynn has written. "These valued and honored recruits were led by an officer corps that was close to the rank and file in social origin and sympathies. Discipline and control eventually kept adequate order without dampening the spirit, and even the idealism, of the common soldier. The campaign of political education fostered patriotism, republicanism, and a sense of cause. But beyond these, it repeatedly expressed the nation's gratitude to its soldiery, which had endured and risked much."[15]

The 1791 tactical manual used by this army became the basis, with several revisions, of Scott, Hardee, and Casey by the 1860s. A member of any volunteer regiment in the Union or Confederate armies would have been able to understand its contents. The Armée du Nord had to incorporate influxes of raw recruits on a regular basis to maintain its troop strength from 1791 to 1794, the years of Lynn's intensive study. Drillmasters could do this in three months of diligent training. Lynn also points out that training combined with experience in the field brought the army to a state of effectiveness. It may not have been as high as that attained by Civil War armies, but it allowed the Armée du Nord to fulfill its basic mission of protecting France's Belgian frontier against heavy pressure from the Allies.[16]

Tactical practices were fairly common between the 1790s and the 1860s. Like

Civil War commanders, eighteenth-century theorists advocated the habitual use of multiple lines separated by about two hundred yards. The Armée du Nord used a combination of lines and columns, although it is unclear if the true ordre mixte (placing lines and columns in the same formation) was used. The army's commanders certainly employed columns of waiting and of maneuver, preferring the double column over the simple column. They often advanced in column only to deploy into battle lines before closing on the target, but they often used columns of attack as well; in fact, they used them more often than did Civil War commanders. The square was rarely used, probably because of its complexity, appearing in only 6 of the 108 battlefield examples of formations and maneuvers that Lynn studied.[17]

The striking similarities between the Armée du Nord and Civil War armies should provide caution for anyone who promotes the idea that the American military experience was unique in Western history. In the same vein, much has been made of the heavily forested terrain of North America as prompting tactical innovation. This idea centers on the conviction that mountains and forests, and the relatively underdeveloped physical culture of America, led armies to adopt two ranks instead of three in the eighteenth century and spurred the development of loose-order tactics. In his study of the British army during the American Revolution, Matthew Spring also argues that the rugged nature of the northern states allowed the Continentals to take up strong defensive positions and compelled the British to adopt the offensive more often than not. British officers used quick offensive tactics (minimal firing followed by a bayonet charge) in part because of the strength of the American positions and partly because they could not spare the men or the time for long, drawn-out engagements.[18]

There may well be some truth to these assertions as applied to the late eighteenth century, but they hardly hold true for the 1860s. Civil War commanders faced a variety of tangled vegetation on most of their battlefields, but there is little evidence that they altered tactics as a result. One does not see Civil War regiments reducing from two to one rank to deal with brush. In fact, battle reports provide vivid evidence that vegetation caused problems for linear formations, but they also provide clear proof that commanders and men alike dealt with it pretty effectively. If it was impossible to maintain formations, they simply waded through a belt of brush and trees in any way possible until they could re-form on the other side.

In most ways, the experience of Civil War armies mirrored that of the large citizen armies of the period from 1792 to 1815 quite well. There also were common traits in the experience of warfare during the dynastic wars of the eighteenth century, which were largely fought with professional, standing armies. One such commonality that has often bedeviled historians of the Civil War is the issue of decisive combat. Most historians believe that the rifle musket offered so much long-range firepower to the defender that no attacks could succeed. Thus the decisive battles that seemed to characterize the Napoleonic era and the wars of the eighteenth century were no longer possible. Modern military technology, in this view, had begun to alter the age of the bayonet charge and the possibility of fighting short, relatively low-cost wars.[19]

Although having already dealt with this thorny issue in *The Rifle Musket in Civil War Combat,* it is worth addressing it here as well. It is wrong to assume that combat in the eighteenth century and the Napoleonic era was necessarily decisive or that Civil War battles were necessarily indecisive. In fact, truly decisive battles—those that can with one stroke win a war—are very rare in any era. That effect is largely the result of a political decision. It would more likely happen if one government had limited goals and was ready to cut its losses at the first sign of military failure. In a conflict such as the Civil War—where fundamental issues were at stake and one government's goal was to eradicate its opponent—the will to suffer and triumph at almost any cost could survive the effect of several major defeats on the battlefield.[20]

On another level, that of the purely military, the idea that one army can "destroy" the other, or defeat it so comprehensively in one engagement as to render it essentially inactive, is a chimera more common in dreams than reality. This was true not only of the Civil War but also of the overwhelming majority of all wars in history. There are many, many reasons for this, and every battle in every conflict has its own set of them. A careful reading of any good operational and tactical study of a major conflict brings these factors out. The various reasons may include the quality of training, the type of weapons used, the number of troops assembled, the quality of leadership and intelligence gathering, the kind of terrain characterizing theaters of operation, and a host of other things that make up the complicated matrix that goes into each battle.[21]

In short, each war has to be taken on its own merits when assessing why victory perched more quickly on some standards than others. The enormous difficulties inherent in managing thousands of men in dangerous territory against thousands of other men who are equally determined to succeed should give us pause. Many factors that affect the outcome of an engagement are but dimly known and often not under the control of the generals. Rather than wonder why battles throughout history have been indecisive, we should wonder that any of them managed to turn out in any kind of a decisive way at all.[22]

The Civil War was a brother's war even in the tactical sense. The Union and

Confederate armies used the same tactical system and studied the same manuals. Both armies were filled by raw recruits at the start of the conflict, men who soon learned how to become effective soldiers along roughly the same learning curve. The Civil War was one of the most symmetrical of all American wars. The North enjoyed the benefit of more resources, and one can make an argument that, in many ways, the Union army was qualitatively better than the Confederate army. But in the area of proficiency on the primary tactical level, there was really little difference between the opposing forces.[23]

Why could Civil War soldiers not translate their proficiency on the primary tactical level into strategic success more rapidly and surely? In short, why could they not exert enough battle force, or combat power, to damage opposing armies more than they did? This question goes to the heart of the supposedly indecisive nature of Civil War combat. In one engagement after another, neither side damaged the other in unequal ways. Many attacks were repulsed, or the attacker achieved limited success that the defender could neutralize by counteraction. Even if badly defeated, the loser often could evacuate the field without being caught or pursued by the victorious army, recover, and be ready for another confrontation in a short time.

Paddy Griffith has suggested a few reasons to explain why Civil War commanders often failed to achieve more in battle. He believes that American officers did not take to heart the French emphasis on quickly driving home attacks as opposed to stopping and trading volleys with the enemy. Griffith is critical of officers for too often allowing battles to degenerate into long, static firefights that failed to degrade the ability of one side or the other to resist. Those prolonged firefights merely racked up a large number of casualties rather than paved the way for spirited attacks.[24]

Griffith also faults Civil War commanders for not understanding how to properly use reserves. Given that they normally formed in multiple lines, they often had ample reserve troops waiting to the rear but did not know exactly when to throw them into the fray. For this they can be forgiven, for detecting the small window of opportunity when the second line could actually help the first overcome resistance was extremely difficult. Often, by the time an officer became aware of this need and the second line moved forward, it arrived too late.[25]

Griffith is on firmer ground when he criticizes Northern and Southern commanders for not keeping back a large army-level reserve and using it opportunely to follow through when the opposing force neared a breakdown. He admits that French Revolutionary armies also suffered the same problem but that Napoleon managed to achieve this high level of coordination very well. "Civil War commanders probably enjoyed just as good means of controlling their battles as had their Napoleonic predecessors," Griffith has surmised, "but felt less sure of themselves when it came to higher battle-handling." As a result, he believes Civil War officers were slightly less successful than Napoleon but more successful in their operations than World War I commanders.[26]

It is true that we rarely see large reserves ably handled on Civil War battlefields. Seldom were there large formations held back to be thrown in at a key moment when an initial attack gained some success. Seldom can we see a large reserve force sent in pursuit of a retreating enemy. When George Thomas unleashed his cavalry to pursue the Army of Tennessee after the Battle of Nashville, James Wilson's troopers hounded the Rebels for many miles but could not catch them or cut off an appreciable number of the routed enemy. Four months later Grant sent his own large cavalry force to pursue Lee from Petersburg. In this case Philip Sheridan managed to cut off Lee's retreat one hundred miles away at Appomattox Station. But it is worth repeating that Appomattox was a unique military operation in the Civil War, rendering Griffith's point more convincing than not.

It is also worth repeating that many of the problems encountered by Civil War officers in handling their troops were similar to those encountered by commanders in other wars. Some of the difficulties may have been more pronounced in the 1860s but not necessarily unusual compared to previous conflicts. Although a severe test for both sides, the length of the war played to the benefit of the North more than the South. The political decision to directly attack slavery and to arm black men probably would not have been made if the conflict had ended early in 1862, and the naval blockade worked more surely to weaken the Confederacy with each passing year. A short Civil War probably would have shaped a very different America than the prolonged conflict that developed in the 1860s.

We cannot blame either the rifle musket or the linear system for the length of the Civil War or for the apparently indecisive nature of its combat. The faults that Griffith identified lay in the realm of higher tactics rather than on the level of formations and maneuvers used by Union and Confederate infantry. While demonstrating proficiency at the primary tactical level, Civil War commanders often failed to handle their armies in a coordinated way on the corps level, and that inhibited their ability to follow through with initial success and more soundly damage their battlefield opponents.

The military system of the United States worked surprisingly well in the 1860s despite its inherent limitations and problems. Just as the colonial military system worked very poorly in times when the threat was minimal and surprisingly well when it was great, so operated the volunteer system of the United States. Small, limited conflicts like the Mexican War were not the most severe test of that system. When faced with the ultimate crisis—national survival on both sides—enough Americans North and South responded to the call and took seriously the enormous task of learning how to be effective soldiers.

Conclusion

A Tactical Summary of the Civil War

One must approach the task of summarizing tactical practice in the Civil War with caution. A conflict involving nearly three million men and some three thousand regiments over four years naturally displayed a certain degree of variety. But that variety lay largely in the area of diverse levels of proficiency among officers and units, not in the area of improvisations on the basic formations and maneuvers as explained in the tactical manuals. It is possible to summarize how Civil War commanders preferred to operate within the range of choices presented to them by the linear system.

Officers much preferred lines over columns for engaging in combat. Lines allowed for maximum use of a unit's firepower and in most ways were easier to maintain than columns. But columns played a large role in Civil War military operations other than as attack formations. They were widely used to hold units ready for combat or to maneuver them on the battlefield before engaging the enemy. In this, Civil War officers followed established practice in European warfare, though they did not duplicate Napoleon's preference for the ordre mixte. Rather than mixing line and column alternately within the same formation, American officers preferred to organize support units in columns within a multiple-line formation.

Successive, or multiple, lines could be seen on almost every battlefield of the Civil War. This formation stacked reinforcements behind the first line at a distance of two hundred or three hundred yards, far enough away to lessen exposure to enemy fire. Columns became an important component of multiple-line formations, for they allowed supporting units the opportunity to rapidly move from point to point on the battlefield.

Civil War officers mostly conducted frontal attacks, not because of a Celtic disposition (among the Confederates) or lack of intelligence (among the Federals), but because it was the easiest way to advance against the enemy. This reason should not be taken lightly, for there were many difficulties associated with the attempt to make a flanking movement. Frontal assaults were not only easier to conduct but also had real chances of success. The rifle musket did not render the defensive supreme on Civil War battlefields. Every attack in every battle of the four-year conflict had its own set of reasons for success or failure, as is true in every war.

In fact, many commanders failed to attack at all. There was a strong tendency for Civil War units to advance within close range of the enemy, come to a halt, and engage in a prolonged firefight rather than press home the assault. There are prominent exceptions to this rule, including Hood's attack at Gaines's Mill and Pickett's attack at Gettysburg. But more often than not, offensive action in the Civil War resulted in firefights rather than assaults. This was not necessarily unwise, for many attacks that were pressed home (as Pickett's assault) ended in failure. One could point to examples of prolonged firefights degrading one side or the other and thus preparing the way for success. Moreover, officers often had little control over the situation as the men advanced, stopped, and opened fire on their own. Theorists had been arguing for centuries about whether it was better to use fire or shock to achieve tactical goals on the battlefield, and neither side in that discussion had a monopoly on wisdom. There were many good points to be made in both arguments, and the Civil War provides no overwhelming evidence that either side was right.

Officers normally moved their men fast when under fire to minimize casualties. That had been the chief concern of Hardee's slight revision of Scott's manual. Regimental and brigade commanders also tried to combine maneuvers, sometimes performing half a dozen different types during the course of a single-day's combat. This level of articulation demonstrates that at least some officers became very proficient in their tactics. It also demonstrates that the rank and file of those regiments learned the drill until they could perform any maneuver under fire without hesitation. Evidence of multiple maneuvers demonstrates a high degree of training, expertise, articulation, and military professionalism.

Civil War commanders improvised now and then, although the level of improvisation was quite low. They sometimes used one rank instead of two for a specialized purpose. They dealt with the effects of inversion of ranks, although experienced regiments could handle this problem better than new ones. Regiments performed squad-level combat or divided into wings if necessary under fire, although squad and wing actions were rare.

The tactical manuals described one way regiments could pass through the line of another, an important issue when arraying men in multiple lines. The authors assumed that officers would maintain proper intervals between units to allow for passage of lines. But Civil War commanders rarely maintained intervals, preferring to connect the flanks of individual regiments. As a result, the passage of lines often was chaotic and unplanned, with one line bursting through another and breaking it up. Some units could not recover from this sudden disruption, but most did, particularly the experienced regiments.

The most common battlefield maneuver in the war was moving by the flank. It was faster, easier, and more flexible than any other way to shift a regiment to right or left or to move it forward through tangled vegetation or around obstacles (such as buildings). Wheeling was not easy to do, but officers often resorted to it as a way to change the direction of a regimental line.

Large formations, meaning the ability to organize corps-sized units for a single task on the battlefield, were comparatively rare in the Civil War. It was more common to see division-level formations dedicated to a single task, such as attacking a partic-ular spot in the enemy position. Articulation on the corps level was more difficult to accomplish. Even so, many division-level operations also broke up and devolved into brigade-level actions. Solid and consistent performance in formations and ma-neuvers are evident only on the regimental and brigade levels during the Civil War.

But the inability of Northern and Southern commanders to regularly organize large formations on the corps level did not necessarily hamper the effectiveness of Civil War armies. The level of articulation on the lower levels, the battalion and the brigade, was very impressive; that was the more important level as well. Combat effectiveness started with the small units, the foundation of armies. As long as regiments and brigades operated effectively, field armies could at least survive if not triumph. The flexible linear system inherited from the Napoleonic era allowed a good deal of latitude to sector commanders to operate as they saw fit within the overall plan of battle. Thus, most Civil War infantry combat consisted of many small-unit engagements more or less taking place within a paradigm set by the army commander. There is little doubt that a higher degree of command and con-trol on the corps level might have made battle more decisive of results, but that remained a problem difficult to fix. It also was a problem experienced by armies in other conflicts. If poor articulation on the higher levels contributed to the length of the war, then the burden fell even more heavily on the small units. Regimental and brigade commanders and their men carried the cause on their shoulders in each successive battle until something broke and hostilities came to an end.

Many commanders placed great emphasis on skirmishing by the midpoint of the conflict. Indeed, the American Civil War involved the most deadly and effective skirmishing in history. To a degree, the rifle musket, in the hands of a soldier naturally apt to use it and eager to engage in this specialized art, accounts for the impressive history of skirmishing in that war. In part, good commanders realized that skirmishing was a less costly alternative to larger action by the battle line. A heavy skirmish line was the optimal way to gain information about terrain and enemy positions, and it could exert something like the pressure a battle line was capable of pushing against the enemy. A commander with a good and strong skirmish line had more opportunity to decide when and where to commit his main force to battle with a better chance of success than a commander with weak and ineffective skirmishers.

Measured per capita, the Civil War was by far the bloodiest conflict in all American history. Yet it is important to keep in mind that it was not unusually bloody compared to other wars. Two-thirds of all the Northern and Southern men who died in the Civil War perished because of disease, not combat. Loss ratios in its battles were not higher than those in engagements fought in the eighteenth century or in the twentieth century. It may seem counterintuitive, but the evidence strongly supports the view that modern weapons do not necessarily kill or injure more opponents on the battlefield than older weapons did three hundred years ago. There certainly is much more volume of fire now than with the smoothbore muskets, but it is unaimed fire, and the percentage of rounds that find a human target is probably lower than in the smoothbore and rifle-musket era. Also, modern tactics emphasize dispersing and taking cover at all opportunities. Far fewer men expose themselves to enemy fire in recent decades than before.

The Civil War was a thoroughly old-fashioned conflict, but that is not to denigrate its character. The old-fashioned way of warfare was impressive in many ways. Modern warfare is not necessarily smarter, more effective in achieving strategic goals, or less wasteful of lives than the older ways of conducting military operations. It is just different.

APPENDIX

A Tactical Glossary of the Civil War

Articulation: The facility with which commanders and men are able to make complicated formations and maneuvers, a measure of the degree of unit effectiveness in primary tactics and of proficiency in the tactical art.

Battalion: Many European armies divided the regiment into three battalions of four companies each for ease of handling, but the American army did not mandate that organization before 1898. At the time of the Civil War, Americans used the term *battalion* to refer to the regiment because *battalion* was the operative word in the French drill manuals that Americans copied. At times Civil War commanders temporarily divided regiments into battalions of several companies each for specific purposes, but that was never permanent. A contemporary definition of the term states: "This word is loosely used. Two companies are sometimes called a battalion, while the whole regiment at drill is also called thus."[1]

Breaking away: Any method of moving a line from one position to another by breaking part of it (whether by file, platoon, or company) from the rest.

By file: Moving a regiment or company into a new position by files.

By the flank: Each man turned right or left in place, forming two long lines that resembled a column. But it was not a column as defined by the tactical manuals. This was a very common way to move a regiment to the right or left, forward or backward, on the battlefield. It was a simple and flexible maneuver to quickly change the position of a regiment and negotiate obstacles in its path.

Change front forward on a subunit: For example, by doing so on the right company of a regiment, moving that subunit to the location of the new line by wheeling, with each company then following in turn. This maneuver could be performed to the right or left, forward or toward the rear.

Column: Defined in the tactical manuals as battle lines stacked closely behind each other. The key difference between a column and a formation of multiple lines was the distance between the lines. In a column the distance varied but always was measured in a few inches or a few yards. In a formation of multiple lines, the distance was measured by hundreds of yards. Also, moving a regiment by the flank was not a column formation because it did not involve battle lines stacked closely behind one another.

Column of attack: French tactical theorists recommended the column formation for attacking particularly strong positions because it allowed the troops to move faster under fire than was possible in a line. While some Civil War commanders favored this formation, mostly because of the sense of power it implied as well as for the received European wisdom, most avoided it. The two main problems with the column of attack were that it allowed only the first two ranks in the formation to fire their weapons (and that could be literally only one company) and it easily devolved into chaos when the first ranks slowed or stopped as they hit obstacles.

Column, division: Every set of two companies was called a division, so the odd-numbered companies of the right wing and the even-numbered companies of the left wing went to the rear of the companies that remained in place. The regimental line remained intact except for alternate gaps, with one company behind another between the gaps. It appears to have rarely been used on Civil War battlefields.

Column, double: Two stacks of battle lines, one beside the other. A regiment in double column had five companies in one stack and five in the other, each stack side by side. This formation allowed for a wider front of two companies with a reduced depth of five companies compared to a simple column, which had half the front but twice the depth.

Column of maneuver: A column whose purpose was to move a unit toward the scene of combat or within the zone of fighting.

Column, simple: Ten company battle lines one behind another, in contrast to a double column wherein five company battle lines were stacked, each stack next to the other. This formed a column with a front of one company and a depth of ten companies.

Column of waiting: A unit in column formation while waiting within the combat zone or near it for orders to go into action.

Common time: With regulation twenty-eight-inch steps, measured from heel to heel, it consisted of ninety steps per minute.

Coup d'oeil: Scott admired this term and defined it as "the faculty of determining, with correctness, distances, numbers, heights, and directions by a glance of the eye." He referred to gauging the formation of troops and the landscape that they moved over as well. He wanted officers to "acquire accuracy and facility in judging the line of direction, and of conducting battalions on every sort of ground with the address and intelligence necessary to prevent faults, or promptly to correct them."[2]

Deploy: To go from column formation into line.

Distance: Referred to as the space between lines that are positioned one behind another, whether it was between ranks (thirteen inches), between battle lines stacked in a column formation (varied from thirteen inches to the frontage of the subunits in the column), or between successive battle lines in a multiple-line formation (typically two hundred or more yards).[3]

Distance, terms referring to within a column: This varied according to purpose. "Closed en masse" meant that the space between the front rank of one line and the rear rank of the line in front of it was the same as the distance between ranks within one battle line (thirteen inches). "Full distance" meant that the spacing was equivalent to the frontage of the line of each subunit so that they could wheel into line quickly from a column (this distance cannot be definitely set because the length of a subunit's line varied according to the number of men and therefore the manuals did not specify inches or feet). "Half distance" is the space halfway between full and closed en masse. Each distance had a purpose—closed en masse was used for attacking a strong position because the officers could control and move their men faster when grouped this way. Full distance was necessary for wheeling into line and allowed the men maximum room for ease of marching long distances. Half distance achieved some of the benefits of each of the other two formations.

Double-quick time: With regulation thirty-three-inch steps, measured from heel to heel, it consisted of 160 steps per minute according to Hardee. Scott did not refer to the term *double-quick time,* but he allowed men to move at 140 steps per minute if needed.

Echelon: To detach units a short distance from the flank of a formation to either the rear or the front. The purpose was to achieve flank protection on defense and to better outflank the enemy on offense. The term derives from the French word for "ladder." A contemporary definition of echelon reads: "A formation of troops, where battalions or brigades follow each other on separate lines, like the steps of a ladder."[4]

Evolutions of the line: Referred to as formations and maneuvers by brigades, divisions, corps, and field armies; in short, everything above the regimental (or battalion) level. A contemporary definition of the term is: "Movements by which troops, consisting of more regiments than one, change their position with order and regularity upon the field of battle."[5]

File: In a two-rank formation, the file consisted of one man in the first rank and the man immediately behind him.

Guides (individuals): Men assigned to stand at and thus mark a spot where the unit would perform a turn or to mark the location of a new line for it.

Guides (units): A company designated as the leader in movement for the regiment, "being regarded as infallible by all the others," wrote Scott, was to move as ordered so that the other companies could model their movements by it. The same applied to subunits of larger formations.

Interval: The distance between the flanks of individual units within a battle line (regulation twenty-two yards), between men in loose-order skirmish lines (five paces), or between groups of four on the skirmish line (from twenty to forty paces).[6]

Inversion of ranks: When, in maneuvering, officers got the second rank in front of the first. It was considered a problem because the regimental line was organized in precise ways and drilled in that precise formation so that each man knew his place and what to expect when orders were issued. Inverting the ranks disrupted this delicate arrangement. But much of this precision was instilled for ceremonial purposes, and volunteer regiments usually gained enough experience under fire so that the men were not overly confused if they had to fight with the ranks reversed.

Loose-order formation: Breaking the touch of elbow, the shoulder-to-shoulder massing of men in a line, by spreading them out so that, on the skirmish line for example, intervals of five paces existed between the soldiers within a grouping of four, and intervals of twenty to forty paces existed between the groupings of fours.

Oblique: A movement designed to shift a line right or left without changing its facing directly toward the front. To accomplish this goal, the men kept their heads and shoulders facing straight ahead, put their right or left foot twenty-six inches in the direction ordered, and the other foot eighteen inches behind the leading foot, retaining their original facing but moving diagonally to right or left. They resumed stepping forward when finished.

Passage of lines: If a unit was formed in multiple or successive lines, the ability to pass one line through the other either forward or backward became important. The only clean way to do so was to move a column through the intervals separating the flanks of individual units within a battle line (regulation twenty-two yards). If no intervals were kept, then commanders passed their lines in any way they could think of, by moving around the flank of the other unit or simply breaking through its line, forcing the affected unit to re-form after the moving unit had passed.

Perpendicular method of deploying from marching column to battle line: Developed by the Prussians in the 1700s, this tactic involved approaching the enemy line by a perpendicular rather than a parallel line of march and deploying into line, with each unit moving obliquely right or left, so as not to expose the flank to enemy fire while approaching and taking position.

Ploy: To go from line formation into column.

Processional method of deploying from marching column to battle line: The old and time-honored way, marching parallel to the enemy and wheeling units into line to confront them. But this exposed the flank while approaching the enemy and forming line.

Quick time: With regulation twenty-eight-inch steps, measured from heel to heel, it consisted of 110 paces per minute.

Rank: Consisting of one line of men touching elbows in shoulder-to-shoulder formation. American armies regularly used only two ranks to form a battle line, but three ranks had been common in European armies immediately preceding the Civil War. Two ranks allowed commanders to extend their line farther and prevented accidents when the third rank opened fire through (or over) the two ranks in front of it.

Refuse line: To bend the flank at an angle with the main line to protect against an enemy threat.

Regiment, organization of: Divided into ten companies of one hundred men each; two companies were known as a division (two hundred men). Each company was divided into two platoons (fifty men each), each platoon divided into two sections (twenty-five men each). Sections were not divided, but the manuals mentioned groupings of four men as the lowest subunit of the regiment. The failure to include a squad formation in the table of organization is difficult to understand, for there was a significant gap between the size of sections (twenty-five men) and the groupings of four men. The manuals, however, recognized squads for temporary purposes, such as drilling new recruits or teaching the fundamentals of the School of the Soldier. A contemporary definition of squad reads: "A small party of men assembled for drill or inspection. Squads of recruits for drill should not number more than four or five."[7]

Route step: Used for marching in column, it was the same rate as common time, ninety steps per minute, though not in cadence, the men allowed to swing their legs at will. Casey recommended that the route step be 110 paces per minute on good roads, and the men could go double quick if needed, though for no longer than fifteen minutes at a time.[8]

Run: Scott defined this as more than 140 steps per minute, while Hardee measured it as the same rate as double-quick time, or 160 steps per minute.[9]

Shoulder-to-shoulder formation: The standard formation of the battle line, with men touching elbows.

Square: A complex formation for 360-degree protection. Large sections of the tactical manuals were devoted to making this difficult formation, but one rarely finds them actually used on Civil War battlefields. Normally recommended for use when infantry was confronted by enemy cavalry, which was comparatively rare.

Turn, left or right: Different than a wheel, the first man on either the right or left flank moving individually to begin forming in the new location as each man to his left or right did the same thing, everyone guiding on the right or left flank and closing up to form the new line.

Wheel: Moving the entire line right or left to change its direction quickly. Could be performed by moving on one flank as a fixed pivot or while marching and using a moving pivot. On a fixed pivot the last man on the pivot flank turned in place, but on a moving pivot that soldier took only nine-inch steps, while the man on the moving flank continued with the regular twenty-eight-inch steps while maintaining touch of elbow. A "full wheel" took the line to rest at an angle of 90 degrees compared to its start. A "half wheel" took it to rest at an angle of 45 degrees, and a "quarter wheel" at an angle of about 22 degrees compared to its start. Taking the line to rest at an angle of 180 degrees was called an "about."

Wing: Half of a unit's battle line, either left or right.

NOTES

ABBREVIATIONS

LC   Library of Congress, Manuscript Division, Washington, D.C.

LSU   Louisiana State University, Louisiana and Lower Mississippi Valley Collections, Special Collections, Baton Rouge, La.

OR   U.S. War Department, *The War of the Rebellion: A Compilation of the Official Records of the Union and Confederate Armies.* 70 vols. in 128 parts. Washington, D.C.: Government Printing Office, 1880–1901. (Unless otherwise cited, all references are to series 1.)

SOR   *Supplement to the Official Records of the Union and Confederate Armies.* 100 vols. Wilmington, N.C.: Broadfoot, 1993–2000.

SRNB   Stones River National Battlefield, Murfreesboro, Tenn.

TSLA   Tennessee State Library and Archives, Nashville

TU   Tulane University, Special Collections, New Orleans, La.

UAF   University of Arkansas, Special Collections, Fayetteville

USMA   U.S. Military Academy, Special Collections and Archives Division, West Point, N.Y.

UTK   University of Tennessee, Special Collections, Knoxville

UW   University of Washington, Special Collections, Seattle

PREFACE

1. Hess, *Rifle Musket,* 107–15; McWhiney and Jamieson, *Attack and Die,* 3–24; Griffith, *Battle Tactics of the Civil War,* 146–47; Grimsley, "Surviving Military Revolution," 176; Nosworthy, *Bloody Crucible,* 278, 573–77, 592.

2. Hess, *Rifle Musket,* 197–215.

3. General Orders No. 36, Headquarters, Hood's Corps, Mar. 7, 1864, *OR,* 32(3):593; Hess, *Rifle Musket,* 108.

4. Hess, *Rifle Musket,* 196–203.

5. Ibid., 223–24. Many veterans of World War II, Korea, and Vietnam have told me that their training stressed the need to engage the enemy at close range in order to be effective on the battlefield. Field Manual 3-21.8, the U.S. Army's current tactical manual for small units, declares that the "infantry's primary role is close combat." *Infantry Rifle Platoon and Squad,* viii.

6. McWhiney and Jamieson, *Attack and Die,* 3–24.

7. Wilcox, *Rifles and Rifle Practice,* 1–146, 167–207, 222–29, 248.

8. *North American Review,* unsigned review of Morris, *Field Tactics for Infantry,* 291.

9. Wagner, *Organization and Tactics,* 87.

10. Joyce, "Tactical Lessons of the War," 43, 46–47.

11. Moseley, "Evolution of the American Civil War Infantry Tactics," 8, 333, 356–57, 402; Mahon, "Civil War Infantry Assault Tactics," 59–66; Davis, *Arming the Union,* 151–53; Ross, *Flintlock to Rifle,* 158.

12. McWhiney and Jamieson, *Attack and Die*, 6, 9, 27.

13. Osterhoudt, "Evolution of U.S. Army Assault Tactics," 72, 82–83. For data on the rate and range of fire in the Civil War that are based on evidence in primary sources, see Hess, *Rifle Musket*, 100–104, 107–15.

14. Hagerman, *American Civil War and the Origins of Modern Warfare*, 10; Frank and Reaves, "*Seeing the Elephant*," 89–90; Haughton, *Training, Tactics, and Leadership*, 32, 36–37.

15. McPherson, *Battle Cry of Freedom*, 477; McPherson, *Ordeal by Fire*, 216–17; Weigley, *Great Civil War*, xix, 131; Weigley, *United States Army*, 235.

16. Griffith, *Battle Tactics of the Civil War*, 74, 148–49, 163, 189.

17. Fratt, "American Civil War Tactics," 6, 15.

18. Nosworthy, *Bloody Crucible*, 277–78, 645–46, 648.

19. Nosworthy, *Anatomy of Victory*, xv.

20. Menning, "Operational Art's Origins," 6–7, 9–11, 15, 17; Morillo and Pavkovic, *What Is Military History?*, 56–58.

21. *Synopsis of the Art of War*, 99; *U.S. Infantry Tactics*, 430; Scott, *Military Dictionary*, 601; Wagner, *Organization and Tactics*, 2.

1. THE EUROPEAN TACTICAL HERITAGE

1. Nosworthy, *Anatomy of Victory*, xvi–xvi, 346.

2. Ibid., 3, 11–12, 18.

3. Rogers, "Tactics and the Face of Battle," 232; Nosworthy, *Anatomy of Victory*, 15–16.

4. Lynn, *Giant of the Grand Siècle*, 475–85; Nosworthy, *Anatomy of Victory*, 4–5, 206, 209; Hughes, *Firepower*, 164.

5 Nosworthy, *Anatomy of Victory*, 80–84.

6. Lynn, *Giant of the Grand Siècle*, 459–61, 467–68, 476, 481, 518–21, 524–25.

7. Ibid., 487, 532–33, 535.

8. Nosworthy, *Anatomy of Victory*, 81–82, 91–92, 263, 330.

9. Duffy, *Army of Frederick the Great*, 83; Lynn, *Giant of the Grand Siècle*, 482; Duffy, *Military Experience*, 111; Nosworthy, *Anatomy of Victory*, 160, 185, 187–88, 196, 313.

10. Lynn, *Giant of the Grand Siècle*, 483; Nosworthy, *Anatomy of Victory*, 244, 249–50; Duffy, *Army of Frederick the Great*, 86–88; Quimby, *Background of Napoleonic Warfare*, 11; Rogers, "Tactics and the Face of Battle," 234–35.

11. Duffy, *Army of Frederick the Great*, 85, 88, 153–55; Nosworthy, *Anatomy of Victory*, 193–95, 250, 349.

12. Nosworthy, *Anatomy of Victory*, 243, 346, 348.

13. Ibid., 262, 267; Quimby, *Background of Napoleonic Warfare*, 23.

14. Ross, *Flintlock to Rifle*, 27, 32.

15. Lynn, *Giant of the Grand Siècle*, 486; Nosworthy, *Anatomy of Victory*, 5–6, 190, 313–16.

16. Nosworthy, *Anatomy of Victory*, 87, 99–101, 104, 107–108, 277, 305.

17. Ibid., 339.

18. Quimby, *Background of Napoleonic Warfare*, 27–35, 62–63, 65–66, 70–71, 73, 76, 84, 87; Duffy, *Military Experience*, 199; Nosworthy, *Anatomy of Victory*, 143–44, 149, 151, 161.

19. Duffy, *Military Experience*, 110, 112, 190, 199–200.

20. Nosworthy, *Anatomy of Victory*, 330, 333, 336, 338–39.

21. Showalter, *Wars of Frederick the Great*, 188–90; Nosworthy, *Anatomy of Victory*, 233–34, 337; Quimby, *Background of Napoleonic Warfare*, 46–48, 91–93.

22. Showalter, *Wars of Frederick the Great*, 67–68, 108–10, 112–13, 205.

23. Quimby, *Background of Napoleonic Warfare*, 94–97, 200.

24. Ibid., 98–100, 102–103.

25. Quimby, *Background of Napoleonic Warfare*, 106, 108, 115–16, 126–28, 156–57, 249–50; Parker, *Cambridge History of Warfare*, 194; Ross, *Flintlock to Rifle*, 35; Zuparko, *George Jeffrey's Tactics*, 27–28.

26. Quimby, *Background of Napoleonic Warfare*, 140–41,163; Duffy, *Military Experience*, 268–69, 275, 278, 279; Nosworthy, *Anatomy of Victory*, 15–16; Showalter, "Seven Years' War in Europe," 40–41; Hakala, "G. M. Sprengtporten," 26–27, 31.

27. Griffith, *Art of War of Revolutionary France*, 282; Nosworthy, *Anatomy of Victory*, 351. Nosworthy argues that the impulse system (or flexible system) was not linear tactics at all, but it seems more accurate to term it an adaptation of the older linear system. Ibid., 259. Certainly no armies in the era discarded linear formations, only the idea of a unitary army.

28. Griffith, *Art of War of Revolutionary France*, 215–21; Muir, *Tactics and the Experience of Battle*, 71; Lynn, *Bayonets of the Republic*, 217.

29. Lynn, *Bayonets of the Republic*, 185–89, 251–53, 257, 282; Quimby, *Background of Napoleonic Warfare*, 328, 332.

30. Lynn, *Bayonets of the Republic*, 191–92; Ross, *Flintlock to Rifle*, 57–58, 60–64, 80.

31. Quimby, *Background of Napoleonic Warfare*, 3–5, 272, 283–84, 306–307, 309; Lynn, *Bayonets of the Republic*, 217.

32. Lynn, *Bayonets of the Republic*, 191–92.

33. Ibid., 263, 265–66, 269–70, 274–75; Nosworthy, *With Musket*, 245–46, 250–51, 253–54, 256; Quimby, *Background of Napoleonic Warfare*, 84–85; Paret, "Relationship between the Revolutionary War and European Military Thought and Practice," 150.

34. Nosworthy, *With Musket*, 125.

35. Ibid., 425; Ross, *Flintlock to Rifle*, 88–89, 92.

36. Nosworthy, *With Musket*, 128, 174; Ross, *Flintlock to Rifle*, 108–109, 116.

37. Nosworthy, *With Musket*, 174.

38. Ibid., 225–26, 231; Ross, *Flintlock to Rifle*, 114–16, 129–30, 137–38, 140–48, 151; Volkogonov, "Tactics of the Russian Forces," 68–69.

39. Nosworthy, *With Musket*, 51–52, 93, 96, 99, 101, 114, 139, 190, 192, 225–26, 231.

40. Ibid., 425, 428–30, 453; Quimby, *Background of Napoleonic Warfare*, 320–26.

41. Muir, *Tactics and the Experience of Battle*, 72–73; Quimby, *Background of Napoleonic Warfare*, 124–25, 332; Rothenburg, *Art of Warfare*, 153; Arnold, "Reappraisal of Column Versus Line," 552; Nosworthy, *With Musket*, 104–107, 124–25, 128, 132–35, 141, 149–50; Chandler, "Column Versus Line," 121, 123–26.

42. Rothenburg, *Art of Warfare*, 156; Zuparko, *George Jeffrey's Tactics*, 119–20, 122, 124.

43. Zuparko, *George Jeffrey's Tactics*, 38, 130–31, 144–45, 147.

44. Ibid., 128, 134–36, 139.

45. Muir, *Tactics and the Experience of Battle*, 74–75; Zuparko, *George Jeffrey's Tactics*, 40, 42–43.

46. Zuparko, *George Jeffrey's Tactics*, 158–19, 161.

47. Rogers, "Tactics and the Face of Battle," 231–35.

2. THE NORTH AMERICAN TACTICAL HERITAGE

1. Wright, "Organization and Doctrine," 222, 224–25; Nicola, *Treatise of Military Exercise*, 2.

2. Nicola, *Treatise of Military Exercise*, vii–viii, 1, 6, 11, 62.

3. Ibid., 51–61.

4. Steuben, *Revolutionary War Drill Manual*, unpaginated publisher's note; Wright, "Organization and Doctrine," 230–32; Graves, "'Dry Books of Tactics,'" pt. 1, 51.

5. Wright, "Organization and Doctrine," 230–32; Graves, "From Steuben to Scott," 223.

6. Steuben, *Revolutionary War Drill Manual*, 6–29.

7. Ibid., 6–9, 31, 33–34.

8. Ibid., 36, 41, 48, 50, 52–62. For a modern version of Steuben's drill manual designed for use by Revolutionary War reenactors, see Schultz, *Illustrated Drill Manual*, 50–55.

9. Spring, *With Zeal and Bayonets*, 76–77, 80–82, 92, 95–98, 102, 139, 141–44.

10. Ibid., 179–83, 252–55, 259.

11. Ibid., 144–47, 152, 201–202, 217–18, 222–24, 228–31.

12. Ibid., 178, 268–79.

13. Gallagher, *Battle of Brooklyn*, 125; Greenman, *Diary of a Common Soldier*, 173.

14. Babits, *Devil of a Whipping*, 81, 83, 91–93, 96, 110–12, 115, 117, 152.

15. Babits and Howard, *Long, Obstinate, and Bloody*, 100–116.

16. Ibid., 100–28, 219–20.

17. Ibid., 142–69, 223, 225.

18. Quimby, *U.S. Army*, 2:513–17, 582n–583n; Graves, "From Steuben to Scott," 226–28; Graves, "'Dry Books of Tactics,'" pt. 1, 53; Graves, "'I Have a Handsome Little Army,'" 45–46, 49; Kimball, "Battle of Chippewa," 172–73, 182.

19. Graves, *Field of Glory*, 221, 223–26, 230, 233; Quimby, *U.S. Army*, 1:340–46.

20. Graves, *Where Right and Glory Lead!*, 120–21, 126, 130, 132–33, 135–37, 139, 141, 145–47, 149, 152–54, 157, 163; Quimby, *U.S. Army*, 2:537.

21. Graves, *Where Right and Glory Lead!*, 167–68, 171, 173–76, 178–80; Quimby, *U.S. Army*, 2:538–42.

22. Graves, *Where Right and Glory Lead!*, 181–82. Brown's regulars had also displayed a high level of tactical performance at the Battle of Chippawa, fought on July 5, 1814. See Kimball, "Battle of Chippewa," 183–86; and Quimby, *U.S. Army*, 2:526–27.

23. Graves, "From Steuben to Scott," 223–24; Graves, "'Dry Books of Tactics,'" pt. 1, 53; Moseley, "Evolution of the American Civil War Infantry Tactics," 242, 247–48.

24. Duane, *American Military Library*, 2:v, 17.

25. Graves, "From Steuben to Scott," 225; Graves, "'Dry Books of Tactics,'" pt. 1, 53; Hsieh, *West Pointers*, 37.

26. Graves, "From Steuben to Scott," 225; Graves, "'Dry Books of Tactics,'" pt. 1, 56; Moseley, "Evolution of the American Civil War Infantry Tactics," 234, 237–40, 241.

27. Graves, "From Steuben to Scott," 226–27; Graves, "'Dry Books of Tactics,'" pt. 1, 56.

28. Graves, "From Steuben to Scott," 228–29; Graves, "'Dry Books of Tactics,'" pt. 2, 173, 175.

29. Moseley, "Evolution of the American Civil War Infantry Tactics," 250, 252–53, 255–57; Hsieh, *West Pointers*, 42.

30. Astoria, "Infantry Tactics," 2; Hsieh, *West Pointers*, 42–46.

31. Astoria, "Infantry Tactics," 3.

32. Winders, *Mr. Polk's Army*, 94; Jamieson, "Background to Bloodshed," 26–27; McWhiney and Jamieson, *Attack and Die*, 33–37, 39; Kirkham, *Mexican War Journal and Letters*, 57.

33. Nosworthy, *Bloody Crucible*, 26–29, 84–86, 96; Hess, *Rifle Musket*, 24–34.

34. Nosworthy, *Bloody Crucible*, 41–42, 45, 50, 52.

35. Haughton, *Training, Tactics, and Leadership*, 29–31; Moseley, "Evolution of the American Civil War Infantry Tactics," 266; Nosworthy, *Bloody Crucible*, 78–79; Hsieh, *West Pointers*, 81.

36. Wilcox, *Rifles and Rifle Practice*, 65–67, 179; Walker, *The Rifle*, 84–85, 142; Nosworthy, *Bloody Crucible*, 30–32.

37. Nosworthy, *Bloody Crucible*, 34–35; Walker, *The Rifle*, 13–25; Busk, *The Rifle*, 201–15; Binney, "Muskets and Musketry," 442–67.

38. Tidball, "Rifle Target Practice," 1–2.

39. Wilcox, *Rifles and Rifle Practice*, 243; [Garesché], *Biography of Lieut. Col. Julius P. Garesché*, 344–47.

40. Busk, *The Rifle*, 22–23; Nosworthy, *Bloody Crucible*, 87–88.

41. Nosworthy, *Bloody Crucible*, 99. See also Ellsworth, *Manual of Arms for Light Infantry*.

42. Wilcox, *Rifles and Rifle Practice*, 243–45.

3. TACTICAL MANUALS AND THE MANAGEMENT OF MEN

1. A. Jackman to Phelps, May 1, 1861, John Wolcott Phelps Correspondence, University of Vermont, Special Collections, Burlington; Scurry to Walker, Mar. 1, 1864, *OR*, 34(2):1016.

2. Hankins, *Simple Story of a Soldier*, 3, 8.

3. Alderson, "Civil War Reminiscences of John Johnston," 76. The 52nd North Carolina also used Hardee's manual. See Hess, *Lee's Tar Heels*, 85.

4. McAllister, *Civil War Letters*, 55; Bryant, *Third Regiment of Wisconsin*, 12; Pope, *Military Memoirs*, 81.

5. Grant, *Personal Memoirs*, 1:166–67.

6. "Memorial to the Congress of the Confederate States," Dec. 14, 1863, Hardee Family Papers, Alabama Department of Archives and History, Montgomery.

7. Ibid.; Bryan, "General William J. Hardee," 267n, 268; William J. Hardee to Harris, May 23, 1861, Box 1, Folder 6, Isham G. Harris Governor's Papers, TSLA.

8. Osterhoudt, "Evolution of U.S. Army Assault Tactics," 75; Moseley, "Evolution of the American Civil War Infantry Tactics," 270–71; Casey, *Infantry Tactics*, 1:5.

9. Astoria, "Infantry Tactics," 3; Osterhoudt, "Evolution of U.S. Army Assault Tactics," 75; Moseley, "Evolution of the American Civil War Infantry Tactics," 270–71; Ross, *Flintlock to Rifle*, 181; Casey, *Infantry Tactics*, 1:5–7, 10–11.

10. Casey, *Infantry Tactics*, 1:5–6, 3:4–175.

11. Ibid., 1:5.

12. Hopkins, *Life of Clinton Bowen Fisk*, 71–72; McGregor, *Fifteenth Regiment New Hampshire*, 291; Circular, Chief Quartermaster's Office, Washington Depot, July 18, 1864, *OR*, 37(2):386. For information on other manuals, see Coppee, *Field Manual*; Monroe, *Company Drill*; Whitehorne, "Efforts to Produce a New Army Drill Manual," 161–62, 167; and Lord, "Army and Navy Textbooks," pt. 2, 100–101.

13. Hardee, *Rifle and Light Infantry Tactics*, 12–13.

14. Ibid., 65.

15. Scott, *Infantry Tactics*, 1:5.

16. Ibid.

17. Ibid.; Hardee, *Rifle and Light Infantry Tactics*, 5. For variations in the way the eight companies were placed within the regimental line, see Ray, "Sixtieth Regiment," 476; and Copp, *Reminiscences*, 23.

18. Paine, *Wisconsin Yankee*, 27–29; William P. Egan Court-Martial transcript, 23rd Kentucky Regimental File, SRNB.

19. Scott, *Infantry Tactics*, 1:5–6; Hardee, *Rifle and Light Infantry Tactics*, 5.

20. Tripp to Baldwin, Jan. 4, 1863; and Stafford to Burns, Jan. 5, 1863, *OR*, 20(1):339, 343; Bidwell to Ward, July 25, 1861, *OR*, 2:412; Walker to Kinsman, July 1, 1863, *OR*, 24(2):304.

21. Hardee, *Rifle and Light Infantry Tactics*, 6; Casey, *Infantry Tactics*, 1:12.

22. Scott, *Infantry Tactics*, 1:6; Hardee, *Rifle and Light Infantry Tactics*, 6; Casey, *Infantry Tactics*, 1:12.

23. Scott, *Infantry Tactics*, 1:6, 8–9, 2:103.

24. Ibid., 1:7; Squier, *This Wilderness of War*, 45; Way, *Thirty-Third Regiment Illinois*, 243.

25. Scott, *Infantry Tactics*, 1:46–48.

26. Morton to Skinner, 1863, *OR*, 16(1):722. The formula Morton explained to estimate unit frontage was generally known. For a Confederate example of this, see General Orders No. 25, Headquarters, First Brigade, Indian Troops, July 14, 1863, *OR*, 22(1):462.

27. Sherman, *Memoirs*, 2:388–89; Scott, *Infantry Tactics*, 1:5.

28. Daniel Harris Reynolds Diary, July 23, 1864, UAF.

29. Orders, Headquarters, Twentieth Corps, June 7, 1864, *OR*, 38(4):432.

30. Wagner, *Organization and Tactics*, 4–5; Jamieson, *Crossing the Deadly Ground*, 109.

31. Benton to Washburn, Oct. 19, 1864, *OR*, 36(1):718.

32. Robertson to Sandidge, Aug. 8, 1862, *OR*, 15:95; Curtis to Sprague, Sept. 22, 1862, *OR*, 19(1):457; Bacon to Moore, June 12, 1864, *OR*, 36(2):303; Jones to Schmitt, Jan. 7, 1863, *OR*, 20(1):315.

33. Sherman to Halleck, Sept. 4, 1864, Sherman, *Sherman's Civil War*, 701; Sherman to Grant, June 2, 1863, *OR*, 24(3):372–73; Sherman, *Memoirs*, 2:384–85; Sherman to Grant, July 22, 1863, *OR*, 24(2):531–32; Force to John Kebler, Aug. 14, 1862, M. F. Force Papers, UW.

34. Maj. Gen. James Patton Anderson's division in the Army of Tennessee, for example, contained twenty-two regiments totaling 2,800 men in early August 1864. Each regiment, therefore, had an average strength of 127 men. Anderson to Ratchford, Feb. 9, 1865, *OR*, 38(3):769.

35. Scott, *Infantry Tactics*, 2:157, 3:257.

36. Ibid., 1:15, 39, 60–61.

37. Hardee, *Rifle and Light Infantry Tactics*, 20–23.

38. Scott, *Infantry Tactics*, 1:60; Hardee, *Rifle and Light Infantry Tactics*, 95.

39. Scott, *Infantry Tactics*, 3:256.

40. Ibid., 2:155–57, 3:254–55.

41. Ibid., 1:17–18, 59, 2:163, 3:287–88.

42. Scribner, *How Soldiers Were Made*, 258.

43. Scott, *Infantry Tactics*, 1:41.

44. Hinman, *Corporal Si Klegg*, 130.

45. Scott, *Infantry Tactics*, 2:168–69. For a detailed description of changing front forward on a company, see Copp, *Reminiscences*, 160, 163.

46. Scott, *Infantry Tactics*, 1:44, 3:271–73.

47. Lyman, *Meade's Army*, 122.

48. Scott, *Infantry Tactics*, 1:40; Casey, *Infantry Tactics*, 2:186; Hazen, *Narrative*, 418.

49. Scott, *Infantry Tactics*, 2:138–39, 152.

50. Ibid., 3:282–84.

51. Ibid., 263; Casey, *Infantry Tactics*, 2:49, 196. If the companies of a regiment contained uneven numbers of men, the resulting column would look a bit ragged because the company lines within it would also be uneven. One can see this in an interesting photograph of the 5th New York (Duryea's Zouaves) forming a simple column on the streets of Baltimore in September 1861. See Bailey, *Forward to Richmond*, 69.

52. Scott, *Infantry Tactics*, 2:170, 172, 3:263.

53. Casey, *Infantry Tactics*, 2:202–203. For a detailed description of forming into a column of division, see Copp, *Reminiscences*, 176. For an interesting discussion of this rare maneuver, see Paine, *Wisconsin Yankee*, 18, 21, 29, 51.

54. Scott, *Infantry Tactics*, 1:65, 2:109–15; Casey, *Infantry Tactics*, 2:30–31.

55. Scott, *Infantry Tactics*, 2:173–78, 3:288–97; Casey, *Infantry Tactics*, 2:229–71.

56. Hazen, *Narrative*, 418.

57. Scott, *Infantry Tactics*, 3:207–97; Casey, *Infantry Tactics*, 1:9–10, 3:156–58.

58. Casey, *Infantry Tactics*, 1:10.

59. Scott, *Infantry Tactics*, 2:183–99; Casey, *Infantry Tactics*, 1:6, 184; Hess, *Rifle Musket*, 127–31.

60. Casey, *Infantry Tactics*, 1:184–87, 189–91, 193.

61. Ibid., 181–83, 185, 196, 198, 200–201.

62. Scott, *Infantry Tactics*, 1:67–68, 71–75, 78–79, 2:120–21, 133; Casey, *Infantry Tactics*, 2:57; Hardee, *Rifle and Light Infantry Tactics*, 118–20. For a description of the duties of the guide while on a march, see Squier, *This Wilderness of War*, 45.

63. Scribner, *How Soldiers Were Made*, 258.

64. Scott, *Infantry Tactics*, 1:75–76, 2:120; Casey, *Infantry Tactics*, 2:61, 63–64.

65. Hardee, *Rifle and Light Infantry Tactics*, 76; Scott, *Infantry Tactics*, 2:122; Granger testimony, Buell Court of Inquiry, Feb. 18, 1863, *OR*, 16(1):438, 441; Ayres testimony, May 17–18, 1880, Warren Court of Inquiry, *SOR*, pt. 1, 8:252, 270.

66. Sherman, *Memoirs*, 2:388.

67. Granger testimony, Feb. 17–18, 1863, Buell Court of Inquiry, *OR*, 16(1):436–37.

68. Ibid., 437.

69. Orders No. 9, Headquarters, First Division, Mar. 16, 1862, *OR*, 52(1):224; General Orders No. 24, Headquarters, Army of the Ohio, June 15, 1862, *OR*, 16(2):26.

70. General Orders No. 113, Headquarters, Army of the Potomac, Apr. 8, 1862, *OR*, 11(3):82–83. For a good description of marching by an enlisted man, see Stephenson, *Civil War Memoir*, 120–21.

71. Granger testimony, Feb. 18, 1863, Buell Court of Inquiry, *OR*, 16(1):441; Orders, Headquarters, Twentieth Corps, May 23, 1864, *OR*, 38(4):291; Orders, Headquarters, Sixth Corps, May 24, 1865, *OR*, 46(3):1204.

72. Warren to Humphreys, June 6, 1864, *OR*, 36(3):649.

73. Sherman, *Memoirs*, 2:388; Scribner, *How Soldiers Were Made*, 262.

74. Casey, *Infantry Tactics*, 3:23, 47–48, 60–73; Scott, *Infantry Tactics*, 2:143–44.

75. Otis Moody, "Account of the Battle of Stones River,"archived at https://web.archive.org/web/20120227114022/http://www.51illinois.org/moody_st_river.html (accessed June 25, 2014); Hall to Embler, July 17, 1863, *OR*, 27(1):439.

76. Circular, Headquarters, Armies of the Confederate States, Feb. 22, 1865, *OR*, 46(2):1248–49.

4. TRAINING

1. McGregor, *Fifteenth Regiment New Hampshire*, 201.

2. Ibid.; Metcalf, "Personal Incidents," 258; Scribner, *How Soldiers Were Made*, 258; Livingston to Stephens, Apr. 16, 1864, *OR*, 34(3):182.

3. Griffith, *Battle Tactics of the Civil War*, 105–109, 111–15; Morrison to McClernand, Feb. 28, 1862, *OR*, 7:212.

4. Bryant, *Third Regiment of Wisconsin*, 11–13. See also Saffell to John, Dec. 16, 1861, Richard Saffell Papers, UTK.

5. Deas to Garnett, May 21, 1862; and "Report of Inspection made at Harpers Ferry, Va, by Lieut. Col. George Deas, Insp. Gen., C.S. Army," contained in Deas to Garnett, May 23, 1861, *OR*, 2:868.

6. Stanley, *Sir Henry Morton Stanley*, 103.

7. Knipe to Scott, Oct. 1, 1862; and Warner to Knipe, Sept. 23, 1862, *OR*, 19(1):487, 493; Williams, *From the Cannon's Mouth*, 126.

8. General Orders No. 3, Headquarters, 78th Pennsylvania, Oct. 26, 1861, Order Book, Company I, 78th Pennsylvania Regimental File, SRNB; circular, Headquarters, Adams's Brigade, Mar. 3, 1863, in "Order Book, 5th Company, B.W.A.," Civil War Papers, Battalion Washington Artillery Collection, LHA Collection, TU; Copp, *Reminiscences*, 25; Orders No. 9, Headquarters, 21st Illinois, June 19, 1861; and Orders No. 23, Headquarters, 21st Illinois, July 9, 1861, Grant, *Papers*, 2:47, 61.

9. Williams, *From the Cannon's Mouth*, 31, 34; Beecham, *As If It Were Glory*, 15; Bull, *Soldiering*, 15.

10. Daniel, *Days of Glory*, 57; Prokopowicz, *All for the Regiment*, 2, 4–5; Garfield, *Wild Life of the Army*, 32, 35.

11. De Forest, *Volunteer's Adventures*, 11, 54.

12. Haughton, *Training, Tactics, and Leadership*, 54–55.

13. Barber, *Holding the Line*, 74, 98.

14. Scott, *Infantry Tactics*, 1:10.

15. Hazen, *Narrative*, 16–18; "Peter Wilson," 404.

16. Otto, *Memoirs of a Dutch Mudsill*, ix, 23; Jacob Van Zwaluwenburg Journal, 27–28, University of Michigan, William L. Clements Library, Ann Arbor.

17. Beatty, *Memoirs of a Volunteer*, 149; Herr, *Nine Campaigns*, 125; Gibson, *Ohio's Silver-Tongued Orator*, 517.

18. "Orphan Brigade Items," 322.

19. McAllister, *Civil War Letters*, 89; "Battalion Commands," Arthur W. Hyatt Papers, LSU; Hartzell, *Ohio Volunteer*, 100.

20. Irving Bronson, "Recollections of the Civil War," 1, Bruce Catton Collection, The Citadel, Archives and Museum, Charleston, S.C.; Copp, *Reminiscences*, 193; Day, *One Hundred and First Ohio*, 40.

21. Hall, *Story of the 26th Louisiana*, 20–21.

22. Paine, *Wisconsin Yankee*, 2–4, 12–13.

23. Ibid., 16–18, 26.

24. Hyde, *Following the Greek Cross*, 236; Boyd, *Civil War Diary*, 131.

25. Brooks to Assistant Adjutant General, Eighteenth Corps, May 25, 1864, *OR*, 36(2):128; Early to Pendleton, Jan. 12, 1863, *OR*, 12(2):715; Stegner to wife, May 22, 1864, Frederick W. Stegner Papers, Navarro College, Pearce Civil War Collection, Corsicana, Tex.; Bryan to Opdycke, Sept. [?], 1864, *OR*, 38(1):319.

26. Hazen to Assistant Adjutant General, Second Division, Left Wing, Jan. 5, 1863, *OR*, 20(1):542, 546–47.

27. Nosworthy, *Bloody Crucible*, 41–42, 45, 50, 52.

28. Hyde, *Following the Greek Cross*, 7, 11, 14; H. B. Hibben to editor, Feb. 16, 1862, *Indianapolis Daily Journal*, Feb. 28, 1862; Durham, *Three Years*, 72–73; Ware, *Lyon Campaign*, 64, 85–86, 133, 325–26, 328.

29. Williams, *From That Terrible Field*, 9; Matrau, *Letters Home*, 20; Hosea, "Regular Brigade," 329; Special Brigade Orders No. 37, Headquarters, Second Division, Massachusetts Volunteer Militia, Apr. 22, 1861, *OR*, 2:590.

30. Floyd, *Fortieth (Mozart) Regiment New York*, 105–106; Miller, *Fighting for Liberty and Right*, 92, 95; Haughton, *Training, Tactics, and Leadership*, 144–47.

31. Garfield, *Wild Life of the Army*, 57.

32. Hall, *Story of the 26th Louisiana*, 39, 47–48.

33. Williams to Schmitt, Sept. 25, 1863, *OR*, 30(1):543.

34. Isaiah Harlan quoted in Haughton, *Training, Tactics, and Leadership*, 56; Chambers, *Blood & Sacrifice*, 121.

35. Southwick to Smith, Apr. 30, 1865, *OR*, 48(2):247.

36. Metcalf, "Personal Incidents," 257–58.

37. Chance, *Second Texas Infantry*, 142; Hess, *Lee's Tar Heels*, 84–86.

38. Dawson to Hindman, June 20, 1862, *OR*, 13:945–46; Terry to Proudfit, Oct. 29, 1864, *OR*, 42(1):818–19.

39. Hartwell, *To My Beloved Wife*, 160, 220; General Orders No. 62, Headquarters, Army of the Potomac, June 12, 1863, *OR*, 27(3):79.

40. General Orders No. 36, Headquarters, Fifth Corps, Sept. 18, 1864, *OR*, 42(2):903.

41. General Orders No. 1, Headquarters, Second Corps, Jan. 1, 1865, *OR*, 46(2):6; Itinerary, Second Brigade, First Division, Second Corps, *OR*, 46(1):79.

42. General Orders No. 4, Headquarters, 78th Pennsylvania, Apr. 10, 1862; and General Orders No. 35, Headquarters, First Division, Fourteenth Corps, Feb. 29, 1864, Order Book, Company I, 78th Pennsylvania Regimental File, SRNB; *Story of the Fifty-Fifth Regiment*, 263.

43. General Orders No. 10, Headquarters, First Brigade, Seventh Division, Dec. 14, 1862; and Circular, Headquarters, Second Brigade, Second Division, Reserve Corps, Aug. 5, 1863, Order, Letter, Circular Books, Third Brigade, Second Division, Fourteenth Corps, Record Group 94, National Archives and Records Administration, Washington, D.C.

44. Carlin, *Memoirs*, 90; Merritt James Simonds Diary, May 5–June 23, 1863, Chickamauga-Chattanooga National Military Park, Fort Oglethorpe, Ga..

45. Hazen, *Narrative*, 99–100, 102.

46. Simmons, *History of the 84th Reg't Ill.*, 160; Philip R. Ward Diary, Mar. 8–18, 1864, Charles S. Harris Collection, University of Tennessee, Special Collections, Chattanooga; Henry Keck Diary, Apr. 20, 1864, Emmett Ross Papers, Mississippi State University, Special Collections, Starkville; Robinson to

Robinson, Dec. 28, 1864, *OR*, 39(1):659; Special Field Orders No. 104, Headquarters, Army of the Ohio, Sept. 8, 1864, Horace Capron Papers, Wisconsin Historical Society, Madison. For another example of continual training, see Special Orders No. 91, Headquarters, Thirteenth Corps, Apr. 28, 1864, *OR*, 34(3):319.

47. Phillips to Curtis, Jan. 19, 1863; and Phillips to unknown, Feb. 6, 1863, *OR*, 22(2):57–58, 101.

48. Lawler to Farrington, Dec. 1, 1864, *OR*, 41(4):738.

49. Burdette, *Drums of the 47th*, 31; Thomas Downs Diary, Jan. 8, 1863, Minnesota Historical Society, Saint Paul; Daniel Howe Diary, Jan. 21, 1863, Daniel Wait Howe Papers, Indiana Historical Society, Indianapolis.

50. Haughton, *Training, Tactics, and Leadership*, 55, 82–84; record of events, Apr. 24, 1863, Company K, 20th Louisiana, *SOR*, pt. 2, 24:464.

51. Womack, *Civil War Diary*, 74; Trimmier to Mary, Mar. 26, Apr. 4, 1863, Theodore Gillard Trimmier Papers, TSLA; Callaway, *Civil War Letters*, 76–77; General Orders No. 12, Headquarters, Adams's Brigade, Mar. 3, 1863, in "Order Book, 5th Company, B.W.A.," Civil War Papers, Battalion Washington Artillery Collection, LHA Collection, TU; W.H. Brooker Diary, Oct. 6, 8, 12, 1863, Rice University, Woodson Research Center, Houston, Tex..

52. General Orders No. 60, Headquarters, District of Indian Territory, Sept. 7, 1864, *OR*, 41(3):914.

53. Edwin H. Rennolds Diary, May 28, 1863, UTK.

54. Hord, "Prize Drill in the Army," 548–49; Giles to wife, Aug. 13, 1863, G. W. Giles Letters, LSU.

55. Mitchell, "Civil War Letters of Thomas Jefferson Newberry," 73.

56. General Orders No. 18, Headquarters, Third Division, Seventeenth Corps, Dec. 3, 1863, M. F. Force Papers, UW; General Orders No. 4, Headquarters, Third Division, Seventeenth Corps, Dec. 3, 1863, *OR*, 52(1):488–89.

57. "Civil War Diary of Charles Henry Snedeker," Dec. 22, 1863, Jan. 22–23, Apr. 5, 1864, Auburn University, Special Collections and Archives, Auburn, Ala.; [Newsome], *Experience in the War*, 60–61. For an example of another drill competition in the West, see Mahon, "Civil War Letters of Samuel Mahon," 245–46.

58. McAllister, *Civil War Letters*, 564–65, 574.

59. Ransom to Clark, May 26, 1863, *OR*, 24(2):298; Spiegel, *Your True Marcus*, 284–85; Wright to Porter, Oct. 9, 1863, *OR*, 30(2):118; Shepard to parents, Dec. 6, 1863, Irwin Shepard Letters, University of Michigan, Bentley Historical Library, Ann Arbor; Miles to Caldwell, Dec. 14, 1862, *OR*, 21:237; Holmes to Harris, Sept. 20, 1862, *OR*, 17(1):111; Sanborn to Clark, May 25, 1863, *OR*, 24(1):729; Bennett to Ratchford, Dec. 6, 1862, *OR*, 19(1):1047; *Story of the Fifty-Fifth Regiment*, 40–41.

60. General Orders No. 27, Headquarters, Second Division, Thirteenth Corps, June 21, 1865, *OR*, 49(2):1021; itinerary, Second Brigade, First Division, Second Corps, *OR*, 46(1):79.

61. McAllister, *Civil War Letters*, 96; Orders, Headquarters, Second Corps, Mar. 22, 1865, *OR*, 46(3):76.

62. Special Orders No. 239, Headquarters of the Army, May 18, 1865; and General Orders No. 27, Headquarters, Army of the Potomac, May 20, 1865, *OR*, 46(3):1171, 1181.

63. General Orders No. 26, Headquarters, Second Corps, May 22, 1865, *OR*, 46(3):1196.

64. Sherman, *Memoirs*, 2:378.

65. Orders, Headquarters, Sixth Corps, May 23, 1865; and General Orders No. 19, Headquarters,

Sixth Corps, June 6, 1865, *OR*, 46(3):1200, 1260.

66. Opdycke, *To Battle for God and the Right*, 290–91.

5. MOVING FORWARD AND THE ART OF SKIRMISHING

1. Collis to Birney, May 6, 1863; and Ellis to Franklin, May 7, 1863, *OR*, 25(1):424, 497; Kimberly and Holloway, *Forty-First Ohio*, 40–41; Palmer to Starling, Jan. 9, 1863, *OR*, 20(1):519.

2. Weitzel to Strong, Oct. 29, 1862, *OR*, 15:168.

3. De Forest, *Volunteer's Adventures*, 64–67.

4. Hunter to Breaux, Aug. 7, 1862, *OR*, 15:103.

5. Pillow to O'Hara, Jan. 11, 1863, *OR*, 20(1):808; Smith to Green, May 24, 1863, *OR*, 24(2):267; Johnson to Sykes, Oct. 5, 1863, *OR*, 30(2):282; McGill to Hale, July 29, 1864, *SOR*, pt. 1, 7:295.

6. Hall to Trousdale, Oct. 4, 1863, *OR*, 30(2):129; O'Neal to Barksdale, July 31, 1864, *OR*, 38(3):941.

7. Thruston to Howard, Dec. 4, 1863, *OR*, 29(1):866; McNeill to [Loughborough], May 31, 1864, *OR*, 38(3):851.

8. Wood to Buck, Oct. 9, 1863, *OR*, 30(2):159–60.

9. Lowery to Benham, Sept. 10, 1864, *OR*, 38(3):727.

10. Willcox to Lydig, Oct. 29, 1864; and Hartranft to Bertolette, Oct. 25, 1864, *OR*, 40(1):571, 576–77. Hartranft apparently learned his lesson about the alignment of his brigade compared to the opposing line. During the Fifth Offensive at Petersburg in September 1864, he noted his alignment as accurately as possible by reporting that it was "about 10 degrees east of north." See Hartranft to Bertolette, Oct. 30, 1864, *OR*, 42(1):56. For another report showing how important it was for the advancing line to be roughly parallel with the target line, see Miller to Wooley, Jan. 12, 1863, *OR*, 20(1):814.

11. General Orders No. 4, Headquarters, Second Division, Nineteenth Corps, June 15, 1863, *OR*, 26(1):560.

12. Hubbard to Thomas, Apr. 18, 1864, *OR*, 34(1):436; Johnson to Brown, July 7, 1862; and McElroy to Barksdale, July 5, 1862, *OR*, 11(2):621, 752.

13. Ronald to O'Brien, July 11, 1862, *OR*, 11(2):578–79.

14. Wells to Andrew, May 21, 1864, *OR*, 37(1):84.

15. Draper to Wheeler, Oct. 30, 1864, *OR*, 42(1):815–16.

16. Thruston to Vance, Sept. 27, 1862, *SOR*, pt. 1, 3:586; Lot Dudley Young Reminiscences, 23, 28, State Historical Society of Missouri, Research Center, Columbia; Lewis to Stake, Jan. 10, 1863, *OR*, 20(1):833; Thompson, *Orphan Brigade*, 179.

17. Hancock to Walker, Dec. 25, 1862, *OR*, 21:228; Gorman to Sedgwick, June 3, 1862, *OR*, 11(1):799; Blanchard to Walker, Apr. 30, 1864, *OR*, 34(1):434–35.

18. Colgrove to Gordon, Aug. 12, 1862, *OR*, 12(2):155–56.

19. Parker, *To Drive the Enemy from Southern Soil*, 405.

20. Lawton to Pendleton, July 28, 1862, *OR*, 11(2):595.

21. Lund to Hollers, Mar. 24, 1865, *OR*, 47(1):499–500.

22. Steuart to Hunter, Dec. 12, 1863; and Thruston to Howard, Dec. 4, 1863, *OR*, 29(1):863, 866–67.

23. Stevens to Evans, Oct. 13, 1862, *OR*, 12(2):631.

24. Bull, *Soldiering*, 44–45; Thompson to unknown, Aug. 8, 1864, *OR*, 36(1):498.

25. Baldwin to Hutchinson, May 9, 1863, *OR*, 24(1):676.

26. Miller to Edsall, July 7, 1863, *OR*, 23(1):503–504.

27. Howard to McKeever, July 26, 1861, *OR*, 2:418.

28. Leasure to Stevens, June 17, 1862, *OR*, 14:72; Griffin to unknown, July 25, 1862, *OR*, 11(2):602; Buford to Loring, June 16, 1863, *OR*, 24(2):83; Colgrove to Gordon, Aug. 12, 1862, *OR*, 12(2):156; Porter to Porter, Oct. 1, 1863, *OR*, 30(2):102; Whitaker to Crowell, Sept. 29, 1863; and Wood to Catching, Sept. 26, 1863, *OR*, 30(1):771, 847.

29. Bowen to Bowler, July 26, 1864, *OR*, 38(3):426.

30. Hoke to Pender, July 8, 1862, *SOR*, pt. 1, 2:455; Holmes to Bolinger, Sept. 5, 1862, *OR*, 51(1):127; Owen to Whittlesey, Dec. 18, 1862, *OR*, 21:278; Cotter to Foote, Jan. 10, 1863, *OR*, 20(1):953.

31. Erwin to Flanagan, May 8, 1863; and Sanborn to Clark, May 25, 1863, *OR*, 24(1):670, 729; Gates to Memminger, Aug. 1, 1863, *OR*, 24(2):119; Perry to unknown, n.d., *SOR*, pt. 1, 5:694.

32. McMillan to Leefe, Sept. 26, 1864; and Mollineaux to Hibbert, Sept. 26, 1864, *OR*, 43(1):314, 330; record of events, Company K, 7th USCT, Sept. 29, 1864, *SOR*, pt. 2, 77:408; Gilbert to Granger, Mar. 17, 1864, *OR*, 34(1):362.

33. Dyckman to Berry, June 27, 1862, *OR*, 11(2):191; Grimes to unknown, June 5, 1862, *OR*, 11(1):956; Bolar to Kirk, Oct. 2, 1862, *OR*, 51(1):155.

34. Fulton to Snowden, Oct. 11, 1862, *OR*, 16(1):1133; Williams to Hudson, Dec. 10, 1862, *OR*, 22(1):91; Quarles to Barksdale, Aug. 6, 1864, *OR*, 38(3):931; Kennedy to Elliott, Mar. 31, 1865, *OR*, 47(1):1109–10.

35. Porter to Porter, Oct. 1, 1863, *OR*, 30(2):102.

36. Baylor to unknown, July 9, 1862, *OR*, 11(2):580.

37. Keigwin to Jordan, May 2, 1863, *OR*, 24(1):587.

38. Read to Edgar, Mar. 29, 1906, *SOR*, pt. 1, 6:855–56; Potter to Hurd, Apr. 2, 1865, *OR*, 46(1):1217.

39. For a full discussion of Civil War skirmishing, see Hess, *Rifle Musket*, 145–74. For the importance of drilling in loose-order formations, see also Scott, *Military Dictionary*, 605.

40. Postscript of Goddard to Wagner, Jan. 12, 1863, *OR*, 20(2):322.

41. Alexander to Martin, May 24, 1863; and Deimling to McCannon, May 25, 1863, *OR*, 24(1):771, 782.

42. Holmes to Harris, Sept. 20, 1862, *OR*, 17(1):111; Wells to Andrew, May 21, 1864, *OR*, 37(1):83–84; Rice to Driver, Oct. 17, 1863, *OR*, 29(1):285.

43. Pillow to Blake, Nov. 10, 1861, *OR*, 3:325.

44. Wagner, *Organization and Tactics*, 88; Sickles to Dickinson, July 7, 1862, *OR*, 11(2):134; Thruston to Vance, Sept. 27, 1862, *SOR*, pt. 1, 3:585.

45. Rice to Sweeny, Oct. 10, 1862, *OR*, 17(1):281; Otis Moody, "Account of the Battle of Stones River,"archived at https://web.archive.org/web/20120227114022/http://www.51illinois.org/moody_st_river.html (accessed June 25, 2014); Bingham to Hatch, May 10, 1863, *OR*, 25(1):340.

46. Reynolds to Reeve, July 27, 1863; Smith to Blair, May 26, 1863; and Ransom to Clark, May 26, 1863, *OR*, 24(2):108, 263, 298; Higbee to Marvin, June 1, 1864, *OR*, 36(3):453.

47. Colgrove to Gordon, Aug. 12, 1862, *OR*, 12(2):155.

48. Wilcox to Sorrel, May 25, 1862, *OR*, 11(1):590; McRae to unknown, Oct. 8, 1862, *OR*, 19(1):1040.

49. Orders, Headquarters, Fifth Corps, June 1, 1864; and Osborn to Cutler, June 1, 1864, *OR*, 36(3):453.

50. George to Archer, May 11, 1863, *OR*, 25(1):931.

51. Hubbard to Thomas, Apr. 18, 1864, *OR*, 34(1):437; Symmes to Creigh, [May (?)], 1863, *OR*, 25(1):736.

52. Clendenin to brigade commanders and division officers of the day, First Division, Sixth Corps, Apr. 1, 1865, *OR*, 46(3):426.

53. Bingham to Hatch, May 10, 1863, *OR*, 25(1):342–43; McCoy to Monteith, Sept. 12, 1864; Cope to Warren, Aug. 24, 1864; Bragg to Monteith, Sept. 6, 1864; and Mead to Monteith, Sept. 4, 1864, *OR*, 42(1):503, 536–40.

54. Hyde to Mundee, Sept. 19, 1862, *OR*, 19(1):412–13.

55. Leasure to Hicks, July 17, 1863; Whittlesey to Adams, July 26, 1863; and Walcutt to Loudon, July 20, 1863, *OR*, 24(2):563–64, 617, 639; Heffron to brother, July 29, 1863, Henry G. Heffron Papers, New York State Library, Albany; Hess, *Rifle Musket*, 156–63.

56. Kiddoo to Vannings, June 22, 1864, *OR*, 40(1):725; Gillmore to Butler, June 2, 1864; and Butler to Gillmore, June 2, 1864, *OR*, 36(3):516, 518.

57. Hess, *Rifle Musket*, 145–46, 156–63.

58. McWhiney and Jamieson, *Attack and Die*, 83–84.

6. MULTIPLE LINES, ECHELONS, AND SQUARES

1. Warren to Crawford and Cutler, May 10, 1864; and Wright to Humphreys, May 10, 1864, *OR*, 36(2):607–608.

2. Hazen, *Narrative*, 332–33; Howard, *Autobiography*, 2:88–89.

3. Anderson to Oldershaw, Oct. 10, 1862, *OR*, 16(1):1062–63; Wood to McClernand, n.d., *OR*, 10(1):141–42.

4. Adams to Notebe, Dec. 9, 1862, *SOR*, pt. 1, 4:80–81; Symmes to Creigh, [May (?)],1863, *OR*, 25(1):736; Gibbon to Carncross, Nov. 7, 1864; and Cutcheon to Matthews, Aug. 7, 1864, *OR*, 36(1):429, 975; Curtis to Shepard, May 19, 1864; and Stedman to Reynolds, May 17, 1864, *OR*, 36(2):100, 163; Holmes to Anderson, Oct. 10, 1863, *OR*, 30(1):880–81.

5. DuBois to Lovell, Oct. 15, 1862, *OR*, 17(1):291.

6. Hawley to Fenton, June 16, 1862, *OR*, 14:67–68; Askew to McGrath, Sept. 12, 1864, *OR*, 38(1):406–407.

7. Weber to Hubbard, Oct. 9, 1862, *OR*, 17(1):201; Greathouse to Harlan, July 17, 1863, *OR*, 24(2):646.

8. Smith to Wallace, Feb. 17, 1862, *OR*, 7:202; Fairchild to Haskell, Sept. 20, 1862; and Bragg to Haskell, Sept. 20, 1862, *OR*, 19(1):253–54.

9. Lamar to Harris, May 13, 1862, *OR*, 11(1):598; Kennard to Hearne, Dec. 2, 1863, *OR*, 31(2):776; Hazen, *Narrative*, 418–19.

10. Sword, *Shiloh*, 113; Jordan, "Notes of a Confederate Staff-Officer," 595, 595n, 599; Chisolm, "Shiloh Battle-Order," 606; Special Orders No. 8, Headquarters, Army of the Mississippi, Apr. 3, 1862; Beauregard to Samuel Cooper, Apr. 11, 1862; and Bragg to Jordan, Apr. 30, 1862, *OR*, 10(1):386, 392–94, 464. While Special Orders No. 8 specified that Bragg should place his corps 1,000 yards behind Hardee, Beauregard's and Bragg's reports indicate the distance was actually 800 yards.

11. Bragg to Jordan, Apr. 30, 1862; and Gibson to unknown, Apr. 12, 1862, *OR*, 10(1):465, 480; Jordan, "Notes of a Confederate Staff-Officer," 602; Lockett, "Surprise and Withdrawal," 605.

12. General Orders No. 8, Headquarters, Army of the Ohio, Apr. 15, 1862, *OR*, 52(1):238–39.

13. Weber to Hubbard, Oct. 9, 1862, *OR*, 17(1):202; Special Orders No. 37, Right Wing, Thirteenth Corps, Dec. 28, 1862; and Blair to Montgomery, Dec. 30, 1862, *OR*, 17(1):622, 656; Hazen to Atkinson, Oct. [?], 1862, *OR*, 16(1):1070; Norton to Hazen, Dec. 30, 1862; and Bragg to Polk, Dec. 27, 1862, *OR*, 20(2):276, 464; Carlin to Morrison, Jan. 6, 1863; Sheridan to Campbell, Jan. 9, 1863; Hascall to Bestow, Dec. 28, 1862; and Cruft to Norton, Jan. 8, 1863, *OR*, 20(1):282, 347, 464–65, 527; Sheridan, *Personal Memoirs*, 1:216.

14. Wilcox to Sorrel, May 25, 1862, *OR*, 11(1):590; Gleason to [Powers], July 5, 1862, *OR*, 11(2):311; Abner Doubleday journal, Aug. 30, 1862, *SOR*, pt. 1, 2:699–700; Doubleday to Dickinson, Sept. 23, 1862; Brown to Cooke, Sept. 15, 1862; and Bartlett to Rodgers, [?] 1862, *OR*, 19(1):221, 386, 388–89.

15. Phelps to Halstead, Sept. 23, 1862; and Kimball to Gorman, Sept. 20, 1862, *OR*, 19(1):233, 313; Williams, *From the Cannon's Mouth*, 128, 189; Ross to Pittman, May 8, 1863, *OR*, 25(1):698.

16. McGinnis to Phillips, May 6, 1863; Stone to Dyer, May 2, 1863; and Logan to Clark, May 26, 1863, *OR*, 24(1):606, 629, 643, 647; Hovey to Scates, May 25, 1863, *OR*, 24(2):41; Palmer to Oldershaw, Sept. 30, 1863; and Knefler to Miller, Sept. 28, 1863, *OR*, 30(1):714, 812.

17. Warner to Mindil, Sept. 8, 1864; Ward to Speed, June 2, 1864; and Hascall to unknown, Sept. 9, 1864, *OR*, 38(2):250, 342, 610–11; Manigault, *Carolinian Goes to War*, 246; Mizner to Morrison, Sept. 2, 1864, *SOR*, pt. 1, 7:13–15; Morgan to McClurg, Sept. 21, 1864, *OR*, 38(1):644–45.

18. Johnson to Hayslip, Sept. 5, 1864, *OR*, 43(1):408; Pulford to Hancock, Aug. 23, 1864; Crawford to Locke, Nov. 2, 1864; McLaughlen to Bertolette, Oct. 16, 1864; Curtin to Wright, Oct. 17, 1864; Hudson to assistant adjutant general, First Brigade, Second Division, Ninth Corps, Oct. 11, 1864; Humphrey to Richards, Aug. 30, 1864, *OR*, 42(1):364, 496, 574, 581–84, 595; Streight to Bestow, Jan. 8, 1865; Smith to Whipple, Jan. 10, 1865, *OR*, 45(1):295, 435; and Pettus to Reeve, Apr. 1, 1865, *OR*, 47(1):1098.

19. Olmsted to [assistant adjutant general, Third Brigade, Second Division, Third Corps], June 26, 1862; Cake to Wilson, June 28, 1862; and Holmes to Toombs, July 23, 1862, *OR*, 11(2):159, 455, 700; Thruston to Vance, Sept. 27, 1862, *SOR*, pt. 1, 3:584–86; Anderson to Coward, Sept. 30, 1862, *OR*, 19(1):908–909; Breitenbach to Parsons, June 28, 1864; and Pier to not stated, n.d., *OR*, 40(1):386, 583–84; Campbell to Phillips, Aug. 30, 1864, *OR*, 42(1):698–99; Keifer to Whittier, Dec. 15, 1864, *OR*, 43(1):227.

20. Kimball to Gorman, Sept. 20, 1862, *OR*, 19(1):313.

21. Smith to Morgan, Aug. 5, 1864, *OR*, 39(1):252.

22. Merritt to Schofield, n.d., *OR*, 3:81.

23. Logan to Williams, Apr. 12, 1862; Kelley to Veatch, Apr. 10, 1862; and Davis to Fox, Apr. 8, 1862, *OR*, 10(1):215, 226, 228.

24. Neff to O'Brien, July 8, 1862; Lawton to Pendleton, July 28, 1862; and Benning to Toombs, July 26, 1862, *OR*, 11(2):584, 595, 703.

25. Taylor to assistant adjutant general, Hooker's Division, Third Corps, Sept. 8, 1862; and Andrews to Sellers, Sept. 5, 1862, *OR*, 12(2):445, 501–502.

26. Branch to Morgan, Aug. 18,1862, *OR*, 12(2):221; F. E. Coffee letter to editor, *National Tribune*, Oct. 4, 1883; Sedgwick to Fairbanks, Jan. 18, 1863; Beatty to Otis, Jan. 9, 1863; and Grider to Sheets, Jan. 1, 1863, *OR*, 20(1):528, 584–85; Richardson to Hoyt, July 6, 1862, *OR*, 11(2):328.

27. Collis to Birney, May 6, 1863, *OR*, 25(1):423.

28. Buell to Bestow, Sept. 27, 1863; Embree to Elwood, Sept. 26, 1863; and Stratton to Miller, Sept. 24, 1863, *OR*, 30(1):654, 661, 819.

29. Henagan to Goggin, July 21, 1864, *SOR*, pt. 1, 6:662–663; Upton to Dalton, Sept. 1, 1864, *OR*, vol. 36,pt. 1, 666.

30. Dawes to Wood, Aug. 8, 1864; and Hofmann to McClellan, Aug. 10, 1864, *OR*, 36(1):621, 626.

31. Warren endorsement on Crawford to Griffin, June 21, 1864, *OR*, 40(2):280.

32. Rogers to Mauran, May 10, 1863, *OR*, 25(1):616; Boynton to Beatty, Sept. 24, 1863, *OR*, 30(1):435; Moulton to Abel, May 11, 1864, *OR*, 36(2):156.

33. McAllister to Hancock, Aug. 11, 1864, *OR*, 36(1):488–89.

34. Rosser to Price, Mar. 21, 1862, *OR*, 8:312; French to unknown, June 3, 1863, *OR*, 11(1):782; Sickles to Locke, July 9, 1862, *OR*, 11(2):140; Leasure to Stevens, June 17, 1862, *OR*, 14:72–73; Ewell to Faulkner, Mar. 6, 1863, *OR*, 12(2):227; Shoup to Newton, Dec. 11, 1862; Frost to Newton, Dec. 15, 1862, *SOR*, pt. 1, 4:58–59, 76; Manigault, *Carolinian Goes to War*, 56.

35. Palmer to Oldershaw, Sept. 30, 1863, *OR*, 30(1):713.

36. Loring to West, Sept. 15, 1864; Featherston to Robinson, July 23, 1864; Huddleston to Neilson, Sept. 15, 1864; French to Jack, July 25, 1864; and Walthall to Gale, Jan. 14, 1865, *OR*, 38(3):876–77, 881–82, 890, 902, 925; Newton to Assistant Adjutant General, Army of the Cumberland, Sept. [?], 1864, *OR*, 38(1):297–98.

37. Bidwell to Mundee, Sept. 28, 1864; and McMillan to Leefe, Sept. 26, 1864, *OR*, 43(1):212, 313; Opdycke to Whitesides, Dec. 5, 1864, *OR*, 45(1):240; Opdycke, *To Battle for God and the Right*, 256–57.

38. Walker to Flynt, Jan. 11, 1863, *OR*, 20(1):442; Draper to Wheeler, Oct. 30, 1864, *OR*, 42(1):815; Hess, *Lee's Tar Heels*, 128.

7. CHANGING FRONT

1 Hill to Chilton, [?] 1862, *OR*, 19(1):1023.

2. Wilcox to Sorrel, May 25, 1862; French to unknown, June 3, 1863, *OR*, 11(1):591, 782; Grant to Read, July 9, 1862, *OR*, 11(2):479.

3. Hayman to unknown, May 6, 1862, *OR*, 11(1):509; Andrews to Gordon, Sept. 23, 1862, *OR*, 19(1):500; Tilton to Mervine, July 9, 1863, *OR*, 27(1):607; Chamberlain to Barnes, n.d., *SOR*, pt. 1, 5:196.

4. Grose to Mason, Sept. 5, 1864, *OR*, 38(1):257–58.

5. Nance to Holmes, Sept. 22, 1862; and Wallace to Evans, Oct. 21, 1862, *OR*, 19(1):868–69, 947; Swayne to Lathrop, Oct. 9, 1862; and Holmes to Harris, Sept. 20, 1862, *OR*, 17(1):111, 190–91; Hascall to Bestow, Dec. 28, 1862; and Lanier to Vaughan, Jan. 9, 1863, *OR*, 20(1):466, 746–47; "C" to editors, Jan. 20, 1863, *Memphis Daily Appeal*, Jan. 29, 1863; Otis Moody, "Account of the Battle of Stones River,"archived at https://web.archive.org/web/20120227114022/http://www.51illinois.org/moody_st_river.html (accessed June 25, 2014); Bento to Scates, July 27, 1863, *OR*, 24(2):609.

6. Phisterer, *Regular Brigade*, 9; Benton to Dyer, May 5, 1863, *OR*, 24(1):625–26.

7. Abner Doubleday journal, Aug. 29, 1862, *SOR*, pt. 1, 2:696; Jefferson to Hubbard, Oct. 13, 1862, *OR*, 17(1):203; Stafford to Burns, Jan. 5, 1863, *OR*, 20(1):343.

8. Blackman to Clay, Apr. 10, 1862, *OR*, 10(1):320.

9. Bradley to Lee, Jan. 8, 1863; Scribner to Taylor, Jan. 9, 1863; and Blake to Kimberly, Jan. 6, 1863, *OR*, 20(1):370, 383, 552; Donaldson, *Inside the Army of the Potomac*, 304–305; Moore to Fisk, July 23, 1864, *OR*, 38(3):257; Hickman to Latta, Sept. 25, 1864; and Clark to Latta, Sept. 26, 1864, *OR*, 43(1):187–89.

10. Manning to Kerr, July 8, 1863, *OR*, 27(2):407.

11. Langley to Swift, Mar. 28, 1865, *OR*, 47(1):541–42; Bradley, *Last Stand*, 229.

12. Special Orders No. 93, Headquarters, Bate's Division, May 6, 1864, *OR*, 38(4):671.

13. Hunter to Breaux, Aug. 7, 1862, *OR*, 15:103; Kershaw to Goggin, Oct. 9, 1862, *OR*, 19(1):865; Turner to Hall, May 18, 1863, *OR*, 24(1):741; Hall to Embler, July 17, 1863, *OR*, 27(1):439; Waters to Boice, Sept. 26, 1863, *OR*, 30(1):787; Nelson to Graham, July 24, 1864, *OR*, 38(3):898; Cumming to Assistant Adjutant General, Stevenson's Division, July 22, 1863, *OR*, 24(2):104.

14. Dougherty to Grant, Dec. [?], 1861, *OR*, 3:292; Marston to Hibbert, n.d.; and Smith to Anderson, June 5, 1862, *OR*, 11(1):477–78, 957–58; Davis to Budlong, June 4, 1863, *OR*, 24(1):711.

15. Fauntleroy to Davis, Oct. 6, 1864, *OR*, 42(1):941.

16. Butterfield to Auchmuty, May 30, 1862, *OR*, 11(1):723; Byrnes to Blake, Dec. 21, 1862, *OR*, 21:246; Leake to Lake, Dec. 9, 1862, *OR*, 22(1):120; McMurray, *Twentieth Tennessee*, 233.

17. Kirby to Voris, Jan. 5, 1863, *OR*, 20(1):284; Hyman to Brevoort, May 8, 1863, *OR*, 25(1):432; Stevenson to Townes, May 6, 1863, *OR*, 24(1):652; Barnes to Otis, Sept. 28, 1863; and Wood to Catching, Sept. 26, 1863, *OR*, 30(1):839, 846; Hill to Sample, May 28, 1864, *OR*, 34(1):329; Otis to [Robinson], Sept. 12, 1864; Huddleston to Neilson, Sept. 15, 1864; and Scott to Robinson, July 23, 1864, *OR*, 38(3):886–87, 890, 895; Daniel Harris Reynolds Diary, July 20, 1864, UAF; De Forest, *Volunteer's Adventures*, 193.

18. McLaughlin to Slack, May 5, 1863; Dollins to Whitehead, May 4, 1863; and Erwin to Flanagan, May 8, 1863, *OR*, 24(1):613, 655, 671; Strickland to Hall, Oct. 10, 1862, *OR*, 16(1):1069; Geary to Rodgers, May 10, 1863, *OR*, 25(1):731; Cutcheon to Bertelotte, Oct. 23, 1864, *OR*, 36(1):970.

19. Crofton to Shepherd, Jan. 10, 1863, *OR*, 20(1):401; "C" to editors, Jan. 20, 1863, *Memphis Daily Appeal*, Jan. 29, 1863.

20. Robinson to Wood, Nov. 18, 1863, *OR*, 27(1):280.

21. Corning to Long, Sept. 20, 1862, *OR*, 19(1):414; Cutcheon to Mathews, Aug. 7, 1864, *OR*, 36(1):976.

22. White to Goodman, Sept. 19, 1862, *OR*, 16(1):985.

23. Hurlbut to Davies, n.d., *OR*, 17(1):297–98.

24. Hawthorn to Thomas, July 9, 1863, *OR*, 22(1):428; Iverson to Peyton, May 13, 1863, *OR*, 25(1):984; Hildebrandt to Seabury, Oct. 22, 1863; and Keifer to Johnson, Dec. 3, 1863, *OR*, 29(1):301, 781.

25. Semmes to Goggin, May 20, 1863, *OR*, 25(1):835; Rowley to Morris, May 8, 1862, *OR*, 11(1):523; Hughs to Johnson, Oct. 12, 1862, *OR*, 16(1):1130–31; Gates to Memminger, Aug. 1, 1863, *OR*, 24(2):118–19.

26. Hughs to Johnson, Oct. 12, 1862, *OR*, 16(1):1131; Williams to Arnall, [May (?)],1863, *OR*, 25(1):1020–21; Kellogg to Disosway, Oct. 21, 1864, *OR*, 43(1):385; McManus to Fetterman, Sept. 3, 1864, *OR*, 38(1):574; Gilbert to Donnan, May 26, 1864, *OR*, 34(1):364.

27. Godwin to Daniel, July 30, 1863, *OR*, 27(2):484.

28. Buck to Cooke, Sept. 16, 1862, *OR*, 19(1):384; Maffett to Holmes, July 31, 1863, *OR*, 27(2):372; Toulmin to Travis, Oct. 5, 1863, *OR*, 30(2):336.

29. Upton, *Infantry Tactics*, 25; Withers to Moore, Dec. 5, 1863, *OR*, 29(1):858–59; Scott, *Infantry Tactics*, 1:42.

30. Davis to Budlong, June 4, 1863, *OR*, 24(1):712–13; Wood to Stone, Dec. 19, 1863, *OR*, 31(2):378.

31. Olson to Watkins, Jan. 9, 1863, *OR*, 20(1):358; Ellis to Franklin, May 7, 1863, *OR*, 25(1):497;

Reid to Walker, Oct. 5, 1863; and Clay to Kerr, Sept. 21, 1863, *OR*, 30(2):349, 517; Spear to Bartlett, Aug. [?], 1864, *OR*, 36(1):576; Gray to Schmitt, Sept. 26, 1863; and Buckner to Edsall, Sept. 27, 1863, *OR*, 30(1):552, 557.

32. Brent to [Withers], Dec. 30, 1862, *OR*, 20(2):469.

33. Williamson to Assistant Adjutant General, Third Brigade, Third Division, Smith's Corps, Army of Tennessee, Jan. 10, 1863, *OR*, 20(1):950.

34. Bunn to Foote, Jan. 15, 1863, *OR*, 20(1):952; Seay, "Private at Stone River," 158.

35. Cleburne to Roy, Jan. 31, 1863, *OR*, 20(1):844–45.

36. Ibid.

37. Ibid.

38. Vaughan to Ingram, Jan. 9, 1863; and Cleburne to Roy, Jan. 31, 1863, *OR*, 20(1):744, 846.

39. Cleburne to Roy, Jan. 31, 1863, *OR*, 20(1):846–47.

40. Ibid., 847–48.

41. Ibid., 848–50.

42. Pickett, "Reminiscences of Murfreesboro," 451.

43. Stewart to Ratchford, June 5, 1864; Clayton to Hatcher, May 19, 1864; and Jones to Macon, May 29, 1864, *OR*, 38(3):817, 832, 842.

44. Stewart to Ratchford, June 5, 1864; Clayton to Hatcher, May 19, 1864; and Jones to Macon, May 29, 1864, *OR*, 38(3):817, 832, 842.

45. Hayes to Hayslip, Aug. 8, 1864, *OR*, 37(1):311.

46. De Forest, *Volunteer's Adventures*, 188–89.

8. COLUMNS

1. Claiborne Diary, Apr. 3, 1864, *SOR*, pt. 1, 6:208–209; Dunphy to Hollers, Sept. 8, 1864, *OR*, 38(1):675.

2. Rosecrans to Thomas, Feb. 12, 1863; and Sheridan to Campbell, Jan. 9, 1863, *OR*, 20(1):195, 348; Powell to Candy, May 29, 1863, *OR*, 25(1):743; Case to McQuiston, May 18, 1864, *OR*, 38(2):557; Logan to Clark, [Sept. 13, 1864], *OR*, 38(3):95; journal of First Brigade, First Division, Fourteenth Corps, Aug. 5, 1864, *OR*, 38(1):532.

3. Kirby to Voris, Jan. 5, 1863; Gibson to Bartlett, Jan. 5, 1863; and Ross to Fairbanks, Jan. 8, 1863, *OR*, 20(1):284, 304, 540; Worden, "Battle of Stone's River," 9; Kirk to Bartlette, n.d., *SOR*, pt. 1, 3:626; Randlett to Moore, Oct. 21, 1864; and Thompson to Lockwood, Oct. 29, 1864, *OR*, 42(1):722, 775–76.

4. Lovell to Cutting, Sept. 25, 1862, *OR*, 19(1):361; Case to McQuiston, May 18, 1864, *OR*, 38(2):557–58.

5. Baldwin to unknown, Mar. 12, 1862, *OR*, 7:338–39; Codman to Parkinson, May 1, 1863, *OR*, 18:350.

6. Blunt to Schofield, July 26, 1863, *OR*, 22(1):447–48.

7. Humphreys to Hays, Apr. 1, 1865; and Grant to Meade, Apr. 2, 1865, *OR*, 46(3):413–14, 452.

8. [Bartlett] to Porter, July 23, 1861, *OR*, 2:388; Lee to Fulton, Aug. 13, 1862, *OR*, 12(2):198; Phelps to Halstead, Sept. 20, 1862; Fairchild to Haskell, Sept. 20, 1862; Callis to Haskell, Sept. 18, 1862; Thomson to Kenny, Oct. 7, 1862; Richardson to Weaver, Sept. 19, 1862; Magilton to Jackson, Sept. 21, 1862; and Gordon to Williams, Sept. 24, 1862, *OR*, 19(1):231, 252, 257, 262–63, 273, 494–95; Clark to unknown, Oct. 2, 1862, *OR*, 51(1):144.

9. Suiter to Gorman, Sept. 20, 1862, *OR*, 19(1):315.

10. Williams, *From the Cannon's Mouth*, 125; Collins to Crane, Sept. 24, 1862, *OR*, 19(1):507.

11. Crawford to Williams, Oct. 21, 1862, *OR*, 19(1):484.

12. Tippin to Birney, May 8, 1863, *OR*, 25(1):420; Robinson to Wood, Nov. 18, 1863; and McAllister to Benedict, Aug. 3, 1863, *OR*, 27(1):279, 553; Williams to Wood, n.d., *SOR*, pt. 1, 5:137.

13. Beal to Leefe, Sept. 26, 1864, *OR*, 43(1):311–12.

14. Doss to Brown, [?] 1862, *OR*, 7:344–45; Barber, *Holding the Line*, 26, 28, 30.

15. Smith to Voris, Sept. 25, 1863; Knefler to Miller, Sept. 28, 1863; and Frambes to King, Sept. 26, 1863, *OR*, 30(1):527, 812, 833; Aiken to Jones, Sept. 26, 18.63, *OR*, 30(2):428.

16 Becht to Malmros, May 25, 1864, *OR*, 34(1):325.

17. Hubbard to Randall, Dec. 27, 1864, *OR*, 45(1):445–46.

18. Burns to Sedgwick, June 3, 1862; and Dana to Sedgwick, June 3, 1862, *OR*, 11(1):806, 808; Grower to Lansing, n.d., *OR*, 12(2):478; Colgrove to Ruger, Aug. 8, 1863, *OR*, 27(1):812; Smith to Johnson, Nov. 10, 1863, *OR*, 29(1):565; Pond to Carleton, Oct. 14, 1864; and James to Proudfit, Oct. 17, 1864, *OR*, 42(1):690, 817; Torbert to Read, Dec. 16, 1862, *OR*, 21:527.

19. Special Orders No. 8, Headquarters, Army of the Mississippi, Apr. 3, 1862, "General Orders from Jan. 6th 1862 to Aug. 24th 1862," Bound Volumes, 196, Louisiana Historical Association, Collection, TU; General Orders No. 8, Headquarters, Army of the Ohio, Apr. 15, 1862, *OR*, 52(1):238–39.

20. Maury to Guillet, Jan. 12, 1863; and Zacharie to Guillet, Feb. 9, 1863, *OR*, 20(1):800–801.

21. Osterhaus to Scates, May 26, 1863, *OR*, 24(2):16; Knefler to Bestow, Sept. 10, 1864; and Fullerton journal, June 15, 1864, *OR*, 38(1):445, 877–78; Streight to Bestow, Jan. 8, 1865, *OR*, 45(1):294.

22. Palmer to Brown, Mar. 7, 1862, *OR*, 7:352–53. In addition to the column of maneuver, the column of waiting, and the column of attack, Nosworthy also writes of the "column of route," a marching formation. See *With Musket*, 91–92.

23. Veatch to Atkins, Apr. 10, 1862, *OR*, 10(1):221; McRae to Snead, July 14, 1863; and Parsons to Snead, July 10, 1863, *OR*, 22(1):417, 420.

24. Upton to Hoffman, Mar. 17, 1862, *OR*, 9:219; Gove to Powers, Apr. 12, 1862; Nugent to McCoy, June 2, 1863; and Gorman to Sedgwick, June 3, 1862, *OR*, 11(1):295, 780, 798–99; Adams to Wilson, July 6, 1862, *OR*, 11(2):453.

25. Robinson to Kearny, July 5, 1862; and Ruehle to Hoyt, July 6, 1862, *OR*, 11(2):176, 325; Condon to unknown, Dec. 24, 1862, *OR*, 21:249; Geary to Rodgers, July 29, 1863, *OR*, 27(1):826; Brown to Morse, Sept. 3, 1864, *OR*, 40(1):717; Thompson to Moore, Aug. 23, 1864; and Shaw to Bailey, Oct. 9, 1864, *OR*, 42(1):710, 772; Edwards to Dalton, Sept. 30, 1864, *OR*, 43(1):184.

26. Palmer to Brown, Mar. 7, 1862, *OR*, 7:352; Jefferson to Hubbard, Oct. 13, 1862; McCalla to Sullivan, Oct. 12, 1862; and Hurlbut to Davies, n.d., *OR*, 17(1):203, 234–35, 297; Sheridan to Campbell, Jan. 9,1863, *OR*, 20(1):350; Benton to Lacey, May 7, 1864, *SOR*, pt. 1, 6:394; Wangelin to Gordon, May 20, 1864, *OR*, 38(3):163; Govan to Buck, Dec. 3, 1863; and Warfield to Sawrie, Dec. 2, 1863, *OR*, 31(2):763, 764; Hood, *Advance and Retreat*, 118.

27. Howard, *Autobiography*, 1:338.

28. Tyler to Kimball, Mar. 26, 1862; and Fulkerson to Pendleton, Mar. 26, 1862, *OR*, 12(1):376–77, 408; Garnett to Pendleton, Mar. 30, 1862, *SOR*, pt. 1, 2:613; Conrad to Gamble, Sept. 30, 1863, *OR*, 30(1):592–93.

29. Sweeny to Lovell, Oct. 15, 1862; and Baldwin to Lovell, Oct. [?], 1862, *OR*, 17(1):272, 290.

30. Fuller to Sinclair, Oct. 13, 1862; and Spaulding to Lathrop, Oct. 9, 1862, *OR*, 17(1):185, 188.

31. Hamilton to Kennett, Oct. 18, 1862; Sweeny to Lovell, Oct. 15, 1862; and Du Bois to Lovell, Oct. 15, 1862, *OR*, 17(1):206, 274, 291.

32. Sedgwick to Williams, May 15, 1863, *OR*, 25(1):559; Shaler to Townsend, Apr. [?], 1878, *SOR*, pt. 1, 4:646.

33. Dawson to Burnham, May 10, 1863, *OR*, 25(1):626; Sears, *Chancellorsville*, 353, 355–57.

34. General Field Order, [May 21, 1863], Grant, *Papers*, 8:246.

35. Osterhaus to Scates, May 26, 1863; and Keigwin to Thompson, May 30, 1863, *OR*, 24(2):20, 232; Spiegel, *Your True Marcus*, 279; Way, *Thirty-Third Regiment Illinois*, 43–44; Buehler to Burbridge, May 25, 1863, *OR*, 24(1):598.

36. Hubbard to Malmros, May 25, 1863, *OR*, 24(1):768; Smith to Green, May 24, 1863, *OR*, 24(2):269–70; Saunier, *Forty-Seventh Regiment Ohio*, 147.

37. Smith to Townes, June 23, 1863; Davis to Budlong, June 4, 1863; and Stevenson to Townes, July 7, 1863, *OR*, 24(1):710, 713, 719; Putnam to Crowell, May 25, 1863; and Humphrey to unknown, Aug. 14, 1863, *OR*, 24(2):67–68, 300; George Carrington Diary, May 22, 1863, Chicago History Museum, Chicago, Ill.; Trimble, *Ninety-Third Regiment Illinois*, 36.

38. Seymour to Turner, Nov. 10, 1863; and Hallowell to Seymour, Nov. 7, 1863, *OR*, 28(1):347, 362; Emery to Seymour, Nov. 9, 1863, *OR*, 53:10.

39. Butler to unknown, Feb. 2, 186[4]; Dandy to Assistant Adjutant General, Headquarters, U.S. Forces on Morris Island, Nov. 4, 1863; and Abbott to Seymour, Nov. 6, 1863, *OR*, 53:6, 11, 12; Abbott to Gilmore, Aug. 16, 1863, *OR*, 28(1):364–65.

40. Sheridan to Fullerton, Feb. 20, 1864; Sherman to Moore, Jan. 22, 1864; Steinwehr to Meysenburg, Dec. 23, 1863; Mindil to Brown, Dec. 18, 1863; and Jones to Brown, Dec. 18, 1863, *OR*, 31(2):189, 194, 359, 362, 366.

41. Wood to Joseph S. Fullerton, Dec. 29, 1863; Willich to Wells, Dec. 31, 1863; Hazen to Assistant Adjutant General, Third Division, Fourth Corps, Dec. 10, 1863; and Beatty to Bestow, Nov. 27, 1863, *OR*, 31(2):254–55, 263, 280–81, 300.

42. Wood to Joseph S. Fullerton, Dec. 29, 1863, *OR*, 31(2):254–55.

43. Rhea, *Cold Harbor*, 198–200, 202.

44. Smith to unknown, Aug. 9, 1864, *SOR*, pt. 1, 6:637–38; Martindale to Bowen, July 1, 1864; and Stannard to Abel, June 20, 1864, *OR*, 51(1):1253, 1261.

45. Upton to Dalton, Sept. 1, 1864, *OR*, 36(1):670–71.

46. Hess, *Kennesaw Mountain*, 64–66.

47. Howard to Whipple, Sept. 18, 1864; Stanley to Fullerton, [?] 1864; Newton to Assistant Adjutant General, Army of the Cumberland, Sept. [?], 1864; Wagner to Lee, Sept. 10, 1864; Clark to Waterman, Sept. 14, 1864; and Fullerton journal, *OR*, 38(1):199, 224, 295, 335, 364, 887; Shellenberger, "Kenesaw Mountain."

48. Davis to McClurg, Sept. [?], 1864; Banning to Wilson, Sept. 9, 1864; and Holmes to Swift, Sept. 7, 1864, *OR*, 38(1):632, 703, 729.

49. Garfield to Crittenden, McCook, Stanley, Sheridan, and Thomas, July 1, 1863, *OR*, 23(2):494; Schriver to King, Aug. 21, 1862, *OR*, 51(1):752.

50. Lyman, *Meade's Army*, 230; Meade to Wright, June 23, 1864, *OR*, 40(2):357.

51. Howard, *Autobiography*, 1:582–83.

52. Luther P. Bradley letter quoted in Wagner, *Organization and Tactics*, 91n.

53. Nathan Kimball letter quoted in ibid.

54. Cox, *Atlanta*, 129.

55. Howard, *Autobiography*, 1:548; *Cincinnati Commercial* correspondent quoted in *Chicago Daily Tribune*, July 6, 1864.

56. McWhiney and Jamieson, *Attack and Die*, 81–89, 91; Hsieh, *West Pointers*, 184.

9. MULTIPLE MANEUVERS

1. Baldwin to unknown, Mar. 12, 1862, *OR*, 7:339.

2. Willich to Gibson, Apr. 10, 1862, *OR*, 10(1):317–18.

3. Campbell to Butterfield, July 5, 1862, *OR*, 11(2):345.

4. Ibid.

5. Ibid.

6. Miles to Caldwell, Sept. 19, 1862, *OR*, 19(1):291.

7. Ibid.

8. Ibid.

9. Condon to unknown, Dec. 24, 1862, *OR*, 21:249.

10. Ibid., 250.

11. Ibid.

12. Ibid.

13. Manderson to Sheets, Jan. 6, 1863, *OR*, 20(1):593.

14. Ibid., 594.

15. Ibid.

16. Ibid.

17. Keeble to Cross, Sept. 28, 1863, *OR*, 30(2):484.

18. Ibid.

19. Chew to Parsons, Oct. 30, 1864, *OR*, 42(1):332–33.

10. LARGE FORMATIONS

1 Prokopowicz, *All for the Regiment*, 46–47, 54.

2. Chamberlaine, *Memoirs*, 94.

3. Norton to Hazen, Dec. 30, 1862, *OR*, 20(2):276.

4. O'Reilly, *Fredericksburg Campaign*, 254–433; Hess, *Pickett's Charge*, 166–80; Rhea, *Battles for Spotsylvania Court House*, 232–307.

5. The standard history of the Army of Tennessee remains Connelly, *Army of the Heartland* and *Autumn of Glory.*

6. For the history of the Army of the Tennessee, see Woodworth, *Nothing but Victory.*

7. For the history of the Army of the Cumberland, see Daniel, *Days of Glory.*

8. There is no single best operational history of the Army of Northern Virginia, but consult studies of its major battles and the *OR.*

9. As with the Army of Northern Virginia, there is yet no single best history of the Army of the Potomac, but consult studies of its major battles and the *OR*.

10. Sears, *Chancellorsville*, 234–35, 261.

11. Rodes to Pendleton, [May (?)], 1863; Ramseur to Peyton, May 23, 1863; and Colston to Pendleton, May 28, 1863, *OR*, 25(1):940–41, 995, 1004.

12. Rodes to Pendleton, [May (?)],1863; and Colston to Pendleton, May 28, 1863, *OR*, 25(1):940–41, 1004.

13. Rodes to Pendleton, [May (?)], 1863; Iverson to Peyton, May 13, 1863; and Christie to Halsey, May 7, 1863, *OR*, 25(1):941, 984–85, 992.

14. Rodes to Pendleton, [May (?)], 1863; Colston to Pendleton, May 28, 1863; Hinrichs to Colston, May 9, 1863; and Brown to Hall, May 12, 1863, *OR*, 25(1):941–42, 1004–1005, 1009, 1032.

15. Schurz to Howard, May 12, 1863; and O'Neal to Peyton, May 12, 1863, *OR*, 25(1):655–56, 951.

16. Hess, *Trench Warfare under Grant and Lee*, 47–48.

17. Rhea, *Battles for Spotsylvania Court House*, 164; Upton to Dalton, Sept. 1, 1864, *OR*, 36(1):667.

18. Upton to Dalton, Sept. 1, 1864, *OR*, 36(1):668; Rhea, *Battles for Spotsylvania Court House*, 168–76.

19. Rhea, *Battles for Spotsylvania Court House*, 214–17.

20. Walker, *History of the Second Army Corps*, 468; Rhea, *Battles for Spotsylvania Court House*, 223; Walker and Walker, "Diary of the War," pt. 4, 180–81; Mason, "Through the Wilderness to the Bloody Angle," 302; Black, "Reminiscences of the Bloody Angle," 423.

21. Hancock to Assistant Adjutant General, Army of the Potomac, Sept. 21, 1865, *OR*, 36(1):335; Mason, "Through the Wilderness to the Bloody Angle," 302–303; Black, "Reminiscences of the Bloody Angle," 424; Walker and Walker, "Diary of the War," pt. 4, 181.

22. Mason, "Through the Wilderness to the Bloody Angle," 303; Walker and Walker, "Diary of the War," pt. 4, 181.

23. Rhea, *Battles for Spotsylvania Court House*, 225–26, 321–22.

24. Hancock to Assistant Adjutant General, Army of the Potomac, Sept. 21, 1865; and Tyler to Marble, Aug. 27, 1864, *OR*, 36(1):335, 477; Hess, *Trench Warfare under Grant and Lee*, 68, 83.

25. Black, "Reminiscences of the Bloody Angle," 427; Alexander, *Fighting for the Confederacy*, 376.

26. Hess, *In the Trenches*, 246.

27. Delafield to Stanton, Oct. 30, 1865, *OR*, ser. 3, 5:178; Walker, "Gordon's Assault on Fort Stedman," 23–24; Hess, *In the Trenches*, 250.

28. Walker, "Gordon's Assault on Fort Stedman," 28; Hess, *In the Trenches*, 250–53.

29. Hess, *In the Trenches*, 251.

30. Bearss and Calkins, *Battle of Five Forks*, 1–13.

31. Warren to Bowers, Dec. 1, 1865; and Kellogg to Lambdin, Apr. 10, 1865, *OR*, 46(1):830, 885.

32. Bearss and Calkins, *Battle of Five Forks*, 86–87; Warren to Bowers, Dec. 1, 1865, *OR*, 46(1):829–31.

33. Warren to Bowers, Dec. 1, 1865, *OR*, 46(1):830; Warren testimony, July 2, 1880, Warren Court of Inquiry, *SOR*, pt. 1, 8:744–46; Bartlett testimony, Nov. 17, 1880; Warren testimony, Nov. 19, 1880, Warren Court of Inquiry, ibid., 9:1168, 1222. Sheridan's chief of staff, James W. Forsyth, testified that Warren prepared a sketch map at Five Forks to avoid misunderstanding of his orders by his subordinates. Forsyth concluded "that it was a guard that he used as between himself and his division commanders." Forsyth testimony, Nov. 5, 1880, Warren Court of Inquiry, ibid., 1048, 1053.

34. Ayres testimony, Nov. 5, 1880, Warren Court of Inquiry, *SOR*, pt. 1, 9:1077, 1080–1081.

35. Coulter to Lambdin, Apr. 26, 1865, *OR*, 46(1):897.

36. Bartlett testimony, Nov. 17, 1880, Warren Court of Inquiry, *SOR*, pt. 1, 9:1169; Chamberlain to Fowler, Apr. 24, 1865; and Bartlett to Fowler, Apr. 10, 1865, *OR*, 46(1):850, 860; Chamberlain testimony, May 18, 1880, Warren Court of Inquiry, *SOR*, pt. 1, 8:272–73; Chamberlain testimony, Nov. 5, 1880, Warren Court of Inquiry, ibid., 9:1085.

37. Bartlett testimony, Nov. 17, 1880; Stickney argument (counsel for Warren), July 26, 1881; and Gardner argument (counsel for Sheridan), July 28, 1881, Warren Court of Inquiry, *SOR*, pt. 1, 9:1169, 1377, 1481; Warren testimony, July 2, 1880, Warren Court of Inquiry, ibid., 8:800.

38. Warren to Bowers, Dec. 1, 1865; and Ayres to Locke, Apr. 12, 1865, *OR*, 46(1):832–33, 869; Ayres testimony, May 17, 1880, Warren Court of Inquiry, *SOR*, pt. 1, 8:254–56.

39. Warren testimony, Nov. 19, 1880, Warren Court of Inquiry, *SOR*, pt. 1, 9:1222, 1228; Warren testimony, July 2, 1880, Warren Court of Inquiry, ibid., 8:750.

40. Chamberlain testimony, May 18, 1880, Warren Court of Inquiry, ibid., 8:273.

41. Tarbell testimony, Oct. 21, 1880; and Denslow testimony, Nov. 9, 1880, Warren Court of Inquiry, *SOR*, pt. 1, 9:997, 1009, 1121.

42. Richardson testimony, May 19, 1880; Denslow testimony, May 21, 1880; Coulter testimony, May 24, 1880; and Warren testimony, July 2, 1880, Warren Court of Inquiry, *SOR*, pt. 1, 8:315, 334–35, 349–50, 750; Tarbell testimony, Oct. 21, 1880, Warren Court of Inquiry, ibid., 9:1008.

43. Warren testimony, July 2, 1880, Warren Court of Inquiry, ibid., 8:750; Warren testimony, Nov. 19, 1880; and Stickney argument (counsel for Warren), July 26, 1881, Warren Court of Inquiry, ibid., 9:1222–23, 1229, 1385.

44. Buell, *"Cannoneer,"* 351.

45. Bartlett to Fowler, Apr. 10, 1865, *OR*, 46(1):861; Buell, *"Cannoneer,"* 352–53.

46. Sawyer testimony, July 2, 1880, Warren Court of Inquiry, *SOR*, pt. 1, 8:411, 415.

47. Bartlett to Fowler, Apr. 10, 1865, *OR*, 46(1):861; Buell, *"Cannoneer,"* 352–53.

48. Chamberlain to Fowler, Apr. 24, 1865, *OR*, 46(1):850; Chamberlain testimony, May 18, 1880, Warren Court of Inquiry, *SOR*, pt. 1, 8:273.

49. Report of Warren Court of Inquiry, prior to Nov. 21, 1882; and Report of the General of the Army, July 15, 1882, Warren Court of Inquiry, *SOR*, pt. 1, 9:1560–61, 1601–1602.

50. Greene, *Breaking the Backbone*, 293–328, 442–51.

51. Ibid., 445–46; Beals, "In a Charge near Fort Hell," 107–108; Hartranft to Bertolette, July 3, 1865, *OR*, 46(1):1061; Miles Clayton Huyette Reminiscences, 11, New-York Historical Society, New York City.

52. Greene, *Breaking the Backbone*, 446, 448, 450; Hess, *In the Trenches*, 267–71.

53. Greene, *Breaking the Backbone*, 265–67, 282; Orders, Headquarters, Sixth Corps, Apr. 1, 1865, *OR*, 46(3):423–24.

54. Greene, *Breaking the Backbone*, 275–76; Getty to Whittelsey, Apr. 17, 1865, *OR*, 46(1):954; Stevens, "Storming of the Lines of Petersburg," 419–22; L. A. Grant to George W. Getty, Dec. 31, 1883, Hazard Stevens Papers, LC.

55. Greene, *Breaking the Backbone*, 267, 276–77; Edwards to Clendenin, Apr. 17, 1865, *OR*, 46(1):941.

56. Confidential Orders, Headquarters, First Division, Sixth Corps, Apr. 1, 1865, *OR*, 46(3):424; Rhodes, *All for the Union*, 225.

57. Greene, *Breaking the Backbone*, 277.

58. Ibid., 273–81; Wright to Webb, Apr. 1, 1865, *OR,* 46(3):423.

59. Hyde to Mundee, Apr. 15, 1865, *OR,* 46(1):975–76.

60. Rhodes, *All for the Union,* 226.

61. Greene, *Breaking the Backbone,* 292, 324.

62. Orders, Headquarters, Sixth Corps, Apr. 5, 1865, *OR,* 46(3):580–81.

11. TACTICAL DEVELOPMENTS AFTER THE CIVIL WAR

1. Hess, *Rifle Musket,* 29–34.

2. Ibid., 107–15.

3. Ibid.

4. Ibid., 97–104.

5. Gist, "Battle of Franklin," 233, 239.

6. Hess, *Rifle Musket,* 218–24.

7. Ibid., 217–18.

8. Wagner, *Organization and Tactics,* 46–47, 111–13.

9. Warner, *Generals in Blue,* 335–36; Morris to father, May 6, 1862, William Hopkins Morris Family Papers, USMA; *In Memoriam, William Hopkins Morris,* Military Order of the Loyal Legion of the United States, New York Commandery, Circular 16, 1900–1901, copy in ibid.

10. Morris to Grant, Feb. 4, 1865, Grant, *Papers,* 13:496–97.

11. Morris to Grant, Jan. 5, 1865, ibid., 495–96.

12. Morris to Grant, Oct. 9, 1865, ibid., 17:45n.

13. Warner, *Generals in Blue,* 535–36.

14. Wallace to Grant, Jan. 11, 1866, Grant, *Papers,* 17:45n.

15. Wallace to Grant, Mar. 2, 1866, ibid., Grant endorsement on board report, Apr. 5, 1866, ibid. Some officers of the era persisted in their belief that columns were effective in attacking heavily defended positions, or in the idea that bayonet attacks could work, or that multiple lines were ineffective. In essence, they seem to have learned relatively little from the actual experience of military operations during the Civil War in contrast to Morris, Wallace, and Upton. See, for example, Lippitt, *Treatise on the Tactical Use of the Three Arms,* 9, 12–15, 18–19; and Palfrey, "Period Which Elapsed," 212.

16. Warner, *Generals in Blue,* 519–20.

17. Michie, *Emory Upton,* 189–90.

18. Ibid., 191–92.

19. Emory Upton to Sherman, Jan. 14, 1865 [actual date 1866], William T. Sherman Papers, LC.

20. Michie, *Emory Upton,* 194–99, 201, 203–206, 211.

21. Upton, *Infantry Tactics,* iii–iv, 1.

22. Ibid., 1–2, 8, 48, 53, 59, 67, 92.

23. Ibid., 57, 59, 82–83, 86, 92, 219, 298, 311.

24. Ibid., 97–98.

25. Ibid., iv.

26. Grant to Stanton, Feb. 4, 1867; and Pope to Grant, May 10, 1866, Grant, *Papers,* 17:44, 47n–48n. Grant also recommended that Upton would be a good teacher of tactics to the Chinese army in 1868. See Badeau to Burlingame, Dec. 28, 1868, ibid., 19:326.

27. Sherman, *Memoirs*, 2:395, 401; Michie, *Emory Upton*, 215–16; Scribner, *How Soldiers Were Made*, 257–58; Morris to Stanton, Jan. 4, 1867; and Casey to Stanton, Jan. 8, 1867, Grant, *Papers*, 17:45n.

28. Jamieson, *Crossing the Deadly Ground*, 11; Osterhoudt, "Evolution of U.S. Army Assault Tactics," 98–99; Griffith, *Battle Tactics of the Civil War*, 104; Lord, "Army and Navy Textbooks," pt. 1, 64.

29. Dederer, "Side Arms, Standard Infantry," 660; Jamieson, *Crossing the Deadly Ground*, 72, 132–33.

30. O'Connor, "Vision of Soldiers," 282, 283n, 294; Greene, *Russian Army*, 195–200, 422; Trenk, "Plevna Delay," unpaginated.

31. Michie, *Emory Upton*, 471–73.

32. Morris, *Tactics for Infantry*, 8–12, 23, 25–26, copy in William Hopkins Morris Family Papers, USMA; John McMurdo to Morris, June 19, 1882, ibid.; Horatio G. Wright to Morris, Aug. 29, 1882, ibid.

33. Jamieson, *Crossing the Deadly Ground*, 43–44, 64, 70–73, 93.

34 Osterhoudt, "Evolution of U.S. Army Assault Tactics," 110–13; Jamieson, *Crossing the Deadly Ground*, 101.

35. Jamieson, *Crossing the Deadly Ground*, 63–64, 73, 104–106, 108–109.

36. Osterhoudt, "Evolution of U.S. Army Assault Tactics," 107, 115.

37. Ibid., 116; Wagner, *Organization and Tactics*, 468.

38. Wagner, *Organization and Tactics*, 120–21, 144–46, 148, 391, 393–94; Osterhoudt, "Evolution of U.S. Army Assault Tactics," 117.

39. Wagner, *Organization and Tactics*, 97–100, 102–104.

40. Wagner, *Santiago Campaign*, 124–26; Jamieson, *Crossing the Deadly Ground*, 132–33, 137–38, 146–48.

41. Osterhoudt, "Evolution of U.S. Army Assault Tactics," 130, 132–34, 136n.

42. Ibid., 150, 156–57.

43. Echevarria, *After Clausewitz*, 21–23, 32, 34, 38, 41, 99–102; Nosworthy, *Bloody Crucible*, 633–35, 639–40; Wawro, *Franco-Prussian War*, 54–57, 59, 62; Boguslawski, *Tactical Deductions*, 133–36; English, *Perspective on Infantry*, 4, 95.

44. Ramsay, *Command and Cohesion*, 76–77, 79, 81, 84–85.

45. Ibid., 86–87.

46. Keegan, *First World War*, 136, 175–78, 195–96; Dastrup, *Field Artillery*, 37, 42–43, 46–47.

47. Griffith, *Battle Tactics of the Western Front*, 54–55.

48. Ibid., 58–62, 194.

49. Ibid., 55, 57, 62–64, 76–79, 96.

50. Ibid., 97–98; Lupfer, *Dynamics of Doctrine*, 54.

51. Gudmundsson, *Stormtroop Tactics*, 8–9, 21–24, 49–50; Lupfer, *Dynamics of Doctrine*, 28.

52. Gudmundsson, *Stormtroop Tactics*, xiii, xv, 71–72, 93, 189; Lupfer, *Dynamics of Doctrine*, 12–14, 29–35, 38–39, 42–43.

53. Gudmundsson, *Stormtroop Tactics*, 84–85, 147–51; Lupfer, *Dynamics of Doctrine*, 48.

54. Gudmundsson, *Stormtroop Tactics*, 97, 101–102, 173–74.

55. Gudmundsson, *Stormtroop Tactics*, 87–88; Lengel, *To Conquer Hell*, 27–29, 45; Nenninger, "American Military Effectiveness," 143, 145; Nenninger, "Tactical Dysfunction," 177–80; Grotelueschen, *AEF Way of War*, 13; Ferrell, *America's Deadliest Battle*, 57; Osterhoudt, "Evolution of U.S. Army Assault Tactics," 162–63, 169, 175, 180, 184–88, 191; *Records of the World War: Field Orders, 2d Army Corps*, 22; *Records of the World War: Field Orders, 5th Division*, 123.

56. Ferrell, *America's Deadliest Battle*, 40–65, 149–54; Lengel, *To Conquer Hell*, 385; Gudmundsson, *Stormtroop Tactics*, 175; Nenninger, "Tactical Dysfunction," 181; Nenninger, "American Military Effectiveness," 144.

57. Grotelueschen, *AEF Way of War*, 44–58, 345–50; Lengel, *To Conquer Hell*, 417; Nenninger, "American Military Effectiveness," 146; Nenninger, "Tactical Dysfunction," 181.

58. Gudmundsson, *Stormtroop Tactics*, 139–40, 162–68, 178; Lupfer, *Dynamics of Doctrine*, 40, 53.

59. Griffith, *Battle Tactics of the Western Front*, 195.

60. Osterhoudt, "Evolution of U.S. Army Assault Tactics," 193, 203; Wheeler, *Infantry Battalion in War*, 50, 55.

61. Wheeler, *Infantry Battalion in War*, xiii, 1–2, 5–7, 9.

62. Finlayson, *Uncertain Trumpet*, xv, 157–58.

63. Doubler, *Closing with the Enemy*, 304–306.

64. Ibid., 269–72; Ford, "US Assessments," 340–44, 355.

65. Hitchman, "Operational Requirements," v, U.S. Army Military History Institute, Carlisle, Pa.

66. Ibid., 9, 15–10.

67. Ibid., 25.

68. Ibid., 2–3, 16, 18–19, 19n.

69. Ibid., 22, 40.

70. In a study of thirty-two battles from 1525 to 1945, George Raudzens has also found that there is no pattern of rising casualty rates over time. See "In Search of Better Quantification," 7.

71. Gudmundsson, *Stormtroop Tactics*, 172.

72. *Infantry Rifle Platoon and Squad*, viii.

73. Ibid., 1.1, 1.14, 1.17, 3.6.

74. Ibid., 3.7–11, 3.14.

75. Ibid.; *Theory and Dynamics of Tactical Operations*, 234–43, 257–68, 275.

12. COMPARISON AND CONTEXT

1. Hsieh, *West Pointers*, 125–26.

2. Cooper, *Rise of the National Guard*, 19–20.

3. Ibid., 5.

4. Ibid., 9–10.

5. Quimby, *U.S. Army*, 1:4.

6. Mahon, *Second Seminole War*, 225, 292, 325.

7. Winders, *Mr. Polk's Army*, 11, 68–69, 72, 82–87; Cooper, *Rise of the National Guard*, 18–19.

8. Newell and Shrader, *Duty Well and Faithfully Done*, xiii.

9. Cooper, *Rise of the National Guard*, 104–105; Cosmas, *Army for Empire*, 10–13, 114–17, 136–37.

10. Coffman, *War to End All Wars*, 28–29.

11. Doubler, *Closing with the Enemy*, 269–72, 279–81; Ford, "US Assessments," 340, 342, 344, 355.

12. Houlding, *Fit for Service*, vii–x, 1, 9–10, 162, 165–66, 294–97, 347–48, 391.

13. Ibid., 376, 389–90.

14. Neely, "Was the Civil War a Total War?," 434–58.

15. Lynn, *Bayonets of the Republic*, 282–83.

16. Ibid., 216, 218, 221–22, 239–40.

17. Ibid., 242–44, 247, 250–53, 257–60, 281.

18. Hsieh, *West Pointers*, 40.

19. McWhiney and Jamieson, *Attack and Die*, 72–73, 82, 103, 121; Weigley, *Great Civil War*, 32.

20. Hess, *Rifle Musket*, 203–208.

21. See, for example, two operational- and tactical-level studies of the Seven Years' War: Showalter, *Wars of Frederick the Great*, 79–84, 177–89, 192–206; and Savory, *His Britannic Majesty's Army*, 27–37, 71–86, 104–109, 126–34, 154–73, 217–24.

22. Weigley, *Age of Battles*, xiii.

23. Hsieh, *West Pointers*, 9, 116, 130.

24. Griffith, *Battle Tactics of the Civil War*, 189–90.

25. Ibid., 60–72.

26. Ibid., 191, 198.

APPENDIX: A TACTICAL GLOSSARY OF THE CIVIL WAR

1. *U.S. Infantry Tactics*, 415.

2. Scott, *Infantry Tactics*, 2:157, 3:257.

3. For the distance between ranks, see Hardee, *Rifle and Light Infantry*, 6.

4. *U.S. Infantry Tactics*, 419.

5. Ibid., 420.

6. Casey, *Infantry Tactics*, 1:185, 187.

7. *U.S. Infantry Tactics*, 430.

8. Casey, *Infantry Tactics*, 2:63–64.

9. Scott, *Infantry Tactics*, 1:61; Hardee, *Rifle and Light Infantry*, 23.

BIBLIOGRAPHY

ARCHIVES

Alabama Department of Archives and History, Montgomery
  Hardee Family Papers
Auburn University, Special Collections and Archives, Auburn, Alabama
  "The Civil War Diary of Charles Henry Snedeker"
Chicago History Museum, Chicago, Illinois
  George Carrington Diary
Chickamauga-Chattanooga National Military Park, Fort Oglethorpe, Georgia
  Merritt James Simonds Diary
The Citadel, Archives and Museum, Charleston, South Carolina
  Irving Bronson, "Recollections of the Civil War," Bruce Catton Collection
Indiana Historical Society, Indianapolis
  Daniel Wait Howe Papers
Library of Congress, Manuscript Division, Washington, D.C.
  William T. Sherman Papers
  Hazard Stevens Papers
Louisiana State University, Louisiana and Lower Mississippi Valley Collections, Special Collections, Baton Rouge, La.
  G. W. Giles Letters
  Arthur W. Hyatt Papers
Minnesota Historical Society, Saint Paul
  Thomas Downs Diary
Mississippi State University, Special Collections, Starkville
  Henry Keck Diary, Emmett Ross Papers
National Archives and Records Administration, Washington, D.C.
  RG 393, Records of U.S. Army Continental Commands, 1821–1920
  Order, Letter, Circular Books, Third Brigade, Second Division, XIV Corps, vol. 42, entry 5748; vol. 43, entry 575; vol. 20, entry 6363
Navarro College, Pearce Civil War Collection, Corsicana, Texas
  Frederick W. Stegner Papers
New-York Historical Society, New York
  Miles Clayton Huyette Reminiscences

New York State Library, Albany

    Henry G. Heffron Papers

Rice University, Woodson Research Center, Houston, Texas

    W. H. Brooker Diary

State Historical Society of Missouri Research Center, Columbia

    Lot Dudley Young Reminiscences

Stones River National Battlefield, Murfreesboro, Tennessee

    William P. Egan Court-Martial Transcript, 23rd Kentucky Regimental File

    Order Book, Company I, 78th Pennsylvania Regimental File

Tennessee State Library and Archives, Nashville

    Isham G. Harris Governor's Papers

    Theodore Gillard Trimmier Papers

Tulane University, Special Collections, New Orleans, Louisiana

    Bailey Diary, Louisiana Historical Association Collection, Civil War Papers, Diaries, box 19, folder 2

    "General Orders from January 6th 1862 to August 24th 1862," Bragg-Beauregard Order Book, Louisiana Historical Association Collection, Bound Volumes

    "Order Book, 5th Company, B.W.A.," Louisiana Historical Association Collection, Civil War Papers, Battalion Washington Artillery Collection, box 12, folder 1

U.S. Army Military History Institute, Carlisle, Pennsylvania

    Norman A. Hitchman, "Operational Requirements for an Infantry Hand Weapon," Operations Research Office, Johns Hopkins University, 1952

U.S. Military Academy, Special Collections and Archives Division, West Point, New York

    William Hopkins Morris Family Papers

University of Arkansas, Special Collections, Fayetteville

    Daniel Harris Reynolds Diary

University of Michigan, Bentley Historical Library, Ann Arbor

    Irwin Shepard Letters

University of Michigan, William L. Clements Library, Ann Arbor

    Jacob Van Zwaluwenburg Journal, James M. Schoff Civil War Collections

University of Tennessee, Special Collections, Chattanooga

    Philip R. Ward Diary, Charles S. Harris Collection

University of Tennessee, Special Collections, Knoxville

    Edwin Hansford Rennolds Sr. Papers

    Richard Saffell Papers

University of Vermont, Special Collections, Burlington

    John Wolcott Phelps Correspondence

University of Washington, Special Collections, Seattle

    M. F. Force Papers

Wisconsin Historical Society, Madison
    Horace Capron Papers

NEWSPAPERS

Chicago Daily Tribune
Cincinnati Commercial
Indianapolis Daily Journal
Memphis Daily Appeal
National Tribune

BOOKS, ESSAYS, ARTICLES, AND ONLINE SOURCES

Alderson, William T., ed. "The Civil War Reminiscences of John Johnston, 1861–1865." *Tennessee Historical Quarterly* 13 (1954): 65–82, 156–78.

Alexander, Edward Porter. *Fighting for the Confederacy: The Personal Recollections of General Edward Porter Alexander.* Edited by Gary W. Gallagher. Chapel Hill: University of North Carolina Press, 1989.

Arnold, James R. "A Reappraisal of Column Versus Line in the Peninsula War." *Journal of Military History* 68, no. 2 (April 2004): 535–52.

Astoria. "Infantry Tactics." *Army and Navy Journal* (August 22, 1868): 2–3.

Babits, Lawrence E. *A Devil of a Whipping: The Battle of Cowpens.* Chapel Hill: University of North Carolina Press, 1998.

Babits, Lawrence E., and Joshua B. Howard. *Long, Obstinate, and Bloody: The Battle of Guilford Courthouse.* Chapel Hill: University of North Carolina Press, 2009.

Bailey, Ronald H. *Forward to Richmond: McClellan's Peninsular Campaign.* Alexandria, Va.: Time-Life Books, 1983.

Barber, Flavel C. *Holding the Line: The Third Tennessee Infantry, 1861–1864.* Edited by Robert H. Ferrell. Kent, Ohio: Kent State University Press, 1994.

Beals, Thomas P. "In a Charge near Fort Hell, Petersburg, April 2, 1865." *War Papers Read before the Commandery of the State of Maine, Military Order of the Loyal Legion of the United States.* 2:105–15. Portland, Maine: Lefavor-Tower, 1902.

Bearss, Ed, and Chris Calkins. *Battle of Five Forks.* 2nd ed. Lynchburg, Va.: H. E. Howard, 1985.

Beatty, John. *Memoirs of a Volunteer, 1861–1863.* New York: W. W. Norton, 1946.

Beecham, R. K. *As If It Were Glory: Robert Beecham's Civil War from the Iron Brigade to the Black Regiments.* Edited by Michael E. Stevens. Madison, Wis.: Madison House, 1998.

Binney, Captain. "Muskets and Musketry." In *Aide-Mémoire to the Military Sciences,* 2:442–67. London: Lockwood, 1860.

Black, John D. "Reminiscences of the Bloody Angle." In *Glimpses of the Nation's Struggle, Fourth Series: Papers Read before the Minnesota Commandery of the Military Order of the Loyal Legion of the United States, 1892–1897*, 420–36. St. Paul: H. L. Collins, 1898.

Boguslawski, Albrecht von. *Tactical Deductions from the War of 1870–71*. Minneapolis, Minn.: Absinthe, 1996.

Boyd, Cyrus F. *The Civil War Diary of Cyrus F. Boyd, Fifteenth Iowa Infantry, 1861–1863*. Edited by Mildred Throne. Baton Rouge: Louisiana State University Press, 1998.

Bradley, Mark L. *Last Stand in the Carolinas: The Battle of Bentonville*. Campbell, Calif.: Savas Woodbury, 1996.

Bryan, Thomas Conn, ed. "General William J. Hardee and Confederate Publication Rights." *Journal of Southern History* 12, no. 2 (May 1946): 263–74.

Bryant, Edwin E. *History of the Third Regiment of Wisconsin Veteran Volunteer Infantry, 1861–1865*. Madison, Wisconsin: Democrat Printing, 1891.

Buell, Augustus. *"The Cannoneer": Recollections of Service in the Army of the Potomac*. Washington, D.C.: National Tribune, 1890.

Bull, Rice C. *Soldiering: The Civil War Diary of Rice C. Bull, 123rd New York Volunteer Infantry*. Edited by K. Jack Bauer. San Rafael, Calif.: Presidio, 1977.

Burdette, Robert J. *The Drums of the 47th*. Urbana: University of Illinois Press, 2000.

Busk, Hans. *The Rifle: And How to Use It*. 8th ed. London: Routledge, Warne, and Routledge, 1862.

Callaway, Joshua K. *The Civil War Letters of Joshua K. Callaway*. Edited by Judith Lee Hallock. Athens: University of Georgia Press, 1997.

Carlin, William Passmore. *The Memoirs of Brigadier General William Passmore Carlin, U.S.A.* Edited by Robert I. Girardi and Nathaniel Cheairs Hughes Jr. Lincoln: University of Nebraska Press, 1999.

Casey, Silas. *Infantry Tactics, for the Instruction, Exercise, and Manoeuvres of the Soldier, a Company, Line of Skirmishers, Battalion, Brigade, or Corps D'Armee*. 3 vols. New York: D. Van Nostrand, 1862.

Chamberlaine, William W. *Memoirs of the Civil War between the Northern and Southern Sections of the United States of America, 1861 to 1865*. Tuscaloosa: University of Alabama Press, 2010.

Chambers, William Pitt. *Blood & Sacrifice: The Civil War Journal of a Confederate Soldier*. Edited by Richard A. Baumgartner. Huntington, W.Va.: Blue Acorn, 1997.

Chance, Joseph E. *The Second Texas Infantry: From Shiloh to Vicksburg*. Austin, Tex.: Eakin, 1984.

Chandler, David G. "Column Versus Line, Oman Versus Modern Historians: The Case of Maida, 1806." In *Acta No. 13: Helsinki 31.V.–6.VI.1988*, compiled by International Commission of Military History, 1:117–27. Helsinki: Finnish Commission of Military History, 1991.

Chisolm, Alexander Robert. "The Shiloh Battle-Order and the Withdrawal Sunday Evening." In *Battles and Leaders of the Civil War*, edited by Robert Underwood Johnson and Clarence Clough Buel, 1:606. Reprint, New York: Thomas Yoseloff, 1956.

Coffman, Edward M. *The War to End All Wars: The American Military Experience in World War I*. New York: Oxford University Press, 1968.

Connelly, Thomas Lawrence. *Army of the Heartland: The Army of Tennessee, 1861–1862*. Baton Rouge: Louisiana State University Press, 1967.

———. *Autumn of Glory: The Army of Tennessee, 1862–1865*. Baton Rouge: Louisiana State University Press, 1971.

Cooper, Jerry. *The Rise of the National Guard: The Evolution of the American Militia, 1865–1920*. Lincoln: University of Nebraska Press, 1997.

Copp, Elbridge J. *Reminiscences of the War of the Rebellion, 1861–1865*. Nashua, N.H.: Telegraph, 1911.

Coppee, Henry. *The Field Manual for Battalion Drill, Containing the Exercises and Manoeuvres in the School of the Battalion*. Philadelphia: J. B. Lippincott, 1864.

Cosmas, Graham A. *An Army for Empire: The United States Army in the Spanish-American War*. Columbia: University of Missouri Press, 1971.

Cox, Jacob D. *Atlanta*. New York: Charles Scribner's Sons, 1882.

Daniel, Larry. *Days of Glory: The Army of the Cumberland, 1861–1865*. Baton Rouge: Louisiana State University Press, 2004.

Dastrup, Boyd L. *The Field Artillery: History and Sourcebook*. Westport, Conn.: Greenwood, 1994.

Davis, Carl. L. *Arming the Union: Small Arms in the Civil War*. Port Washington, N.Y.: Kennikat, 1973.

Day, L. W. *Story of the One Hundred and First Ohio Infantry*. Cleveland: W. M. Bayne, 1894.

Dederer, John Morgan. "Side Arms, Standard Infantry." In *The Oxford Companion to American Military History*, edited by John Whiteclay Chambers II, 659–61. New York: Oxford University Press, 1999.

De Forest, John William. *A Volunteer's Adventures: A Union Captain's Record of the Civil War*. Edited by James H. Croushore. New Haven, Conn.: Yale University Press, 1946.

Donaldson, Francis Adams. *Inside the Army of the Potomac: The Civil War Experience of Captain Francis Adams Donaldson*. Edited by J. Gregory Acken. Mechanicsburg, Pa.: Stackpole, 1998.

Doubler, Michael D. *Closing with the Enemy: How GIs Fought the War in Europe, 1944–1945*. Lawrence: University Press of Kansas, 1994.

Duane, William. *The American Military Library; Or, Compendium of the Modern Tactics*. 2 vols. Philadelphia: By the author, 1809.

Duffy, Christopher. *The Army of Frederick the Great*. London: David and Charles, 1974.

———. *The Military Experience in the Age of Reason*. London: Routledge and Kegan Paul, 1987.

Durham, Thomas Wise. *Three Years with Wallace's Zouaves: The Civil War Memoirs of Thomas Wise Durham.* Edited by Jeffrey L. Patrick. Macon, Ga.: Mercer University Press, 2003.

Echevarria, Antulio J., II. *After Clausewitz: German Military Thinkers before the Great War.* Lawrence: University Press of Kansas, 2000.

Ellsworth, E. E. *Manual of Arms for Light Infantry, Adapted to the Rifled Musket, with, or without, the Priming Attachment, Arranged for the U.S. Zouave Cadets, Governors Guard of Illinois.* N.p., 1859.

English, John A. *A Perspective on Infantry.* New York: Praeger, 1981.

Ferrell, Robert H. *America's Deadliest Battle: Meuse-Argonne, 1918.* Lawrence: University Press of Kansas, 2007.

Finlayson, Kenneth. *An Uncertain Trumpet: The Evolution of U.S. Army Infantry Doctrine, 1919–1941.* Westport, Conn.: Greenwood, 2001.

Floyd, Fred C. *History of the Fortieth (Mozart) Regiment New York Volunteers.* Boston: F. H. Gilson, 1909.

Ford, Douglas. "US Assessments of Japanese Ground Warfare Tactics and the Army's Campaigns in the Pacific Theatres, 1943–1945: Lessons Learned and Methods Applied." *War in History.* 16, no. 3 (2009): 325–58.

Frank, Joseph Allan, and George A. Reaves. *"Seeing the Elephant": Raw Recruits at the Battle of Shiloh.* Westport, Conn.: Greenwood, 1989.

Fratt, Steve. "American Civil War Tactics: The Theory of W. J. Hardee and the Experience of E. C. Bennett." *Indiana Military History Journal* 10, no. 1 (1985): 4–15.

Gallagher, John J. *The Battle of Brooklyn, 1776.* New York: Sarpedon, 1995.

[Garesché, Louis]. *Biography of Lieut. Col. Julius P. Garesché, Assistant Adjutant-General, U.S. Army.* Philadelphia: J. B. Lippincott, 1887.

Garfield, James A. *The Wild Life of the Army: Civil War Letters of James A. Garfield.* Edited by Frederick D. Williams. East Lansing: Michigan State University Press, 1964.

Gibson, William H. *Ohio's Silver-Tongued Orator: Life and Speeches of General William H. Gibson.* Edited by David Dwight Bigger. Dayton, Ohio: United Brethren Publishing House, 1901.

Gist, W. W. "The Battle of Franklin." *Tennessee Historical Magazine* 6, no. 3 (1920): 213–65.

Grant, Ulysses S. *The Papers of Ulysses S. Grant.* Edited by John Y. Simon. 28 vols. Carbondale: Southern Illinois University Press, 1967–2005.

———. *Personal Memoirs.* 2 vols. Reprint, New York: Viking, 1990.

Graves, Donald E. "'Dry Books of Tactics': U.S. Infantry Manuals of the War of 1812 and After." Parts 1 and 2. *Military Collector & Historian* 38 (1986): 50–61, 173–77.

———. *Field of Glory: The Battle of Crysler's Farm, 1813.* Toronto: Robin Brass Studio, 2000.

———. "From Steuben to Scott: The Adoption of French Infantry Tactics by the U.S. Army, 1807–1816." In *Acta No. 13: Helsinki 31.V.–6.VI.1988,* compiled by International Commission of Military History, 1:223–32. Helsinki: Finnish Commission of Military History, 1991.

———. "'I Have a Handsome Little Army. . . .': A Re-examination of Winfield Scott's Camp at Buffalo in 1914." In *War along the Niagara: Essays on the War of 1812 and Its Legacy*, edited by R. Arthur Bowler, 42–52. Youngstown, N.Y.: Old Fort Niagara Association, 1991.

———. *Where Right and Glory Lead! The Battle of Lundy's Lane, 1814*. Toronto: Robin Brass Studio, 1999.

Greene, A. Wilson. *Breaking the Backbone of the Rebellion: The Final Battles of the Petersburg Campaign*. Mason City, Iowa: Savas, 2000.

Greene, F. V. *The Russian Army and Its Campaigns in Turkey in 1877–1878*. New York: D. Appleton, 1879.

Greenman, Jeremiah. *Diary of a Common Soldier in the American Revolution, 1775–1783: An Annotated Edition of the Military Journal of Jeremiah Greenman*. Edited by Robert C. Bray and Paul E. Bushnell. DeKalb: Northern Illinois University Press, 1978.

Griffith, Paddy. *The Art of War of Revolutionary France, 1789–1802*. London: Greenhill, 1998.

———. *Battle Tactics of the Civil War*. New Haven, Conn.: Yale University Press, 1989.

———. *Battle Tactics of the Western Front: The British Army's Art of Attack, 1916–1918*. New Haven, Conn.: Yale University Press, 1994.

Grimsley, Mark. "Surviving Military Revolution: The U.S. Civil War." In *The Dynamics of Military Revolution, 1300–2050*, edited by Macgregor Knox and Williamson Murray, 74–91. Cambridge, UK: Cambridge University Press, 2001.

Grotelueschen, Mark Ethan. *The AEF Way of War: The American Army and Combat in World War I*. New York: Cambridge University Press, 2007.

Gudmundsson, Bruce I. *Stormtroop Tactics: Innovation in the German Army, 1914–1918*. New York: Praeger, 1989.

Hagerman, Edward. *The American Civil War and the Origins of Modern Warfare: Ideas, Organization, and Field Command*. Bloomington: Indiana University Press, 1988.

Hakala, Ilmari. "G. M. Sprengtporten—a Tactician—Some Aspects about the Swedish-Finnish Tactics in the Latter Part of the 18th Century." In *Acta No. 13: Helsinki 31.V.–6. VI.1988*, compiled by International Commission of Military History, 1:25–33. Helsinki: Finnish Commission of Military History, 1991:.

Hall, Winchester. *The Story of the 26th Louisiana Infantry, in the Service of the Confederate States*. N.p., n.d.

Hankins, Samuel W. *Simple Story of a Soldier: Life and Service in the 2d Mississippi Infantry*. Tuscaloosa: University of Alabama Press, 2004.

Hardee, William J. *Rifle and Light Infantry Tactics, for the Instruction, Exercises, and Manoeuvres of Riflemen and Light Infantry, including School of the Soldier and School of the Company*. New York: J. O. Kane, 1862.

Hartwell, John F. L. *To My Beloved Wife and Boy at Home: The Letters and Diaries of Orderly Sergeant John F. L. Hartwell*. Edited by Ann Harwell Britton and Thomas J. Reed. Madison, N.J.: Fairleigh Dickinson University Press, 1997.

Hartzell, John Calvin. *Ohio Volunteer: The Childhood & Civil War Memoirs of Captain John Calvin Hartzell, OVI*. Edited by Charles I. Switzer. Athens: Ohio University Press, 2005.

Haughton, Andrew. *Training, Tactics, and Leadership in the Confederate Army of Tennessee: Seeds of Failure*. Portland, Ore.: Frank Cass, 2000.

Hazen, W. B. *A Narrative of Military Service*. Boston: Ticknor, 1885.

Herr, George W. *Nine Campaigns in Nine States*. San Francisco: Bancroft, 1890.

Hess, Earl J. *In the Trenches at Petersburg: Field Fortifications & Confederate Defeat*. Chapel Hill: University of North Carolina Press, 2009.

———. *Kennesaw Mountain: Sherman, Johnston, and the Atlanta Campaign*. Chapel Hill: University of North Carolina Press, 2013.

———. *Lee's Tar Heels: The Pettigrew-Kirkland-MacRae Brigade*. Chapel Hill: University of North Carolina Press, 2002.

———. *Pickett's Charge—The Last Attack at Gettysburg*. Chapel Hill: University of North Carolina Press, 2001.

———. *The Rifle Musket in Civil War Combat—Reality and Myth*. Lawrence: University Press of Kansas, 2008.

———. *Trench Warfare under Grant and Lee: Field Fortifications in the Overland Campaign*. Chapel Hill: University of North Carolina Press, 2007.

Hinman, Wilbur F. *Corporal Si Klegg and His Pard*. Cleveland: Williams, 1887.

Hood, J. B. *Advance and Retreat: Personal Experiences in the United States and Confederate Armies*. Philadelphia: Burk and McFetridge, 1880.

Hopkins, Alphonso A. *The Life of Clinton Bowen Fisk*. New York: Funk and Wagnalls, 1888.

Hord, Henry Ewell. "Prize Drill in the Army." *Confederate Veteran* 10 (1902): 548–49.

Hosea, Lewis M. "The Regular Brigade of the Army of the Cumberland." In *Sketches of War History, 1861–1865: Papers Prepared for the Commandery of the State of Ohio, Military Order of the Loyal Legion of the United States, 1896–1903*. 5: 328–60. Wilmington, N.C.: Broadfoot, 1992.

Howard, Oliver Otis. *Autobiography*. 2 vols. New York: Baker and Taylor, 1907.

Hsieh, Wayne Wei-siang. *West Pointers and the Civil War: The Old Army in War and Peace*. Chapel Hill: University of North Carolina Press, 2009.

Hughes, B. P. *Firepower: Weapons Effectiveness on the Battlefield, 1630–1850*. New York: Sarpedon, 1997.

Hyde, Thomas W. *Following the Greek Cross: Or, Memories of the Sixth Army Corps*. Columbia: University of South Carolina Press, 2005.

The Infantry Rifle Platoon and Squad. Field Manual No. 3-21.8. Headquarters, Department of the Army, March 28, 2007.

Jamieson, Perry D. "Background to Bloodshed: The Tactics of the U.S.–Mexican War and the 1850s." *North and South* 4, no. 6 (August 2001): 24–31.

———. *Crossing the Deadly Ground: United States Army Tactics, 1865–1899*. Tuscaloosa: University of Alabama Press, 1994.

Jordan, Thomas. "Notes of a Confederate Staff-Officer at Shiloh." In *Battles and Leaders of the Civil War*, edited by Robert Underwood Johnson and Clarence Clough Buel, 1:594–603. New York: Thomas Yoseloff, 1956.

Joyce, Marion D. "Tactical Lessons of the War." *Civil War Times Illustrated* 2, no. 10 (February 1964): 42–47.

Keegan, John. *The First World War.* New York: Alfred A. Knopf, 1999.

Kimball, Jeffrey. "The Battle of Chippawa: Infantry Tactics in the War of 1812." *Military Affairs* 31, no. 4 (Winter 1967–68): 169–86.

Kimberly, Robert L., and Ephraim S. Holloway. *The Forty-First Ohio Veteran Volunteer Infantry in the War of the Rebellion, 1861–1865.* Cleveland: W. R. Smellie, 1897.

Kirkham, Ralph W. *The Mexican War Journal and Letters of Ralph W. Kirkham.* Edited by Robert Royal Miller. College Station: Texas A&M University Press, 1991.

Lengel, Edward G. *To Conquer Hell: The Meuse-Argonne, 1918.* New York: Henry Holt, 2008.

Lippitt, Francis J. *A Treatise on the Tactical Use of the Three Arms: Infantry, Artillery, and Cavalry.* Harrah, Okla.: Brandy Station Bookshelf, 1994.

Lockett, S. H. "Surprise and Withdrawal at Shiloh." In *Battles and Leaders of the Civil War*, edited by Robert Underwood Johnson and Clarence Clough Buel, 1:604–606. New York: Thomas Yoseloff, 1956.

Lord, Francis A. "Army and Navy Textbooks and Manuals Used by the North during the Civil War." Parts 1 and 2. *Military Collector & Historian* 9 (1957): 61–67, 95–102.

Lupfer, Timothy T. *The Dynamics of Doctrine: The Changes in German Tactical Doctrine during the First World War.* Leavenworth Papers 4. Fort Leavenworth, Kans.: U.S. Army Command and General Staff College, 1981.

Lyman, Theodore. *Meade's Army: The Private Notebooks of Lt. Col. Theodore Lyman.* Edited by David W. Lowe. Kent, Ohio: Kent State University Press, 2007.

Lynn, John A. *The Bayonets of the Republic: Motivation and Tactics in the Army of Revolutionary France, 1791–1794.* Urbana: University of Illinois Press, 1984.

———. *Giant of the Grand Siècle: The French Army, 1610–1715.* New York: Cambridge University Press, 1997.

Mahon, John K. "Civil War Infantry Assault Tactics." *Military Affairs* 25, no. 2 (Summer 1961): 57–68.

———, ed. "The Civil War Letters of Samuel Mahon, Seventh Iowa Infantry." *Iowa Journal of History* 51, no. 3 (July 1953): 233–66.

———. *History of the Second Seminole War, 1835–1842.* Gainesville: University of Florida Press, 1967.

Manigault, Arthur Middleton. *A Carolinian Goes to War: The Civil War Narrative of Arthur Middleton Manigault, Brigadier General, C.S.A.* Edited by R. Lockwood Tower. Columbia: University of South Carolina Press, 1988.

Mason, Edwin C. "Through the Wilderness to the Bloody Angle at Spotsylvania Court House." In *Glimpses of the Nation's Struggle, Fourth Series: A Series of Papers Read before* the Minnesota Commandery of the Military Order of the Loyal Legion of the United States, 1892–1897, 281–312. St. Paul, Minn.: H. L. Collins, 1898.

Matrau, Henry. *Letters Home: Henry Matrau of the Iron Brigade*. Edited by Marcia Reid-Green. Lincoln: University of Nebraska Press, 1993.

McAllister, Robert. *The Civil War Letters of General Robert McAllister*. Edited by James I. Robertson Jr, New Brunswick, N.J.: Rutgers University Press, 1965.

McGregor, Charles. *History of the Fifteenth Regiment New Hampshire Volunteers, 1862–1863*. [Concord, N.H.: Ira C. Evans], 1900.

McMurray, W. J. *History of the Twentieth Tennessee Regiment Volunteer Infantry, C.S.A.* Nashville, Tenn.: Publication Committee, 1904.

McPherson, James M. *Battle Cry of Freedom: The Civil War Era*. New York: Oxford University Press, 1988.

———. *Ordeal by Fire: The Civil War and Reconstruction*. New York: McGraw-Hill, 1982.

McWhiney, Grady, and Perry D. Jamieson. *Attack and Die: Civil War Military Tactics and the Southern Heritage*. University: University of Alabama Press, 1982.

Menning, Bruce W. "Operational Art's Origins." In *Historical Perspectives of the Operational Art*, edited by Michael D. Krause and R. Cody Phillips, 3–21. Washington, D.C.: U.S. Army Center of Military History, 2005. www.history.army.mil/html/books/070/70-89-1/cmhPub_70-89.pdf. Accessed December 2, 2013.

Metcalf, Edwin. "Personal Incidents in the Early Campaigns of the Third Regiment Rhode Island Volunteers and the Tenth Corps." In *Personal Narratives of Events in the War of the Rebellion, Being Papers Read before the Rhode Island Soldiers and Sailors Historical Society*, 1:245–71. Wilmington, N.C.: Broadfoot, 1993.

Michie, Peter S. *The Life and Letters of Emory Upton*. New York: D. Appleton, 1885.

Miller, William B. *Fighting for Liberty and Right: The Civil War Diary of William Bluffton Miller, First Sergeant, Company K, Seventy-Fifth Indiana Volunteer Infantry*. Edited by Jeffrey L. Patrick and Robert J. Willey. Knoxville: University of Tennessee Press, 2005.

Mitchell, Enoch L., ed. "The Civil War Letters of Thomas Jefferson Newberry." *Journal of Mississippi History* 10, no. 1 (January 1948): 44–80.

Monroe, J. *The Company Drill of the Infantry of the Line. Together with the Skirmishing Drill of the Company and Battalion, after the Method of Gen. LeLouteril, Bayonet Fencing, with a Supplement on the Handling and Service of Light Infantry*. New York: D. Van Nostrand, 1863.

Moody, Otis. "Account of the Battle of Stones River." www.51illinois.org/moody_st_river.html. Accessed December 2, 2013 (site discontinued). Archived at https://web.archive.org/web/20120227114022/http://www.51illinois.org/moody_st_river.html. Accessed June 25, 2014.

Morillo, Stephen, and Michael F. Pavkovic. *What Is Military History?* 2nd ed. Cambridge, UK: Polity Press, 2013.

Moseley, Thomas Vernon. "Evolution of the American Civil War Infantry Tactics." Ph.D. diss., University of North Carolina, Chapel Hill, 1967.

Muir, Rory. *Tactics and the Experience of Battle in the Age of Napoleon.* New Haven, Conn.: Yale University Press, 1998.

Neely, Mark E., Jr. "Was the Civil War a Total War?" *Civil War History* 50, no. 4 (December 2004): 434–58.

Nenninger, Timothy K. "American Military Effectiveness in the First World War." In *Military Effectiveness, Volume 1: The First World War,* edited by Allan R. Millett and Williamson Murray, 116–56. Boston: Allen and Unwin, 1988.

———. "Tactical Dysfunction in the AEF, 1917–1918." *Military Affairs* 51, no. 4 (October 1987): 177–81.

Newell, Clayton R., and Charles R. Shrader. *Of Duty Well and Faithfully Done: A History of the Regular Army in the Civil War.* Lincoln: University of Nebraska Press, 2011.

[Newsome, Edmund]. *Experience in the War of the Great Rebellion, by a Soldier of the Eighty-First Regiment Illinois Volunteer Infantry.* Carbondale, Ill.: E. Newsome, 1879.

Nicola, Lewis. *A Treatise of Military Exercise, Calculated for the Use of the Americans.* Philadelphia: Stymer and Cist, 1776.

North American Review. Unsigned review of *Field Tactics for Infantry,* by William H. Morris. 99 (July 1864): 291.

Nosworthy, Brent. *The Anatomy of Victory: Battle Tactics, 1689–1763.* New York: Hippocrene Books, 1992.

———. *The Bloody Crucible of Courage: Fighting Methods and Combat Experience of the Civil War.* New York: Carroll and Graf, 2003.

———. *With Musket, Cannon, and Sword: Battle Tactics of Napoleon and His Enemies.* New York: Sarpedon, 1996.

O'Connor, Maureen P. "The Vision of Soldiers: Britain, France, Germany, and the United States Observe the Russo-Turkish War." *War in History* 4, no. 3 (1997): 264–95.

Opdycke, Emerson. *To Battle for God and the Right: The Civil War Letterbooks of Emerson Opdycke.* Edited by Glenn V. Longacre and John E. Haas. Urbana: University of Illinois Press, 2003.

O'Reilly, Francis Augustin. *The Fredericksburg Campaign: Winter War on the Rappahannock.* Baton Rouge: Louisiana State University Press, 2003.

"Orphan Brigade Items." *Southern Bivouac* 3, no. 7 (March 1885): 322.

Osterhoudt, Henry Jerry. "The Evolution of U.S. Army Assault Tactics, 1778–1919: The Search for Sound Doctrine." Ph.D. diss., Duke University, 1986.

Otto, John Henry. *Memoirs of a Dutch Mudsill: The "War Memories" of John Henry Otto, Captain, Company D, 21st Regiment Wisconsin Volunteer Infantry.* Edited by David Gould and James B. Kennedy. Kent, Ohio: Kent State University Press, 2004.

Paine, Halbert E. *A Wisconsin Yankee in Confederate Bayou Country: The Civil War Reminis-*

cences of a Union General. Edited by Samuel C. Hyde Jr. Baton Rouge: Louisiana State University Press, 2009.

Palfrey, Francis Winthrop. "The Period Which Elapsed between the Fall of Yorktown and the Beginning of the Seven Days' Battle." In *Campaigns in Virginia, 1861–1862: Papers of the Military Historical Society of Massachusetts*, 1:153–215. Boston: Houghton, Mifflin, 1895.

Paret, Peter. "The Relationship between the Revolutionary War and European Military Thought and Practice in the Second Half of the Eighteenth Century." In *Reconsiderations on the Revolutionary War: Selected Essays*, edited by Don Higginbotham, 144–57. Westport, Conn.: Greenwood, 1978.

Parker, Francis M. *To Drive the Enemy from Southern Soil: The Letters of Col. Francis Marion Parker and the History of the 30th Regiment North Carolina Troops*. Edited by Michael W. Taylor. Dayton, Ohio: Morningside, 1998.

Parker, Geoffrey, ed. *The Cambridge History of Warfare*. New York: Cambridge University Press, 2005.

"Peter Wilson in the Civil War." *Iowa Journal of History and Politics* 40, no. 4 (October 1942): 339–414.

Phisterer, Frederick. *The Regular Brigade of the Fourteenth Army Corps, the Army of the Cumberland, in the Battle of Stone River, Or Murfreesboro, Tennessee*. N.p., [1883].

Pickett, W. D. "Reminiscences of Murfreesboro." *Confederate Veteran* 16 (1908): 449–54.

Pope, John. *The Military Memoirs of General John Pope*. Edited by Peter Cozzens and Robert I. Girardi. Chapel Hill: University of North Carolina Press, 1998.

Prokopowicz, Gerald J. *All for the Regiment: The Army of the Ohio, 1861–1862*. Chapel Hill: University of North Carolina Press, 2001.

Quimby, Robert S. *The Background of Napoleonic Warfare: The Theory of Military Tactics in Eighteenth-Century France*. New York: Columbia University Press, 1957.

———. *The U.S. Army in the War of 1812: An Operational and Command Study*. 2 vols. East Lansing: Michigan State University Press, 1997.

Ramsay, M. A. *Command and Cohesion: The Citizen Soldier and Minor Tactics in the British Army, 1870–1918*. Westport, Conn.: Praeger, 2002.

Raudzens, George. "In Search of Better Quantification for War History: Numerical Superiority and Casualty Rates in Early Modern Europe." *War & Society* 15, no. 1 (May 1997): 1–30.

Ray, James M. "Sixtieth Regiment." In *Histories of the Several Regiments and Battalions from North Carolina in the Great War, 1861–'65*, edited by Walter Clark, 3:473–98. Goldsboro, N.C.: Nash Brothers, 1901.

Records of the World War: Field Orders, 2d Army Corps. Washington, D.C.: Government Printing Office, 1921.

Records of the World War: Field Orders, 5th Division, 1918. Washington, D.C.: Government Printing Office, 1921.

Rhea, Gordon C. *The Battles for Spotsylvania Court House and the Road to Yellow Tavern, May 7–12, 1864.* Baton Rouge: Louisiana State University Press, 1997.

———. *Cold Harbor: Grant and Lee, May 26–June 3, 1864.* Baton Rouge: Louisiana State University Press, 2002.

Rhodes, Elisha Hunt. *All for the Union: The Civil War Diary and Letters of Elisha Hunt Rhodes.* Edited by Robert Hunt Rhodes. New York: Orion Books, 1985.

Rogers, Clifford J. "Tactics and the Face of Battle." In *European Warfare, 1350–1750,* edited by Frank Tallett and D. J. B. Trim, 203–35. New York: Cambridge University Press, 2010.

Ross, Steven. *From Flintlock to Rifle: Infantry Tactics, 1740–1866.* Rutherford, N.J.: Fairleigh Dickinson University Press, 1979.

Rothenburg, Gunther E. *The Art of Warfare in the Age of Napoleon.* Bloomington: Indiana University Press, 1980.

Saunier, Joseph A., ed. *A History of the Forty-Seventh Regiment Ohio Veteran Volunteer Infantry.* Hillsboro, Ohio: Lyle, [1903].

Savory, Sir Reginald. *His Britannic Majesty's Army in Germany during the Seven Years War.* Oxford, UK: Clarendon, 1966.

Schultz, A. N., ed. *Illustrated Drill Manual and Regulations for the American Soldier of the Revolutionary War.* Union City, Tenn.: Pioneer, 1982.

Scott, H. L. *Military Dictionary: Comprising Technical Definitions; Information on Raising and Keeping Troops; Actual Service, including Makeshifts and Improved Materiel; and Law, Government, Regulation, and Administration Relating to Land Forces.* New York: D. Van Nostrand, 1861.

Scott, Winfield. *Infantry Tactics: Rules for the Exercise and Manoeuvres of the United States' Infantry.* 3 vols. Washington, D.C.: Gales and Seaton, 1835.

Scribner, B. F. *How Soldiers Were Made: Or the War as I Saw It.* Chicago: Donohue and Henneberry, 1887.

Sears, Stephen W. *Chancellorsville.* Boston: Houghton Mifflin, 1996.

Seay, Samuel. "A Private at Stone River." *Southern Bivouac* 4, no. 3 (August 1885): 156–60.

Shellenberger, John L. "Kenesaw Mountain: The Causes That Led to the Repulse of Harker's Brigade." *National Tribune.* December 11, 1890.

Sheridan, P. H. *Personal Memoirs.* 2 vols. Reprint, Wilmington, N.C.: Broadfoot, 1992.

Sherman, William T. *Memoirs.* 2 vols. New York: D. Appleton, 1875.

———. *Sherman's Civil War: Selected Correspondence of William T. Sherman, 1860–1865.* Edited by Brooks D. Simpson and Jean V. Berlin. Chapel Hill: University of North Carolina Press, 1999.

Showalter, Dennis. "The Seven Years' War in Europe." In *West Point History of Warfare,* edited by Clifford Rodgers and J. T. Seidule. West Point, N.Y.: History Department, U.S. Military Academy, 2013.

———. *The Wars of Frederick the Great.* London: Longman, 1996.

Simmons, L. A. *The History of the 84th Reg't Ill. Vols.* Macomb, Ill.: Hampton Brothers, 1866.

Spiegel, Marcus M. *Your True Marcus: The Civil War Letters of a Jewish Colonel.* Edited by Frank L. Byrne and Jean Powers Soman. Kent, Ohio: Kent State University Press, 1985.

Spring, Matthew H. *With Zeal and Bayonets Only: The British Army on Campaign in North America, 1775–1783.* Norman: University of Oklahoma Press, 2008.

Squier, George W. *This Wilderness of War: The Civil War Letters of George W. Squier, Hoosier Volunteer.* Edited by Julie A. Doyle, John David Smith, and Richard M. McMurry. Knoxville: University of Tennessee Press, 1998.

Stanley, Sir Henry Morton. *Sir Henry Morton Stanley, Confederate.* Edited by Nathaniel Cheairs Hughes Jr. Baton Rouge: Louisiana State University Press, 2000.

Stephenson, Philip Daingerfield. *The Civil War Memoir of Philip Daingerfield Stephenson, D.D.* Edited by Nathaniel Cheairs Hughes Jr. Conway: University of Central Arkansas Press, 1995.

Steuben, Baron von. *Revolutionary War Drill Manual.* New York: Dover, 1985.

Stevens, Hazard. "The Storming of the Lines of Petersburg by the Sixth Corps, April 2, 1865." In *The Shenandoah Campaigns of 1862 and 1864 and the Appomattox Campaign, 1865: Papers of the Military Historical Society of Massachusetts,* 6:411–35. Boston: Military Historical Society of Massachusetts, 1907.

The Story of the Fifty-Fifth Regiment Illinois Volunteer Infantry in the Civil War, 1861–1865. Clinton, Mass.: W. J. Coulter, 1887.

Supplement to the Official Records of the Union and Confederate Armies. 100 vols. Wilmington, N.C.: Broadfoot, 1993–2000.

Sword, Wiley. *Shiloh: Bloody April.* Dayton, Ohio: Morningside, 1983.

A Synopsis of the Art of War. Columbia, S.C.: Evans and Cogswell, 1864.

Theory and Dynamics of Tactical Operations: ROTC Manual No. 145-160, March 10, 1972. Washington, D.C.: Government Printing Office, 1972.

Thompson, Ed. Porter. *History of the Orphan Brigade.* Louisville, Ky.: Lewis N. Thompson, 1898.

Tidball, John C. "Rifle Target Practice in the Army." *Ordnance Notes* 237. January 30, 1883.

Trenk, Richard T., Sr. "The Plevna Delay: Winchesters and Peabody-Martinis in the Russo-Turkish War." *Man at Arms Magazine* 19, no. 4 (August 1997): unpaginated online. http://www.militaryrifles.com/Turkey/Plevna/ThePlevnaDelay.html. Accessed June 21, 2013.

Trimble, Harvey M., ed. *History of the Ninety-Third Regiment Illinois Volunteer Infantry from Organization to Muster Out.* Chicago: Blakely Printing, 1898.

U.S. Infantry Tactics, for the Instruction, Exercise, and Manoeuvres of the United States Infantry, including Infantry of the Line, Light Infantry, and Riflemen. Philadelphia: J. B. Lippincott, 1863.

U.S. War Department. *The War of the Rebellion: A Compilation of the Official Records of the Union and Confederate Armies.* 70 vols. in 128 parts. Washington, D.C.: Government Printing Office, 1880–1901.

Upton, Emory. *A New System of Infantry Tactics, Double and Single Rank, Adapted to American Topography and Improved Fire-Arms.* New York: D. Appleton, 1867.

Volkogonov, Dmitri A. "Tactics of the Russian Forces in the Battle of Borodino." In *Acta No. 13: Helsinki 31.V.–6.VI.1988,* compiled by International Commission of Military History, 1:68–69. Helsinki: Finnish Commission of Military History, 1991.

Wagner, Arthur L. *Organization and Tactics.* New York: B. Westermann, 1895.

———. *Report of the Santiago Campaign, 1898.* Kansas City, Mo.: Franklin-Hudson, 1908.

Walker, Arthur. *The Rifle: Its Theory and Practice.* Westminster, UK: J. B. Nichols and Sons, 1864.

Walker, Charles N., and Rosemary Walker, eds. "Diary of the War, by Robt. S. Robertson." Pts. 3 and 4. *Old Fort News* 28 (1965): 119–74.

Walker, Francis A. *History of the Second Army Corps in the Army of the Potomac.* New York: Charles Scribner's Sons, 1887.

Walker, James A. "Gordon's Assault on Fort Stedman." *Southern Historical Society Papers* 30 (1903): 19–31.

Ware, E. F. *The Lyon Campaign in Missouri: Being a History of the First Iowa Infantry.* Iowa City, Iowa: Press of the Camp Pope Bookshop, 1991.

Warner, Ezra J. *Generals in Blue: Lives of the Union Commanders.* Baton Rouge: Louisiana State University Press, 1964.

Wawro, Geoffrey. *The Franco-Prussian War: The German Conquest of France in 1870–1871.* Cambridge, UK: Cambridge University Press, 2003.

Way, Virgil G. *History of the Thirty-Third Regiment Illinois Veteran Volunteer Infantry.* Gibson City, Ill.: Gibson Courier, 1902.

Weigley, Russell F. *The Age of Battles: The Quest for Decisive Warfare from Breitenfeld to Waterloo.* Bloomington: Indiana University Press, 1991.

———. *A Great Civil War: A Military and Political History, 1861–1865.* Bloomington: Indiana University Press, 2000.

———. *History of the United States Army.* Enlarged ed. Bloomington: Indiana University Press, 1984.

Wheeler, Walter R. *The Infantry Battalion in War.* Washington, D.C.: Infantry Journal, 1936.

Whitehorne, J. W. A. "Inspector General Sylvester Churchill's Efforts to Produce a New Army Drill Manual, 1850–1862." *Civil War History* 32, no. 2 (June 1986): 159–68.

Wilcox, C. M. *Rifles and Rifle Practice: An Elementary Treatise upon the Theory of Rifle Firing.* New York: D. Van Nostrand, 1859.

Williams, Alpheus S. *From the Cannon's Mouth: The Civil War Letters of General Alpheus S. Williams.* Edited by Milo M, Quaife. Detroit: Wayne State University Press, 1959.

Williams, James M. *From That Terrible Field: Civil War Letters of James M. Williams, Twenty-First Alabama Infantry Volunteers.* Edited by John Kent Folmar. Tuscaloosa: University of Alabama Press, 1981.

Winders, Richard Bruce. *Mr. Polk's Army: The American Military Experience in the Mexican War.* College Station: Texas A&M University Press, 1997.

Womack, J. J. *The Civil War Diary of Capt. J. J. Womack.* McMinnville, Tenn.: Womack Printing, 1961.

Woodworth, Steven E. *Nothing but Victory: The Army of the Tennessee, 1861–1865.* New York: Alfred A. Knopf, 2005.

Worden, James A. "The Battle of Stone's River." *Military Essays and Recollections of the Pennsylvania Commandery, Military Order of the Loyal Legion of the United States,* 2:1–10. Wilmington, N.C.: Broadfoot, 1995.

Wright, Robert Kenneth, Jr. "Organization and Doctrine in the Continental Army, 1774–1784." Ph.D. diss., College of William and Mary, 1980.

Zuparko, Ned, ed. *George Jeffrey's Tactics and Grand Tactics of the Napoleonic Wars.* Brockton, Mass.: Courier, 1982.

INDEX

Adams, Alexander D., 149

Adams, Daniel W., 147–48

Alabama units: 22nd, 133; 28th, 134; 32nd, 138; 35th, 44; 41st, 75; 52nd, 138

Alexander, E. Porter, 186

Alexander, Jesse, 96

American Expeditionary Force, 219, 221, 230

American Revolutionary War, 20–25, 227–29

Andrews, George L., 115

Antietam, battle of, 63, 88, 94, 100, 111–13, 123, 131, 143–45, 161, 167–69

Appomattox campaign, 199, 237

Arkansas units: 3rd, 126; 4th, 135; 30th, 93

Armée du Nord, 12, 14, 233–34

Armstrong, John, 28

Army of Northern Virginia, 179–80, 268n8

Army of the Ohio, 109–10, 147, 177–79

Army of the Potomac, 180, 200, 269n9

Army of Tennessee, 75, 135, 138, 178, 254n34

Army of the Tennessee, 178

Articulation, 62, 165–75, 176–77, 200, 240–41, 243

Atlanta, battle of, 92, 126

Atlanta campaign, xii, 100–102, 112–13

Ayres, Romeyn B., 56, 188–89, 191–92

Babcock, Conrad, 219

Baldwin, William E., 91, 162

Banning, Henry, 158–59

Barber, Flavel C., 65, 145

Barlow, Francis C., 159, 167–69, 184–85

Bate, William B., 127

Baton Rouge, battle of, 84

Battalion, 3, 9, 13, 15, 21, 38–39, 43, 212, 220, 223, 243

Baylor, William S. H., 94–95

Bayonet charge, 7–8, 165, 234, 271n15

Bayou De Glaize, battle of, 130, 133

Beal, George L., 145

Beatty, Samuel, 116, 145

Beauregard, Pierre G. T., 107–9, 147

Becht, John C., 146

Belmont, battle of, 96–97, 127

Benning, Henry L., 115

Benton, William P., 125

Bentonville, battle of, 89, 94, 113, 126

Bermuda Hundred campaign, 118

Bingham, Daniel G., 97, 99

Bishop, Judson, 75

Black, John D., 184–85

Blackman, Albert M., 126

Blair, Frank P., Jr., 110

Blake, W. H., 81

Blue Book, 20–22

Blunt, James G., 143

Bonaparte, Napoleon, 14–15, 236

Borodino, battle of, 15

Bowen, Edwin A., 92

Boynton, Henry V. N., 118

Bradley, Luther P., 97, 160

Bragg, Braxton, 110

Bragg, Edward S., 100, 105

British army, 16–17, 22–23, 32, 214–17, 219–20, 223, 231, 234

Bronson, Irving, 67

Brooklyn, battle of, 23

Brown, Jacob, 25–26, 229

Bryant, Edwin, 35, 62

Buckner, Allen, 135

Buell, Don C., 56, 109–10, 147

Buford, Abraham, 92

Bull, Rice C., 90

Bunker Hill, battle of, xiii

Bunn, H. G., 135

Burdette, Robert J., 75

Burgess's Mill, battle of, 173–75

By the flank, 49, 127–133, 164, 167–69, 171–75, 199, 209, 241, 243

Caldwell, John C., 170

Cambrai, battle of, 219

Campbell, Hugh S., 166–67

Casey, Silas, xiii, xxi, 36–38, 51, 53–56, 59, 64, 208–10

Cedar Mountain, battle of, 88, 97

Chamberlain, Joshua L., 124, 190–91, 194

Chamberlaine, William W., 177

Chambers, William Pitt, 71

Champion Hill, battle of, 92, 112, 127, 134

Chancellorsville, battle of, 81–82, 90, 97–99, 112, 116–18, 130, 132, 134, 145, 151–53, 161, 180–83, 200

Change front forward on a subunit, 124–27, 164, 167–69, 174–75, 243, 254n45

Chapultepec, battle of, 30

Chasseurs-à-pied training, 32–22

Chattanooga campaign, 134, 155–57

Cheatham, Benjamin F., xii, 203

Chew, Henry, 174–75

Chickamauga, battle of, 84–85, 92–94, 112, 116, 118–19, 130, 133–35, 145–46, 151, 172–73

Chickasaw Bluffs, battle of, 110

Chippawa, battle of, 252n22

Christie, Daniel H., 181

Citizen soldiers, 227, 231

Clark, John, 143

Clayton, Henry D., 138–39

Cleburne, Patrick R., 135–37

Clendenin, George J., 99

Cold Harbor, battle of, 97–98, 134, 156–58

Colgrove, Silas, 88, 98

Collis, H. T., 82, 116

Colston, Raleigh E., 32, 181

Columns, frontispiece, 8–10, 11–13, 16–17, 21, 29–30, 49–51, 106–7, 128, 140–61, 163, 165–66, 170, 200, 224–25, 234, 239, 243–45, 255n51, 266n22, 271n15

Condon, Patrick J., 170

Connecticut units: 7th, 105, 149; 11th, 104; 12th, 64, 82–84, 130, 139

Continental Army, 227–28, 234

Copp, Elbridge, 67

Corinth, battle of, 97, 105, 125, 131, 150–52

Corning, Joseph W., 131

Cornwallis, Charles, 24

Coulter, Richard, 193

Coup d'oeil, 45, 244–45

Cowpens, battle of, 23

Cox, Jacob, 160

Crawford, Samuel, 117, 144, 188, 192

Crofton, Robert E. A., 130

Crysler's Farm, battle of, 25

Curtis, Joseph B., 44

Davis, Carl L., xvi

Davis, Jefferson, 30

Davis, Jefferson C., 158

Davis, Samuel, 136

Davis, William P., 128

Dawson, C. L., 72

Day, L. W., 67

Dearborn, Henry, 27

Deas, George, 62–63

Decisive battles, 235–36

Deep Bottom, Second Battle of, 149

DeForest, John W., 64

Deimling, Francis C., 96

DeLacroix, Amelot, 25, 27

Donaldson, Francis Adams, 126

Doubleday, Abner, 125

Doubler, Michael, 230

Doughty, Henry, 127

Dresden, battle of, 15

Drill manuals, xx, 19–22, 26–33, 34–38, 64–65, 122, 133–34, 163, 176–77, 205–12, 220–21, 233, 240, 252n8, 253n3, 253n12

Drummond, Gordon, 26

Du Bois, Cornelius, 42

Duane, William, 27–28

Duffy, Christopher, 11

Dutch Revolt, 2

Dyckman, Garrett, 94

Echelon, 5, 17, 118–21, 163, 245

Ellis, A. Van Horne, 81

Ellsworth, Elmer, 32, 69–70

Emery, Sabine, 155

Eustis, William, 27

Evolutions of the line, 28, 53, 75, 176–201, 245–46

Fair Oaks, battle of, 88, 124, 149

Fairchild, Lucius, 105

Fauntleroy, Robert B., 128

Files, 7

Finlayson, Kenneth, 220

Firepower, 7–8, 16, 22

Fire-team, 205, 223–24

First Bull Run, battle of, 92

First Kernstown, battle of, 150

Fisher's Hill, battle of, 130

Fisk, Clinton B., 38

Five Forks, battle of, 187–95, 200, 269n33

Flintlock, 2–3

Folard, Chevalier de, 8–11

Fontenoy, battle of, 7

Forsyth, James W., 269n33

Fort DeRussy, battle of, 93

Fort Donelson, battle of, 97, 105, 145, 148, 162

Fort McAllister, battle of, 103–4

Fort Stedman, battle of, 186–87, 200

Fort Wagner, battle of, 155–56

Fours, 209, 212, 223

Franco-Prussian War, 213

Frank, Joseph Allan, xvii

Frank, Paul, 118

Franklin, battle of, xii, 119–20, 203

Fratt, Steve, xviii

Frederick the Great, 4–7, 10

Fredericksburg, battle of, 88, 93, 146, 150, 169–71, 177

French army, 9–10, 16–17, 32, 69, 236

French Revolutionary Wars, xi, 5, 11–14, 233–34

Frontage of units, 42–43, 82–83

Fulkerson, Samuel V., 150

Fuller, John W., 151–52

Fulton, John S., 173

Gaines's Mill, battle of, 86, 89, 92, 94–95, 115, 149, 166–67

Garesché, Julius P., 32

Garfield, James A., 64, 70

Garland, Samuel, 98, 123

George, N. J., 98–99

Georgia Landing, battle of, 82–84

Georgia units: 17th, 115; 26th, 92

German army, 214, 217–20

Gettysburg, battle of, xiii, 88–89, 121, 124, 126, 131, 133, 145, 177

Gibbon, John, 104

Gibson, William H., 66

Gilbert, James I., 93, 133

Godwin, Archibald, C., 133

Goetzel, S. H., 36

Gordon, George H., 97–98, 144

Gordon, John B., 179–80, 186–87

Gorman, Willis A., 149

Gove, Jesse A., 149

Gracie, Archibald, 146

Granbury, Hiram, 85

Granger, Gordon, 56–57

Grant, Lewis A., 124

Grant, Ulysses S., 35, 38, 153, 204–5, 210, 237, 271n26

Graves, Donald, 25

Gray, Samuel F., 124

Greathouse, Lucien, 105

Greene, Nathaniel, 23–24

Greenman, Jeremiah, 23

Griffin, Charles, 188–89, 190, 193

Griffith, Paddy, xii, xviii, 12, 62, 210, 216, 219, 236–37

Grimes, Bryan, 94

Grimsley, Mark, xii

Grose, William, 124

Grotelueschen, Mark Ethan, 219

Gudmundsson, Bruce, 217–19, 223

Guibert, Comte de, 10–11, 13

Guides, 41–42, 46–47, 81–86, 191, 193–94, 199, 246, 255n62

Guilford Courthouse, battle of, 23–24

Hagerman, Edward, xvii

Hall, John G., 84

Hall, Norman J., 59

Hall, Winchester, 67, 70

Hancock, Winfield S., 88, 184–85

Hankins, Samuel W., 34

Hardee, William J., xiii, xviii, 30–32, 35–38, 40, 45, 53, 56, 75–76, 245

Harker, Charles G., 179

Harlan, Isaiah, 71

Harris, James L., 89

Hartranft, John F., 85–86, 259n10

Hartzell, John Calvin, 67

Hatch, John, 125

Haughton, Andrew, xvii

Hawthorn, A. T., 132

Hayes, Rutherford B., 139

Hayman, Samuel B., 124

Hazen, William B., 49, 52–53, 65, 69, 73–74, 103, 106, 110, 157, 179

Helena, battle of, 132, 149

Henagan, John W., 117

Herr, George, 66

Heth, Henry, 32

Hill, Daniel Harvey, 123

Hinman, Wilbur F., 48

Hitchman, Norman, 221–23

Hofmann, J. William, 117

Holman, John H., 121

Honey Springs, battle of, 143

Hood, John Bell, xii, 119–20, 150

Hooker, Joseph, 43, 58, 72, 161

Hord, Henry Ewell, 76

Houlding, John A., 231

Howard, Oliver O., 92, 103, 134, 147–48, 150, 158, 160–61, 179

Howe, Daniel Wait, 75

Hsieh, Wayne Wei-siang, 161

Hubbard, Lucius F., 146, 154

Hubbard, Thomas H., 99

Humphreys, Andrew A., 143

Hunt, Henry J., 208

Hunter, S. E., 84

Hurlbut, Frederick J., 131–32

Hyatt, Arthur W., 66–67

Hyde, Thomas W., 68, 100

Illinois units: 8th, 130; 15th, 115; 16th, 89; 17th, 104; 32nd, 115; 34th, 91; 45th, 105; 46th, 115; 47th, 125; 48th, 105; 51st, 97; 52nd, 92; 57th, 131; 79th, 135; 123rd, 104; 124th, 77; 125th, 126

Indiana units: 6th, 125; 11th, 70; 19th, 105; 23rd, 128, 134; 27th, 88, 98; 32nd, 165–66; 39th, 44; 47th, 130; 49th, 95; 58th, 116; 59th, 96; 79th, 112, 172

Ingram, John, 35

Intervals, 3–4, 53, 55, 113, 118, 122, 209, 241, 246–47

Inversion of ranks, 11, 20, 27, 68, 104, 131, 134, 163, 166, 175, 209, 240, 246

Iowa units: 1st, 114–15; 7th, 97; 27th, 93, 133; 29th, 150

Iuka, battle of, 96

Iverson, Alfred, 132

Jackson campaign, 105

Jamieson, Perry D., xii, xv, xvii, 161

Jefferson, John W., 125

Johnson, Richard W., 73

Johnston, John, 34

Jones, Bushrod, 138

Jonesboro, battle of, 85

Jordan, Thomas, 109

Joyce, Marion, xvi

Kansas units: 1st, 114

Keeble, R. H., 172–73

Keifer, J. Warren, 132

Keigwin, James, 95

Keitt, Lawrence, 157

Kennedy, John D., 94

Kennesaw Mountain, battle of, 158–59, 160–61

Kentucky units: 3rd (C.S.), 76; 4th (C.S.), 88; 8th (U.S.), 130; 14th (U.S.), 64

Kernstown, First Battle of, 150

Kernstown, Second Battle of, 139

Kiddoo, Joseph B., 87, 100

Kimball, Nathan, 160

Knefler, Frederick, 148

Knipe, Joseph, 63

Korean War, xiii, 203, 221, 249n5

Laffargue, Andre, 217

Laiboldt, Bernard, 151

Langley, James W., 126

Large-unit effectiveness, 176–201, 241

Laumann, Jacob, 97

Lawler, Michael K., 74

Lawton, Alexander R., 89, 115

Lee, Robert E., 59–60

Leggett, Mortimer D., 76–77

Leipzig, battle of, 15

Lengel, Edward, 214

Leuthen, battle of, 10

Liberty Gap, battle of, 91

Liddell, St. John, 137

Light infantry, 8, 11, 22, 29

Line and column, mix of, 146–59

Livingston, R. R., 62

Loose order, 54, 212–13, 246, 260n39

Loss ratios in battle, 222, 273n70

Louis XIV, 3

Louisiana units: 16th, 148; 17th, 91; 25th, 148

Love, John W., 34

Ludendorff, Erich, 217

Lundy's Lane, battle of, 25–26

Lyman, Theodore, 48, 159

Lynn, John A., 12, 14, 233–34

Madison, James, 27

Magersfontein Kopje, battle of, 215

Mahan, Dennis Hart, 29

Mahon, John K., xvi

Maine units: 1st Sharpshooters, 194; 7th, 100; 20th, 124; 30th, 99

Malvern Hill, battle of, 86–87, 115–16

Manderson, Charles F., 171–72

Manigault, Arthur M., 119

Manning, Van H., 126

Mansfield, James K. F., 144

Mansfield, battle of, 86

Marching, 2, 4, 7, 23, 31, 45–46, 55–58

Marksville, battle of, 146

Marsh, Jason, 68

Martindale, John H., 157

Maryland units: 1st (C.S.), 86

Mason, Edwin C., 184

Massachusetts units: 15th, 113; 22nd, 149; 25th, 118; 27th, 118; 34th, 87, 96; 45th, 142; 54th, 155

Matchlock, 1, 3

Maurice of Nassau, 1–2

Maxey, Samuel B., 75–76

McAllister, Robert, 35, 66, 77, 118

McClellan, George B., 57

McComb, William, 128

McCook, Daniel, 73, 117

McDonald, John, 28

McGregor, Charles, 61

McLane, John W., 166

McLaughlin, John A., 130

McNair, Evander, 135

McPherson, James M., xvii

McRae, Dandridge, 119

McWhiney, Grady, xii, xv, xvii, 161

Meade, George G., 160

Mechanicsville, battle of, 93

Meredith, Solomon, 66

Merritt, William H., 114

Mesnil-Durand, Baron de, 8, 10–11

Metcalf, Edwin, 71

Meuse-Argonne offensive, 218–19

Mexican War, 29–30, 227, 229, 238

Michie, Peter S., 207, 211

Michigan units: 2nd, 85; 4th, 116; 7th, 144; 14th, 89; 20th, 131

Miles, Nelson A., 78, 167–69

Militia Act of 1792, 228

Mine Run campaign, 84–85, 89–90, 132

Mississippi units: 9th, 131; 13th, 86; 14th, 145; 15th, 76; 19th, 98; 22nd, 129–30

Missouri units: 3rd (C.S.), 130; 5th (C.S.), 130; 8th (U.S.), 70; 10th (U.S.), 96; 11th (U.S.), 105

Mitchell, John, 158–59

Molino del Rey, battle of, 30

Mollwitz, battle of, 7

Monroe, James, 28

Monterey, battle of, 29

Moody, Otis, 59

Morgan, Daniel, 23

Morgan, James D., 141

Morris, William Hopkins, xvi, 205–6, 208–11, 271n15

Morrison, William R., 62

Morton, James St. Clair, 42, 85, 254n26

Moseley, Thomas Vernon, xvi

Moulton, Orson, 118

Multiple lines, 2–3, 9, 47, 106–14, 121–22, 163, 200, 209, 213, 234, 239, 243, 245, 261n10, 271n15

Munfordville, battle of, 131

Napoleonic Wars, xi, 5, 14–18, 160, 200, 233, 241

Nashville, battle of, 113, 146, 148, 237

Native Americans, 74–76

Neff, John, 115

Nenninger, Timothy K., 218

New Hope Church, battle of, 161

New Jersey units: 2nd, 133; 12th, 174–75

New Market, battle of, 87, 95

New York units: 2nd Excelsior, 115; 5th, 82, 255n51; 7th, 168; 10th, 175; 14th, 190; 26th, 141, 143; 27th, 143, 149; 33rd, 131; 34th, 144; 37th, 124; 52nd, 124; 59th, 113–14; 61st, 167–69; 63rd, 169–71; 64th, 99, 167–69; 82nd, 88; 95th, 125, 190; 121st, 117; 123rd, 90; 124th, 116, 134

Nicola, Lewis, 19–20

North Anna, battle of, 117

North Carolina units: 3rd, 90, 97; 4th, 94; 5th, 98, 123; 52nd, 121, 253n3

Nosworthy, Brent, xii, xviii–xix, 15–16, 251n27, 266n22

Oak Grove, battle of, 94, 97, 113

Oatis, Martin A., 130

Oblique movement, 6, 93–95, 102, 168, 170, 192, 246

Obstacles, 87–91, 170, 172–73

Ohio units: 1st, 125; 15th, 105; 19th, 116, 171–72; 27th, 152; 35th, 118; 43rd, 152; 46th, 100; 49th, 44, 124, 126; 51st, 130; 54th, 126; 63rd, 152; 93rd, 125; 110th, 132; 120th, 77; 121st, 158; 122nd, 132

Olmstead, William A., 113

Olson, Peter C., 134

O'Neal, Edward, 182

O'Neill, Joseph O., 169–70

Opdycke, Emerson, 79–80, 119–20, 179

Orchard Knob, battle of, 155–57

Ordinance of 1754, 8

Ordinance of 1766, 10

Ordinance of 1791, 13, 16, 27–28, 233

Ordre mixte, 9, 146–48, 239

Osterhaus, Peter J., 154

Osterhoudt, Henry Jerry, xvii, 210

Otto, John Henry, 65

Overland campaign, 102, 117, 131

Paine, Halbert E., 40, 67–68

Palmer, John M., 81, 112, 119

Palmer, Joseph B., 148

Parsons, M. Monroe, 149

Passage of lines, 47, 114–18, 164, 172, 241, 246–47

Patrick, S. L., 91

Peachtree Creek, battle of, 84, 119–20, 129–30

Pennsylvania units: 3rd Reserves, 143; 11th Reserves, 94; 36th, *frontispiece*; 49th, 126; 50th, 131; 56th, 189; 61st, 153; 83rd, 166–67; 88th,

189; 95th, 117; 100th, 92; 110th, 83; 114th, 116; 118th, 126; 119th, 126; 121st, 190; 128th, 63; 139th, 121; 142nd, 190

Perpendicular method, 4, 6–7, 37, 59, 247

Perry, William F., 93

Perryville, battle of, 104, 110

Pershing, John J., 218

Petersburg campaign, 85–87, 95, 99–100, 102, 117, 121, 128, 143, 160, 186–201, 259n10

Pettus, Edmund, 113

Phelps, John W., 64

Phillips, William A., 74

Pickett, W. D., 137

Pickett's Mill, battle of, 105, 150, 179

Pillow, Gideon J., 84, 96–97

Pine Mountain, battle of, 147–48

Place of honor, 3–4, 20, 40, 42

Plains Indian Wars, 212

Pleasant Hill, battle of, 99

Plevna, battle of, 211

Pope, John, 35, 38, 210

Port Gibson, battle of, 91, 95, 112, 125, 130

Port Hudson, siege of, 86

Porter, George C., 94

Potter, Andrew, 95

Prague, battle of, 7

Prairie D'Ane, battle of, 150

Prairie Grove, battle of, 119

Processional method, 4–7, 23, 59, 247

Prokopowicz, Gerald, 177

Prussian army, 4, 9–10, 16

Putnam, Haldimand S., 155

Quimby, Robert S., 10, 13, 16

Ramseur, Stephen, 88–89

Range of infantry combat, xii–xvi, 202–4, 211, 213–15, 221–23, 249n5, 250n13

Ranks, 2–3, 12, 16, 19, 27, 29, 37, 41, 103–4, 164, 175, 206–9, 247, 290

Ransom, Thomas E. G., 77

Rate of advance, 91–93, 100–102, 165, 240, 244–45, 247–48

Raudzens, George, 273n70

Raymond, battle of, 128

Read, Edmund S., 95

Reaves, George A., xvii

Refusing a flank, 123–24, 163, 247

Regiment, organization of, 39–41, 43–45, 247–48, 254n17

Regulations of 1764, 10

Reid, Hugh T., 68

Rennolds, Edwin H., 76

Resaca, battle of, 124, 138

Reviews, 78–80

Reynolds, Alexander W., 140

Reynolds, Daniel H., 43

Rhode Island units: 2nd, 117–18, 142, 198–99; 3rd, 71; 4th, 44

Rice, Elliott W., 97

Rice, Samuel A., 38

Rifle, repeating, 204, 207–8, 210–11, 213

Rifle musket, xi–xvi, 30–33, 202–3, 232, 235, 240, 242, 250n13

Ringgold, battle of, 106

Ripley, Eleazar W., 26

Robertson, J. W., 44

Robinson, James S., 74

Robinson, William W., 131

Rocky Face Ridge, battle of, 148

Rogers, Horatio, Jr., 118

Rohr, Willy Martin, 217

Ronald, Charles A., 87

Rosecrans, William S., 150, 177

Ross, Steven, xvi

Rossbach, battle of, 9–10

Russo-Turkish War, 211

Savage's Station, battle of, 124

Sawyer, Charles F., 194

Saxe, Marshal Maurice de, 10

Schofield, John M., 74

Scott, Henry L., xxi

Scott, Winfield, xiii, 25–26, 28–29, 36–37, 40–43, 45–46, 48–49, 51–53, 55, 59, 65, 114, 244–45

Scribner, Benjamin, 47, 56, 62, 210

Scurry, William R., 34

Secessionville, battle of, 92, 105

Second Boer War, 215

Second Bull Run, battle of, 90, 93, 110, 115

Second Seminole War, 228

Sedgewick, Thomas D., 116

Semmes, Paul J., 132

Seven Pines, battle of, 94

Seven Years' War, 9–11, 274n21

Shaw, Robert G., 155

Sheridan, Philip H., 188–89, 195, 237

Sherman, Thomas W., 208

Sherman, William T., 42, 44, 56–57, 58, 79, 208, 210

Shiloh, battle of, 104, 107–10, 115, 126, 147, 149, 165–66, 261n10

Showalter, Dennis, 10

Sickles, Daniel E., 97, 118–19

Simonds, Merritt James, 73

Skirmishing, 10–11, 13–14, 27, 53–55, 72, 95–102, 152, 203, 208–9, 211, 214, 242, 260n39

Small-unit effectiveness, xiv, xxi, 13, 177, 226–27, 240–41

Smith, Andrew J., 114

Smith, John E., 105, 154

Smith, Thomas B., 129

Smith, Thomas Kilby, 84

Smith, William F., 100, 157

Smyth, Alexander, 27

Sniping, 203

South Carolina units: 3rd, 133; 17th, 90; 18th, 90, 124; 23rd, 90; Holcomb Legion, 90

South Mountain, battle of, 97–98, 105, 111, 123–24, 133

Spanish-American War, 213–14, 229–30

Spiegel, Marcus M., 77

Spotsylvania, battle of, 103, 159–61, 178, 182–86

Spring, Matthew, 22, 234

Squads, 105, 214

Squares, 52–53, 120–21, 248

Squier, George W., 42

Stacy, George, 82

Stanley, Henry Morton, 63

Stannard, George, 157

Stanton, Edwin M., 53

Stanton, George, 66

State volunteers, 228–30

Stedman, Griffin A., 104

Stegner, Frederick W., 68

Steuart, George H., 84, 89–90

Steuben, Frederick William Augustus von, 20–21, 228–29

Stevens, P. F., 90

Stevenson, Carter L., 127

Stevenson, John D., 154

Stewart, Alexander P., 138

Stones River, battle of, 81, 84, 88, 93, 97, 110, 116, 119, 121, 125, 129–30, 134–38, 147–48, 150, 171–72, 177

Stratton, Henry G., 116

Streight, Abel D., 113, 148

Suiter, James A., 144

Sumner, Edwin V., 114, 150

Sweeny, Thomas W., 152

Tactics, definition, xx–xxi

Tactics, flexible linear, 14–18, 241, 251n27

Tactics, infiltration, 204, 216–20

Tactics, linear, xi, xiv–xxi, 1, 4, 9, 11–12, 100, 203–25, 251n27

Taylor, Nelson, 115

Tennessee units: 1st (Turney's), 98–99; 3rd, 65, 145; 17th, 136; 18th, 148; 20th, 129; 23rd, 172–73; 44th, 136

Tercio, 1

Texas units: 2nd, 72; 5th, 134

Third Winchester, battle of, 126, 139, 145

Thirty Years' War, 2

Thompson, A. P., 76

Thompson, Thomas C., 91

Thomson, T. P., 123

Thruston, Stephen D., 84–85, 88, 97

Torbert, A. T. A., 146

Torgau, battle of, 7

Training, 15, 61–80, 176–77, 226–27, 233, 240, 249n5, 258n57, 260n39

Trimmier, Theodore Gillard, 75

Tripp, Hagerman, 41–42

Tupelo, battle of, 114

Twiggs, David E., 29

Tyler, E. B., 151

Unitary army, xi, 9–10, 12, 18, 251n27

United States Army units: 1st Colored Troops, 87; 11th Colored Heavy Artillery, 71; 16th Infantry, 130; 17th Infantry, 115; 18th Infantry, 125; 22nd Colored Troops, 72, 87, 100; 37th Colored Troops, 121

Upton, Emory, 133–34, 157–58, 182–83, 207–11, 223, 271n15, 271n26

Van Dorn, Earl, 151

Vegesack, Ernest von, 167

Vegetation, 128–30, 164, 234

Vicksburg campaign and siege, 84, 97, 153–55

Vietnamese War, xiii, 203, 249n5

Virginia units: 4th, 87; 5th, 94–95; 26th Battalion, 95; 33rd, 115; 55th, 128

Wagner, Arthur L., xvi, xxi, 43, 160, 212–14

Wagram, battle of, 15

Walcutt, Charles C., 100

Walker, James A., 186–87

Walker, Moses B., 120

Wallace, Lewis, 206–7, 209, 271n15

Wallace, W. H., 124

Walthall, Edward C., 76

War of 1812, 25–26, 228–29, 252n22

War of the Austrian Succession, 8

War of the Rebellion, xiii, xiv

Ward, Philip R., 74

Ware, Eugene F., 70

Warren, Gouverneur K., 58, 72, 98, 103, 117, 188–89, 191–93, 195, 269n33

Weber, Andrew J., 105

Weigley, Russell, xviii

Weitzel, Godfrey, 64, 82–83

Wells, George D., 87, 96

Wheaton, Frank, 197

Wheeler, Walter R., 220

Wheeling, 17, 20 48, 85–86, 133–39, 164, 166, 193–94, 209, 241, 248

White, Thomas W., 131

Wilcox, Cadmus M., xv–xvi, 31

Wilderness, battle of the, 117–18

Wilkinson, James, 25

Williams, Alpheus S., 63–64, 112, 144–45

Williamsburg, battle of, 98, 106, 124

Willich, August, 71, 157, 165–66

Wilson, James, 237

Wilson, Peter, 65

Wilson's Creek, battle of, 114–15

Wings, 52–53, 87, 105–6, 248

Wisconsin units: 2nd, 105, 131; 6th, 105; 7th, 131; 8th, 125, 150

Wood, Enos P., 104

Wood, James, Jr., 134

Wood, S. A. M., 85, 94

World War I, 61, 204, 215–21, 230–33

World War II, xiii, 61, 203, 205, 221, 226, 230–31, 249n5

Wright, Horatio G., 58, 198

Yorktown campaign, 149

Young, Lot Dudley, 88

Zouaves, 32–33, 69–70, 82, 116